ON TOUR WITH THE CLASH, 1981.

WHAT
ROCK 'N' ROLL PEOPLE
SAID ABOUT

'He's a heavy duty journalist.'

JOE STRUMMER, 1981

'You could be a Traveling Wilbury.'

TOM PETTY, 1988

'You're a party animal!'

DUSTY SPRINGFIELD, 1990

'Me and Ian (Hunter) would be better off with you as the head of a major record company.'

MICK RONSON, 1990

'You're a marginal prophet, Mike. You could be the next David Lynch.'

IAN McCULLOCH, 1993

MY LIFE WITH

ROCK
N'ROLL

P E O P L E

M I K E   N I C H O L L S

GHOSTWRITER™

GHOSTWRITER™

First published 2019 by Ghostwriter™

ISBN: 978-1-5272-4049-0

Cover design and typeset by Jamtastic Design Ltd, Aylesbury, Bucks.

Printed and bound in Great Britain by
Biddles Books Ltd of King's Lynn, Norfolk

Front cover picture by Pete Vernon. Back cover picture by Andy Phillips.

All pictures taken from author's private collection unless otherwise stated.
Every effort has been made by the author and publisher to clear permissions.

Visit www.ghostwriterbooks.net to read more about
our books and to buy them. You will also find news of any
author events and you can sign up to a mailing list so that
you're always first to hear about our new releases.

To Kira, Jasmine and Grace
For putting up with my occasionally strange behaviour.
It will all work out in the end, until the very end.

Respect to the editors

The Don – Alf Martin.
Partners in crime – Kira Nicholls and Ria Higgins.

Thanks also to Julie Lodge for the design.

CONTENTS

INTRODUCTION 1

1. ADAM ANT 3

2. AL STEWART 7

3. ANDY WARHOL 11

4. BILL WYMAN 14

5. BILLY IDOL 20

6. BOB GELDOF & PAULA YATES 24

7. BOBBY WOMACK & RONNIE WOOD 30

8. BOY GEORGE 34

9. BRUCE DICKINSON 39

10. BRYAN FERRY & BRIAN ENO 42

11. CHRIS DIFFORD & GLENN TILBROOK 46

12. CHRIS POPE 49

13. CHRIS REA 54

14. CHRISSIE HYNDE 57

15. DARYL HALL 61

16. DAVE GAHAN 65

17. DAVE STEWART 68

18. DAVID BOWIE 72

19. DAVID GILMOUR 76

20. DEBBIE HARRY 80

21. DENNIS EDWARDS 84

22. DIANA ROSS 88

23. DONOVAN 92

24. DUSTY SPRINGFIELD 96

25.   ELVIS COSTELLO 99

26.   ERIC CLAPTON 103

27.   ERIC STEWART & 10cc 106

28.   FEARGAL SHARKEY 110

29.   FRANCIS ROSSI 113

30.   GEORGE MICHAEL 116

31.   HER MAJESTY THE QUEEN & VISCOUNT LINLEY.............. 120

32.   HOWARD DEVOTO 126

33.   IAN BROUDIE 130

34.   IAN DURY 132

35.   IAN HUNTER 136

36.   IAN McCULLOCH 142

37.   IGGY POP 145

38.   JACK BRUCE 148

39.   JACKIE COLLINS 151

40.   JEAN-JACQUES BURNEL... 155

41.   JEFF BECK 159

42.   JEFF LYNNE 162

43.   JOE STRUMMER 165

44.   JOHN CALE... 174

45.   JOHN COOPER CLARKE 178

46.   JOHN LYDON... 184

47.   JOHN MARTYN 193

48.   JOHNNY THUNDERS 197

49.   JULIAN COPE 201

50.   KATE BUSH.. 204

51.   KEITH RICHARDS.. 211

52.   KEVIN ROWLAND.. 215

53.   KIM WILDE.. 219

54.	LEMMY	223
55.	LEONARD COHEN	228
56.	LOU REED	231
57.	MADONNA	235
58.	MALCOLM McLAREN	238
59.	MARC ALMOND	243
60.	MARIANNE FAITHFULL	250
61.	MARK KNOPFLER	253
62.	MARTYN WARE	256
63.	MEAT LOAF	262
64.	MICHAEL JACKSON	266
65.	MICK FLEETWOOD	270
66.	MICK JAGGER	274
67.	MICK JONES	282
68.	MICK RONSON	287
69.	NEIL YOUNG	293
70.	NILS LOFGREN	297
71.	NOEL GALLAGHER	300
72.	PAUL CARRACK	303
73.	PAUL McCARTNEY	306
74.	PAUL WELLER, BRUCE FOXTON & RICK BUCKLER	318
75.	PAULINE BLACK	326
76.	PETER HOOK	331
77.	PETE WYLIE	336
78.	PHIL LYNOTT	341
79.	PHIL & RONNIE SPECTOR	344
80.	RAY DAVIES	349
81.	RICHARD THOMPSON	354
82.	RICKIE LEE JONES	357

83.   RICK WAKEMAN 360

84.   ROBERT PALMER 364

85.   ROBERT PLANT 371

86.   ROBERT SMITH 374

87.   ROD STEWART 377

88.   ROGER DALTREY 381

89.   ROGER WATERS 383

90.   STEVE HARLEY 386

91.   STEVE MARRIOTT 390

92.   STEVE WINWOOD 393

93.   STEVEN MORRISSEY 396

94.   STEVIE NICKS 399

95.   STING, ANDY SUMMERS & STEWART COPELAND 402

96.   TINA TURNER 407

97.   TOM PETTY 409

98.   TOM VERLAINE 417

99.   WILLY DeVILLE 420

100. ZODIAC MINDWARP 423

INTRODUCTION

So who are these rock 'n' roll people? Well, there are one hundred here and I've met and interviewed them all. Naturally, each one is an individual but they have a lot in common. First of all, you can see it in their eyes, a twinkle here, a hint of mischief there. Then there's that profound and sincere look of integrity matching a heart full of soul.

Real rock 'n' roll people were born rebels; tell them to sit down and they stand up. Recommend a trade and they'll give a little shimmy, a quick twirl and head for the nearest party. Actually, ma, you didn't make plans for Michael because like a lot of rock 'n' roll people, I didn't get on with my father either. Some of these people didn't even get to know their fathers, literally as well as metaphorically. No wonder they became modern-day minstrels and court jesters singing along, saying what they felt and damn the consequences.

What else do we know about rock 'n' roll people? Personally, I believe they are non-PC, in fact too cool to succumb to the drag of any kind of politics. What they *should* be are poets, philosophers and business men (and women), especially if they are to survive the parasites inevitably drawn towards them. Historically, the list of casualties is endless but at least we can learn from their mistakes.

Ideally, the rock 'n' roll people in this book are your heroes as well as mine. As I say, I've interviewed them all, sometimes several times, for newspapers and magazines such as *Record Mirror*, the tabloids, *Penthouse, Hello!, The Times, Evening Standard* and *The Sunday Times*. You can read about my life with all of them either by proceeding from A to Z, or just diving into your personal favourites. Search and enjoy, suggests rock's forgotten boy.

MIKE NICHOLLS

1

ADAM ANT

Like his biblical namesake, Adam was always one of the originals. Gigging with The Sex Pistols, steering punk towards fetishism, then suddenly switching from cult figure to full-on superstar. Musically and visually, Adam and his Ants gate-crashed the consciousness of different generations with everything from Burundi rhythms to presenting fictional characters such as Prince Charming and Kings of The Wild Frontier. Following a number of hits, his early 1980s Christmas tour owed as much to pantomime as rock 'n' roll, the stage dominated by a pirate ship straight out of *Mutiny on the Bounty*.

Reviewing an early gig for *Record Mirror*, I remarked how enchanted many of the younger kids had seemed; from then on ordinary gigs could prove something of an anti-climax. This observation was duly noted by Mr Ant (*né* Stuart Leslie Goddard) during an interview for the same magazine in May 1982. Adam actually thanked me – again, quite original – and said he had personally sent a copy of the review to his agent in LA. Adam was hoping to get more film work having already appeared in *Jubilee*, Derek Jarman's dystopian punk movie.

'I hope the tour was a sincere gesture inasmuch as I lost a hundred grand even after selling every seat in the house in thirty cities,' he asserted with his usual candour. 'But I think that was an investment in my career.'

It was certainly a sea change from the sex 'n' leather routine of the early days and records such as 'Deutsche Girls'... 'That was inspired by Mel Brooks's *The Producers* which dealt with taboos,' he replied. 'I thought that was what the whole punk thing was about. SEX (the Malcom McLaren and Vivienne Westwood shop in London's Kings Road) was taboo fashion and it was a case of taking that shock element and using things like leather and rubber clothes in an anarchic manner. It was stylish and as important an artistic movement amongst young people as Dadaism, Surrealism, Futurism or anything.'

By this time, Adam had parted company with the Ants. 'Too many business things came into it,' he explained. 'I ended up talking more to their lawyers and managers than them. Then again, they were given no say in anything because, after all, I'm the leader and it never was a democracy.

'I did encourage a family ('a wild nobility, we are the family', to quote the frontier hit). I gave them a percentage and made sure they were financially secure. But it was wholly abused because apart from Marco who continues to be half of Antmusic and producer Chris Hughes, I played nearly everything. It got to ludicrous lengths when if I asked someone to do a session, they'd check their contract first.'

The interview coincided with the release of the next single, 'Goody Two Shoes'. This was inspired by a gig both of us had attended at The Old Vic – Dexys Midnight Runners led by Kevin Rowland, an artiste who had impressed Adam with his musical passion and honesty, or in the words of the song:

> When I saw you kneeling
> Crying words that you mean
> Opening the eyeballs
> Pretending you're Al Green[1]

---

[1] Copyright EMI Music

'This is going to be Dexys' year,' reckoned Adam, accurately as it turned out, since within a couple of months the self-styled Celtic Soul Brothers had reached Nos. 1 *and* 2 respectively in the UK Top 20 singles and album charts. 'They're dealing with intense emotions and although I'm not, I can appreciate it. It's soul for Christ's sake. But they're not just adding to a style, they're trying to update it. They're also a group. If you had Dexys Midnight Runners down an alley and they were attacked, they'd fight for themselves and each other. I don't think that was the case in my band although it was at one stage.' I then asked him what he thought he'd be doing in five years' time, another film perhaps? Once again, he showed prescience. 'I will do a film one day with a director I want to work with.'

Fast forward seven years and we met again. Following a musical fall from grace, Adam had been in America since 1985 as an actor. He had appeared in Steven Spielberg's *Amazing Stories* and other high-profile TV programmes. I'd been updating my own life too, from the music press via the tabloids to *The Times* newspaper, with regular columns on the arts and weekend pages.

However, Adam was the one wearing the immaculate blue-black Jean Paul Gaultier overcoat and at thirty-five he could have been ten years younger. Did he ever wear jeans, I wondered? 'Maybe if I was gardening,' he replied, showing his usual obsession for style, 'but even then, it would require performing in a certain way.' He had evidently been moving in the right circles, proof of his celebrity status, supported by the fact that he had been invited for an audience with the then undoubted King of Pop, Michael Jackson.

'Oh, it was the usual trip,' he elaborated. 'I met the llama and the parrots, and Michael's a very charming lovely guy. He usually gives off this timid thing but there was one moment when the other side of him came through. I asked him how he had become so successful and he fixed me with a really serious expression and said, "I only work with the best people". It's something I've tried to do ever since. Unlike a lot of pop singers who have tried to get into films, I've not been playing the part of myself. There's been a whole range of characters, including killers, thugs and general nasties. With each movie, I've had more lines. After all, acting is a craft and in LA the beaches are awash with singers and directors who have tried to take short cuts. Being number one in the charts equips you for nothing except looking good; and a model could do that.'

Clearly this son of a domestic cleaning lady continues to be far more than that. In recent decades, there have been autobiographies, TV and radio documentaries about him and a return to live music, which included playing in front of a crowd of 45,000 people in Hyde Park. There have also been problems with mental health, with music rather than medication eventually proving to be the best solution. Nevertheless, Adam appreciated that not everyone in society shares his talent and good fortune. 'Mental health needs a great deal of attention,' he told me during a chance meeting at a North London hospital. 'No one can afford simply to look the other way.'

In an age when hardly a day goes by without some media story about mental illness, Adam Ant certainly remains one of the originals, resiliently ahead of life's inexorable game.

CHAPTER 2

AL STEWART

A singer-songwriter with an unusual passion for both history and wine, Al Stewart has another claim to fame. He's the only person to have performed at Warwick University for nine years on the trot. During that time, I interviewed him for the local radio station and afterwards we went in search of sustenance and further detailed conversation. It came to pass that we shared a mutual appreciation for cheese and tomato sandwiches and the music of Bob Dylan, or Bobby the Zee as Al referred to him.

It was 1975 and *Blood On The Tracks* had just been released. Mr Stewart, born in Glasgow but with a distinctly southern accent, reckoned 'Simple Twist of Fate' was the Zimm's best song since his heyday. It was around about this period that Al had released an album, *Bedsitter Images*, reflecting his own 60s lifestyle. 'Every night I'd buy half a pound of sausages and wash them down with a bottle of wine bought from an excellent shop in Belsize Park,' he recalled in an understated fashion as if reading the news. 'That's how I got ideas for my next song.'

To a certain extent this is a tragic story. Within staggering distance of both Hampstead and Primrose Hill, this north London village was an even cooler place to live then than it is now. Al knew The Beatles and opened shows for the Rolling Stones, and neighbours would have included future rock stars like Leonard Cohen. There were also some notable flats of multiple occupation housing members of Fairport Convention and other cult figures of the day. While all around him the first generation of 24-hour party people were living the life, Al was imbibing alone. It's almost as sad a tale as The Kinks' Ray Davies confessing to have missed out on the 60s because he was too busy writing about them.

But we digress. The next time Al's name came up was when I went to America for the first time in 1978. I had some rock 'n' roll cousins in LA, including Judi Lesta, a photographer for the *NME*. Her jeep bore the number plates 'BOLLOX', which went down well with visiting British acts who cheerfully posed in front of the car. Judi also happened to be shacked up with Al's tour manager. This proved to be a useful fund of further Al tales, including his obsession with the sea which has often been an inspiration for his music and semi-poetic lyrics. His favourite track on his early *Modern Times* album was about 'The Dark and Rolling Sea'. Stewart's current LP, *Time Passages*, included a track entitled 'Life in Dark Water', one of the first to have been written in his now native LA.

A couple of years later I caught up with him in London when he was peddling more eccentricity with an album called *24 Carrots*. His move to California seemed a good place to start. 'My original record company dropped me after six albums because I'd never had a hit single,' he explained. 'Silly, really, because they were still making money out of me. The guy supposedly looking after my career simply said, "We've got this new band that's going to be huge and we want to put all our efforts into them." Who were they? The Wombles!

'So I recorded my next record at my own expense and offered it to Virgin for £5,000 but Richard Branson turned it down. So I took it to the States where it sold millions.' The disc in question was, of course, 'The Year of The Cat'. Not only does the single remain one of the biggest airplay hits in rock radio history but forty-two years later, Al is still playing tracks from the album on world tours. Some of the gigs take place in wineries. 'My interests in life have been music, history, literature and wine,' he told me in the 90s. 'I've probably spent half of my disposable income on the latter. The rest I've wasted!'

An avid collector of French reds, the first thing Al did when he moved to LA was to build a house with a cellar which at one point stored more than 3,000 bottles. He described the location as being 'the cheap bit of Bel Air', half way up Mulholland Drive in a place called Rosco Mare Canyon. Further probing revealed ownership of one and a half acres of land on a private track surrounded by a forest full of wild deer, raccoons and coyotes. 'I suppose I went from being a folkie to the first yuppie. Yes, I know it's an awful thought and it sometimes gives me nightmares, but the facts of the matter are that yuppies were supposed to drive Porsches, drink Perrier Jouet and dine in nice French restaurants, and I was doing all that in 1971 when everyone else was a hippie.

'Now that everybody else in LA is a yuppie, in my own fevered imagination I've become more rustic. I only go to certain restaurants, usually with my own wine freshly decanted. I give a glass to the chef and one to the *maître d'*, and three things generally happen. I always get a great table, terrific service and, of course, no charge for the wine, which is great as LA restaurants can rip you off cruelly.'

Al reckons he got his taste for good living from his stepfather who married his mother when Al was nine. 'My father died before I was born, in action in a Lancaster bomber just before the end of the Second World War. My stepfather had a hotel in Gloucester and a cake shop in Bournemouth. Then, after twenty years in catering, he flipped in mid-career and became a probation officer.

'The people I admire most are those who have lived several lifetimes in one,' says the man who has dedicated most of his life to wine and song. 'I'm into quality rather than quantity and when

I'm not on the road, I set aside one day a week to spend with other Californian wine collectors to indulge in what are amusingly known as vertical tastings. We try about twelve different wines and decide which ones to buy in bulk. I suppose the most valuable bottle I've ever had was a '61 Château Pétrus,' continued the troubadour who has won numerous awards in France. 'That was a particularly good year and cost about $2,000. Mind you, that's nothing. A German mate spent $70,000 on something from American President Thomas Jefferson's private collection. He said it tasted like warm sawdust.

'I studied wine for about two hours a day for about ten years and have tried every Mouton Rothschild from '45 onwards. It's insanity. Obsessive.' He went on to find an alternative distraction – marriage. Al met his wife Chris in the late 80s after a gig she attended in Reno, Nevada. 'I persuaded her to leave university and come and look after me,' said Al who was still a bachelor at forty-three. Although nineteen years his junior, the relationship, which has produced two children, seems to have coincided with a reduction in the number of bottles in his collection. By 1995, when I interviewed Al for the *Evening Standard*, his collection had gone down to half its original size. The following year, they moved to a suburb of San Francisco but now the kids are fully grown, he's been able to go back on the road.

Al reckons at his age, seventy-five this year (2019), he only needs to do enough gigs 'to make ends meet. I'm happy to break even just so long as I'm not poor. I wouldn't want to be reduced to a single room in the San Fernando valley, or even a small flat in Belsize Park however much it goes up in value.'

ANDY WARHOL

It was a no-brainer, as they say. I was in the Sixth Form when a documentary about Andy Warhol was banned from being shown on TV. Two months later in March 1973, the decision was reversed so obviously all the hip brigade at my, frankly, cool grammar school tuned in.

Before then, the only lead I had on the chap came courtesy of a track on David Bowie's *Hunky Dory* LP, which included the line, 'put you all inside my show'. I'd always been one for rounding up the troops for some degree of mayhem, so Andy was obviously a kindred spirit. The fact that his signature also appeared on the cover of the first Velvet Underground album didn't do any harm either. It soon became clear that Mr Warhol, then in his mid-forties, was an artist with a difference. Instead of applying paint to canvas, his schtick was silk-screen prints. These ranged from pictures of soup cans to images of dead actresses such as Marilyn Monroe and graveside presidential widows. Each one would be repeated in vertical and horizontal rows like a sheet of postage stamps, while the overlaying of bright contrasting colours created a dazzling effect.

Printing then proceeded on an industrial scale in The Factory, as his studios were called, where most of the work was undertaken by star-struck young staff. As well as acting as patron to *avant-garde* musos like the Velvets, Warhol was also into making bizarre art movies such as *Chelsea Girls*, *Flesh* and *Pork*, and fraternising with the rich and famous. Nor was he short of a few bob himself. When he died in 1987, the estate of his foundation was estimated to be around $300 million, with auctions of his works still taking place at the Sotheby's and Christie's of this world.

The previous summer Warhol had made what was destined to be his last visit to Britain for the opening of an exhibition of self-portraits at the Anthony d'Offay Gallery in London's West End. This was preceded by an unforgettable press conference attended by a gang of rowdy rock journalists as well as the more refined employees of art publications. Representing the *Mail on Sunday*, I planned to ask a few questions and persuade our host to sign my stainless steel Aiwa tape machine.

Without too much ado Andy ambled in, pale yet charismatic beneath his trademark silver-white wig. Flanked by the most elegantly dressed and least intimidating minders imaginable, he took a seat behind a gleaming glass dining table. As one, the guests involuntarily heaved forward and the table was history, one broken end somehow propping up a Coca Cola can. 'It's art!', bellowed a prominent paparazzo photographer, ending any semblance of decorum. While most of the journos busied themselves getting their press packs autographed, I made some discreet enquiries as to the whereabouts of that evening's inevitable celebrity beano. In an age of specialist security companies and clipboard Nazis, it's hard to reconcile how easy it was to gatecrash the VIP party at the timelessly stylish Café Royale.

Having acquainted ourselves earlier, it wasn't difficult to secure an audience with the diminutive fellow. Although surrounded by what appeared to be auspicious members of the art squad, there was no vibe of impenetrability. Indeed, I found myself effortlessly entering the clique and soon understood why; Andy wasn't really talking to anybody, his conversation restricted to replies like, 'Oh', 'Gee', 'Well', 'I dunno' or 'Why?'.

I asked a couple of entry-level questions too banal to bear repetition before moving on to the subject of parties. Is there an art to parties I asked, thinking this was reasonably safe ground. 'No!', he shouted and that to all intents and purposes was that. But in some far-flung cupboard amongst the memorabilia of a roller-coaster career, there rests a tape-recorder bearing the authentic, bold, black signature of Andy Warhol.

BILL WYMAN

Bassist Bill Wyman may have been the oldest of the Rolling Stones but he never exploited his seniority. Brian Jones was the original leader while Mick Jagger and Keith Richards wrote the songs. At a time when the establishment saw the Stones as the epitome of teenage delinquency, Bill had the longest hair. Paradoxically he hid towards the back of the stage, hardly moving. It was exactly what he wanted. 'I suppose I've always been visually dull,' he told me in 1981. 'But I don't like the idea of not moving about naturally. Mick and Keith are instinctive movers whereas I know my limitations and try not to exceed them.'

This conversation took place in the St James's Club near Jermyn Street in one of the smartest parts of London. Bill had invited me for lunch following our introduction at a movie premiere the night before. The film was *Green Ice,* a James Bond-type thriller for which Bill had composed the soundtrack. He had wanted to do something like this for years.

'I'd been looking for the chance to write descriptive music for a visual project for a while,' he explained. 'I got turned on by all those spaghetti westerns by Sergio Leone. It was also a chance to experiment with some of the new synthesizers I've collected for my home studio.' Home at that time was mainly his villa in the South of France, his favourite neighbour being the artist Marc Chagall. Apart from talking about film music, Bill was also promoting his debut single, the tongue-in-cheek '(Si Si) Je suis un Rock Star' which reached No. 3 in the charts, making him a more successful solo artist than any of the other Stones.

Over Dover sole and the most upmarket Chablis available, I suggested a hit could be a means of breaking into the band's songwriting team. 'Basically, there's no place for another songwriter in the band,' he replied tactfully. 'I'd like to be involved if I could and I'm sure Ronnie would too. It's a bit of a drag but if you only record one album every eighteen months or so, there's not much room for anyone else. I've no desire to do my own music within the context of the Stones.'

After lunch Bill and his chauffeur dropped me back at the *Record Mirror* office in a limo. Tragically there was no one around I knew to see me disembark. Devastating, but not for long. A few months later I joined the Stones on the road for a tour of the American Midwest. This partly came about as a result of our mutual friendship with their support band, The Stray Cats. Mick and Keith had always been into backing fresh talent and the New York rockabilly trio were the latest act to be thus honoured. They had been in London for about a year and been royally checked out by all the band, plus myself. So we all reconvened in Chicago and flew on to Cedar Falls, Iowa. You can catch up with this little adventure in the Mick Jagger chapter. In the meantime, let's get back to Bill and his favourite pastimes like Willy and the Poor Boys, cricket... and crumpet.

In the mid-80s the Rolling Stones took a sabbatical while Jagger recorded his first solo album, *She's the Boss*. This left Bill at a loose end so he formed Willy and the Poor Boys with mates like Andy Fairweather-Low, the Welsh geezer with the unmistakable high-pitched voice. In the 60s he had hits with Amen Corner such as '(If Paradise Is) Half as Nice' before going solo and celebrating Christmas '75 with the classic 'Wide-Eyed and Legless'. The last time I saw Andy was at Wembley Arena in the 90s when he was playing guitar with Van Morrison. An in-demand sort of guy, he went on to tour with Roger Waters and Eric Clapton.

The first time I met Fairweather-Low was at a Willy and the Poor Boys party at the Video Café, near the Palladium in Soho. I was invited by Bill and picked up the gold-leaf invitation from his office in The King's Road, Chelsea. No point risking the post with a bash like that. Until I got to the beano I had no idea our Fairweather friend would be there, still less Jimmy Page of Led Zeppelin, Paul Rodgers of Free and Bad Company, and incredibly Steve Winwood of Traffic and Blind Faith, a talented chap but nonetheless a recluse who hardly ever spoke to journalists. Of course, that didn't stop me taking his photograph with Rodgers and Page, who had just put together a band called The Firm, recording one classic song, 'Radioactive'. Naturally, their name had nothing to do with the fact that they were signed to Swan Song, the label owned by feared old-school gangster-manager Peter Grant.

Actually, I got on quite well with Peter and he was well chuffed that I went over and had a chat with him and his daughter at the *Kerrang!* Awards in 1996, the annual bash for the UKs leading heavy rock contingent. We'd already met at the first In The City conference inaugurated by ITV presenter Tony Wilson in Manchester a few years earlier.

Anyway, the Willy and the Poor Boys party was one of very few I bothered taking my trusty Cannon Sureshot to, one of the best idiot-proof cameras since the Kodak Instamatic. Looking at the pictures I think you'll agree that for ninety quid it wasn't a bad investment, even if they were taken by a technological halfwit.

The following year, Bill invited me to his fiftieth birthday party in the last week of October 1986. It took place at the House of St Barnabas, a Grade I listed building in the heart of Soho which had originally been built as a charitable institution to keep families together when the husband went into a workhouse. More recently part of the imposing mansion had been a women's hostel which must have amused Bill no end. To pile on the irony, Mr Wyman probably wouldn't have wanted me there if he'd known what was about to appear in the subsequent issue of *Penthouse*.

Two months earlier he had been at the heart of a scandal when he admitted to a Sunday newspaper that he'd been having an affair with a girl since she was thirteen. I knew all about this since I'd met her myself the previous May. The occasion was a party thrown by Richard Branson at the Kensington Roof Gardens to celebrate the fifth anniversary of his ownership of the club. The unusual establishment was a sort of Art Deco Hanging Gardens of Babylon overlooking most of prime West London's real estate. As Branson had already given me complimentary membership for an article I'd written about his new Virgin airlines, I was a guest of honour, as were a bottomless list of celebrities from cricketers Ian Botham and Viv Richards to computer geek Clive Sinclair, and comedians Lenny Henry and Ade Edmondson.

More to the point, Bill and Who drummer Kenney Jones were there sharing a table with this new Lolita, Mandy Smith. While the two musicians droned on about drum machines or whatever, I started chatting to Mandy under the watchful eye of one of the editors of the *News of the World*. She soon came clean about having gone out with Wyman for a couple of years and bingo, front page news. Their first date had been at the club Tramp with fellow Stone Keith Richards and his wife Patti, and they frequently dined with Mick Jagger and Jerry Hall. During the week, Mandy stayed with Bill at his Chelsea apartment above the office and at weekends they repaired to his country pile, Gedding Hall in East Anglia.

When all this came out in the papers, they fled ever further afield to Bill's villa on the French Riviera. Two Tory MPs demanded a full investigation into underage sex allegations but got nowhere. Detectives admitted there was nothing they could do unless Mandy or any member of her family filed a formal complaint, which never happened. At the same time, legal experts reckoned that the Director of Public Prosecutions would not see it as being in the public interest to take things any further. All this appeared in my *Penthouse* report which came out just after Bill's fiftieth birthday party. Although he was not best pleased at the time, we had a good laugh about it all at the Brit Awards aftershow party a few years later.

Then in 1992 there was a charity cricket match at Kenfield Cricket Ground near Canterbury. Those participating included football legend Gary Lineker, jockey Peter Scudamore and John Keble of Spandau Ballet. By this stage Bill and Mandy had married and separated, and he had another fiancée on the go. On this occasion Bill didn't look too happy to see me. Never mind the man from Spandau, this was one pirouette too many.

Another cricketing aficionado was Rolling Stones drummer Charlie Watts. By the age of fourteen he had become a confirmed jazz fan, playing in various bands around North London. These included the widely respected Blues Incorporated with Alexis Korner. Through this lot he met the rest of the Stones in the early 60s.

For some time now his main extra-curricular activity had been The Charlie Watts Quintet whose ranks had been swelled by the likes of Courtney Pine and Jack Bruce. I joined Charlie for a Bloody Mary or three at the late lamented Halcyon, one of London's first boutique hotels. The event was the release of his *Warm and Tender* album featuring a portrait of his rather beautiful daughter on the cover. With me not being an expert on pre-jazz-rock jazz, we found ourselves talking about a whole range of other subjects such as architecture, Ronnie Wood's eye for a good property and why, despite residing in Devonshire, Charlie prefers not to live on the coast.

'The sea air erodes houses,' he pointed out. Watts and Shirley, his wife of more than half a century, therefore live inland where they run a stud farm. As Bill Wyman would probably agree, it's an appropriate hobby for a Rolling Stone.

BILLY IDOL

It wasn't the most exhilarating of first encounters. I met Billy Idol in the upstairs room of a North London pub following The Boomtown Rats' Christmas show at The Rainbow Theatre in 1978. Bob Geldof's band was celebrating a successful year, their second album having yielded 'Rat Trap', the first single by an Irish group to reach No. 1. Along with his girlfriend, Paula Yates, Geldof had become a key figure in punk society. The least he could do was throw a party albeit in a run-down part of the inner city.

Guests included Jimmy 'Jack the Lad' Pursey of Sham 69, who had also scored a few hits that year, and singer Billy Idol, whose band Generation X were no strangers to *Top of the Pops* either, occupying the opposite end of the New Wave spectrum. Whereas Sham projected an image of skinhead reprobates, Idol's look was that of a peroxide pretty boy. Apart from the Gen X sound being influenced by 60s pop, Idol's identikit punk-like style contrived to attract a flamboyant teenybop following, mainly female. This was enhanced by a veneer of artiness, clothes, records, sleeves and photoshoots courtesy of some of the trendiest designers in town.

I asked Mr Idol, *né* Broad, a former associate of punk pioneers the Bromley Contingent, whether Generation X had cornered the market in punk pop. He was not best pleased. 'We're not pop, we're a rock 'n' roll band which is why we're currently recording our second album with Ian Hunter,' he asserted, referring to the Mott The Hoople legend who in recent decades has become one of the most cherished figures in the history of rock. 'If you're talking about current pop, look no further than Blondie. 'Hanging on the Telephone' is their best single to date.'

Actually, I've always found it one of their most annoying, not holding a candle to the sublime '(I'm Always Touched by Your) Presence Dear' or the even more recent 'Picture This'.

The conversation gradually petered out and the next time we met was in January 1981 following a couple of difficult years on Planet X. The Hunter-produced *Valley of The Dolls* album was a commercial failure and musical differences saw the departure of guitarist Derwood Andrews, a proposed third album remaining unfinished. A fierce legal battle with their ex-manager had taken its toll with Billy commenting, 'I never thought I'd joined a group to spend days in a lawyer's office.' Add to this almost being dropped by their record company and the stage could have been set for something of an edgy interview.

On the upside, the meeting took place at a distractingly historic venue in London's tranquil Little Venice, the house previously inhabited by former Sex Pistol Sid Vicious and his girlfriend Nancy Spungen. Its current occupant was Gen X bassist, Tony James, who opened the proceedings with the kind of tour of the premises not normally offered by estate agents. The main feature was the bloodstains ingrained in the various walls where the warring couple had conducted their courtship. Then there was the spacious upstairs window from which some other punter, a drug-dealer escaping the police, had jumped to his death.

In contrast, Messrs Idol and James seemed confidently full of life. A new album, *Kiss Me Deadly*, had finally been released with tracks previewed on around a dozen provincial gigs. With the rise of new, more sophisticated acts like Elvis Costello and Talking Heads, the intervening years had witnessed many changes in the music scene. So who were the current Generation X fans?

'Well, there were certainly a number of our original fans and die-hard punks,' Billy replied. 'But also quite a lot of younger kids, some of whom followed us to other gigs. It wasn't just a case of playing old hits because half of the material is new. Although you have to play for the audience to a certain extent, you also have to play for yourself.'

With the benefit of hindsight, this remark proved loaded with irony. For having enlisted a premier league manager – Bill Aucoin, who was guiding the career of American megaband Kiss – Billy relocated to New York City to become a solo artist. One of the cuts from *Kiss Me Deadly*, 'Dancing with Myself', was gaining airplay so Idol decided to follow the money, taking with him Keith Forsey, Gen X's highly acclaimed producer. Film director David Mallet completed the team, another astute move since the 80s was about to become the age of the video. The year 1982 saw 'White Wedding' from his debut solo album gain what was to become known as 'heavy rotation' on MTV, the new and vitally influential video channel. Billy's second LP, *Rebel Yell*, was an even bigger success yielding Top 10 hits like the title track and 'Eyes Without A Face', not only in the US and the UK but in other parts of the world including Europe and Japan.

The next time I chanced upon the singer was in the rarefied confines of the VIP Room at The Limelight Club, which opened in London in the summer of 1986. Possibly as a result of having downed a drink or three, he came charging over to give me a massive hug and enthusiastically kiss the girl I was with, the art director of a well-known women's magazine. She was still dining out on the experience the following month.

By then Idol had released the *Whiplash Smile* album which boasted hits 'To Be A Lover' and 'Don't Need A Gun'. It also featured crack guitarist Steve Stevens who would go on to work with Michael Jackson. The rest of the decade saw Billy father both a son and a daughter by two different girlfriends prior to being involved with a motorcycle nightmare which nearly cost him a leg.

The last time we met was after his show at The Astoria in Charing Cross Road in the mid-90s. Unusually for a rock star, he waited for the audience to disappear before catching up with a few of his old muso mates in the bar. For someone who had spent the best part of the past twenty years as an international star, it was a modest touch.

Old punks never die or even fade away; they just rock up for last orders.

CHAPTER 6

BOB GELDOF &
PAULA YATES

Towards the end of the last century, at the height of the dot com boom, there was a high falutin' internet conference at the prestigious Queen Elizabeth II Centre next to Parliament Square, central London. It was hosted by the then Chancellor of the Exchequer, Gordon Brown, with speakers assembled from all over the globe. These were mainly early online millionaire entrepreneurs and pompous American academics who probably wished they had put their money where their motormouths were.

Reporting for a computer magazine irresistibly entitled *Revolution*, during the lunchbreak I targeted a clique of familiar faces. One of these belonged to Martha Lane Fox who at the time was the most famous young businesswoman on the planet, having co-founded lastminute.com, the iconic travel company which a few years later sold for £600 million. She was chatting away with someone even more famous, my old mucker from the class of '77, Bob Geldof. Inviting myself into their conversation, I made some cheeky enquiry about the lastminute share price. Ms Fox glanced at Geldof as if to say, 'Who is this nutter?' Bob swiftly came to my aid with the words, 'It's all right, I've known this man for longer than I've known my own father.' A classic piece of exaggeration even by Geldof's standards – but he had a point.

We'd originally met at the Manchester Apollo more than twenty years earlier during the Tonic for The Troops tour. His band, the Boomtown Rats, was about to secure the first new wave No. 1 and I was a trainee at the *Altrincham Guardian*. In those far off days of record company excess his label had a regional representative who ushered me backstage to be introduced to The Bob. I mentioned that The Beatles had played this venue in the 60s and Geldof almost hit the roof. 'I'm not their biggest fan at the moment,' he seethed. 'I met George Harrison the other night and he made some remark along the lines of his group having done the world a favour by putting Irish show bands out of business.'

We met again later that year (1978) in very different circumstances. By then I had joined *Record Mirror* and part of the job was entertaining pop stars who seemed to enjoy dropping into the office for a bit of free PR and a cuppa. The Skids, The Undertones, Buzzcocks, Debbie Harry, Boy George... they all used to make an appearance, sometimes to complain about an indifferent review but usually for a bit of a social and to remind us how wonderful they were.

Geldof was quite a regular even before his girlfriend, Paula Yates, started writing for us. Her Natural Blonde column was supposed to be a rollicking good gossip revealing whatever naughtiness went on at celebrity parties. When Bob was not on the road, she preferred early nights at their new house in Clapham so guess what? I selflessly volunteered to go to a lot of the shindigs in her place. Part of the deal was contributing whatever scandalous stories I could remember from these over-lubricated events and before long we were a pretty good team.

When the Boomtown Rats undertook their next UK tour, I decided to drive back to my native Manchester to review an early gig – with the passenger seat reserved for Paula. There followed some of the most scurrilous hours of my sheltered life to date, the non-stop dialogue taking no prisoners. Nobody's sex life went unmentioned, not that the music business had ever been the height of propriety in the first place. The accompanying cabaret wasn't bad either, the hem of Ms Yates's short dress gradually rising up those inviting thighs as she teased and twittered all the way up the backbone of Britain's dull motorway network. At one point we stopped to use the facilities and our strictly metropolitan madam was shocked. 'Who are these people?' she gasped, clocking the kind of clientele one only tends to see in the back of beyond.

When we arrived in Manchester, my mother informed us that Bob had been on the phone and the Rats were running a little late. Why not nip round and see my grandmother while we're waiting? Paula took the suggestion rather well, especially when I pointed out that she was no ordinary granny so the conversation was likely to be similar to the one we'd had on the journey up.

After tea, scones and family gossip, Paula and I departed for the venue where Geldof gave a typically extrovert performance that included his signature throwing of shapes. For much of the gig I fended off gaggles of excitable young girls keen to ask Paula about her hats and other sartorial matters.

My main memory of the aftershow party was of Geldof monkeying around with one of those multi-gallon urns of tea that you used to see in factory canteens and pre-designer hotels. Bob was not a boozer, a fact confirmed when I went to see the band play in Belfast the following spring, one of the few big rock concerts to have taken place in the Northern Ireland capital since the start of the Troubles a decade earlier. Apart from being pulled up by constant police patrols, we were all staying at The Europa which had the reputation of being the most bombed hotel this side of Beirut – an excuse for having a good drink if ever there was one.

With his usual devil-may-care attitude, Geldof didn't seem too perturbed about possible explosions, showing more concern for the quality of recent releases by new wave rivals such as The Police and Elvis Costello. We continued talking until late about everything and nothing, the standard routine with rock 'n' roll people. Unlike with family or even close friends, there's no pressure to compete, impress or justify what you are doing with your life. It's like ships in the night except with the knowledge that before long you will meet again in some other port of call.

The port of Newcastle to be precise where Paula used to travel for Channel 4's exuberant flagship pop show *The Tube*. Presented by the still natural blonde and the equally effervescent Jools Holland, the combination of music and media guests made it a happy hunting ground for mischievous chat. Having parted company with *Record Mirror* (following the arrival of a new editor and the winning of an industrial tribunal), I was freelancing for a fresh generation of pop pages. *The Sun* and *Daily Mirror* copied *London's Evening Standard* in running a daily column. The editors of these outlets were insufficiently connected and so they relied upon rock journalists to fill the gaps. It was a case of trebles all round since the ensuing tabloid rivalry meant everyone involved was frothing to cross your palm with silver. As an increasing number of pop journos jumped aboard the red top bandwagon, I beat a path to the *Daily Express* where amidst the ties and pinstripes, my new boots and biker jacket caused a bit of a stir.

This was balanced by the contents of my contacts book and within a few months, I was ghosting a new section. Next, I was conducting interviews and writing live reviews with my own byline. Describing the singer of a heavy metal band as 'wearing trousers so tight you could tell his religion' proved a useful turn of phrase when it came to securing more commissions.

With column inches to top up, visiting TV shows, including *Top of the Pops,* was a given, ditto anything half memorable happening at *The Tube*. I remember Bob turning up to a party at the end of the first series but it was at Wembley Stadium where we had our next historic chat.

The occasion was Live Aid, the internationally screened all-day rock 'n' roll show raising funds for the victims of famine in Ethiopia. Featured artists included Queen, U2 and George Michael, while in America we had Bob Dylan and the Beach Boys. The event in the summer of '85 was mainly Geldof's idea and soon afterwards the actual Queen awarded him the KBE, the equivalent of a knighthood for those born outside the UK. Live Aid was introduced on the day by the monarch's son, Prince Charles. At an impromptu press call between acts I asked Bob what he'd done with his mate Chazza. 'Probably gone to his mother's for lunch,' he replied without missing a beat.

He continued chatting about the day ahead (no digital updates back then), which was pretty admirable considering the amount of organisation involved. By nightfall he looked ready to die but, in the process, he became a household name. His subsequent autobiography sold millions and was translated into dozens of languages. Meanwhile the Boomtown Rats disbanded and Geldof decided to return to a musical career with a new single, 'The Great Song of Indifference' – surely a tongue-in-cheek title in the wake of his major charitable contribution? I put this question to him during an interview for *The Times* in 1990. 'I'm the least indifferent person,' he agreed, 'but if you are completely apathetic, then please use the song as a personal anthem. I would anticipate holidaying hooligans in Ibiza drunkenly singing along. In the past I was never proud to be from Dublin. I didn't like the parochialism of the place or the attitude of the people, which basically meant that anyone attempting to do anything different was a non-starter. The Boomtown Rats had a very hard time before moving to London. It's only in the wake of U2 that Irish kids have become aware of the potential of making music for a living.'

At their peak in the late 70s, few new wave bands could match the success of the Boomtown Rats yet by Live Aid, their fortune was on the wane. Is that why he wrote his autobiography entitled *Is That It?* 'Yes, it was dictated by finance,' he admitted, 'after my first solo album *Deep in The Heart of Nowhere* only sold moderately in the UK. I wasn't sure what direction to take. Most of the people around me were urging me towards a career in politics but I've never harboured any such ambitions.

'I would find it utterly boring having to do those surgeries where people moan about the lights outside their house. Also, I'm useless on committees as I'd rather have my own way,' he went on, the outspokenness flowing thick and fast. 'Then there's the parliamentary whip system and having to agree with a bill just because the party supports it. I'd just say bollocks. Perhaps more important with single issue politics, like famine, you are more powerful outside the political process. Famine is an issue of morality and politicians don't deal with morality, they are more about the art of pragmatism,' he observed. 'At the end of the day, politics is about managing the economy and all other issues can only be promoted via a giant lobby.'

This interview appeared in *The Times* nearly thirty years ago, in June 1990. An old folk song springs to mind, the one with the chorus 'When will they ever learn?' There's a more recent record too: Blur's *Modern Life is Rubbish*. Some will argue that it always was. Then again, current trends suggest an increasing awareness of immoral pragmatism. It's good to think a rock 'n' roll person had a hand in that.

CHAPTER 7

BOBBY WOMACK & RONNIE WOOD

Fashion can be a cruel mistress for some. Others, like myself, tend to ignore it especially where artists are concerned, which explains why I was able to devote an unusual amount of time to Bobby Womack in the autumn of 1986. Not to mention his friend Ronnie Wood, guitarist with the Rolling Stones. Womack was in London so his record company set aside a couple of days for interviews. Yet very few journos wanted to talk to him despite the fact that he had one of the most remarkable CVs of modern times.

Discovered in his early teens by legendary soul crooner Sam Cooke, Womack went on to write the Stones' first No. 1 single 'It's All Over Now', before spending the rest of the 60s touring and recording with Ray Charles, Elvis Presley, Aretha Franklin and Dusty Springfield. The next couple of decades saw success with his own albums including *The Poet II*, voted by one of the music papers as the best album of 1984. Talk about the fickleness of fashion.

Actually Bob, Ronnie *et moi* found a lot more to talk about that day to the extent that by evening I felt like a walking encyclopaedia of rock 'n' roll, R&B, country blues, gospel and any other musical style suited to Bobby's emotive baritone voice. There was only one thing for it. We'd have to go out and listen to more sounds even if the current charts were driven by a mixed bag of artificially produced strings and drumbeats, a practice becoming known as sampling.

Having already made steady inroads into the hotel's minibar, the first stop had to be the Spanish Bar between Soho and Fitzrovia, home of London's finest jukebox and a clientele sporting enough to sing along proudly to 'Stand by Your Man' and 'That's Amore'. Then on to The Limelight where the non-stop dance music wasn't really cut out for dancing. So, flashing my gold VIP card, we ascended to the VIP Room where my fellow Mancunian Mick Hucknall was trying to find his London legs. He was delighted to meet Bobby who he described in my *Mail on Sunday* piece as one of his all-time heroes, a photograph of the pair of them accompanying the story. More drinks and anecdotes all round, and then at the end of the evening Ronnie had a lightbulb moment. Would I like to join him and Bobby the following night in West Side Studios which they had booked to record some new material? It was a bit like George Best wondering if you fancied a game of five-a-side football.

I drove over to the Shepherd's Bush studios without realising Ron would be mixing the most refreshing bourbon cocktails known to mankind. I didn't even know I liked Tennessee sipping whiskey until whatever was left of any inhibitions rapidly evaporated. Although it was ostensibly Womack's session, it appeared to be Ronnie doing the singing. Even more unpredictably, there didn't seem to be a record producer organising Ron, Bobby and the other musicians who had turned up. So I decided to step into the breach. Perhaps imagining it was no more difficult than suggesting to a colleague how to start an article, I began instructing Ronnie, a Rolling Stone, how to sing. 'This is R&B – you've got to sound more black,' I proclaimed, the alcohol talking even louder. As far as I can recall, the advice was accepted graciously, at least no one showed me the door. On the other hand, I never got to hear the resulting tapes or indeed whether anyone planned to release them. But

I did get to interview Bobby's brother, Cecil, when Womack & Womack came to town.

WOMACK & WOMACK

The other half of the duo with Cecil was Linda, with whom Bobby had once had an affair. She was also the daughter of Sam Cooke whose widow Bobby had married after the crooner had been assassinated by a jealous lover. Families, eh? Try telling that to Cecil and Linda who produced seven children together. One of these, less than a year old at the time, appeared onstage in Linda's arms at London's Dingwalls in early 1989, starting a craze for that sort of thing.

Famous friends in the audience included Eric Clapton who, along with artists as diverse as George Benson and The Beautiful South, had recorded some of Womack & Womack's songs. Their track 'Teardrops', which reached No. 3 in the UK singles charts, was covered by Elton John while another top name, Dave Stewart of The Eurythmics, devised a TV programme about them. It showed the family staring into a crackling bonfire on their farm in Virginia. 'It's in a small town near the border with North Carolina,' said Linda when I interviewed Womack & Womack for *Hello!* magazine in 1991. 'We decided the rural life was more suitable for raising a family and liked the idea of fixing up our own place. The closest city is Nashville and that's about 300 miles away.'

It was also a case of going back to their roots. Having established their musical career in California, Cecil fancied returning to the home of his forefathers. 'My dad and his before him worked in the coal mines of Virginia. While they worked, they sang – which is where our music originated. Dad used to tell me how every time they struck the coal with an axe, they would sing a note. Then in the evening they would gather round and sing gospel songs.'

Unsurprisingly, they were promoting a new album entitled *Family Spirit*, although in keeping with the times, it had more in common with dance music than their gospel roots. Ever since their 1980s hit, 'Love Wars', Cecil and Linda had experienced more success in the UK than America, which explains why they were planning to buy a house in London. 'After all those years in the countryside we're ready to return to a town,' Cecil remarked. 'London seems like a good base since we sell more records in Europe than anywhere else. The only problem is that we don't want to abandon the rural lifestyle completely; we'll need somewhere to raise sheep. Do you think we would be able to keep them on Hampstead Heath?'

Definitely the strangest question I've ever been asked by a rock 'n' roll person.

CHAPTER 8

BOY GEORGE

Rock 'n' roll people like to distance themselves from ordinary civilians. I mean, who really needs to have their creative integrity compromised by self-styled authority figures like parents, teachers, bosses and random bully-cowards poncing around in risible hi-viz jackets. Unfortunately, the gap is not always easy to close. It's called human nature, that twisted riddle responsible for politics, manipulation, ego, insecurity and all the foibles deployed by those around us. These negative attributes explain why most rock stars have had difficult relationships with their fathers, a classic example being the one Bruce Springsteen reveals in almost embarrassing detail in his autobiography *Born to Run*.

When addressing teenage rebellion, punks should have enjoyed a double whammy. In the late 1970s the average Sex Pistol fan would have experienced at least some of the events of the Swinging Sixties, heralding the dawn of youth culture. Punk refined the process with a different sound and look. Yet those running the show proved no less controlling than their predecessors, especially Malcolm McLaren. The shock tactics which birthed both his Kings Road shop and the anarchic antics of the Pistols soon gave way to familiar tactics of divide and rule.

Adam lost his first nest of Ants when McLaren lured them away to join Bow Wow Wow, the band fronted by the fourteen-year-old Annabella Lwin who Malcolm discovered singing along to the radio in a dry cleaner's shop. However, when Ms Lwin and her mother proved to be a bit of a handful, McLaren brought in Lieutenant

Lush as a means of playing both ends against the middle.

Born George O'Dowd he became the androgynous star of the New Romantics, shrewdly securing employment as cloakroom attendant at Blitz, the Covent Garden nightclub at the centre of the next musical big thing. With heavy make-up and distinctly non-masculine clothes, Boy (initially mistaken for a girl) nevertheless had a striking look, 'a pouf with muscles' as he articulated in the mainstream media. As bands like Spandau Ballet and Depeche Mode started playing at cultish venues all around town, George made sure he was seen in all the right places.

I first met him at the Sundown Club near Leicester Square in early 1981. By then he had left Bow Wow Wow having been used by McLaren to put Annabella in her place. The two singers had fronted the band at the Rainbow Theatre in Finsbury Park a few months earlier and it was obvious that even the large stage at the famous London theatre wasn't big enough for both of them. Still George seemed happy enough to be interviewed and photographed by *Record Mirror* adding that he was DJ-ing at a trendy club called Planets. The week after the article appeared, he came swanning into our magazine's office, rendering most of my colleagues speechless.

Making it clear that he was up for as much publicity as he could possibly wangle, George paused only to call the editor, Alf Martin, on his private line offering to sleep with him. Except that wasn't the actual word he used. Within eighteen months not only had Boy George formed Culture Club but also released the finest debut single of the year, the reggae-tinged 'Do You Really Want To Hurt Me?'. A couple of weeks before its rapid ascent to the top of the charts, I persuaded the showbiz editor of the *Daily Express* to make space for a feature, otherwise we'd lose out to the other papers. By this stage, the Boy George PR machine was in full swing and the only time available for an interview was during a taxi ride across town to the *Daily Mirror*. Fortunately, the rival tabloid just wanted to run a photo story for its Saturday pop club page enabling my *Express* piece to scoop them the day before.

En route we stopped off at George's flat where he applied full make-up for the red top piece and produced a scrapbook showing pictures of himself with his rival Jeremy Healey. Not only had Healey's band Haysi Fantayzee beaten Culture Club to the Top 40 but, like O'Dowd, Healey also sported luxuriant dreadlocks. However, George was able to prove that Healey had short, straight hair indicating that it was he himself who had the original white dreadlock image. While caking on the slap, he found time to play me the next proposed single, the even more soulful 'Time (Clock of The Heart)'.

By 1984 Boy George was the most famous new star in the firmament, on the way to selling 50 million records. These included the catchy yet profound 'Karma Chameleon' which caught the *zeitgeist* to the extent that one of the characters started singing it in Jack Rosenthal's *The Chain*, a popular TV comedy-drama. It also won a Brit Award for Best British Single and helped spark a second British invasion in the USA, the first having been the one led by The Beatles a generation earlier. An example of Culture Club's success was George's appearance on an American awards show that was beamed all over the States. It was on this occasion that I next saw the singer, not performing but being interviewed live by fellow star Lionel Richie. Surprisingly this didn't take place at a major event but at an empty club in London – an early example of a live satellite broadcast.

It was almost unnerving to be accompanying one of the biggest stars in the world at the usually teeming Hippodrome even if he was dressed to the nines in his latest gaudy outfit, a lime green lurex suit with calf-length coat and white boots. But it was an ideal interview environment with pictures courtesy of Richard Young, the king of the rock 'n' roll paparazzi. Despite his lofty position in the tabloid media, Young always remained first and foremost a fan. He compared the excitement and historic nature of the evening with what a Beatles event must have been like for a previous generation.

Born in June 1961, George missed out on Beatlemania but wasn't too young to appreciate the emergence of David Bowie at the end of the decade. 'My older brother Richard had a copy of 'The Man Who Sold The World' which I inherited when he moved on to edgier rockers like Alice Cooper,' he told me. 'I saw Bowie at the Lewisham Odeon on the Ziggy Stardust tour and I became a huge fan. He said it was okay to be gay and I was experimenting at the age of fifteen, by which time I'd left school to stack shelves in a supermarket. Then punk came to the rescue which, of course, was a very colourful time although quite dangerous. So many people wanted to punch you. The Teddy Boys came down very hard on punks and then when the New Romantic scene started we had trouble with straights because of the way we looked.'

That night at the Hippodrome, George pointed out that the New Romantic crowd – 'not a name we called ourselves, it was more of a press invention' – never numbered more than about 200 but most of those involved at the start went on to make a name for themselves as fashion designers, pop stars and make-up artists. 'I told the careers officer at school that I wanted to be a make-up artist and he looked at me as if I was a Martian. That was when I started using make-up myself! Anyway, those 200 all had big ambitions and dreams, and although there weren't many of us, we more than made up for it by being full of our own self-importance. I might have missed out on the 60s but I feel lucky to have grown up in the 1970s. My generation burst out of the closet and jumped for joy at being able to be ourselves.'

Richard Young took many photos of the New Romantics, and the various other music tribes and celebrities inhabiting London until the end of the century. In 2004, I was involved in his exhibition of celebrity photography at The Hospital entertainment complex in Covent Garden. And the last time I saw George? Addressing the students' union at Oxford University. Arriving by train I gave him a quick tour of the dreaming spires but only the students were allowed to ask questions following his talk. So I had a night off for a change.

CHAPTER 9

BRUCE DICKINSON

Nineteen eighty was a landmark year for heavy metal. The new decade ushered in *Kerrang!*, the magazine which grew out of a headline. It also grew out of the *Record Mirror* office about two metres from my desk. The genre had been around for years but HM received a shot in the arm from rock's next big thing – the New Wave of British Heavy Metal or NWOBHM, represented by a generation of loud new guitar bands such as Iron Maiden, Saxon and Samson. Nineteen eighty was also an important year for the first of these acts; it was the year they poached singer Bruce Dickinson from Samson.

Their first single together, 'Run to The Hills', sold 250,000 copies and European dates soon followed a UK tour. At the age of twenty-two, Dickinson's experience of going abroad had been limited to a school trip. Then came a tour of the USA, 'a place so impossibly exotic, I couldn't sleep for a week thinking about it.'

I think the first time I spoke to Bruce was at the Reading Festival. We'd already met because he tended to refer to me as 'Nicholls'. Old habits die hard with ex-public schoolboys. I remember him scampering around in the backstage area, rather loud and confrontational for someone who was only five foot six inches tall. What he lacked in stature was offset by charisma, long hair and biker jacket identifying him as a future star of heavy metal. That weekend was probably the most important of his life: he was invited to audition for Iron Maiden, uniquely, as there were no other contenders.

Almost forty years later, Iron Maiden remain one of the biggest names in rock, having released almost as many albums and played to audiences of up to 300,000. Dickinson has done much to enhance his individual status. Apart from enjoying a parallel career as a solo artist, he has also built up his own aviation business, qualifying as an airline captain. In addition, he has become a top international fencer, with other sidelines including brewing beer, writing novels and making movies.

His multi-tasking lifestyle can at least partly be attributed to the fact that early on in his career he was struck with the realisation that 'access to money and drugs can seriously damage your mental health.' Another lightbulb moment was grasping the importance of looking after his voice: it's one of his favourite subjects when he's not undergoing a period of enforced silence.

Although we've met at countless gigs and parties over the years, the one time we did a serious sit-down interview, the angle was vocal tips. The article appeared in a magazine called *The Band*, a specialist publication about 'gigging, recording and... making it'. 'The best way to preserve a voice is to get loads of sleep in a quiet room with no air conditioning,' he advised. 'That and a diet with plenty of fresh vegetables and few dairy products which tend to produce excess mucus.' In his recent autobiography called *What Does This Button Do?*, Bruce points out that drugs are eventually fatal to the voice, 'especially cocaine and speed which are snorted into the delicate mucosa in the sinus cavities. I've never had singing lessons but my girlfriend had them at school and told me all about the dangers of nodes on the vocal chords.

'I listened to all my favourite singers and decided they'd all shagged up their voices except for one or two who had done it the right way. Top singers like Paul Rodgers and Peter Gabriel have got something to teach you – as has any vocalist who has made a song their own. Young singers always try to find their physical limits but it's the emotional extremes that are more important. The emotive range increases with age and that's ultimately what the audience identifies with. With practice, singers find their own sound from within the shape and space of their own bodies. But the diaphragm is always the engine room of the voice and singers breathe in a way more familiar to people who meditate or do yoga. The diaphragm has to be trained to become stronger. It can be done by standing with the lower back slightly flattened to permit maximum expansion of the lung cavity. This means eating before a show can be a very uncomfortable activity.'

Having taken such care of his voice and himself for so long, it was with some frustration that Bruce found out that he had cancer – of the tongue. He discovered that his chance of survival was 60 per cent but, since he was a fit non-smoker, possibly 90 per cent. Thirty-three sessions of radiation therapy and a few weeks of chemotherapy eventually gave him the vital last 10 per cent. Four months after the start of the treatment, Bruce got the all clear. Ten months after that, he was flying abroad and within another two his voice was almost back to normal. When diagnosed with cancer Bruce decided: 'I would treat it as an uninvited guest and firmly dismiss it from my house.'

Talking about houses, Iron Maiden founder Steve Harris has quite a pile in Essex. Along with the recording studio and a full-size football pitch, Steve has built his own country pub complete with barmaids. It was the ideal location for an at home feature in *Hello!* magazine, for which I was the music writer for several years. Everything went according to plan. Photographs of Steve and Bruce in the bar were duly taken but unfortunately never appeared in the magazine. 'Even for Essex girls, the barmaids look a bit too common for *Hello!*,' the female editor complained.

CHAPTER 10

BRYAN FERRY &
BRIAN ENO

I finally got to meet Bryan Ferry when Roxy Music reformed in 1979. We were introduced backstage at the Manchester Apollo the week before I relocated to London to join the staff of *Record Mirror*. It was only seven years since Roxy, a fusion of 'rock' and 'sexy', had exploded onto the scene but it seemed like a lifetime. During that period, Ferry had recorded a dozen albums including five solo projects. Backstage a pushy guy from a local paper was organising a photocall and since I was chatting to Ferry at the time, I found myself included in the picture.

I looked awful as I discovered the following week when the photo appeared in *Music Week*, the record industry trade magazine. Then again, who would look at their best alongside a singer variously described as a 'lounge lizard' and 'disgracefully handsome'. That taught me a thing a thing or two about asking artists obscure questions about their work. Most Ferry interviews had been devoted to his image and private life. All very well but he also wrote fascinating lyrics referencing stylish movies. For example, '2HB' was less about a pencil than the actor Humphrey Bogart in *Casablanca*. And what about the *Stranded* album? Was it really based on the film *Death in Venice*? With all the pre-gig activity spilling over, I couldn't absorb Bryan's exact answer ('Something along those lines.') but I do remember his advice with regard to my move to the capital. 'Don't get lost in London,' he said, perhaps as one northerner to another.

Originally from Washington, County Durham, Ferry remains one of rock 'n' roll's most famous art school graduates. Many of his early Roxy songs were inspired by the beliefs of surrealists like Marcel Duchamp, specifically that the purest form of love is that which remains unrequited. Hence the combination of anguish, melancholy and nostalgia seeping from songs like 'Mother of Pearl' and the hackneyed romanticism of 'If There is Something'. The objects of Bryan's affection tended to be *femmes fatales* whose glamour mirrored his actual relationships. The appearance of Jerry Hall on the cover of *Siren* gives some idea of how life reflected art in the Roxy world, earlier albums having showcased previous cover girl lovers such as Amanda Lear.

The solo LPs also featured their fair share of crooning sorrow, especially covers like 'River of Salt' and 'Smoke Gets in Your Eyes'. All the more surprising then to discover that in real life Ferry can be as charming and funny as the contents of his wardrobe. He could also be very candid, particularly on the subject of old flames and new. 'Most of my girlfriends have been models because I find great-looking girls stimulating. It would be nice to find a woman I can talk to but I'm not much of a conversationalist. I suppose I'm too involved with my work. It's the only thing I can do, really. I feel guilty when I'm not working.'

This conversation took place in Glasgow following an uproarious date at the city's main theatre as part of the tour following the release of *Flesh and Blood*, Roxy Music's second album since they reunited. Interestingly, the sleeve did not feature the party girls of the past but rather a pair of serious-looking Amazons armed with javelins. Musically the album had strength to match, the best tracks 'Oh Yeah', 'The Same Old Scene' and 'My Only Love' all fraught with disillusion and the haunting memories of failed affairs. Following his embarrassingly public parting with Jerry Hall, did he not feel it was time to move on and settle down? 'I don't think marriage is for me,' he replied. 'As people get older, they become set in their ways and find themselves used to living alone. As time goes by, marriage becomes less likely to happen.'

Within two years, Ferry married a socialite as well as a model, Lucy Helmore, and went on to have four sons. It's one of the regrets of my career that we only spoke in passing and never got around to conducting a full interview.

BRIAN ENO

Another key partner in Ferry's life has been Brian Eno, one of the original members of Roxy Music. Apart from a striking dress code, his main contribution was processing the band's sound with an early VCS 3 synthesizer which ultimately led to his early departure due to creative differences. Decorating the first two albums with a surfeit of electronic sound effects led to disagreements with Ferry and Eno went on to establish a highly original solo career. This included inventing ambient music whose purpose was to be 'as ignorable as it is interesting'. He also collaborated with David Bowie on his Berlin trilogy before working with major 80s artists like David Byrne and U2. By this stage Eno's role was practically that of a professor of sound, serious fans elevating his status to that of musical guru.

I met him on a few occasions during the 90s, in typically unusual circumstances. In the spring of 1995, Channel 4 screened a new series called *The White Room*. It featured contemporary up-and-coming Britpop bands like Elastica and Sleeper, and was recorded in one of a number of studios in a west London complex. Invited to the first programme, I promptly bowled into the wrong studio. The windowless room was bathed in absolute darkness – i.e. by no means white – and I wondered if this was some kind of ironic wind-up. Enquiring whether I was in the correct place, a disembodied voice replied, 'Certainly not ... ah yes, I thought I recognised your voice.' Adjusting to the lack of light, it became apparent that I was talking to Mr Eno. If anyone was to identify me in a blacked-out room, it would have to be a prominent 'sound doctor'. It worked out he was producing a new album for a slightly left-field rock band, James, and they were experimenting with performing in the dark.

Our next rendezvous took place on the other side of London at the Flowers Gallery in Hackney. It was a charity event for War Child which provided assistance to children in areas of conflict. This particular fundraiser was for a school in Mostar, Bosnia, where Muslim children had suffered during the war in the former Yugoslavia. The school, specialising in music therapy, was opened by the opera singer Pavarotti while England donated 'Little Pieces from Big Stars', paintings by leading performers such as Paul McCartney, Paul Weller and members of Oasis. These were exhibited and later sold at Flowers. Hosting the opening were none other than David Bowie and Brian Eno, while McCartney and Kate Bush were also present. Unfortunately, Kate did a runner before there was time to get stuck into the stress-relieving cocktails but Eno was on fine form, wondering if I'd had any problems finding the gallery, situated as it was in a remote part of East London miles from the nearest underground station. Clearly a man more at home with the sound of voices in studios than sat navs.

CHRIS DIFFORD &
GLENN TILBROOK

Chris Difford is the lyrical half of Squeeze, the melodic rock and pop band which has been together for more than thirty years. They released their first singles on an indie label at the height of the punk boom but otherwise had little connection with their new wave contemporaries. Squeeze were always more about music than image and some of the earlier songs didn't escape criticism. Their first hit, 'Cool For Cats', was allegedly sexist making pointed references to faithless women and social diseases. But Chris wasn't writing from personal experience as he was glad to clarify when I first interviewed him for *Record Mirror* in 1979. 'Those songs were mainly a reflection of the company we were keeping at the time,' he said, 'the sort of men you meet in south London pubs when you're taking a break from recording.' Within a couple of years, Squeeze were making profound observations about relationships, songs like 'Tempted' and 'Labelled With Love' from the classic *East Side Story* album inviting comparisons with The Beatles.

With the benefit of hindsight, it has been no surprise that for the past few decades the band have enjoyed most success in America. In 1988, I bumped into them at Indochine, one of the trendiest clubs in New York City. They had just played to 15,000 fans at a venue called Meadowlands. The following night they were to play the even more capacious Madison Square Garden, yet they stayed loyal to their songwriting roots. 'Instead of going out for expensive dinners with record company executives, Glenn (Tilbrook, the melodic side of Squeeze) and I have been getting up in clubs and playing new material to between 600 and 1,000 people, me on acoustic guitar and Glenn singing at the piano. It's been gut-wrenching going onstage without a full band. It's more nerve-wracking than playing a stadium.'

Four years and a few marriages later, I sat down with the duo again as they were starting to get the hang of life without the backing of a major record company. 'After Polygram bought A&M Records, we were dropped before being snapped up by Warners. We recorded an album for them (*Play*, featuring the excellent track 'The Truth') and three months later were dropped again. Apparently, we were too left-field for radio. But we're still there,' Difford continues, 'delivering the goods with thirteen albums and twenty-three tours behind us. I suppose we're a bit like Marks & Spencer, not the most fashionable brand but still respected for our quality. Squeeze can still produce the tastiest sandwich, which is what you want really.'

If you are to judge a man by the company he keeps, perhaps the same applies to his neighbours. In the early 90s, Chris and his girlfriend decided to take a break from London and move to Peasmarsh in Kent. He found himself practically sharing a driveway with Paul McCartney. 'He sent me a welcoming letter saying he was going to come over for a cup of tea but the nearest I've got to him so far is seeing him in a huge BMW with black windows and initialled number plates. He's also got a Land Rover and second-hand tractor from the 50s. I thought that's where he should have the personalised registration.'

GLENN TILBROOK

The last time I saw Glenn was in the Victorian house he had recently bought with his partner earlier this century. Situated in

Charlton, in Squeeze's cherished south London, Glenn admitted not spending as much time at home as he would wish, mainly as a result of his addiction to going on the road.

As well as Squeeze still being a going concern, Glenn had been touring America with his band, The Fluffers. Their chosen mode of transport was a six-bedroom Damon Challenger Motorhome, economically acquired for $18,000. 'There's room for everybody and it's transformed the way you can tour,' he explained. 'I never really enjoyed the hotel experience and the facilities are just as good when we stop in National Parks, especially in states like Colorado, Nevada and Texas. You actually get a better view of your surroundings too. I've seen more in the last three years than I did in the previous twenty. We can cook for ourselves and swim in the nearest lake.'

Glenn has recorded five solo albums which have appeared on his own label and been sold either online or from the back of the motorhome when on tour. It's very different from Squeeze in the 80s but the singer claims his enthusiasm is undented. 'You can spend your money how you want as opposed to spending weeks in top studios trying to get the perfect drum sound when imperfection is sometimes better anyway. The major labels are scared of indies as they can't deal with records that don't sell in vast quantities, which can only help people like me,' concluded the musician who had recently played dates in Australia, the Far East and the occasional UK festival. And those were just the dates with Squeeze, almost half a century since first teaming up with Chris Difford.

CHAPTER 12

CHRIS POPE

One of the worst experiences for a writer is when someone reminds you of a long-forgotten review. Apparently, after seeing The Chords in 1980, I concluded 'the kids are *not* alright', referring to both their Mod image and the Who single which partly inspired the remark.

Fast-forward seven years and The Chords' guitarist and songwriter Chris Pope was wondering whether, despite that review, I would like to manage his new group, Gatecrash Heaven. They were a tight rock band and the three songs on their demo were a mere taster for the dozen or so cuts which lit up their live shows. They were playing regular gigs at the Marquee, Dingwalls, the Mean Fiddler and other outposts of the London club circuit.

Chris was, and remains, a classy guitarist, clearly influenced by the Pages and Townshends of this world. The Chords released two albums through Polydor, the second of which died a death and sealed their fate. Pope suspected record company politics, especially as the second LP was released at the same time as the entire Jam back catalogue. The Jam were also a Mod band, who had recently completed a farewell tour. It would stand to reason that the Polydor promotions and marketing departments would have been biased towards them.

Meanwhile, Gatecrash seemed to have a loyal following, especially in the department marked Rock Chick. I discovered this when Chris became my lodger and the house was suddenly full of comely females. Weekends saw an influx of Italian girls, all golden thighs and even fresher pasta. As well as having his rent paid by the local council, Chris was also writing for *For The Record*, the music industry trade magazine of which I was the editor. He became adept at directing good questions towards managers, producers, record company bosses and anyone else who could spill the right sort of beans to a band and manager in search of a recording contract. As luck would have it, the late 80s was not the best time to be looking for a record deal. The charts were full of easily manipulated boys and girls who looked good on video. It was easier to promote new talent on the ever-increasing number of pop TV shows than to subsidise bands on the road as part of an expensive support tour.

One of Gatecrash Heaven's best songs was 'Swinging London', written a full decade before the 60s expression was revived in favour of the new onslaught of Britpop bands. 'Wine bars kill guitars,' harangued Chris and some rock 'n' roll people agreed. Primarily Graham Gouldman, songwriter, producer and 25 per cent of 10cc. He was an old mate of mine from Manchester and offered to remix the track in his own studio for £1,000. Then his manager got involved, things got messy and the whole idea fell to pieces.

Instead, we spent the money on Virgin flights to America (£100 outward, $100 return) and made some wonderful contacts in New York. Amongst these was Kate Hyman, one of the most gorgeous, sensitive and sexy women in the business. She was working at Chrysalis at the time and we saw each other a few times over the next decade. It was while I was in her office that I spotted the phone number of Mott The Hoople legend, Ian Hunter, on her pin board. I thought what the hell, give the dude a call and he picked up the phone himself with the unforgettable greeting, 'Unter 'ere.' It was a useful link in a friendship which you can read about in his own chapter.

Meanwhile, me and the Gatecrash gang had a near-miss at The Limelight Club, when it came to jamming with Guns N' Roses. Slash, a down-to-earth quality geezer from Stoke-on-Trent near Manchester, was up for it but it was just before they broke big and they were only playing a short set. Six months later, Guns N' Roses stole the show at the annual Monsters of Rock festival at Castle Donnington and spawned at least two generations of look-alikes and sound-alikes.

Going from the sublime to the ridiculous, New York was followed by a couple of dates in Warsaw as part of a cultural exchange. It was organised by somebody in a Brixton record studio who swiftly became known as Swinging Halpin. The contrast between America and Poland in 1988 was like turning up the volume to minus eleven. The grocery shops were virtually empty, so it was lucky someone had the bright idea of bringing over a jumbo-sized bag of confectionary and other blood sugar essentials. On the other hand, the beer and the vodka in the bars were ridiculously cheap, something certainly appreciated by legendary *Melody Maker* journalist Carol Clerk, who effortlessly drank us all under the stout wooden tables.

The rest of the year saw little progress on the record company front, although there was feedback from New York. A former manager of Diana Ross was impressed with the tape and offered financial backing in the form of accommodation and sustenance. I urged them to go for it. I had taken things as far as I could and, anyway, was more suited to being a journalist, especially as my old boss at the *Daily Express* was now editing the weekend entertainment section of *The Times*.

Gatecrash Heaven regularly phoned home and seemed to be having a great time. There was some momentum which eventually led to a showcase at a club in LA. The only problem was the lead vocalist deserted the stage during the fourth song, resulting in goodnight Gatecrash. One of my oldest friends in London explained to me that sometimes musicians are so desperate to make it that when the time comes, they get frightened and blow it. Talk about being careful about what you wish for...

Chris eventually returned to London and found gainful employment with a reputable computer company. He also managed to shack up with a leggy brunette who occupied a flat across the road from one of our favourite pubs – The Crown and Sceptre on Brixton Hill. It is namechecked on the Clash song 'Stay Free'. On the day in June 1996 that the Sex Pistols played their big homecoming gig in Finsbury Park, Pope stood me up: he'd just become a father.

By the beginning of this century, the entire live rock 'n' roll scene was in a state of unparalleled nostalgia. If you weren't a tribute band, then you were making a living returning to the real thing; The Chords were duly reborn. Not with the original line-up (the singer had moved to Japan), but with Chris now a confident singer as well as the songwriter and guitarist, he could reasonably claim the name. Following a couple of solo albums on his own E-Pop (Pope backwards) label, he recently put out a second album of new material by The Chords UK.

During the past few years, I've seen them at the Rebellion Punk Festival in Blackpool, Islington Town Hall in front of a 1,000 mainly fifty-somethings and at London's 100 Club, where the whole punk/Mod scene originally took off in the late 70s. Decades come and go, and fly past at ever great speed, but in a noisy corner at a Chords UK gig there will always be a sound which links their 70s hit 'Maybe Tomorrow' with 'Dreams Of Yesterday', an homage to the redoubtable Ian Hunter.

Stop Press: Just as I'm wondering what to write next, the postman arrives with the latest Chords' UK *meisterwerk*, an album entitled *Nowhere Land*. It would appear to be about the UK, and when I give Chris a quick thank-you call, he's at the airport trying to get out of this once green and pleasant land. In fact, he's on his way back to America for a series of gigs. After forty years of 'gatecrashing Chord-ery', whatever next?

CHRIS REA

The best Chris Rea story I've heard came from his marketing manager following a reception for the singer-songwriter. The record company threw the bash at a posh restaurant in Highgate village in London, following the release of Rea's then latest album. The only beer available was foreign bottled lager. Chris, who hardly knew any of the guests, took said marketeer to one side and demanded, 'Is there anywhere we can go around here for a decent fuckin' pint?' The anecdote wouldn't be half as ridiculous if it wasn't for the fact that the executive didn't have a music industry background; he had recently been poached from an advertising agency after winning an award for his sterling contribution to reviving the fortunes of a once popular cream cracker.

When Chris's next album, *Auberge*, was released I met him at his studio in Berkshire, a world away from the music industry, yet only half an hour from central London. He arrived in the Caterham Seven convertible sports car, pictured on the sleeve of the album. The car was capable of racing from 0 to 60 in 4.2 seconds, and in the right place could exceed 135mph. That place, not being the 'Road to Hell', Rea's eulogy to the M4 motorway. At the time you could pick up a UK Caterham for about £12,000 – a quarter of the price of a Porsche or a Ferrari.

'I've always been a pound for pound person,' Rea pointed out, which partially explains why he prefers pubs to restaurants. Hailing from Middlesbrough, in the once industrial north, from an early age, Rea wanted to be a writer of films and film music.

JO, MY FIRST WIFE, WITH
ADAM ANT, MARCH 1982.

*Debbie Harry pictures
by Howard Barlow.*

DEBBIE HARRY, MANCHESTER
FREE TRADE HALL, 1977.

DISCUSSING GUITARISTS FOR BOB GELDOF'S FIRST SOLO ALBUM, LONDON 1986.

WITH BLONDIE'S NIGEL HARRISON, EMBASSY CLUB, 1981.

BILL WYMAN BASH AT LONDON'S VIDEO CAFE, 1985.

ANDY FAIRWEATHER-LOW WITH BILL WYMAN.

JIMMY PAGE AND STEVE WINWOOD.

PAUL RODGERS, BILL WYMAN AND JIMMY PAGE.

Pictures by Mike Nicholls.

CATCHING UP WITH BRYAN FERRY AFTER THE 1982 WEMBLEY ARENA SHOW.

BRYAN FERRY WITH CHRIS SPEDDING, WEMBLEY ARENA, 1982.

THE IRREPRESSIBLE
RECORD MIRROR TEAM
TEN PIN BOWLING,
STREATHAM, 1981.

RECORD MIRROR
TEAM IN LONDON'S
SLOANE STREET,
SUMMER OF 1979.

Picture by Terry Lott.

MY 37TH BIRTHDAY AT THE SPANISH BAR, HANWAY STREET, 23 JUNE 1992.

FLANKED BY THE CHORDS' CHRIS POPE AND PARTNER-IN-CRIME JUSTIN 'FOCUS' THOMAS.

JUSTIN THOMAS, RIA HIGGINS AND CHRIS POPE.

WITH THE FOCUS.

CAROUSING WITH PHOTOGRAPHER DUNCAN RABAN.

TOO MUCH 'POP' FOR POPE.

DAVID BOWIE, NEW BINGLEY
HALL, STAFFORDSHIRE,
SPRING 1978.

Picture by Howard Barlow.

'But it wasn't really the right city for that sort of career,' the singer pointed out, in his typically understated way. On the other hand, it shouldn't be a surprise that he has written hits like, 'On The Beach', which is so evocative you can almost hear the sea.

Chris's dad had an ice-cream business and dreamed of his son transforming it into a global brand. 'But it wasn't to be and one day he caught me in the stock room practising on my guitar.' After joining a couple local bands, a solo career beckoned. The only problem was that in the late 70s and early 80s, the UK was very image orientated and Chris was anything but. In fact, his first few albums made very little impression, the early Rea history being one of record company meddling in the face of artistic belief. 'It was only later they realised that my act was based on innovative songs and slide guitar,' he reflected. 'That I was my own man and not one of those puppets.'

Chris's UK breakthrough didn't occur until 1985 when he charted with 'Stainsby Girls', a song about the school attended by his teenage girlfriend and future wife, Joan. Before then he had enjoyed an American hit with 'Fool If You Think It's Over' whose success was soon to turn into a bit of a nightmare. 'It might have spent five weeks in the American Top 10, but it caused four years of problems,' Rea revealed. 'After that, I was regarded as a glossy middle-of-the-road artist. The record company saw me as being the next Elton John or Billy Joel whereas I was naturally writing blues, jazz and R&B. It was an uneasy time.

'Then I started to meet people in TV studios, like Mark Knopfler and Tom Robinson, who told me I didn't need to do glitzy showbiz things, but what did I know? I'd come down to London at the age of twenty-five and was signed right away. I thought it was wonderful. I mean anything would have been if it meant making more money than on the dole. By the third album it was a case of: "If you don't play our game..." and I was almost ready to give up. Then I got a call from my label in Ireland suggesting I go over there for some dates.

'It was my wife who made up my mind,' he admitted. 'She reckoned I should try and get a band together, if only for a year, and find a manager who didn't just talk about big deals; far more important to work out how to get a PA to the next gig. So we played twenty-eight shows which is more than I'd done in the previous three years. The record company's idea of promotion had been interview tours and TV chart shows.'

Concentrating on music rather than window dressing also worked in Europe, especially Germany where he believes popularity primarily spread via word of mouth. 'I like to go there if I'm invited on to a TV programme or something,' he said. 'We live quite close to Heathrow airport, so I can always nip over there for the day and get back in time to see the kids before they go to bed.' Chris was eager to point out that his daughters were anything but standard issue rock-biz brats. 'They grew up during a not-so-successful part of my career, so they've never viewed me as some sort of celebrity. If I'm invited to a music bash involving the royals and it clashes with a motor racing event, then you know which one I'll choose.'

Apart from his Caterham Seven, Chris has raced, owned and restored classic Ferraris – a far cry from the Triumph Herald which starred in *Soft Top, Hard Shoulder*, the film whose soundtrack Chris became involved in. 'I was watching breakfast TV and saw an item about independent film companies having trouble with budgets. So I drove down to Shepperton and sold myself on the spot.' The film marked a watershed in the career of Peter Capaldi who went on to achieve fame with TV series such as *The Thick of It* and *Dr Who*. Further proof, if ever needed, that word of mouth can shout louder than corporate millions.

CHAPTER 14

CHRISSIE HYNDE

Introducing my mother to rock chick colleagues like Paula Yates was one thing. I'm not sure quite how she would have reacted to smouldering biker bird Chrissie Hynde. In her autobiography, *Reckless* (Ebury Press), the Pretender included graphic scenes of just about every aspect of the dark side of rock 'n' roll. The drugs, thugs, squalid squats and even gang rapes at the hands of psychotic Hells Angels. No wonder she waited until her parents had died before writing her memoir. The word gang is also synonymous. Unlike a lot of musicians, she always wanted to front a band rather than be a solo star. By the time she was in her early twenties, the American realised she would have a better chance of making it in London than her native Midwest and, following a few crash landings, hit the ground running.

Hynde's arrival in England coincided with the emergence of the punk scene. Originally writing reviews for the *NME*, she networked her way around the city and enjoyed a brief songwriting partnership with Mick Jones, later of The Clash. Unluckily for her, there was a rival waiting in the wings. 'Joe Strummer put the aggression in and the songs were better with me out,' she commented with her usual candour. So, thank God for Hereford, home of the three talented musicians who completed The Pretenders in the late 70s.

Following success with the debut single 'Stop Your Sobbing', written by future lover Ray Davies and produced by Nick Lowe, The Pretenders started the new decade topping both the singles and albums charts. The band barely had time to catch breath before there was a similar outcome in the USA. 'The market was wide open for a band like ours,' explained Chrissie who had no qualms about The Pretenders losing her original punk sensibility. 'A girl vocalist and solid, simple straight-ahead rock songs. It sounds perfect on the radio too, which is why it happened in America. I mean the album sold 300,000 copies in California alone, probably because it didn't jar when played next to Styx or Foreigner.'

It also helped that there were some standout songs on the album, none of which seemed trapped in a particular trend. 'Take a Bow', 'Precious', 'Mystery Achievement' and the singular 'Private Life', memorably covered by Grace Jones.

One of the loosely knit gangs of rock 'n' roll people I used to hang out with at the time was the band's guitarist James Honeyman-Scott, who I'd met at an Ian Hunter party. Apart from being a neighbour in the then totally ungentrified Notting Hill Gate, James was also a regular on the Camden/Soho gig circuit, checking out new and newly signed bands at places such as Dingwalls and the Music Machine.

The week his band achieved their double chart whammy, I saw him at the Marquee watching yet another band of hopefuls. A year or two younger than myself, I congratulated him on the group's great success. He was very grateful and tipped me off about a Pretenders gig in Coventry a couple of days later. This was the third time I'd seen the band in six months. The previous occasion being a 'secret' one at Dingwalls just before Christmas.

Success can be a double-edged sword and although Chrissie was always going to have the strength to cope with it, there was nothing to say the same would apply to her cohorts. By 1982, the lifestyle had got the better of Jimmy and he died of an overdose in a friend's flat. Meanwhile the resilient Miss Hynde learned to roll with rock's punches and forty years later remains highly productive, enjoying the worlds of film, fashion and art, as well as music and children.

We first met in New York city in the spring of 1980; both of us happened to be staying at the Gramercy Park Hotel, at the time one of the world's premier rock 'n' roll hotels. More three-star seedy than deluxe, it wasn't the sort of place to leave valuables lying around. By the same token, the management seemed to turn a blind eye to how many people were staying in your room. Chrissie was about to embark on a US tour with The Pretenders and I'd been sent to NYC for a week to report on all matters musical. Amazingly, that was how things worked in those days.

Coincidentally, I'd started seeing a girl called Lauren who was in the same band as Diane Athey, Chrissie's best friend from Akron, Ohio, where both of them went to school. Lauren and Diane were in a group called Nervous Rex, signed to a label owned by Mike Chapman who had recently produced Blondie's monumental *Parallel Lines* album. So Chrissie and I had something to talk about. If it hadn't been for the tour, Chrissie and I could have continued where Jimmy and I had left off in London; prowling the streets of Manhattan catching every hip band gigging between Greenwich Village and the Bowery.

Always a vegetarian and something of an environmental activist, later on in the 80s Hynde became involved in Ark, rock 'n' roll's answer to Greenpeace. Other contemporaries included Sting, Kirsty MacColl and Godley and Creme, and there was a lively launch party at Antony Worrall Thompson's dell'Ugo restaurant in Soho. By then, I had a weekly pop column in celebrity pop magazine *Hello!* and Chrissie agreeably claimed to be a big fan of it. 'Oh, I love *Hello!*', she beamed, somewhat to the distaste of Ms MacColl, who said, 'I bought it once and thought it was a load of rubbish.'

Somewhat controversially, Chrissie went on to tell some TV presenter that non-eco operations like McDonald's 'should be fire bombed'. Since she happened to be representing Ark, rock's main pro-vegetarian operation was obliged to close down soon afterwards. A bit of a blip, but as Bob Dylan once pointed out: 'To live outside the law you must be honest.' Without that kind of honesty, it's inconceivable that Chrissie Hynde would have invaded England to become the uncrowned queen of rock 'n' roll.

CHAPTER 15

DARYL HALL

In conjunction with his on/off partner John Oates, Daryl Hall has sold more albums than any duo in musical history – quite an achievement for a self-taught musician from Pottsdown, a Philadelphia suburb he describes as being 'the equivalent of Swindon.' Hall knows about obscure English towns as he has lived in this country for many years. When not making records, the singer- songwriter and multi-instrumentalist enjoys renovating property, particularly Georgian houses. He has one of his own on the banks of the River Thames in London's Chelsea.

It is, however, to Philadelphia that Hall owes his career, spending years in church choirs from an early age. 'My mother was the director of a choir in a Methodist church so I grew up surrounded by harmony and that whole religious sound. It was part of the black-oriented gospel tradition, Philadelphia being unusually well-integrated, not just between blacks and whites but also between the middle and lower classes. Chelsea has many architectural similarities with Philly,' says the man who started working with Kenny Gamble in the mid-60s, long before the producer started the Philadelphia soul label the following decade. Hall met John Oates in New York in 1969 and together they became one of the biggest AOR acts in America, early hits like 'She's Gone', 'Sara Smile' and 'Rich Girl' being followed by classic albums like *Beauty on a Back Street*, *Voices* and *H_2O*.

A personal favourite is 1985's *Live At The Apollo* on which they were joined by Eddie Kendricks and David Ruffin of The Temptations. It included Daryl's fabulously emotional interpretation of 'Every Time You Go Away', also a hit for British soul singer Paul Young. Soon afterwards, Hall and Oates decided to take an extended separation from their joint career. 'We had spent a long time on the road and felt that some of the spark had gone out of our creative relationship,' Hall explained. 'If we work together again, we must have something to say. Right now, that's difficult because I'm living in London and John is 6,000 miles away on the West Coast.'

Our conversation took place in 1993 when the singer had just released his third solo album *Soul Alone*. It included one of his best ever songs, 'Written In Stone'. 'It's a little less polished than stuff I'd recorded before but I tend to like raw voices like Otis and Marvin. In the past I've probably been more comparable with Luther Vandross but with this record I've tried to keep more of a street edge to stop it sliding into MOR. That can be a problem when producers take the technology too far. I'm not a fan of that digital tight sound. CD can be a bit cold and I can't listen to it for more than about an hour. CD is only interesting if you want to be analytical about music and hear what every instrument is doing,' reckoned the multi-instrumentalist.

Daryl Hall is one of the few artists to have worked with three separate major record companies. The latest of these was Sony/Epic at a time when all the labels were starting to face competition from the internet and wondering where to go next. 'It's a very interesting time for music right now because everything is so eclectic. It's also very healthy that the record companies are confused and don't know what's going to be a hit because a touch of unpredictability never did any harm. If there's no formula to hide behind then you're forced to go with your instinct, whether it's grass roots, soul, rock or whatever.

'In the 1970s everything was a lot more flexible,' he continued. 'You could experiment more which is how bands like Steely Dan and ourselves were able to take off. Record companies allowed you to try things and there was FM underground radio which was not so heavily dictated by playlists. Then the industry grew and it all became about ratings and money. In America all the indie labels are satellites of the majors and if you look at the bands who have been successful in recent years, like REM, they took years to happen.'

With the benefit of hindsight, Daryl was right on target. The record company system has disintegrated today but there's more live music available than ever before.

'I tend to listen to what's around me, in clubs, down on the street or on the radio. You can hear plenty of good music without trying to categorise it,' said the musician who around this time could be seen at clubs as varied as Bank (serious funk) or Fred's, a bar on two storeys offering background music for those honing their networking skills.

Hall was also between marriages when we met. He was married for the first time in his early twenties for three years and, more recently, to the daughter of casino mogul John Aspinall for six years. In between, he enjoyed a thirty-year relationship with Sara Allen, the inspiration for Sara Smile. A further relationship produced his son Darren, now in his thirties. 'There's a constant pull between emotional attachment and the desire to write and be alone,' Darryl explained. 'For me, romance is a battlefield and I don't know how to deal with it. The problem can be masked if you have a flexible partner and Sara was gracious enough to allow me to be me without trying to change me or force me to face the situation.' This is clearly putting it mildly. Much of their time together was spent apart, Sara spending a lot of time in California with a sick relative. 'I've seen so many friends separate because they just couldn't handle it anymore.' Or, to quote his own words:

Everybody's high on consolation
Everybody's trying to tell me what's right for me.[1]

---

[1] © Unichappel, 1973

DAVE GAHAN

The 1980s were a rollercoasting baptism of fire for many a rock star, none more so than Dave Gahan. The lead singer of Depeche Mode started the decade sharing a council house with his mother in the working-class suburb of Basildon, Essex. Fifty million album sales later, he was one of the biggest UK rock stars in America, but at huge cost to his personal life. He started the new decade divorced and addicted to heroin. 'I was on a death trip,' he admitted with the benefit of hindsight. 'I wanted to go the whole way, do it rock 'n' roll style, live in Los Angeles, everything. My ego was way out of control.'

Compared with the clean-cut image of the early Mode, his appearance shocked his nearest and dearest too, shoulder length hair, beard and tattoos completing the stereotypical rock star persona. At one point, his heart stopped for two minutes, the result of drunken and narcotic excess.

Fast forward to 2017 and several spells of rehab later and, incredibly, none of his near-death experiences appeared to have affected Depeche Mode's career. On the contrary, they sold 1.5 million tickets for less than fifty shows that year and became the first ever act to sell out four consecutive nights at the Hollywood Bowl.

It was all a far cry from the day Depeche Mode trooped into the White Lion, the favoured *Record Mirror* pub in Covent Garden. This was in spring 1981 when they had just been signed by Daniel Miller's fledgling indie label Mute Records. A few years earlier, Miller had made a name for himself with his own single 'TVOD', under the name The Normal. He accompanied his mainly teenage band to the pub where we used to go on our break, several times a day.

The ball started rolling for the band at a club called Croc's in Rayleigh, in their native Essex. 'We were the first band to play there on Thursday's futurist night,' recalled Dave. 'The resident DJ, Rusty Egan, was renowned for running clubs like Blitz and Billy's in central London. He liked us and went on to give us a spot at one of his other nights at The Venue, Richard Branson's club.'

It occurred to me that I ought to check out the band in their native habitat, and so on a balmy spring day found myself taking the train from Fenchurch Street to Basildon where they greeted me at the local station. They were accompanied by Dave's girlfriend and future wife, Jo, who had taken the afternoon off school to participate in this historic event. It began with a cup of tea *chez* Mrs Gahan before proceeding to a local café.

It turned out that half the band used to sing in church, 'but then the devil got them,' Dave laughed, making his friends blush. They played guitars to begin with until one day, Martin Gore, who later became the main songwriter following the departure of Vince Clarke, turned up with a basic synthesizer. 'They're a lot easier to play from scratch, as well as being more portable,' he declared. 'We can fit all our gear into a few suitcases and drop them into the back of the car,' Dave added. 'No need for amplifiers, back-lines or much else,' illustrating how a massive career can grow from such practical beginnings.

Dave was the last member to join, turning up to rehearsals and jamming on covers like David Bowie's 'Heroes'. They'd all known each other since school days but, instead of joining the church choir, Dave used to bunk off Sunday school, sowing the seeds for his future career as a rock 'n' roll rebel.

Actually, truancy was not the only one of his early misdemeanours. During his teens, Gahan got into a fair amount of trouble with the law, stealing cars, joy-riding and setting them alight. 'I loved the excitement of nicking a motor. I was a bit of spanner,' he confessed. 'I remember being chased by the police and hiding behind a wall with my heart beating, wondering whether they'd get me.' This particular phase of his life ended with weekend custody at a secure facility after trashing the office of his probation officer. 'Eventually, music saved me,' Dave claimed, without realising what the 90s would hold in store for him.

CHAPTER 17

DAVE STEWART

Our chance meeting should be mentioned in the same breath as the rendezvous of New York journalist Henry Stanley and British missionary David Livingstone. Only instead of taking place in nineteenth-century Africa, it occurred in the A&E department of the Royal Free Hospital, Hampstead in late December 1985.

I was staggering around with broken ribs, Dave was horizontal on a trolley. 'Collapsed lung,' he gasped, anticipating my opening question. 'How about you?' 'Got beaten up during an interview with Oliver Reed for *Penthouse*,' I replied, supplying the Eurythmic with an exclusive story about my visit to the home of the notorious actor. It was one which appeared in various tabloid newspapers the following week and went on to make me a legend in my own lunchtime, mainly at The Groucho Club. Martin Kemp of Spandau Ballet (and later *EastEnders*) was particularly impressed and clearly a fan of said magazine. The same applied to his brother Gary. 'Sting, have you met street-fighting man Mike Nicholls?', he enquired when re-introducing us to one another at a party a few weeks later.

Meanwhile, Mr Stewart looked horrified and sank back under his blanket. Obviously, it wasn't the first time we had met. That happened in a disused railway station in Aylesbury, Buckinghamshire, where his original band, The Tourists, were shooting a video for their future hit single, 'So Good to be Back Home'. The Tourists, which also included Annie Lennox, weren't a bad little pop/rock group, opening for Roxy Music's come-back tour in 1979. But they endured major record company problems which ultimately may have proved to be a blessing in disguise. If they hadn't been forced to disband, the chances are we would never have got to enjoy the refined talents of Dave and Annie who went on to distil their skills as a duo.

Stewart, of course, went on to do much more, working as a producer for the likes of Bob Dylan and Mick Jagger, and showcasing his entrepreneurial expertise with projects like The Church studio and The Hospital arts complex. As a result of the aforementioned problems, the Eurythmics started out in debt and realised a useful way of recouping funds was to record in their own studio. They found a room above a noisy timber factory in Chalk Farm, north London. 'We used to have to wait for them to turn off their machinery before we could record the vocals,' Dave joked. Nevertheless, using relatively primitive eight-track equipment, they managed to create hits like 'Sweet Dreams (Are Made Of This)' and 'Love Is a Stranger'.

When it came to going on tour, Dave and Annie displayed their natural charisma to attract some of the finest post-punk musicians of the day, including Clem Burke of Blondie and Mickey Gallagher from Ian Dury's Blockheads. Even backing vocalist Eddie Reader became a bit of a star, fronting the chart-topping Fairground Attraction later in the 80s.

While Annie became a media darling, as a result of various daring roles in a succession of hit videos, Dave became a studio star, buying a twenty-one-year lease on a church in Crouch End and turning it into one of the most acclaimed recording facilities in town. It attracted ripped-jean mega stars like Eric Clapton and Bob Dylan who, at one point, was rumoured to be buying a house in the hip north London suburb. 'It cost us a lot of money but we figured out it was an investment,' explained Dave. 'When we weren't using it ourselves, we would be able to hire it out to other musicians.'

Touring abroad influenced the Eurythmics' sounds with funk, soul, calypso and gospel gradually joining their original electronic vocabulary. Their musical empathy was all the more impressive bearing in mind their private relationship had broken down, not that anyone would have suspected interpersonal tensions. In 1984, the duo appeared on Channel 4's *The Tube* with the legendary Tina Turner, who was also recording a separate show following her well-publicised return to music. Dancing non-stop throughout Turner's performance, Annie was clearly a fan of the soul legend and afterwards we all ended up sharing a slap-up feed at a quality Chinese restaurant.

Over the course of the next decade or two, both Dave and Annie saw their careers develop at a spectacular rate, Annie enjoying solo success with albums such as *Diva* and *Medusa*, and Dave co-writing and producing with some of the biggest names in rock. Everyone from Bob Geldof and Bryan Ferry to Bono and Tom Petty shared space with the Eurythmics on award-winning recordings; Stewart even received major record company finance for his own label, Anxious.

The last time I saw him was at the annual Midem music industry conference in Cannes, where he was overseeing the purchase of a mansion in neighbouring La Napoule. This, in itself, proved something of a coincidence. Stewart and I are both northerners who moved to London in the 70s. He chose to live in Crouch End, at the bottom of the hill, whereas I selected Muswell Hill at the top. With our respective purchases of French residences, history has repeated itself. His place is near the coast, whereas my villa nestles in the fragrant hills near Grasse, acknowledged as the world's perfume capital. With Dave's address book reading like a *Who's Who* of rock 'n' roll, I wait in expectation for a reciprocal visit from the maestro. He is, of course, invited to bring an illustrious plus one, perhaps a Geldof or a Dylan.

Incidentally, Bob buying in Crouch End would never have been for the best. As any property-owning dude knows, you should always buy at the top of the hill to avoid biblical floods and that kind of thing further below. Then again, you don't want to be too close to the edge, despite the excellent views. During the dry summer of 1990, houses in Muswell Hill suffered sustained subsidence and even started moving south. Like everything, Bob, life is about getting the balance right, whether to be a born-again Christian or a fully-subscribed member of the Kosher Nostra on a never-ending tour.

DAVID BOWIE

I was still at school the first time I met David Bowie, too shy to have a conversation but old enough to click. It was the summer of 1972 and the Ziggy Stardust tour had arrived at Manchester's spanking new high-tech venue, The Hard Rock, recently converted from a bowling alley. Our exchange involved a Velvet Underground tune. He wondered if anyone was familiar with their music as he was about to play one of their songs. Since I was very near the front, I suggested 'White Light, White Heat'. Actually, 'Waiting For The Man' would have been the right answer, but it was a start.

Several monumental albums and stage shows later, I finally got to enjoy a proper conversation with David on the Glass Spider tour. By that time I had progressed from Bowie fan to editor of the trade magazine, *For The Record*. We had a section on CD and DAT so it was a good excuse to talk about his back catalogue and how it would adapt to the new digital formats. It was a question which wasn't fully addressed until the 90s when EMI finally got around to releasing Bowie on CD.

Musically this was the decade when David took something of a back seat, albums like *Outside* and *Hours* hardly in the same class as *Young Americans*, *Station to Station* or the Berlin trilogy. On the other hand, if you were an art critic then it was a case of numerous Christmases coming at once. My artier colleagues were only too pleased to take me to some of the exhibitions they were obliged to attend.

One of these took place at Flowers Gallery in Hackney, the War Child fundraiser for the children caught up in the war in the former Yugoslavia. David had produced a painting which was being printed up and sold as posters to raise money for the new music therapy school in Bosnia. Co-hosting the event with his friend and collaborator, Brian Eno, Bowie was on sparkling form and definitely up for a chinwag. If I had known he was going to be present, I might have prepared a series of questions but instead ended up relying on memory and questions I'd wanted to ask for more than twenty years. The relatively intellectual atmosphere of the established art gallery took me back to Bowie's early recordings and interviews with a generation of journalists who tended to be quite educated. Songs like 'Quicksand' (on *Hunky Dory*) suggested a flirtation with existentialism, particularly the lyric, 'Knowledge comes with death's release'.

How did David feel in the early 70s about being described as the Jean-Paul Sartre of rock? 'I was probably quite flattered,' he replied, 'because songwriting was never something that came naturally. I had to make an effort to be able to do it. I've never thought there are that many independent-thinking songwriters. They're all influenced by each other because it's such a disposable medium.'

What about all the talk at the time of the cut-up approach to writing lyrics, assembling random phrases together? 'It was more a case of loving art, theatre, fashion and the way we express ourselves,' he explained. 'Rock music was a means of keeping hold of all those things. It's always been a very versatile culture. You can analyse it but people will forget what you said after a few weeks. That's part of the fun of rock 'n' roll, there's no permanent philosophy behind it. Hence the whole cut-up thing. But that was blown out of all proportion. I think there were about two songs where I used that technique. Most of what I wrote about in the 70s was based on personal observation, on what I'd seen during the endless tours. Having said that, when writing, the melody always came first. The words, sometimes poems, would then be written to fit the melodies.'

During this conversation, David was accompanied by his PR man, Alan Edwards. I'd known Alan for almost twenty years, ever since he came up from London to attend the last night of Manchester's punk venue, the Electric Circus. He was the first punk PR of any significance, early clients including The Stranglers, Buzzcocks, Blondie and many others. He went on to perform the same duties for the Rolling Stones and Bowie, alerting the world when David passed away in 2016. I had always had a good relationship with Alan, unusually we had visited each other's homes.

I'd never been one for becoming too involved in the symbiotic relationships which can blur the boundaries necessary to maintain the professionalism between the journalist and PR. This public service announcement underlies the circumstances of the occasion in which Alan said something to Bowie along the lines of, 'You do realise you're talking to a journalist, don't you?', to which David replied, gesturing grandly in my direction, 'Oh, it's okay – he's luverly!' And that, ladies and gentlemen, is why you are able to read this right now.

In 1995 there was another significant exhibition, this time on the other side of London. It comprised nearly all the pictures David had painted during the previous decades. Most of them were owned by private collectors who lent them back to the artist for this retrospective exhibition at the prestigious Cork Street gallery in Mayfair. Celebrities and music journalists from most of Fleet Street's newspapers flocked to this epicentre of London's art scene but, amazingly, I didn't see a single hack engage Bowie in conversation. Except for me, doing my usual hale and hearty how's-it-going-old-boy routine.

David recognised me from our previous encounter and gave me a brief guide to his interpretation of German Expressionism, as revealed by the paintings around us. My favourite was the father and son in a dimly lit bar in Kreuzberg, the Turkish quarter of Berlin, their gaunt faces and the intensity of their interaction contrasting with the gloomy surroundings. It was near the Hansa Studio where he recorded the late 70s masterpieces *Low* and *Heroes*. The canvas was massive by anyone's standards and quite unforgettable. Presumably the owner has a period house with high ceilings and picture rails. If ever he needs to sell it, I wouldn't mind having first shout. Better a Bowie masterpiece in my sitting room than a classic Ferrari gathering dust in the garage.

CHAPTER 19

DAVID GILMOUR

When CD sales started to take off in the mid to late 80s, it wasn't just the new acts who benefitted from the supposedly new improved digital format. Record companies made a fortune by essentially recycling their back catalogues, particularly classic albums of the previous two decades. When the Beatles' *Sgt. Pepper* came out on CD, it was the twentieth anniversary of the original vinyl release and the whole exercise was a masterclass in marketing, something the record industry was really getting to grips with, arguably far more than the vital business of searching, signing and developing new talent.

Behind the scenes, some of what had been the great cult acts were filling their boots, too. Take a bow, bands such as Led Zeppelin and Pink Floyd, whose instrumental prowess was further enhanced by digital remastering and all the other seemingly magical processes.

In 1989, *The Times* commissioned me to write a series of articles about what was occurring in the music industry, a whole generation after the original pop/rock explosion. Instead of talking to corporate PRs and associated propogandists, I went to the source – fans at gigs and staff at record stores. The outcome was a foregone conclusion.

The original fans of Zeppelin and Floyd had passed the word on to their kids who would appear to have been far more impressed with these so-called dinosaurs than they were with most of the chart fodder being pushed at them at the time.

Employees working the tills at point of sale were staggered at the popularity of middle-aged acts with people their own age purchasing the newly-minted CDs. When I sought information from record industry bodies, like the BPI, about the percentage of sales breakdown between new and old artists, guess what? There was none available. *The Times* was offered access to the results of a possible survey but we would have had to pay for it ourselves. The editor replied, 'Thanks but no thanks,' as we already had the story, one which would be repeatedly picked up by the rest of the music media.

I was glad Pink Floyd were a classic example of the new CD sales phenomenon for two reasons. Firstly, I had personally been a fan since the late 60s, with the release of the *Saucerful Of Secrets* LP. Secondly, our classically-trained music teacher at school had dedicated a whole lesson to it, which meant our parents were obliged to stump up and buy their conscientious kids a copy. Over the next few years I was pleased to return the favour to our hip teacher by taking in future albums, like *Atom Heart Mother* and *Meddle*, for the purposes of play and discussion. From 1970 onwards, I saw every Pink Floyd tour and in 1986 got to meet David Gilmour. It is his guitar playing which epitomises the unmistakable core of the Floyd sound and which, from time to time, has made him the go-to gun-slinger for other musicians.

On this occasion, he was playing at Midem for an all-star band assembled by The Who's Pete Townshend. Since Gilmour wasn't officially promoting anything of his own, he arrived at the industry conference without promotional people or any of the usual hangers-on. This enabled me to go to the reception of the hotel he was staying at, find out his room number and invite him down for a drink at the bar. At the time, I was writing for *International Musician* whose editor was keen for me to manage his band. Turning up to an international music conference to meet some of the biggest names in music seemed like a useful manoeuvre.

With David Gilmour being more of a musician than a showbiz personality, much of the conversation revolved around studios, instruments and gadgets. David saw his role as transferring other people's ideas into music. 'Yes, I would say Roger Waters came up with most of the concepts for the Floyd albums and it was my job to turn the ideas into music. Since he left the band, I've been doing the same thing with other artists, like Bryan Ferry and Grace Jones.' The name of the latter also came up when we were talking about sampling, the new form of recording where sounds were taken from old records and grafted on to new material. 'Gadgets and machinery are not really my forte,' he admitted, 'but I suppose the arrival of sampling was inevitable. It means it's very easy to delude yourself about the difference between what *is* good and what sounds good. That's the secret.' he claimed. 'The quality of the sound makes all the difference when it comes to emotional content.'

Indeed, one only has to listen to Floyd classics, like 'Us and Them' on *Dark Side of the Moon* to realise Gilmour is one of the most emotional players in the rock canon. Talk then turned to other aspects of the contemporary business, like the role of independent labels. 'I don't mind the way the majors are using them as A&R departments,' he said candidly. 'At least it stops them fucking up so many of the good artists who get signed.'

Otherwise Gilmour didn't believe he was in a position to say much about the music scene since the Floyd have always been at least one step removed from it. 'We are a very closed off, insular unit,' he reflected. 'We never socialise much with other musicians. Sometimes we weren't that much different amongst ourselves, which is why albums like *Ummagumma* were partially devoted to solo projects. Personally, I don't think I really found my niche until *Echoes*.' That album was recorded in 1971, almost half a century ago, and they have been developing creatively ever since. Those of us who have followed the band from the start would probably agree that their entire career is encapsulated in the title of their latest opus, *Endless River*.

CHAPTER 20

DEBBIE HARRY

It was a Damascene moment in my family history. My younger daughter, Grace, is a serious rock fan: twentieth-century music mainly, Dylan, Leonard Cohen, The Clash, The Doors and Roxy Music, to name but a few. You are probably thinking Dad has got something to do with this but actually I have never pushed or tried to influence her taste or even given her a tour of my exemplary vinyl collection. She has just picked up on names over her twenty-five years and collected CDs. None of this downloading; Grace is an art school graduate and loves a good record cover.

One name – and face – that came to her attention was Blondie. Grace particularly liked a picture of Debbie Harry which was taken live at Manchester's Free Trade Hall on Blondie's first UK tour in 1977. In fact, the photographer, Howard Barlow, my long-term partner in crime, turned it into a T-shirt for her. Like Marilyn Monroe, Debbie cast her spell over girls and boys alike; while boys fancied her, girls wanted to be her.

Grace knows I've known Debbie for a long time and tries not to be too envious. She particularly likes the story about the time I went backstage after a gig and Debbie instantly offered me a beer. So, for the last ten years, whenever we've hung out, my daughter has bought me a beer. In fact, when she was very young, she used to drink apple juice because it was the closest in colour to beer. A stunning rock star, a classy daughter and a cold pint streaming with condensation. Do rock 'n' roll stories come any cooler than that?

Forty odd years ago, things were very different. Blondie were in the UK supporting Television. Debbie looked fine but her stage act left much to be desired, mainly comprising martial arts chops and blows. The reason for this eventually proved quite simple. 'Our equipment was pushed to the front of the stage because Television wanted me to confine my movements to a small space so that Tom Verlaine (Television's front person) could look striking, standing alone in a large space when he came on,' the singer explained later. So, no room to tease or dance resulted in polite applause at most. When Blondie came off stage, there was neither the time nor inclination to make even eye contact, especially as I was pencilled in to interview Mr Verlaine.

Within nine months Blondie had topped the charts with 'Denis' and by the autumn of 1978 scored more hits from their third album *Parallel Lines*. Another UK tour followed, this time seeing them headline the Free Trade Hall. By then I had made a bit of a name for myself in Manchester both working for a local newspaper and as the Northern correspondent for *Record Mirror*. From Factory nights at The Russell Club to big halls like The Apollo, I was putting in more hours backstage at venues than in my own home! Security guys, promotors *et al* automatically waved me through.

Meanwhile, Britain was becoming a second home to Blondie and the band was delighted that in a remarkably short space of time their career had eased into top gear. 'The Clash, Jam and other groups we've come up with have become institutions and yet the kids continue to be loyal to us. In fact, I feel we are communicating more directly to them than to our American audience,' Debbie remarked that night. The guys in the band were also on a high and asked me, as a local, what I'd got lined up for the rest of the night. I told them I was off to The Russell Club to see Yachts, an up-and-coming Liverpool band with a catchy keyboard sound. Blondie's keyboard player, Jimmy Destri, recognised the name right away having already bought their indie single called 'Suffice To Say'.

I packed Jimmy and rhythm section Clem Burke and Nigel Harrison, into my car and off we roared to the notorious inner-city club – a Jamaican joint where local etiquette demanded Special Brew was imbibed straight from the bottle. More bourgeois establishments were to catch up with this trend the following decade. The Blondie boys obviously enjoyed themselves because for the next few years I always got a call from them whenever they were in town, wondering what to do that night, first in Manchester and later in London.

Meanwhile, Blondie were developing as musicians. *Parallel Lines* featured an old song with a new arrangement, the disco oriented 'Heart of Glass'. The band might have started life as a new wave act but that did not preclude utilising the currently fashionable syncopated sound of the Bee Gees and Donna Summer. 'It's a psychic thing that has to do with the beat,' reasoned Debbie. 'The 4/4 heartbeat rhythm has a calming effect on the listener. It's almost biological.'

Being a versatile crew living in a creative city (New York), the various members of Blondie got into extra-curricular activities. The actress within Debbie led to her starring in the mystery/romance film *Union City*, while her partner, guitarist and songwriter Chris Stein, started producing other musicians, including Walter Steding who was managed by Andy Warhol. Other key contacts were Nile Rodgers and Bernard Edwards who went on to produce Harry's first solo album *KooKoo*. Throughout the 1980s, Blondie remained on hold as the various members went about their individual projects. It was during the first year of the following decade that I caught up with Debbie on her solo UK tour. Writing for *The Times*, the powers that be had decided she ought to be the lead story on the Friday arts page, unusual for a live review, so I drove up to Norwich for their first show at the University of East Anglia.

Since most of the students would still have been at primary school when the singer was pop's favourite pin-up, there wasn't the usual mad rush to get into the dressing room at the end of the gig. In fact, I pretty much had the singer to myself, along with that historic beer. By this point in her career, Debbie had scored a couple of solo hits with 'French Kissing in the USA' and I Want That Man'. Unfortunately, neither of these songs were inspired by your author... but at least the beer was cold.

CHAPTER 21

DENNIS EDWARDS

If the name escapes you, then you should recognise the voice. It was as rich as double cream flowing over a juicy peach. Dennis was one of the great Motown singers, leading The Temptations through their genre-busting, psychedelic pop-funk-soul period. Without 'Papa Was A Rolling Stone', there could have been no theme tune from *Shaft,* while other hits of the era included 'Cloud Nine', 'Ball of Confusion' and 'Just My Imagination'. We should add to this classics such as 'Get Ready' and 'I'm Gonna Make You Love Me', that exceptional late 60s double act with Diana Ross & The Supremes.

I was aware of all this when I met Dennis over dinner in Cervia, an Italian restaurant in west London, in the mid-90s. What I didn't realise was, in Temptations terms, he was the new boy, only joining the group in 1968 after David Ruffin departed for a solo career. Dennis also related some great anecdotes about his fellow stars of the day – The Beatles, The Stones, those kind of people – and was surprisingly candid about the pitfalls of being an artist at that point in time. Paramount amongst these was ownership of name, which explained why he was appearing at Harlesden's Mean Fiddler as The Temptations Revue featuring Dennis Edwards. This followed a legal wrangle with former colleague Otis Williams, the original founder of the group, who unlike Dennis rarely sang lead vocals.

'When I meet people and tell them my name, the first thing they say is, "Ah, The Temptations". I also tell them there are two words to take care of: "show" and "business". It hurts that I can't use the name but obviously I'm proud to have been part of them and my name appears alongside theirs in the Rock 'n' Roll Hall Of Fame.

'One of the great things about our music was the way it reflected the times,' he went on. 'As well as love songs like 'My Girl', one of the biggest-selling hits ever, the late 60s was the time of the Vietnam War, racial tension and poverty, and we couldn't ignore that kind of stuff. I come from Alabama and the only way to be true to your race was to express it through what you knew best – music. I don't think we ever went too far but we did make some kind of statement to contribute something positive. And we were thankful. My parents moved to Detroit so my father could work in the automobile industry, which was the first time there were good jobs for black men who could get away from being share-croppers in the South.'

The motor city was also, of course, where Berry Gordy founded the Tamla Motown label, the first step to stardom for people with Edwards' talent. In the same way that every rose has its thorns, success can be a double-edged sword, especially when it comes to relationships. 'I've been married three times,' came the confessional. 'All failures. On each occasion I never took the time to know my wife, I just wasn't listening. A lot of men are like that. There's more to love than wonderful sex,' added Dennis, who was fifty-one at the time and had been with his latest partner for twelve years. 'Two people have to learn how to love one another and it takes a while. Sometimes you marry for the wrong reasons. I married one of the wives because she was pregnant and my mother was like, "You're having a baby, you've got to marry her and give her your name,' but that doesn't mean you love them. It has taken me a lifetime to learn about relationships yet it's hard to admit that, especially when you're a connoisseur of love songs.'

Like many of the Motown family, Edwards found himself moving to California, the go-to place for many a man of good fortune in the 1970s. Something to do with the weather as well as the after-school activities. 'Living in LA meant parties going on for days on end,' he recalled. 'This restaurant opening, that launch, which I needed twenty years ago. Then I'd go on tour where there was a woman in London, another in Paris, another in Rome...'

Nice work if you could get it but for some of The Temptations it was a case of live now, pay later. 'Paul Williams shot himself after years of depression and drug abuse, David Ruffin who recommended me as his replacement in the band, died of a crack overdose after serving time in jail and Eddie Kendricks succumbed to cancer two years ago. I'll never forget the last time I saw him in hospital. He weighed about 65 lbs and said, "I'm not going to make it, but don't you stop. Keep going even if they do own the name."'

He waved at two policemen walking past the restaurant window. 'Don't those guys have guns now? Ours carry Uzis because of the war on drugs. It's ruining the world. What can you do about it? Everybody's affected. Even if it's not in your family, there's someone you know and the people who are into it will steal everything from your house. Then you go to somewhere like Geneva and even a chef is on a six-figure salary.'

On a happier note, London also reminded him of the first time he appeared on *Top of the Pops* and especially meeting The Beatles. 'It must have been the start of the rift which people have said was caused by Yoko. John Lennon, Paul McCartney and Ringo Starr were pushing one another around the place before going on stage. Then on another occasion, Mick Jagger walked in flashing a bottle of amyl nitrate. He said, "Do you do drugs?" and here's me, a young kid bowing to peer pressure. I said, "Oh yeah, I'll try it," but actually I'd never done anything. That was the era. Anyone who says they went through the 60s or 70s without doing drugs is lying. Then there was the President who said: "I didn't inhale." I guess that was when the rot really set in.'

CHAPTER 22

DIANA ROSS

Diana Ross may have had one of the sweetest voices in the history of pop and soul, but her uncompromising attitude is straight out of the manual of rock 'n' roll. She was still at school when she decided to become a singer and had a useful neighbour in Smokey Robinson. He helped Diana and a group of her friends secure an audition at Motown, attended by the label's founder, Berry Gordy. Advised to finish her studies, Ms Ross blagged a summer job as an office girl and persuaded Gordy to produce a single. It didn't get very far and neither did the next couple of attempts.

By this stage Motown had earned the nickname 'Hitsville USA', underpinned by the songwriting team of Holland, Dozier and Holland. Ross encouraged them to sprinkle a little gold-dust over her group The Supremes and from then on, their luck changed. Their run of success began in 1965 with the No. 1 hit 'Where Did Our Love Go?'. What made them different was Diana's light yet sexy voice, something which made her stand out from the deeper soul sound of most of her contemporaries. Her endearing catchiness ensured Ross kept returning to the charts for the rest of the decade and beyond.

Record sales were bolstered by many sensational live shows. Not only were they almost theatrical in their extravagance but the singer always seemed enthusiastic about interacting with her audience. The variety of material stretched from The Supremes' hits to Broadway tunes and tributes to influences such as Bessie

Smith. Then there were the films. Having established Tamla Motown as one of the most popular and successful labels in recording history, Gordy decided to get into movies, with Ross in the starring role. Although Diana was still young, she took on the part of one of the greatest blues singers of the century, Billie Holiday. Diana's portrayal of Holiday in *Lady Sings the Blues* astounded both the movie- and music-loving public, as did *Mahogany*, a rags-to-riches tale of a model written with Ross in mind.

Despite the fabulous success delivered by their partnership, Ross did not always see eye to creative eye with mentor Gordy. For example, he didn't want to release 1970's 'Reach Out and Touch' because it was in waltz time as opposed to being the kind of music with which her fans were familiar. Diana, however, felt the song's message was significant, especially with regard to the social alienation caused by the Vietnam War. Hence her reluctance to compromise, a quality which arguably assisted her rise to superstardom in the 1980s. By this time, she had left Motown for musical as well as business reasons. The previous decade had seen a cultural shift from soul to disco, leading Diana to team up with Nile Rodgers and Bernard Edwards, the hit makers behind Chic and Sister Sledge. Then on *Silk Electric* she started to write more of her own material and it was at the launch of this album that we met at Claridge's Hotel in 1982.

It was supposed to be a small gathering for the European press but, as luck would have it, there was some cock-up with a gilt-edged invitation finding its way into the *Record Mirror* office. Rounding up the usual suspects, I arrived at the palatial hotel at midday, greeted by immaculately clad waiters dispensing goldfish-bowl sized glasses of the most refreshing in-house cocktail – gin, champagne and fresh lime, a slight twist on a French 75. After several of these, it was time to meet La Ross who wondered if I was a Spaniard. We talked about the ever-changing music scene and some of the new groups around. She was glad to share the same record label with Duran Duran and said she adored the extravagant clothes of the New Romantics.

Had she heard of Soft Cell or their rendition of her own 'Where Did Our Love Go?' on the B-side of their chart-topping 'Tainted Love'?

'Soft Cell? Tainted Love? That all sounds amazing,' she gasped like a child hearing a particularly enchanting fairy tale. Then again it could have been the thermonuclear drinks. She certainly gave the impression of enjoying a sherbet or two, a matter confirmed when she rocked up at Midem in the early 1990s. On this occasion, Ross was hosting a dinner to celebrate her thirty years as a recording artist at the equally grand Carlton International hotel in Cannes. It followed an edgy press conference in which a particularly sleazy tabloid hack questioned her about the behaviour of her mate Michael Jackson and his predilection for much younger friends. 'I'm not here to talk about Michael but if you're asking me about whether I support him, of course I do.' Following an unsettling silence, a less controversial member of the Euro media came to the rescue. 'I want to thank you for all the years of great music,' he gushed in classic continental journo style, while another member of the audience started wibbling narcissistically away about how hard it had been for her to become a pop star herself.

Next, somebody pointed out that Diana was wearing a fur coat. 'Actually, it's not real fur but it's funny you should mention that. When The Supremes first became successful, one of the first things I wanted was a coat with a fur collar... but of course times have changed. When you're brought up poor, you want to look your best and I still love wearing evening gowns. Otherwise I don't think my lifestyle has changed that much. I always used to take my children to school or the market and

I'm very happy with the type of fame I've had in my life. I've never thought people have wanted to hurt me, they just want to touch me. I don't allow myself a lot of security because I don't think I have the kind of personality which provokes negativity. Somehow I've been able to have a nice balanced life. I can be normal and I like who I am. I'm a very happy person and I don't think I hang on to anger. I think it's to do with background. I come from good stock and take good care of myself mentally as well as physically.'

A more helpful question was how a woman with such a healthy appetite managed to keep her weight down. 'It must be my genes and my metabolism,' she replied. 'I stay active and I eat very well. Vegetables not junk food. My favourite meals include pickles and olives, so I get a lot of flavour without resorting to rich sauces and never tend to gain a lot of weight.'

Unfortunately for Diana, pickles and olives didn't appear on the menu at that evening's gala dinner. However, there was no shortage of the local rosé wine to maintain the singer's celebrated twinkle. In fact, for dessert, she gave us a turn, an acapella version of 'Chain Reaction', sashaying between the lines of banqueting tables and openly flirting with the guests. That transition from soul to disco certainly had a lasting effect.

CHAPTER 23

DONOVAN

School trips and late-night gigs were never an obvious match, especially in the windswept Hebrides of Scotland, but take a van-load of embryonic rockers and a local star, and something is bound to happen. Add to the mix an easy-going teacher partial to post-hike pints and we're in business. In Portree, capital of the Isle of Skye to be precise.

There had been talk of Donovan buying a castle nearby, presumably the spoils of a four-year run of hits ranging from 'Catch The Wind' and 'Colours' through to 'Mellow Yellow' and 'Hurdy Gurdy Man'. Suddenly a gig was announced at the village hall, all the more appealing to us teenage fans following a music free week in tents.

The singer-songwriter did not come on until bedtime but there was plenty to drink and requests for his songs were conscientiously met. Of course, the Scottish troubadour would never be as hip as Dylan even if the pair did hang out together when the American legend toured Britain. But Donovan did record with members of Led Zeppelin and enjoyed a successful joint venture with Jeff Beck with the single 'Barabajagal'. Donovan also worked with The Beatles, teaching Lennon and McCartney the finger-picking guitar technique deployed on *White Album* tracks such as 'Dear Prudence' and 'Happiness is a Warm Gun'. In fact, it was John Lennon who claimed, 'Donovan was way ahead of The Beatles and all the other artists with his music, fashion and views on life.'

With the benefit of hindsight, the talented musician can also be seen as an early pioneer of World Music. Check out the use of congas, uilleann pipes and other Celtic instruments on 'There is a Mountain', another of his 1960s hits. We talked about this and other subjects when we finally met for an interview for *Hello!* magazine in 1992. His forty-date tour included four separate shows in the capital alone. Understandably, he was no longer living on Skye, having moved to bring up his children. So how did he feel about the comparisons with Dylan? A help or a hindrance after all this time?

'We were both influenced by Woody Guthrie,' replied Donovan, who like Guthrie used to feature the legend 'This Machine Kills' on his acoustic guitar. Guthrie, however, added the word 'fascists' to the end of that statement. 'Not only with singing protest songs but also the look, wearing a cap plus the harmonica on a neck holder so we could play guitar at the same time. Joan Baez and Pete Seeger left their mark too, giving us encouragement.' Another name from the past also came into the equation, Buffy Sainte-Marie. In the early 1970s she sang the soundtrack to the controversial native American Western film, *Soldier Blue*, but the previous decade she wrote another song about conflict, 'Universal Soldier', the title track of Donovan's debut album. This was round about the same time as Dylan was releasing his best political songs.

'Then came the anti-Vietnam marches,' Donovan continued, 'until we realised that more could be achieved through art, song and festivals, which is pretty much how the whole folk-rock scene came about. A group of us were doing the same things in different countries. In Greenwich Village there was Roger McGuinn of The Byrds, whose 'Mr Tambourine Man' was the first folk-rock hit, and singer John Sebastian. Canada brought us Neil Young and Steve Stills with 'Stop Children, What's That

Sound?' while in England guitarists like Jimmy Page started amplifying folk music. Although Led Zeppelin are regarded as being the first heavy metal band, their music was influenced by folk as well as blues, which is particularly prevalent on their third album. Meanwhile I liked blues and jazz, especially when it came to experimenting with different kinds of rhythms.'

Unfortunately, all this pioneering and musical experimentation had its drawbacks. 'The kind of pop-roots fusion we were aiming at was such a new concept that it was hard to put a band together, let alone get gigs. In London there were clubs like Les Cousins and The Troubadour but nobody made any money. In fact, even as a solo performer with no band to pay, I hardly ever got paid. Before making records, the only way I earned anything was by busking.'

At the time we spoke, Donovan was looking forward to touring with his twenty-one-year-old daughter, Astrella Celeste, on percussion and vocals. 'She worked with me during her school years, playing and singing with other young musicians like Andy Williams's two sons. Unlike her friends, she's not into dance music, she's more into Celtic sounds like her dad! I can't deny it's down to upbringing. We've mainly lived in Ireland which has always influenced my music. I know people used to laugh at the time but the long flowing robes I used to wear were part of that attitude. Whereas The Who favoured pop art gear, I dressed in what I suppose you'd call mythological romantic clothes which reflected what I was singing about. The Celtic cultural look!' Comprising eco-friendly natural fabrics, no less, at a time when most of the population were sweating in unhealthy man-made fibres. 'The only other environmentally conscious celebrity I knew in those days was Brigitte Bardot,' the singer reveals referring to one of the most gorgeous pouting actresses of the era. 'Our common concerns brought us together but our relationship never went further than that. I'd already met my wife.'

Another name that cropped up was Pink Floyd's David Gilmour who had just contributed to Donovan's latest album. An old mucker from the 60s perchance? 'No, I actually only just met him recently through the violinist Nigel Kennedy. It's quite amusing that it took someone half our age to bring the two of us together but it shows that, if you stay around long enough, anything can happen.' Including being interviewed by an old punk who saw him onstage during his schooldays.

CHAPTER 24

DUSTY SPRINGFIELD

As a teenager Dusty Springfield sang folk music in coffee houses, the most fashionable kind of venue during the pre-Beatles era. When the 1960s got underway she started to enjoy the most successful run of hit singles ever achieved by a solo female artist. In the fullness of time most of them came to be regarded as classics, including 'You Don't Have to Say You Love Me' and 'Son of a Preacher Man'. As a result, she could easily be categorised as a pop star in the same vein as Cilla Black or Sandie Shaw, except Dusty possessed the unmistakable soaring pipes of a torch singer, closer in genre to the likes of Scott Walker or Julie London. She was a perfectionist to boot, choosing to interpret songs by some of the most talented writers of the day like Burt Bacharach and Carole King.

More than half a century later, the performance and production of these mini-masterpieces hold their own with anything recorded using modern technology. Yet, midway through her career, Dusty decided to turn her back on guaranteed success in order to experiment with blues and soul. While her contemporaries were queuing up to take part in the Eurovision Song Contest, Springfield went Stateside to work with R&B pioneers Jerry Wexler, Tom Dowd and Arif Mardin. Between them they had guided the careers of everybody from Otis Redding and Aretha Franklin to Ray Charles and the Bee Gees. At their behest, the former folk-singer recorded *Dusty In Memphis*, still regarded as a classic of its time. This is why I have decided to label her as a full-blown rock 'n' roll person. Dusty Springfield is one of the few female singers ever to have blended talent, versatility and courage across a career covering multiple genres.

When I interviewed the singer in the early 1990s, she had been working with the Pet Shop Boys on the soundtrack to the film *Scandal*. This was based on the true story of a cabinet minister's affair with a courtesan which brought down the government of the day. How did an icon of the 60s come to join forces with one of the most idiosyncratic duos of the 80s?

'Like all the good things in life which have happened to me, the opportunity just came along,' she smiled. 'My manager received a phone call saying a tape was coming over and could we give an answer within twenty-four hours.' The track was 'Nothing Has Been Proved', which was commissioned by Steve Woolley, the producer of *Scandal*. Neil Tennant of the PSBs then had the idea of using Dusty on vocals. Their collaboration also yielded a further hit, 'In Private', both songs appearing on Dusty's 1990 album, *Reputation*. Her association with the Pet Shop Boys actually began earlier in the 1980s when she duetted with Tennant on 'What Have I Done to Deserve This?', a single which charted on both sides of the Atlantic.

'That was my re-entry into the music industry,' Dusty pointed out. 'I didn't have to do much. Just sing the chorus in the middle. It was an ideal way of making a comeback, much easier than having to devise some project of my own. If you sit around waiting for something to happen, you can bet it's not going to.'

Success with the Pet Shop Boys led to Dusty coming back to live in England following many years in America. When we met, she was in the process of moving to the countryside near Windsor, a quicker journey into the West End than from north London where she was originally brought up. She had recently turned fifty and reckoned she had benefitted from taking time off. 'The 1980s wasn't a great time for artists signed to small labels,' she admitted. 'I found myself with one company after another taken over by corporations who had little interest in the rosters they had inherited. It happened to a lot of people.'

I mentioned that apart from conducting interviews for *Hello!* magazine, I was writing corporate music stories for *The Times*, highlighting the increasing regularity of record companies being run by lawyers and accountants, in the same way as the film industry had been taken over following the unprecedented success of *Jaws*. 'Oh good, expose them all!' she enthused. 'I expect you have to go out and meet a lot of people... Oh, you do?... so you're a party animal?' Guilty as charged, your Honour!

'I did an incredible amount of partying back in the day,' Dusty admitted. 'The Ad Lib Club, the Scotch of St James... all those places,' she laughed. 'I knew everybody. I remember meeting Mick Jagger at one of those poll winner concerts at the Albert Hall. He was leering at me from the corner of the dressing room and as soon as we made eye contact, he asked me out. No, I didn't take him up on his offer. He had this terrible "bad boy" image and he frightened the life out of me!'

A case of survival of the smartest as well as the fittest.

ELVIS COSTELLO

If ever the expression 'an enigma wrapped in a conundrum' was to apply to an English rock star, it would be Elvis Costello. Since 1977, when his singles sales were sufficient for him to appear on *Top of the Pops*, he has released an average of one album a year but rarely been a household name. The parents of my generation have heard of The Beatles and the Stones, and even Dylan and Springsteen, but Costello? Paradoxically they are more likely to be familiar with Joe Loss, whose orchestra featured Elvis's dad as vocalist.

Costello was not only the first solo singer-songwriter to emerge from the new wave but also one with a massive collection of songs. By early 1981 he had released five classic albums and toured the world. I first saw him at Rafters, a basement club in Manchester, in 1978 and then in Berlin two years later. After the German show, I managed to get backstage for a brief conversation before being shooed away by his notoriously officious management team. I made no protests about interviews or being from *Record Mirror*. That would have been like a red rag to a bull, as future events would prove.

They say revenge is a dish best served cold, so I thought I'd try again later. The opportunity came when Elvis was promoting the *Trust* album the following year. Despite boasting epic cuts like 'Shot With His Own Gun' and 'Big Sister's Clothes', the record hadn't sold nearly as well as its predecessors so there was the possibility he would be more co-operative when it came to fraternising with fans. It had already been made clear that press interviews were off the agenda so I would have to masquerade as just another fan, preferably not in London where I'd be more likely to be rumbled by a record company PR or someone else in the business. I targeted Manchester, my old stamping ground, where I knew the manager of the Apollo Theatre would give me a backstage pass.

After the show I left a polite gap before ascending the familiar stone stairs to the dressing room. There I was greeted by Elvis's manager, Jake Riviera, who invited me to pour myself a drink. Boy, did I need one! I sloshed the best part of a pint of wine into a plastic tumbler. Meanwhile, Elvis had appeared and was enjoying being hugged by a couple of teenage girls. This proved rather useful since it allowed me to keep a low profile, my concealed tape machine doing most of the work.

During the concert Costello had alluded to the disappointing sales of *Trust* before playing 'Watch Your Step', that brilliant encapsulation of paranoia. Had that been inspired by a recent experience, I asked? 'No, I wrote it about five years ago, actually,' he replied. 'It just seemed to fit in with the mood of the new material so I decided to include it in the set.'

Ah, so it was one of the famous stockpile of 400 songs rumoured to have existed at the start of your career? 'Sort of. We definitely have a lot of material which is why we're able to vary the set each night. I also like to include covers by favourite artists like Merle Haggard and Bobby Blue Band. We play longer sets these days as opposed to shooting through the show at breakneck speed, which we used to do a couple of years ago. We got called back eight times earlier in this tour.' Which should help revive sales of *Trust*... 'Well that's what tours are designed to do but, to be honest, one of the main reasons we're on the road is because we haven't played for two years. We did most of Europe during 1980 and started this year with an American tour. We were able to play theatres, which was pretty good, considering.'

That last qualifying word was included for good reason. In 1979 Costello almost blew his career in America following a drunken episode in a hotel bar. Elvis was being wound up by ageing US musicians Bonnie Bramlett and Steve Stills, and retorted by slagging off America, its customs and its entertainers. Two of those he singled out were Ray Charles and James Brown. One he insulted as being 'a blind, ignorant nigger', the other 'a jive-ass nigger'. The media got wind of these thoughtless remarks and the incident became a national outrage resulting in death threats and the picketing of later gigs. Did he believe the mishap had caused long-term damage? 'Yeah, there's no doubt about it,' he admitted. 'I mean I got into this stupid argument and to try and finish it I thought I'd shock them into submission. But I was touring and working so much at the time it wasn't always easy to stay in control.'

Without looking in his direction, I could practically feel Mr Riviera tuning into this confessional so I thought I'd better steer it into less controversial waters. As a Liverpudlian, Costello was a schoolboy when he met The Beatles in a local television studio. This was mainly due to his father's status as a singer who was often on TV. What did Elvis think of the current lively Liverpool scene? 'I really like that record 'Reward' by The Teardrop Explodes,' he enthused. 'Wah! Heat sounds good too. I'm not sure about Echo & The Bunnymen or Orchestral Manoeuvres in the Dark but The Original Mirrors are okay. Their singer, Steve Allen, used to be in Deaf School with Clive Langer who is now a great producer,' said the singer about the man who would soon go on to produce some of his own records. 'My favourite songwriter at the moment is Chris Difford of Squeeze. As a lyricist he really is the business.'

By this stage arrangements were being made to board the tour bus to go back to the hotel. Being in possession of my own wheels, I went ahead, narrowly beating Elvis to the bar at the Post House Hotel in South Manchester. He bought me another drink and just as the mood was becoming a little more relaxed, his attitude suddenly changed. He confronted me with a glazed, quizzical look and challenged me with the words, 'You're from *Record Mirror*! You're too suss and your paper has got it in for me.' I pointed out that his last three albums had received five-star reviews. However, my cover had been blown, presumably by another musician in the bar who I'd interviewed the previous year. The next thing I knew, I got whacked in the side of the head by Riviera and narrowly avoided a kick in the groin. Whether by reflex or design, I attempted to retaliate but suddenly found myself grabbed from behind. I half-turned only to encounter a Viking looming over me. It was one of the Swedish security guys on loan from ABBA.

'You're coming outside,' roared Riviera – but luckily the moment had passed. Bar staff and other bystanders intervened demanding we cool it. A good time to make an exit, I felt, pausing only to check that my tape machine was still in place.

Over the next couple of decades Costello's career was to bloom and flourish, from working with Paul McCartney and Burt Bacharach to recording highbrow classical albums with the likes of The Brodski Quartet. Strangely enough, our paths have never crossed since that night, although I did review his *Brutal Youth* album in 1994. It was his reprise punk CD, an appropriate conclusion one might say.

ERIC CLAPTON

One of the most outstanding musicians in the history of rock, Eric Clapton's virtuosity has been matched by an ability to change musical styles. Initially revered as a blues guitarist throughout the 1960s and 70s, he confounded fans by moving on to soul, folk and country while establishing a separate career as a singer-songwriter and reluctant celebrity. It was in the latter role that I enjoyed a raucous conversation with the legend originally nicknamed 'God'.

This was in the mid-1980s when he still enjoyed a drink or two. He happened to be sitting at the next table in media haunt The Groucho Club, dining with David English, a music industry executive. English had previously been an employee of Eric's first manager, Robert Stigwood, and appears in the Bill Wyman chapter of this book. An exuberant reunion was soon underway, a refreshed and twinkling Clapton joking about my resemblance to a certain American actor. Somebody ordered a cappuccino and Eric shot to his feet, toasting, 'Yes, let's all have an Al Pacino!' Once again, I regretted not having kept in touch with teenage schoolmates, Clapton fans one and all.

We would all have been about fourteen years old when the coolest act on the planet was Cream, the trio Eric put together with fellow instrumentalists and genii Jack Bruce and Ginger Baker. Though only together for three years, their four-album career was a rock 'n' roll odyssey, raging from *avante-garde* hits like 'I Feel Free' and 'Strange Brew' to extended improvisations such as 'Spoonful' and 'I'm So Glad' from their renowned live shows. There were also catchy singles like 'Badge' featuring Beatle George Harrison, which was ironic since Clapton had quit chart dandies The Yardbirds when he was nineteen as his passion for the blues was more powerful than any ambition to be a pop star. His next move was the pre-Cream album John Mayall's *Blues Breakers with Eric Clapton*, which successive generations of artists still regard as one of the finest LPs of the genre. Yet, in the same way as the blues gave Clapton a yearning to apply his style to rock, the demise of Cream led to a decision to start again almost from scratch. He joined a couple of unknown musicians, Delaney and Bonnie, on tour and returned to life as a session musician with the likes of Aretha Franklin on *Lady Soul*.

These tours of duty in turn led to the singer-songwriter stage of his journey. For an artist whose tastes were honed on American bluesmen such as Big Bill Broonzey, Robert Johnson and BB King, an album like *461 Ocean Boulevard* came as a surprise. Following the cure of his heroin addiction, it represented a renewed optimism in life and still has the light and laidback feeling its title suggests, from the soaring melodic 'Let It Grow' to the reggae pop of Bob Marley's 'I Shot The Sheriff'. By 1997's *Slowhand*, Clapton's musical interests had switched to country music, although historic crowd-pleaser 'Wonderful Tonight' was practically an MOR ballad. Here, once again, former heavy rocker Eric was throwing the market a curve and reinventing himself.

To all intents and purposes, Eric's solo career had begun with *Layla and Other Assorted Love Songs* credited to Derek and The Dominoes. Layla was based on an Indian story of unrequited love. In real life it referred to George Harrison's wife Patti who Eric went on to marry. The first time I met Eric and Patti was at a charity event at a Park Lane hotel in 1984. They were sitting quietly at a table when, not believing my eyes, I blundered over and introduced myself as being from the *Daily Express*. Eric got up, shook hands, introduced me to Patti and invited me to join them. A waiter arrived with a bottle of champagne and we started to talk, the conversation growing louder as the fizz kicked in. This gradually attracted the attention of most of the famous people in the room who, tuning into a certain amount of name-dropping, came and joined us for what turned into an anecdote-swapping masterclass.

A surfeit of booze led to partial amnesia but I remember Glyn Johns, top record producer for The Who, Stones, Zeppelin, Dylan and The Clash to name but a few, asking me to repeat a story about a famous band giving their even more famous label boss a hard time in the recording studio. By the end of the night, fellow guests were wondering why I didn't have a career as a TV presenter. The simple answer is it probably wouldn't have suited my liver as much as my ego. Still, two good nights out with Eric is worth far more than being just another yesterday's man on the telly.

CHAPTER 27

ERIC STEWART
& 10cc

It's quite simple, really. Anyone who lived in Liverpool in the 1960s had some connection with The Beatles. In the school holidays I would go and stay with Cousin Henry in Menlove Avenue, a few yards from where John Lennon grew up. His family had previously lived next door to Brian Epstein who couldn't believe Henry listened only to classical music. If I took a taxi from Lime Street station, the driver would be almost apologetic about the fact that he or she were part of the generation who used to see the group at The Cavern.

In Manchester everybody knew 10cc. My three best friends all went to the same school as Kevin Godley who, along with bandmate Lol Creme, went on to become one of the biggest directors of pop videos. Lol Creme's sister used to hang out in the same clubs and bars as me and my friends. Graham Gouldman, another member of 10cc, was married to the daughter of someone who lived in the same block of flats as my mother. Guitarist Eric Stewart, who so memorably took the lead vocal on 'I'm Not in Love', well, he was the 'yoch' or gentile to be more polite. 'We were originally going to call ourselves Three Yids and a Yoch,' he joked when we met for an interview in 1993, 'but our manager didn't like the idea very much.'

This was an interesting year for music inasmuch as it highlighted a lot of problems which would lead to the downfall of the industry, in particular the major record companies. It was around this time I started writing a weekly column for the *Evening Standard* exposing the corporate idiocy of the music business, especially the prioritising of the promotion and marketing of records over the actual music itself. So Eric and I had quite a lot to talk about, not least because of a recent incident in 10cc history. 'A year ago, a record company suggested the original line-up should reunite to make a new album. Our previous one had gone platinum. So we went to Todd Rundgren's studio in Bearsville, upstate New York, and worked with producer Gary Katz of Steely Dan fame.

'The record company gave us all the money we needed but by the time it was finished there had been a change in managing directors. So we had a meeting with the A&R department about what single to choose and a financial adviser sat in. He asked, "How many copies do you expect to sell?", to which we replied, "Maybe a quarter of a million." The money guy reckoned the promotional cost would be too high so the whole thing was scrapped. Pathetic. Bear in mind we'd been having hits like 'Rubber Bullets', 'Wall Street Shuffle' and 'I'm Mandy, Fly Me' for twenty years, so what chance would a new band have of building a fan base if the record company couldn't believe in a band like 10cc?

'If it's not accountants calling the shots, it's others who are just as poorly qualified. I was listening to George Michael talk about his problems with Sony, basically a hi-fi manufacturer who had taken over CBS so they could have access to their back catalogue. And they're telling George how to make records! They might as well be battery farming. Let's get back to music people running the music industry and maybe record sales will improve. These days in order to get to No. 1, a single only needs to sell 30,000 copies. 'I'm Not In Love' sold a million during the first week it was out!'

One should add to this that 10cc were respected and taken seriously by other musicians and music critics alike. It helped that in the early days they owned their own studio and were able to experiment and pioneer their high-tech sounds, while simultaneously remaining catchy and commercial. Stewart was also at a loss to know why CDs were so much more expensive than vinyl albums when they were so much cheaper to produce. 'The accountants are encouraging the labels to make a fast buck which will end up simply killing their own market.' The rest, of course, is history, the record companies winding up in too poor a state to be able to take on the internet. But at least 10cc were from an era when bands could make hay while the sun shone. Eric went on to work on two of Paul McCartney's most successful solo albums and produced an album for Agnetha of ABBA, 'the blonde one with the big bum! I asked all my mates in the business to write a song each... Jeff Lynne, Eddie Grant, Justin Hayward...' A far cry from the teenager who took over lead vocals in The Mindbenders following the departure of Wayne Fontana. Eric sang on the evergreen 'Groovy Kind of Love' which jump-started his career by topping the charts.

In contrast, bassist Graham Gouldman started out as a songwriter composing 'For Your Love' and 'Heart Full of Soul' for The Yardbirds, one of the hippest bands of the 1960s. He also wrote the lyrically smart 'Bus Stop' for The Hollies and even produced a Ramones album.

By the mid-1980s, Godley and Creme were mainly making a living directing ground-breaking videos for everybody from The Police to Duran Duran and Frankie Goes To Hollywood. It was around this time that I took a starring role in a mini press conference mainly attended by writers for European magazines. None of them seemed up to asking many questions and were quite relieved that I was doing most of their work. The non-stop dialogue was doubtless enhanced when the duo opened the proceedings by rolling a spliff the size of a pool cue.

Kevin was very much a face about town and, for a while, I would bump into him on more occasions than any other Mancunian, including members of my own family. He was a regular at The Groucho Club and one evening I spent hours there sitting at the same table as him and Ronnie Wood of the Rolling Stones. Shame he didn't have his video camera with him but I guess we're all entitled to a night off.

Fast forward to 1992 and the launch of U2's video of their Zoo tour at Madame Tussaud's. Mr Godley turned up with a camera and crew, and this time it was my turn to be interviewed, mainly about U2 and their music. I never got to see the resulting footage but, in case anyone out there gets lucky, I'd welcome the feedback.

CHAPTER 28

FEARGAL SHARKEY

One of the oldest jokes in rock 'n' roll involves ownership of the van. Bill Wyman of the Rolling Stones felt he only got the job of bass player because he had a van in which they could drive all the gear to gigs. Usually, it's the drummer who has the van as he wouldn't be able to take much of his kit on board a bus. With The Undertones it was the opposite. Singer Feargal Sharkey was the youngster with the van; as a teenager he had a day job as a TV repair and delivery man. By night he would drive the band to gigs all over their native Northern Ireland.

Although very young, The Undertones were one of the first acts to break through following the first flush of punk. Their indie single 'Teenage Kicks' found the ears of Radio One hero John Peel and a major recording contract duly followed. By 1979 they were regularly on the road which was when I caught them at Manchester's Factory, shortly before I moved down to London. I got chatting to Feargal after the show and found him rather shy. In his distinctly non-rock 'n' roll anorak he looked about sixteen but was actually four years older.

The last time I saw Feargal Sharkey was in my back garden in East Finchley, attending my fiftieth birthday party. He arrived with his wife who is Scottish. I don't normally get on with Scottish girls in London, finding them feisty and defensive. In contrast, she was very charming. I don't think she was his first wife because I remember seeing him around for a while with a girl of Middle Eastern appearance, possibly Iranian. But of all the rock stars I've ever met, Feargal was the least likely to talk about personal matters.

In the early 1990s he became poacher-turned-gamekeeper, switching from being a singer to entering the business side of the industry. First, he became an A&R man and later started working with industry bodies such as The Radio Authority and the Live Music Forum. Apart from being neighbours we had radio and live gigs in common. I had gradually made the transition from interviewing artists to investigating the *modus operandi* of the music industry: Sharkey had changed careers altogether. After being the singer in a relatively low-key pop group (imagine The Ramones without the haircuts and leathers) Feargal enjoyed a couple of years as a fully-fledged rock star.

Following the fourth Undertones album he left his teenage pals and sought thrills anew, briefly with ex-Depeche Mode musician Vince Clarke and then with a brace of American heavyweights. Sharkey's first hit was written by Maria McKee, one of the first alt-country stylists, whose brother Bryan McLean was the guitarist in West Coast legends, Love. His next hit was 'You Little Thief' about his relationship with McKee, written by Benmont Tench, keyboard player with Tom Petty and the Heartbreakers. At least that was Tom's summary of the situation when we touched base at a music and media conference in Amsterdam in the late 1980s.

Whatever the case, Feargal had certainly gained in confidence from The Undertones days. When he sang his hits on *Top of the Pops*, gone was the chronic leisurewear in favour of designer suits, bootlace ties and extravagant choreography. By the time he had assumed the industry roles, the singer had added public speaking skills to his sharp new repertoire. I remember one year at Tony Wilson's annual In The City media bash in Manchester, Feargal practically stole the show with his extrovert behaviour. He certainly helped us get the best table at the Yang

Sing restaurant which had just won an award for being the best Chinese restaurant in Britain.

Working for the Radio Authority as the 'live music czar' was like being a paralegal. I remember one morning we caught the same underground train going into central London. I was trying to keep my voice down while asking him about his various exploits. He, in turn, answered with all the volume and articulacy of a talk show host. Most of the people around us in the crowded carriage pretended not to be listening but their looks of concentration suggested otherwise. Travelling by Tube may have its drawbacks but you'll never get to hone your speech skills delivering tellies in a van.

CHAPTER 29

FRANCIS ROSSI

It is not surprising that Status Quo would have been together for half a century if Rick Parfitt had not succumbed to a fatal infection a couple of years ago. Nor that the seeds of the group were sown when Francis Rossi had barely reached his teens, for this lead singer and guitarist is the epitome of a rock 'n' roll person, his temperament ranging from hyperactive to absolutely crackers.

I interviewed Rossi a few times between the 1970s and the 1990s, and it was like being caught in a flood. However energetic Quo appeared onstage, in person his control panel is cranked up to eleven. At least. It is all the more ridiculous considering his staunch Roman Catholic parents named him after Saint Francis of Assisi. I first met him soon after I arrived at *Record Mirror* in 1979. The paper was about to celebrate its twenty-fifth anniversary so it seemed appropriate to include the British band which had been together the longest. Other contenders like the Stones, The Who and The Kinks had all started up around the same time but had endured more changes of personnel.

So, Mr Rossi, you're in charge of the longest surviving line-up of continuously gigging musicians in UK rock history... what do you think of that? 'What do I think?' he replied. 'There's no one more surprised than me. There was nobody less likely to break into the business than ourselves and, having done that, it was even more unlikely we'd be able to sustain it.' Really? One would have thought that with their basic, earthy catchy simplicity Quo would have been onto a winner from the start.

'Oh yeah,' he agreed. 'Our sound was basic enough, but not easy to do and make happen every time. I suppose there was a chemistry and that's obviously what the kids went for.'

It wasn't instant karma, however. After a couple of hits towards the end of the 1960s – the psychedelically-inclined 'Pictures of Matchstick Men' and 'Ice in the Sun' – Quo went through a lean period. So lean, in fact, that the band were reduced to wearing jeans onstage. 'Yes,' Francis reflected, 'In those days you were conditioned towards dressing up. We went through that whole frilly shirt and three-piece suit scene but, by about 1971, we were so broke we *had* to come on in denims.' This accidentally set the style for a whole generation of boogie bands, the sort with their own brand of head-banging stagecraft. Quo's pared-down look also suited the infectious refrains of 'Caroline', 'Down Down', 'Rockin' All Over the World' and all the rest of their classics.

'Well, there's been a few happy accidents. Not long ago we got fed up with the old routine of single, album, single and so on, so we thought we'd put out an EP – quite unheard of at that time. As it happened, it was our thirteenth year together, our thirteenth 45 and the running time totalled thirteen minutes! None of that was planned, it just worked out that way. It was the same with our Rockin' All Over the World campaign. It was what we were doing so we named the album after it. There was no masterplan but it did show we could handle a world tour. It's funny, I bumped into a bloke from The Boomtown Rats the other day – no, not the gobby one – and he said, "You've always broken the rules, haven't you?" but our attitude has always been: "Things have a way of sorting themselves out so let's just let them." Let's face it, we'd been together since we were twelve or thirteen so what else were we going to do? As much as anything, we let things happen out of a sense of security.'

Clearly, it's worked. Quo have gone on to sell 120 million

albums, not that success ever seems to have gone to their heads. 'No matter how big you are to one set of people, to another lot you're nothing at all,' he said when we met a few years later. This was when Status Quo were headlining at the Milton Keynes bowl in 1984. 'A few miles down the road there will be people who won't even be aware that this show is going on. It's vital to realise that there are other things going on in the world. I mean, some bleeding hippo in darkest Africa doesn't know about us, neither does a woman in India with three starving kids.

'On the other hand, when you've found a successful formula, you'd be a fool to dump it. People talk about our 'style' but how do you actually define it? We play shuffles; it's what we like to play. People liked it when they came to see us so we carried on doing it. After we'd struggled to get to that stage, there was no way we were suddenly going to turn around and try to be cool and do something else.' Francis then revealed that one night he was listening to the radio and a DJ joked, "There go the lads again, same old three chords." ...But actually, it was double that. There were three basic chords and also three minor chords for which The Beatles were often praised for introducing to pop.' This is the appeal of Status Quo: the immediate simplicity that meets the ear is actually more complex to create than one realises.

Soon after this conversation, Quo extended the joke by releasing an album entitled *In Search of the Fourth Chord*. Then they went the whole hog and formed a record label of their own bearing the same name. 'Frankly, I don't like to boast but I've seen it all before,' said Francis. 'In 1969 I met this geezer in Berlin who told us he was planning to do a cover version of our song 'Down the Dustpipe'. As it happened, it didn't work out – his first album didn't sell well either. The next thing we knew, he was in America set to become one of the biggest stars of all time. His name? Elton John!'

CHAPTER 30

GEORGE MICHAEL

I first met George Michael and Andrew Ridgely, his partner in crime, early in their career in the summer of 1982. They called themselves Wham! and were part of a new generation of pop stars that included Spandau Ballet and Duran Duran. Their debut single, 'Wham Rap', was the English equivalent of what was starting to emerge in America with bands like Grandmaster Flash. Only Wham! were more commercial than political despite references to 'soul on the dole' and asking their audience 'Do you enjoy what you do?'

Following another hit, 'Young Guns (Go for It)', again about teenage hedonism, I decided to write a piece for *Flexipop!*, an irreverent take on teen magazines published by two former *Record Mirror* colleagues. We decided it would be fun to do a parody on the photo love story enduringly popular in teenage girls' magazines such as *Jackie*. George and Andrew would be having a typical boys' night out at the Camden Palace only instead of meeting two lovestruck girls, they would get horribly drunk, throw up and have to be escorted home. The combination of self-deprecating humour and originality went down well with the duo and we kept in touch. When I bumped into them one night at a party, they told me a good tale about some contretemps they had had with one of their fashion designers which was about to end up in court. The Ad Lib gossip column in the *Evening Standard* went for it like a shot.

The following year Wham! scored another autobiographical hit with 'Bad Boys' shortly before their first album, *Fantastic*, entered the charts at No. 1. The tour which followed included home movies of the boys' childhood – a far cry from the overblown videos produced by some of their contemporaries who were clearly itching to be taken seriously as actors. 'Above all, our image is humorous,' they explained. 'We're playing the game of pop as it should be played.' The video for their next single, 'Club Tropicana', showed them falling off lilos in a glamorous hotel swimming pool and spilling expensive cocktails as irresponsible youngsters are wont to do. Meanwhile, George started to think in terms of being a serious songwriter and decided to release the soon-to-become classic 'Careless Whisper' as a solo artist. It gave Michael the distinction of being the first ever pop star to enter the UK charts both as a member of a group and a soloist in the same year. 'Careless Whisper' appeared on Wham's follow-up album, *Make It Big*, most of which continued to show George's intention to move on as a writer rather than a pop star.

'I'd rather write songs than make videos,' he told me when I interviewed him for the leading Japanese magazine, *Music Life*. 'When you've been making an album and working non-stop for three months, the last thing you want to do is sit round on a film set and prove yourself all over again. My music is very much inspired by the 1960s and 1970s – my favourite singer at the moment is Diana Ross who specialised in black pop as opposed to black disco – but finding the words can be hard. Having decided not to bore people any more by writing about our lifestyle as we did in the early singles, I've got to find something the audience can relate to. Just about the only thing we share with people our own age is the way you deal with relationships, so that's my most popular theme. The problem is there's a limit to the supply of situations that one can refer to. Perhaps I should write a song about a murder mystery! At the end of the day it's melodies that really turn people on, especially if it strikes a certain chord with them.'

Another example of George's maturity was Wham! playing for striking miners during the summer of 1984. 'It wasn't a case of wanting to get mixed up with politics,' he pointed out, 'we just decided we wanted to raise money to buy food for the miners' families. We can't claim to know the political ins and outs of the whole situation, but we saw the opportunity to help out. I didn't like the miners' leader, Arthur Scargill, at all. His determination to bring the government down was even worse than the intransigence of the Prime Minister. You couldn't have had a worse situation.' Having said that, George was clearly more comfortable talking about music than politics, especially the artists who had influenced him. These included idols of a previous generation such as Paul McCartney and Elton John who, eventually, would sing George's praises. 'I think the people who have respect for my songwriting are older writers because I'm very much a traditionalist. A lot of the music happening now might be relevant to today but won't necessarily stand the test of time. I don't really write for now, I just concentrate on structure and melody.'

This approach became evident in 1987 following the break-up of Wham! and the release of George's first solo album, *Faith*. By this time, I was the editor of the trade magazine *For The Record* and was invited to the record companies' annual sales conferences. The promotion and marketing of *Faith* was obviously a priority for Epic Records and by now George had realised that the videos for both the title track and the next single, 'Father Figure', were important sales tools and consequently required high production values.

I had a chat with George in the hotel bar, specifically about where he acquired the cowboy boots he wore in the *Faith* promo. He in turn admired my haircut and subtly gave the impression that he was coming on to me, something I'd been aware of

RECORD MIRROR

SHAKIN' STEVENS ▷ MADNESS

APRIL 4, 1981.

ELVIS COSTELLO EXCLUSIVE INTERVIEW

ISSN 0144 5804

TRAVOX ▷ BUCKS FIZZ ▽ P.I.L.

Another knock-out Mike Nicholls interview.

ALMOST BEATEN TO THE PUNCH

CONTINUED OVER

THE ELVIS
COSTELLO
INCIDENT, 1981.

WHAM WOMEN & SONG

BORING? UGLY? CRAP AT PULLING GIRLS?

Don't be depressed. We understand how tough it is for inadequate cretins like you. And we can help.

We asked dashing disco stars around town WHAM to help us to help you. They spent an evening demonstrating the correct way to achieve success with the opposite sex. In this special feature we cover all aspects of forming Meaningful Relationships - from the initial approach to the final consummation.

It is with some pride then, that we present this carefully researched and hopefully useful manual - tentatively titled

Featuring George (left) and Andy (right) of Wham.
Pix by Neil Matthews
Therapissed: Mike Nicholls
With thanks to the Camden Palace

LESSON 1: A smart, well groomed apppearance is paramount. Therefore, before any 'pull' or 'blag' is attempted, a visit to the toilets is advisable. Andy is seen here removing an unsightly blackhead.

LESSON 2: Basic reconnaissance work; potential prey is selected and hemmed in. The 'I'm a famous rockstar' line is tried - and pays off (for non-famous rock star readers –this need not be true).

WHAM! PHOTOSTORY PARODY: GEORGE MICHAEL AND ANDREW RIDGELEY TAKING THE RAP.

Picture by Howard Barlow.

PETE SHELLEY OF
THE BUZZCOCKS, ROCK
AGAINST RACISM GIG,
MANCHESTER, SUMMER
1978.

WITH JEFF BECK, ELECTRIC
BALLROOM, LONDON 1980.

JEAN-JACQUES
BURNEL AND
HUGH CORNWELL,
MANCHESTER
APOLLO, 1977.

Please admit

Mr Mike Nicholls

on 29th July 1999

RICS
12 Great George Street
Parliament Square
London SW1P 3AD

INVITATION TO SEE HER MAJESTY THE
QUEEN AT THE RICS OFFICE PARTY.

Pictures by Kevin Cummins.

IAN HUNTER,
MANCHESTER FREE
TRADE HALL. SUMMER 1977.

IF IT'S BARCELONA, IT
MUST BE THE CLASH!
SUMMER 1981.

GETTING THE DRINKS IN ON THE CLASH TOUR. VALENCIA, 1981.

Pictures by Pete Vernon.

JOE STRUMMER CONSIDERS ANOTHER TEQUILA SLAMMER. BARCELONA, 1981.

Pictures by Howard Barlow.

IGGY POP LIVE AT THE APOLLO. MANCHESTER. 1977.

Picture by Paul Slattery.

ON THE ROAD WITH IGGY POP AND JOHN GILL OF TIME OUT MAGAZINE, 1980.

at the Fashion Aid party at The Groucho Club the previous year. As we were getting stuck into the cocktails, I realised the record company staff were discretely eavesdropping on our conversation, presumably anxious that I was trying to scoop up some story and sell it to the tabloids. The next thing I knew, his security folk came over to have a quiet word and escorted me away. Looking back, I saw George at the other end of the room gazing after me in consternation, at a loss to understand why I had apparently done a runner.

It wasn't to be the last occasion that George disagreed with record company policy. By the early 1990s, Sony had taken Epic over and he had started a legal battle against the corporation. This was largely the result of arguments about his right to determine his own career path, with George refusing to appear in videos for future singles releases. He eventually moved to Virgin Records where his 1999 *Songs from the Last Century* proved to be his worst-selling solo effort. Four years later he was back with Sony but despite further releases, charity records and occasional touring, he never regained the success of his early solo career. Various health and drug problems led to a tragically premature death on Christmas Day in 2016. He was only fifty-three.

CHAPTER 31

HER MAJESTY THE QUEEN & VISCOUNT LINLEY

It may not have been love at first sight but Her Majesty The Queen was definitely my first poster girl. At primary school there was only one picture on the wall in the grim dining hall, that of our Queen on Coronation Day. She looked radiant, the blue diagonal sash on her white gown framing her beautiful smile. Never mind the Crown Jewels, here was a face we could never forget. She might now be in her nineties but there's no mistaking the link with that original iconic image.

Moving on to 1976, it's Wembley and Manchester United have just been ridiculously beaten by Southampton in the F.A. Cup Final. My father and I decided to make a quick getaway and found ourselves in a deserted street. A black limousine glided past and who should be seated in the back but The Queen, who had obviously just done a runner herself after handing out the trophy. Our eyes met, she waved that wave and two generations of Nicholls were temporarily speechless. My exuberant dad blurted out, 'She *must* have been waving at us!' There was no one else in sight, so I grunted in agreement. This was still the pre-celebrity stage of my life, so it never occurred to me to try to secure an exclusive interview – that was all to come. In the meantime, United might have lost the match but at least, as the old nursery rhyme has it, I went to London and saw The Queen.

Fast forward to the last year of the last century and I was the press officer at the Royal Institution of Chartered Surveyors

(RICS). You might have heard of them. Every month they produce a report on the state of the housing market based on feedback from the nation's surveyors and estate agents. I used to turn the figures into the press release you probably heard quoted on the news or read in the newspapers. When I got the gig, I gleefully called up my old muckers on the Street of Shame to relate this latest chapter in my unpredictable life. There were some amused responses.

Since RICS is a royal institution, a visit from Her Majesty was soon on the cards. Not everybody there was a royalist, let alone a rock 'n' royalist. This meant all the staff were given the choice of taking a day's leave or participating in the royal bash. I replied to my line manager that of course I wished to greet 'the nation's top bird'. Unfortunately, my enthusiasm rang one or two alarm bells. The powers that be were anxious I would go into Mike Nicholls mode, stroll up to our sovereign and initiate a conversation about rock 'n' roll, property prices, best new cocktails and all the rest. It was therefore decided that my role would be to report from the mezzanine floor overlooking the hall where the main event was taking place. This at least meant I would have a bird's eye view of the whole affair while those penned in downstairs would get to see very little.

Now it's a biological fact that when surrounded by lots of excitable, unattractive people you don't really want to associate with, the natural reaction is to look up. Think about the last time you were stuck in a queue for some ticket desk or, more likely, a bar. Hemmed in as she was, Her Majesty automatically looked up – straight into the eyes of one of her most loyal subjects. She instinctively smiled and I, of course, smiled back, half-raising a waving hand in the process. I could have shot a Paul McCartney style double thumbs-up, but this was The Queen after all. Better to follow her example and be a little on the understated side for once. I mean, she's not David Bowie or Mick Jagger, but she definitely has rock 'n' roll credentials: since The Beatles received their MBEs in the mid-1960s, The Queen has handed out countless awards to members of the rock 'n' roll aristocracy and was herself immortalised by the Sex Pistols in print as well as song.

Recently someone asked The Queen the secret of her successful seventy-year marriage to Prince Philip. She answered that he always made her laugh. You can't get much more rock 'n' roll than that.

DAVID ARMSTRONG-JONES, VISCOUNT LINLEY

In the summer of 1986, I found myself doing the PR for the VIP Room at The Limelight, the central London deconsecrated church which had suddenly become the most talked about club in town. The tabloids adored it, if only because it was a fast-track way of filling up their pop columns. In the days before mobile phones, I would have a different paparazzi photographer on patrol each night awaiting celebrity arrivals, especially those who were a little worse for wear. These ranged from a Princess Di lookalike performing a striptease to actor Mickey Rourke, fresh from the controversial movie *9½ Weeks*, arriving with an entire posse of distinctly ungodly Hell's Angels. After Mick Hucknall of Simply Red appeared in *The Sun* cosying up to the stunning girlfriend of Wham!'s Andrew Ridgely, the singer apparently left London in favour of a lower profile back up north.

Another eventful evening under my watch was the birthday party of Nile Rodgers, the Chic legend who had also produced major albums by Bowie, Jagger, Ferry, Madonna and so on. Nervously seated alone in one corner of the VIP Room was David Armstrong-Jones, nephew of The Queen and better known as Viscount Linley. Since the recent death of his father he is now the second Earl of Snowdon, an upmarket carpenter who in terms of business is probably the most successful self-made royal on the planet. Back then he was a young-looking twenty-five-year-old who simply called himself David Linley on his business card and was eager to make contacts. This became clear a few years later when he turned up to the annual Midem music festival in the south of France. I met him for the second time at a party hosted by Willie Robertson, the rock 'n' roll insurance broker, on board his luxury yacht. An old Harrovian, Robertson made his fortune insuring millions of pounds worth of equipment for bands like The Who, Pink Floyd and Roxy Music. He also pioneered the concept of artists being insured for a no show, like the time Rod Stewart had to cancel dates after some high jinks led to broken toes.

Nobody was really bothering with the still-shy Linley, so I thought I'd steam in and reintroduce myself. Looking askance at my usual uniform of biker jacket, 501s and cowboy boots, he laughed politely when I told him I was reporting for the *Financial Times* as well as my usual *Hello!* column. He took me more seriously when the chief steward came over and enquired, 'Your usual, Mr Nicholls?' He was, of course, referring to a suitably nautical Bombay Sapphire and tonic. I suggested to my new Viscount pal that he partake of the same, cheekily adding that his mother, Princess Margaret, was not impartial to a drop of gin. In fact, he opted for a glass of rosé, the local beverage. Little did the royal, still youthful in his thirties, realise the potential danger therein. By being famously quaffable, far more so than most of the rubbish the French export over here, the pale fragrant rosé has a good kick as well as a pleasant nose. It's also incredibly more-ish.

This was very much in evidence as young David started giggling and his pallid complexion soon attained a similar colour to that of his drink. By evening he was still on the go, arms around the shoulders of a pair of good-looking local fillies. Later that night Factory Records were hosting a showcase for some of their newer acts at the elegant Martinez Hotel. Let's just say that the Viscount's behaviour was more entertaining than that of The New Fast Automatic Daffodils. By then I had switched allegiance to another bunch of familiar faces; it seemed a better alternative than being charged with leading a young royal astray and spending many a year in the Tower of London as a guest of his auntie.

Later that same year there was a launch of a photographic exhibition at Sotheby's which I attended with my paparazzi colleague, Richard Young, who appeared earlier in the chapter on Boy George. Also there was the boy Linley with his then girlfriend, future fashion guru Susannah Constantine. After Richard had offered advice to David about how to handle the press, I asked about his carpentry business. He admitted trade had suffered somewhat during the recent recession, so I suggested the construction of quality CD shelving for his pals in the record industry. Nothing like a royal seal of approval to get the troops furnishing their homes with smart cabinets to contain all the free CDs they received. He could practically name his price! Ms Constantine was rather taken with this idea, vigorously nodding her head in approval. It was now up to me to offer my services as agent and the Viscount duly presented me with one of his gold-embossed business cards.

Even yours truly has his moments of doubt and to be honest, I never followed up the idea, possibly through being too involved with my own projects, not to mention fathering two daughters over the next couple of years. I did see David again, however, at the annual Nordoff-Robbins charity auction. The rock 'n' roll charity provides premises and facilities for autistic children to learn to communicate via music therapy. The great and good of the music industry donate prizes which are then auctioned for considerable sums of money. Viscount Linley's donation was a fortnight's holiday at his family's retreat on the Caribbean island of Mustique. Lucky for me and my pride it wasn't a fancy piece of furniture for name-dropping CD collectors.

CHAPTER 32

HOWARD DEVOTO

Howard Devoto's original music career commenced with Buzzcocks, the first non-metropolitan punk band. Although Howard was from Scunthorpe, the band was formed in Manchester, Devoto, *né* Trafford, having been a student at Bolton College of Technology with guitarist Pete Shelley. Buzzcocks appeared on both the Sex Pistols' Anarchy tour and The Clash's White Riot tour, and were the first punk band to release an indie single in early 1977. Soon afterwards Devoto left to form his own band, Magazine, with a very different sound from Buzzcocks' catchy punk-pop.

I first met Howard backstage at the Manchester Apollo, at an Iggy Pop gig in September of the same year. I immediately recognised him from his widow's peak hairdo and he told me he'd formed a new band. Later that evening he had supper with Iggy and gave him a copy of the indie EP *Spiral Scratch*. He made the presentation with the immortal words, 'I've got all your records, now you've got all mine.' A couple of weeks later, Magazine appeared at the last night of the Electric Circus, the exceptional venue situated in the middle of an unrestored World War II bomb site in North East Manchester. They played three songs, including Captain Beefheart's 'I Love You, You Big Dummy' and 'Shot by Both Sides', Magazine's future debut single on Virgin Records.

Punk made Manchester an even greater city than it had been while I was at school and I spent the next year or so bumping into members of Manchester bands. I saw Howard at the opening night of The Factory where he was involved in a friendly brawl with an inebriated Shelley. Like a true gent, Devoto offered his hand as a gesture of reconciliation. By this stage his cult status had gone stratospheric, the *NME* referring to him as 'the most important man alive'. That seemed like a pretty good starting point for our next conversation and I wondered how he felt about being thus described. 'It's like being in a movie, but it doesn't move me,' he replied: he clearly felt the appellation was excessive and certainly had no thoughts of taking it seriously.

At times punk could be a Stalinist affair, none of its participants claiming to have had much time for any of the music which came beforehand. Devoto, however, had no qualms about being a big fan of Dylan, Bowie and Frank Zappa. At twenty-six, he was older than the average punk, so this was to be expected. The first Magazine album was striking, not least because of the distinguished post-prog rock keyboards of Dave Formula and the innovative circular guitar riffs of John McGeoch, later a key member of Siouxsie and The Banshees and Public Image Ltd. McGeoch's intro to 'The Thin Air' was one of the highlights of 1979's *Secondhand Daylight*, two further albums appearing before Devoto's surprising decision to split the band. We met at the Institute of Contemporary Arts to discuss the matter. For me it was like the end of an era having seen the band regularly since their first-ever gig. 'It actually feels like a new beginning to me,' Devoto maintained. 'I went through all my crises several weeks ago when telling the others. I felt I was letting the band down a bit but, at the same time, to have gone on doing things half-heartedly wouldn't have been very good. Everyone else was keen to go on tour so it's hard not to feel bad about it.'

The elephant in the room was that despite Magazine's incredible critical success and the number of name-checks they have gone on to receive from successive generations of bands like U2 and the Red Hot Chilli Peppers, they never were a commercial proposition to match. The last album, *Magic, Murder and The Weather*, was no exception but Howard was obviously proud of it and keen to explain what it was all about. 'The weather is there in a lot of songs. The track 'Come Alive' concerns the dawn of Cro-Magnon man asking the question, "What have I done to deserve the rain? What have I done to deserve the sun?"'

Almost on cue the sun came out so we left the ICA and its exhibition of record sleeves (including all of Magazine's) to take a walk in St James's Park. The solar power had a positive effect on Devoto's turn of phrase. Many interviewees stutter and mutter their way through conversations, saving their best for stage and studio. Howard spoke deliberately and precisely, carefully choosing every word and occasionally breaking into graphic prose. He sounded more like an actor, perhaps one playing a detective expounding a hypothesis. 'You might think I'm in a state of inertia but at the moment I'm vibrating at an incredibly high frequency,' was one of his more memorable quotes. His view of the exhibition was equally opinionated. 'I don't know if record sleeves should be put behind glass and hung from walls,' he complained. 'They belong in record shops.' At least Devoto had not lost his belief in music. Howard eventually moved on to other projects like Luxuria and even joined Morrissey onstage at one London gig. As in Manchester, he continued to be a fan around town. We had a chat at the Electric Ballroom in 1988, entertained by Joe Strummer's Latino Rockabilly War.

The last time I saw Howard was almost a decade later at a gig by a band called Mansun at London's Astoria Theatre. The promising young rock band had worked with him on a couple of songs and he'd come to check out the live results. Despite an impressive run of singles including 'She Makes My Nose Bleed',

Mansun were destined to follow in the footsteps of Magazine and remain a footnote in musical history. At least Devoto can claim to have influenced others, which at the close of play means it was a case of only being shot by *one* side.

IAN BROUDIE

Ian Broudie is probably the most talented poptician to have come out of Liverpool since The Beatles. If his name is not instantly familiar then his tunes will be, including 'Three Lions (Football's Coming Home)' which he co-wrote with a pair of stand-up comics from a later generation. Broudie also sang and wrote 'Life of Riley', for many years the TV theme for the BBC's Goal of The Month competition.

Ian was one of the founders of the Scouse new wave scene, forming Big in Japan, a loopy extrovert bunch most of whom went on to make names for themselves, like a supergroup in reverse. Take a bow Holly Johnson (Frankie Goes to Hollywood), Budgie (Siouxsie and The Banshees) and Bill Drummond who managed both Echo & The Bunnymen and Teardrop Explodes before finding notoriety in KLF. Remarkably, the teenage Broudie was drawn more to production than performance. 'I found the band culture a little off-putting at the time,' he revealed during one of our meetings in the 1990s. 'I didn't like the idea of sitting in a van all day.' This explains why by the early 1980s he could be found producing the third Bunnymen album, *Crocodiles*, and their biggest hit, 'The Cutter'. Yet before that he signed a major record deal as part of a band called The Original Mirrors whose A&R man had previously signed Dire Straits.

Expectations must have been high, so much so that on an early *Record Mirror* assignment I was flown to Paris to interview The Original Mirrors at top Euro punk venue, Bain Douche – literally a former public bathhouse. Once again it was a case of too many cooks. After two albums The Mirrors cracked, singer Steve Allen went on to start a dance label and the drummer received a substantial wage for a stint with Status Quo. 'I realised that what I was best at was writing songs,' Ian reflected. 'But I got side-tracked for the whole of the 1980s.' Hence the planting of The Lightning Seeds, of which Broudie was initially the sole member. 'For the first two LPs I wanted to see if I could cut it as a pop musician, then after a run of hit singles I decided I might as well turn it into a proper full-time group. Having enlisted a bunch of people I really liked and who were talented, the next step was to let them write their own songs and generally realise their potential.'

These musicians involved classically trained backing vocalist and keyboard player Angie Pollack who he met through producing The Colour Field, the band led by former Specials and Fun Boy Three singer Terry Hall. Another Seed was Martyn Campbell, bassist with fellow Liverpudlians The La's. Just in case the whole Merseyside networking scenario isn't entirely clear, Broudie's choice of drummer was Zak Starkey, son of a certain Ringo Starr. The Lightning Seeds' reputation was bolstered by two hit albums, *Jollification* and *Dizzy Heights*. The son of an apparently off-beat family, Ian's songwriting techniques tended towards the eccentric. If possessed by a catchy tune while away from the recording studio, he would use a telephone kiosk to sing it into his answering machine at home.

Otherwise he would be quite happy to take on board musicians he encountered along rock 'n' roll's highway. Stephen Jones of Babybird's 'You're Gorgeous' fame is an occasional co-songwriter while Nicky Wire of the Manic Street Preachers wrote the profound 'Waiting for Today to Happen'. An odd title for a Broudie track, to be sure, since much of his career has been spent behind the scenes, not really worrying about whether anything was likely to happen.

IAN DURY

Variously describing himself as a 'wordsmith' and a 'street-corner philosopher', Ian Dury was definitely one of the originals. Apart from coining the phrase 'sex and drugs and rock 'n' roll', he was one of a handful of artists who was established pre-punk yet was also a pillar of the new wave scene. Almost Dickensianly working-class in appearance, his lyrics betrayed a highbrow intellect even if he was one of the most down-to-earth singers ever to have topped the charts.

We originally met when his band Kilburn & The High Roads played Warwick University in 1975 but didn't sit down for an interview until three years later for the *Record Mirror* Christmas issue. It was at a key point in his career. Ian Dury and The Blockheads had recently been at No. 1 with 'Hit Me With Your Rhythm Stick' and had spent much of the year on the road promoting his debut album, *New Boots and Panties!!* This record introduced to the world such impressively poetic characters as Plaistow Patricia and Billericay Dickie, affectionate thumbnail sketches of real people and real life, bursting with humour and rhyme. The following summer would see the release of *Do It Yourself* where the emphasis was on the music, showcasing the dexterity of a very talented band.

We parlayed at Gants Hill Odeon in east London the day before Christmas Eve, 1978. Ian and his band were about to complete a week-long jaunt around London following a six-month tour of America and Europe. 'The only thing that makes me happy is being active,' he revealed. So why just a week in London, I wondered? What about the rest of the country? 'We ain't ready yet,' he replied, 'We haven't got enough new material to do a whole tour of England. The deal I did with Stiff Records was that there wouldn't be any pressure to put out albums, which means I can produce them when I'm ready rather than worry about some phoney deadline.'

Indeed. Until recently artists were continually badgered to get an album out in time for Christmas even if that led to a compromise on quality. 'Doing two albums of songs a year *can* be done,' he said. 'The Beatles did it and Ray Davies managed to put out all those classic Kinks singles but that's not the same as LPs, of course. At the same time, we don't want to stockpile stuff. I mean, what would happen to the songs if I got killed tomorrow like Buddy Holly? Somebody might go and put violins on them!'

One new song already in the bag was the relatively unsung 'This Is What We Find', the ode to home improvement about Harry Hill of Harold Hill who came home to find 'another geezer's kippers in the grill'. 'It took me days to knock out each set of rhyming couplets,' Ian admitted. 'I'd done a little bit of delinquent poetry before going into the music business but when I looked at it, I thought it was a bit of a wank-off so I left it. I don't like poetry, personally. I just make things rhyme if I can to keep me interested.'

Like many a premier league rock star, Ian went to art college. 'In Walthamstow, east London, although I actually grew up in Upminster which is in Essex, so I'm not really a cockney. Then after leaving college, me and my wife moved to the country for a while. We had a kid and not a load of money, and if you haven't got much money in London it's no fun for the kid. So we went out to near Aylesbury and got a vicarage for a fiver a week with eight rooms and two acres of grounds. They slung us out after four years, the result of rehearsing there with the Kilburns. Still, there can't be many rock 'n' roll people whose careers began in a vicarage!'

Still in the foothills of my own career as a rock journalist, I was prone to asking philosophical questions like 'What is your motivation in writing and performing?' Sometimes I got an honest answer. 'It's to make myself happy, I suppose, which is wiser than trying to make a lot of other people happy. Because if you do that you could go round thinking "I'm the bloke who makes people happy," and that's power. I don't think there's any good in power being exercised over other people by anybody; you just end up hurting people.'

He illustrates this issue with regard to himself. 'Sometimes I can feel all the power I've got as a lyricist come out the wrong way. I can really have a go at people. Like, when I was younger and got drunk, I could be really vicious. So if you've got a gift, say, as a verb artist, you've got to be careful you don't use it to hurt other people. That's why I don't drink any more.' Nor, despite the title of one of his most favourite songs, does Dury take drugs. 'Last week I met three famous people in the hotel where I was staying – a rock 'n' rolly hotel. Every one of them asked, "Do you want some nose food?" That was their first topic of conversation. Seems tragic to me. I suppose if you were asked, "Do you want to do sex and drugs all day or work for Ford Motors?", I'd choose the former but not otherwise. We played a theatre in Paris called The Mogador. It didn't take long before we renamed it The Mogadon,' he goes on, referring to a popular brand of narcotic.

Unsually for the time – the height of the Troubles – Ian Dury and The Blockheads also played Belfast, one of the few bands to do so during the 1970s. 'I reckon all the trouble over there is about work. It might not be my business to say so, but I believe it's an economic thing created by poverty as much as anything else. We went to a mixed youth place where a non-sectarian church was being built. They ain't finished it yet – but they had finished the bar... actually, they all seemed to be having a great time. All jumping into bed with one another!

'Seriously, though, that religious nonsense is disappearing so quickly that if they mixed the schools, it would all be over. The kids from the Falls Road or the Ardoyne, or wherever, are all enjoying it together. Hotels don't get bombed when there's a band staying, which basically means that the kids are the most important thing to everybody.'

It's not only the youth that were to drop their sectarianism. Music did so too. When punk first happened, everything that had gone before was soundly denigrated. Then, through bands like The Clash, rock 'n' roll guitars regained their respectability. Danceability also found its way back on to the guest list. 'Someone accused 'Rhythm Stick' of being disco,' Dury said. 'If it is, then I'm pleased because that's uncharted territory for us. If our records are being played in discos where the real blockheads of this world go banging around, that's great.' He then goes on to explain how the name of his band came about. 'Charlie Charles, our West Indian drummer, came to a session wearing exactly the same clothing described in the song 'Blockheads': those jeans with patches that aren't really patches and a pair of those pig-nosed shoes and he reads the lyrics and says, "Hey, this guy's dressed just like me," and I replied "Er, yeah," and I thought we should call ourselves The Blockheads. If you take the mickey out of yourselves, people forgive you anything. It's nothing heavy, just street corner philosophy.'

Quite.

IAN HUNTER

The former frontman of enduring cult heroes Mott The Hoople occupies a unique position in rock 'n' roll. Mott were originally an albums band that didn't sell many albums. I first discovered them via 'At the Crossroads', a track on the iconic Island records sampler, *Nice Enough to Eat*, where a track from their first self-titled LP appeared alongside five-star cuts, by the likes of Traffic, Free, King Crimson, Nick Drake and a few others.

Whereas their contemporaries connected to the newly-emerging underground audience, Mott The Hoople stalled. History repeated itself on their next three albums whereupon Hunter was tempted to call it a day. Then the cavalry arrived in the form of mega-fan David Bowie who wrote them a hit single, 'All The Young Dudes'. The story is told on a later Mott song, 'Saturday Gigs', which climaxes with the exclamation 'And then we went to Croydon!' a reference to the gift from Bowie and almost biblical in its narration. Indeed, for some fans it is one of the greatest rock 'n' roll stories ever told.

'All the Young Dudes' was followed by a succession of other hits, including 'All the Way from Memphis' and 'Roll Away the Stone'. A change of record companies boosted new album sales, but in the mid-70s, time was called on the band when Hunter left to form a duo with former Bowie guitarist, Mick Ronson. There have been subsequent Mott The Hoople reunions, but for the last four decades, both live and in the studio, Ian Hunter has been primarily a solo artist, and a prolific one at that. He is after all, knocking eighty.

I got to meet him after a show at a packed and excited Manchester Free Trade Hall in the spring of 1977. Once again, he was at the crossroads, to coin his phrase. On the one hand, he was promoting *Overnight Angels*, now a long-forgotten album recorded with Queen producer Roy Thomas Baker. On the other hand, he was squeezed into black leather trousers, an emblem of the gathering punk movement. He dedicated one of his songs to Little Richard, 'the first-ever punk'. Whereas former glam-rocker Bowie scored instant cred with the art school end of the new wave, Hunter would have to wait. When we talked afterwards backstage, our conversation was partly about Bowie and his aptitude for media manipulation. I got the impression Ian was eager to get the media back on-side but he wasn't going to push it.

It didn't help that I was in the process of developing my search and destroy give-us-an-interview technique on the night when his elderly parents had come to see him. They both seemed embarrassed to be there, especially Hunter senior, a tall, sour-faced ex-policeman. Some years later I learned that he had been a strict and, by today's standards, abusive father. A lack of paternal affection seems to be one of the motivating factors for a life in rock 'n' roll. Take a bow, John Lennon, Bruce Springsteen, Tom Petty, Joe Strummer, me... all may be well that ends well, but it wasn't much fun growing up – assuming, that is, any of us ever did.

Two years later, Ian was back on track with his landmark *You're Never Alone with a Schizophrenic* album. He delighted a packed Hammersmith Odeon and there was a great party in a West End club afterwards. Other stars showed up, and I remember sinking a few with Pete Townshend who was enjoying a full-on rock 'n' roll lifestyle at the time. The tour did so well that in 1980 it became a live album, *Welcome to the Club*. As part of the promotion, I was invited to join Hunter-Ronson in Germany to review their performance on the classic *Rockpalast* show. It proved to be a fateful weekend leading to me working with Mick Ronson later in the 80s.

Hunter-Ronson were sandwiched in between ZZ Top and Joan Armatrading which meant plenty of time for socialising. Since *Record Mirror* only required a live review, it was a relief not to have to record a serious interview. Instead, we traded gossip and anecdotes while tucking into a selection of German beers, sparkling wines and cocktails. The relaxed atmosphere was conducive to making enquiries about Bob Dylan, who Mick Ronson had accompanied on the Rolling Thunder Revue tour. Mick's overall view on Dylan was, 'He's alright, you know, Bob. I mean he does hang out.' Well, that was one in the eye for this Dylan freak who had always imagined he was an enigmatic recluse. Ian, like Ronno, was also concise in conversation but had a strange Dylan tale to tell. 'I remember meeting him one night in New York and he started shouting "Mott The Hoople, Mott The Hoople!" and naming all the tracks on the first album. Things weren't going very well for the band at the time, so I just said something like, "Give it a rest, Bob, I'm not having a good day." '

In contrast, we had a great night with many a stunning German girl entering the equation. I mentioned to Hunter that the following month *Record Mirror* were sending me to New York for a week to 'promote the brand' and cover the local scene. 'Well, we're starting a tour in Denver Colorado, the following week,' Ian revealed. 'Why not come and join us on the road?' I almost sobered up.

The next time I saw Mick and Ian, I was gently simmering in an outdoor jacuzzi at the Holiday Inn, Denver. For a second, I didn't recognise the singer without his shades and then realising my mistake, suddenly exclaimed, 'Hello!' 'Hello? That could only be an Englishman,' Hunter laughed before turning to Ronson and asking, 'Do you think we should invite this young waif to dinner?' I recall it was largely a liquid repast.

The next night's gig saw Hunter fronting an E Street sized band, with two guitarists and two keyboard players. A few hardcore fans had earlier come backstage with generous quantities of marching powder but the gig itself almost turned ugly. During the show-stopping song called 'Cleveland Rocks', Hunter provocatively added the phrase, 'Iran rocks', only for serious heckling to begin. This was borderline redneck country and America's relationship with Iran, which had included storming embassies, was about as attractive as a lanced boil. Fortunately, Hunter's showmanship enabled him to turn the situation around, which was useful when confronted with a sea of burly farm-workers in hobnailed boots.

Later that night, the tour bus set off for Phoenix, Arizona, with everyone in high spirits. The atmosphere was reminiscent of a sixth form excursion, except how many of us recall school trips dawning with orange juice rendered effervescent with chilled champagne. At least that was the Ronson-Nicholls definition of breakfast. Hunter, never a diminutive chap, had loftier ideas. One of the conditions of him originally joining Mott The Hoople was that if he was going to be the frontman he'd have to lose to weight. As a strapping Shropshire lad he'd always had a bit of a battle with the bulge. So, it was now on with the trainers for a calorie-crunching run before the sun got too high over the New Mexico desert. Then it was on to the Grand Canyon, where Ian announced another gallop. Afterwards, he swallowed a small mountain of vitamin pills, claiming, 'I'm the Barbara Cartland of rock,' referring to the romantic novelist famed for her health kicks. 'You'd better not write that!'

It was the LA gig, at the famous Roxy on Sunset Boulevard, which was the highlight of the trip, not to mention the party afterwards. We didn't even have to travel very far, for it was upstairs at the On The Rox club, the celebrity haunt of the West Coast. You can refer to the Mick Ronson chapter for further details. My next rendezvous with Ian and Mick was at the White Lion in Covent Garden, the *Record Mirror* local pub. I'd just been promoted to assistant editor of the paper and Ian was very pleased for me. 'You'll be working for *Time* magazine next!' he exclaimed before politely turning down a celebratory plate of corned beef hash, the Irish pub's speciality. 'Mick and I are planning to go to Khan's later,' Ian added, with reference to the popular Westbourne Grove curry house, 'but we'll be looking for somewhere to go later. Any gigs on tonight?' I recommended checking out a couple of new bands at The Venue, London's answer to New York's Bottom Line, a club with a restaurant area behind the dance floor. The groups in question were, Afraid of Mice and Everest the Hard Way. Ian almost doubled up in laughter at the names, rich coming from a man who found fame with a group called Mott The Hoople.

Later in the 1980s, Hunter and Ronson played London gigs at the Dominion Theatre and the Town & Country Club. The latter saw the presence backstage of Mick Jones of The Clash and Big Audio Dynamite, not to mention an early member of the Mott fan club. He was accompanied by his oldest friend, Tony James, who had just made a bit of a name for himself with the overhyped Sigue Sigue Sputnik.

Come the next decade and Hunter almost proved prophetic with his *Time* magazine remark. In fact, he was only one letter out. For our next interview was for *The Times*, in which he contributed to my debate about the antics of radio stations. Whereas in the past, popular shows were programmed by DJs and producers who lived for music, 1990 playlists were dictated by the results of market research and computer printouts. Ian was not impressed, 'In order for new artists to be successful they have to play, not what they want, but what some consultant seems to think they want. Obviously, this is ridiculous. Bands should be making records for themselves, not for some speculative sales figures. Radio stations were once fun places of organised chaos. Now they are like laboratories, slick, sterile and glossy. But the public aren't stupid. People will switch off unless someone decides to take them seriously again.'

Once again, Hunter could see a glimpse of the future. Soon afterwards, we saw the introduction of XFM, and descendants like 6 Music, Absolute and a whole new generation of digital stations. I think it's fair to say they were custom-made for all the young dudes, past as well as present.

IAN McCULLOCH

Even by Liverpool standards, Ian McCulloch is an unrepentant scally with an acerbic opinion about everything and everybody. His band, Echo & The Bunnymen, became music press darlings before U2 and he has never forgiven Bono's bunch for overtaking them. 'If he'd been based in Liverpool or, rather if they'd been based in Liverpool, he'd have been laughed out of town,' McCulloch wheezed, in 1993, when we met up in London's Olympic Studios. While talking in the hospitality suite, Mick Jagger entered the foyer with somebody who was clearly not his wife. 'Well, what can any of his birds expect?' Ian announced. 'That's not a bad bit of heft,' he remarked, referring to Carla Bruni, the future First Lady of France.

Bobby Gillespie, the singer with Primal Scream, a cornerstone of the dance rock scene, didn't fare too well, either. 'He's got in there, but he hasn't got it right. His music sounds cheap and he's no icon. He'll always be an extra from The Jesus and Mary Chain, and they were never that good anyway.'

Hero Lou Reed? 'I liked *New Sensations*, *The Blue Mask*, and *The Bells*, but not *New York* (usually regarded as Lou's great comeback album). And I've never forgiven David Bowie for the Serious Moonlight tour.' Ian also decimated Bill Drummond, the Bunnymen's manager for several years, in a similar fashion. 'Bill was one of the most clever, inarticulate bastards there's ever been. He doesn't really know how to say how he feels. He can only do it through other people, like he did with us. If it hadn't been for him managing us, he wouldn't be in the business now.' In contrast to all these put-downs, I got quite a good school report. 'You're a marginal prophet, Mike, I think we should team up. You could be the next David Lynch,' he enthused, referring to the director of the monumental *Blue Velvet*, and the subsequent TV soap with a twist, *Twin Peaks*.

McCulloch and I originally met at the old BBC TV centre in White City, West London. Echo & The Bunnymen had just appeared on *Top of the Pops* performing 'The Cutter', one of their biggest hits. Ian had distinguished himself by partly removing his top, cheekily parodying the legendary behaviour of Debbie Harry on the same programme a few years earlier. Over the first of many vodkas in the BBC bar, Ian enquired, 'What did you think of the art statement?', while simultaneously pointing out that he had no intention of doing an interview. A few drinks later there was no stopping him, especially when his press officer pointed out I was from the *Daily Express*. 'Ah, so we've landed the big fish,' McCulloch stated, suddenly changing his tune. 'Are you from Manchester? You've done alright. I thought everybody from there was a hairdresser. I mean, it's not a hard place, like Liverpool, or as proud. I saw some kid the other day who looked like he wanted to kill everybody in the world. That's what I used to be like when I was fifteen!'

But not for long. No sooner was punk happening and McCulloch, or Mac, as he came to be known, was an ardent fan of Mark Smith and his group The Fall. Urban myth has it that The Bunnymen started out roadie-ing for The Fall. Not true, apparently. 'I met him at Eric's, (the legendary Liverpool club) and he was getting the bevs in and I told him, "That was the best show I've ever seen, and I saw the Pistols and The Clash here." Smith replied, "Hey cock, that makes it all worthwhile. Come and have a drink in the dressing room." I sent him a tape of

'Read It in Books' and he thought I had a lovely voice. That was very flattering considering I told him he looked like a gargoyle.'

McCulloch, of course, looked like nothing of the sort. With his doe eyes and full lips – 'Look at that. Pure sex!' he exclaimed, admiring his reflection in the mirror in the BBC bar – he's one of the better-looking men in rock. His image was completed by a spiky-topped haircut, completing his male model look. 'You know how I get my barnet like that?' he revealed. 'I lie off the end of the bed and rinse it with sugar and Coca Cola. Quicker and cheaper than some Manchester hairdresser.'

Japanese girls certainly appreciated Ian's pulchritude. 'We played to 7,000 people over three nights in Tokyo. We couldn't do that in Liverpool,' he admitted at the time. 'The best part of Japan was eating beef curry in a bullet train going 150 miles an hour. That, and the respect people seem to have for each other. Children are brought up strictly, whereas here they are raised as brats. Maybe it's all down to unemployment and bad education, but there's a loss of pride in this country. Where there was once hope, Britain now seems negative and apathetic. Still, there are things to be grateful for, like Liverpool FC and Echo & The Bunnymen.'

The following year, we met to discuss his band's best album, 1984's *Ocean Rain*. 'Needless to say, every song is a classic,' he deadpanned, selecting 'The Killing Moon' for particular praise. 'That was one of the best songs for years, wasn't it? Class without the type of modern production which blands everything out,' he said, appreciating that this particular interview was for *International Musician*. 'In fact, we used one or two old-fashioned tricks, like playing the tape backwards in order to get that elongated twangy effect on the guitars. You've got to be a brave engineer to suggest that sort of thing. Can you imagine someone having told John Lennon to stop playing a solo so that the tape could be turned back in order to create a Beatles classic?'

IGGY POP

The first time I made eye contact with Iggy Pop he threw a chair at me. Back in 1977, being a member of the press meant you could get away with anything. At the lip of the stage at the Manchester Apollo there was an orchestra pit, a relic of bygone days when a theatrical show would include a full band, sound-tracking the main event. If you were pushy enough, photographers and journalists could talk their way into hunkering down for a bird's-eye view of a gig. Although the flying chair only missed me by inches, it was the lens men I felt sorry for, trying to ply their trade amidst the threat of smashed cameras. 'I hate you, you and you,' the singer raged, before addressing his enthralled, paying public with the words, 'But I love you!'

Love was hardly the operative word for a man mainly famous for his demonic, atonal sounds inspired by the eternal noise of the traffic blighting his trailer park adolescence. Add to this, an anti-social performance fuelled by self-harm and drug abuse, and 'songs' which defied the Trade Descriptions Act, and it's hardly surprising that I portrayed him in the *Altrincham Guardian* as 'Detroit's manic, metallic mad man'. This, in a local newspaper whose readers were more accustomed to me wittering on about music on a summer evening for the blue rinse brigade.

It was the second time I'd seen The Pop that year because I'd earlier witnessed him at London's Rainbow Theatre when he was joined on keyboards by David Bowie. The Bowie connection was the reason for my interest in the man born James Osterberg.

David had taken him under his manager's wing on a journey which would eventually lead to the release of *The Idiot*, the first of two Iggy albums to appear in 1977. *The Idiot* featured the exceptional 'China Girl' which resurfaced on Bowie's *Let's Dance*, his biggest-selling album to date. However, the highlight of the Apollo show was 'I Wanna Be Your Dog', which would eventually evolve into an erotic duet with Blondie's Debbie Harry, dribbling more than a hint of oral sex.

Naturally, Iggy also performed material from the other album of that year, *Lust for Life*. Some two decades later, the title track from this LP introduced the world to the hyper-kinetic movie *Trainspotting*. Apart from the fact that, historically, Iggy had been dubbed 'The Godfather of Punk', it wouldn't be unreasonable to claim that Iggy has always been ahead of his time. 'I knew damn well *The Idiot* wasn't going to be a million-seller, but I still believed in Iggy Pop,' he told Nick Kent of the *NME*, back in 1979. 'I started reading about me being the godfather of punk and I figured if that's the case I'm going to be a real godfather, Mafia style.'

A few major record company deals later and the summer of 1993 saw me in the balcony of The Forum in Kentish Town, London. My then partner was pregnant with our second daughter, who has subsequently enlightened punks of all ages with the story of how she attended an Iggy concert while still in her mother's womb. Her tale is generally spiced with the information that he pulled off his usual party trick of exposing himself.

The last time I saw The Igster was in June 1996 when he was one of the opening acts for the Sex Pistols at their London reunion show in Finsbury Park. A book by his former bassist, Alvin Gibbs, had just been published and I wondered what Iggy thought of it. He was about as talkative as Andy Warhol had been at the Café Royal but at least he didn't throw a chair at me. During our brief exchange Paul McCartney's daughter, Mary, came over for a chat. At the time, she was a bit of a girl about town and we often bumped into one another. Then, who else should have joined this VIP gathering but Noel Gallagher, another acquaintance of mine from many a rock 'n' roll night out. At the time, Oasis were the most popular band in the land, so between us we formed quite a quartet.

You can't plan these situations, you just greet them as a pleasant surprise. As is the continued survival of Iggy Pop, still the Godfather of Punk. Mafia-style? I don't see why not.

JACK BRUCE

Considering he was the principal singer and songwriter in pioneering blues-rock trio Cream, it is extraordinary that Jack Bruce is not as well-known as his former colleague Eric Clapton. In fact, the bass player almost hooked up with someone even more famous than both of them. 'In the late 1960s, I was talking to Jimi Hendrix about putting a band together with Steve Winwood and a couple of others but the following year, Jimi died. It was a much tinier scene then and we all knew each other. Come to think of it, I had quite a few offers from all sorts of other groups. Led Zeppelin; Crosby, Stills, Nash & Young; and Emerson, Lake & Palmer all approached me to go on the road with them, but I was tired of travelling. Cream had done a seven-month tour of the USA, one night in every town. That's how you broke a band in those days. In contrast, albums were no trouble: I did my first solo record in ten days.'

This was the incomparable *Songs for a Tailor* which, for me, is one of the finest ever LPs by a UK artist. Then came the urge to go back on tour, so Jack joined jazz drummer Tony Williams and *avant-garde* guitarist John McLaughlin. 'Ah, the great days of what they called fusion,' reminisced Jack, who also played piano and cello. Our interview took place in 1992 prior to a one-off gig at The Grand in Clapham. This was a former dance hall only able to accommodate a modest 1,200 people – a fraction of the number he was more accustomed to entertaining. 'We thought we'd begin modestly since we haven't worked much here,' he explained. 'Europe, the States and Japan are our usual venues but there's been no demand in the UK. It's very much a case of being in fashion and I can't remember the last time I was flavour of the month, if ever! But we've just played Warsaw and we're off to Sardinia tomorrow. It's London I'm nervous about after not performing here for so long.'

It all seemed a far cry from the early 1970s when a documentary about Jack was screened on primetime TV. Entitled *Rope Ladder to The Moon* after one of his songs, he celebrated the occasion by buying a Scottish island. 'I thought it would be nice,' he said. 'It was called Sander and geographically about fourteen miles from Northern Ireland. I'd been looking for somewhere private in Scotland but I had long hair, so nobody would sell me an actual estate. Then the opportunity of the island came up. It was nice to have for a while but proved totally impractical. I'd want to go for a couple of weeks but would have to wait three or four days on the mainland until the weather improved. Another problem was that the people who lived there didn't have many rights. Landowners in Scotland are not renowned for developing the countryside to give people homes. They'd rather keep it for shooting. It's different in Glasgow where I was born, and which is like a new place now. Growing up there was pretty rough but during the 1980s people took risks and money came in. A lot of it was used for yuppifying but on the credit side, a lot of the old tenements were nice sandstone buildings. Instead of knocking them down and replacing them with concrete, they've cleaned them up and turned them into smart apartments.'

At the time of our conversation, Jack was living in Suffolk between Sudbury and Colchester. Coincidentally, it's close to where I moved with my wife in 2017. Jack arrived in 1970 and proceeded to get married and have five children, another reason why he's careful about how much time he spends on the road.

His wife is German and 'likes to be near the shops', which tend not to exist on remote islands. Compared with Germany, Jack thinks people are ripped off in this country. 'Wages over there are double and stuff is half the price,' he complained. 'Everything is about multinational conglomerates and the profit motive. My father, who was an engineer, worked very hard but there was never any money around. All those countries that were behind us, like Spain, have now overtaken us. I was in Bari in the south of Italy the other week. Considering it's supposed to be really poor, everyone was going around in nice clothes and sitting in cafés. Quality of life seems to have evaded the UK. We're in the EU, everything should be the same price.'

The Bruces, however, like Suffolk. 'It's still a bit real,' he opined. 'It's not all weekend cottages owned by stockbrokers. So, I don't mind not working all the time. My family is the most important thing to me. I've been in this business a long time and you expect to have periods when things can be quieter. I'm pretty laid back about it all.'

Meanwhile, his old mate Eric remains the stressful type, a troubled workaholic, even if he has been more successful than the average stockbroker.

CHAPTER 39

JACKIE COLLINS

"Would you like to lie on the floor? I could get you a couple of pillows..."

JACKIE COLLINS, 1986

The second time I met Jackie Collins, the novelist vowed, 'You're going to be one of the characters in my next book.' Indeed, she was as good as her word. Pick up a copy of Jackie's *Rock Star*, turn to page forty-seven and there I am. Not too subtly disguised as Nicholls Kline. The character is a nightclub manager, the Kline borrowed from a certain rock 'n' roll manager who worked for The Beatles and the Rolling Stones.

The author's lightbulb moment came during lunch at the Royal Garden Hotel, in Knightsbridge. Between the champagne and smoked salmon, she wondered what I had been up to since our previous, and first, meeting the year before. On that occasion, we had convened at the even flashier Berkeley Hotel so I could interview her for *Penthouse*. We got on famously, she enjoyed the feature and promised we'd meet again.

In answer to her question, I had, indeed, been up to quite a lot. The previous week alone, I had broken the Bill Wyman and Mandy Smith story, having spotted them together at a Richard Branson party. That was in addition to working as the VIP Room PR at the newly opened Limelight Club (hence the nightclub manager bit) and managing the rock band Gatecrash Heaven, featuring Chris Pope, hence the Kline component. Readers of

Collins's books will be aware that most of the characters are based on hybrids of actual stars. For example, the hero of *Rock Star* is a cross between Rod Stewart, Tom Jones and possibly Robert Plant of Led Zeppelin. Then, here comes yours truly, referred to in a book by an author whose sales have exceeded 500 million, never mind all the films, TV mini-series, and so on.

The first time we met was also in unusual circumstances. I'd arrived to do the *Penthouse* interview with an aching back, the result of just having completed a 50,000 word book in five days. She offered the possibility of conducting the interview with me lying on my back on the floor. As it happened, laughter proved to be the best medicine and there was plenty of that. The rendezvous commenced with lots of gossip about my cousin, John, who at the time worked for Jackie's then husband, Oscar Lurman. Oscar owned celebrity haunt Tramp in Hollywood where cousin John was *maître d'*. We also talked about mutual acquaintance George Best whom I had known since I was fifteen, as well as Michael Caine, Sean Connery and Simon Le Bon of Duran Duran. 'He just doesn't seem to have it,' said Jackie about the New Romantic singer, 'but I must tell you about Prince. I saw him at a party recently and he only danced to his own records...'

Jackie also mentioned the band Spandau Ballet, specifically the blonde saxophonist Steve Norman. I happened to see them all in The Groucho Club the following week. Singer and guitarist Gary Kemp was particularly amused that the famous author had enquired about Steve. With sneaky aplomb Jackie also made enquiries about George Michael. 'I keep reading speculation in the British press that he's gay. What is all this?' But it wasn't her who should have been asking the questions, at least not on this occasion. That was my role and there was quite a lot for me to ask. For example, where did Jackie obtain the raw material for books like *Hollywood Wives* and *The World is Full of Married*

Men, the airport bookshop potboiler which kickstarted her career in the 1960s?

'I get invited to a lot of parties but I'm quite selective. I will accept an invitation if I think it will be fun and informative. Then I have a lot of friends who call me every day and tell me everything that is going on. One of my best friends in Hollywood is a guy who is friendly with a famous madame and she tells him all kinds of things. I mean there's one man, a very famous film producer, who can only get it up by hiding in the closet dressed in his wife's clothes. The closet has an eye piece, so they have a male hooker and he comes into the bedroom and makes out with his wife. The guy never comes out of the closet, just watches.'

Needless to say, Jackie didn't chance upon this kind of livelihood overnight. 'I've enjoyed writing ever since I was a young girl at school,' she says. 'I'd get hold of filthy stories, write them out and sell them to the other kids. I was always a vulture. I'd see what people were up to and go home and write about it. My father was a theatrical agent so there were always famous people coming and going into the house. I guess you could say I started writing professionally when I was about fifteen.'

This is when Collins happened to get expelled from school for 'smoking and playing truant', she went on gleefully. By this stage, elder sister Joan was already living in LA '...trying to become a movie star, so I went to join her. When I got to LA, she picked me up at the airport and said, "Here are the keys to the apartment, some more for the car, go and learn to drive." I had all this freedom and my parents were only too pleased to be rid of me as I'd said I wanted to be a writer and it got me out of their hair.'

In the 1990s Joan, by now one of the biggest stars in the world as a result of *Dynasty*, decided to appear in a series of six dramas for the BBC. Working for the *Daily Express*, I went to the launch party at Television Centre, the corporation's west London studios, my old stomping ground from *Top of the Pops* days. Ignoring the phalanx of security, I marched up to Joan and engaged *the grand dame* in conversation. Having secured a few quotes for my article, I told her my anecdotes about her younger sister which amused her, because, hey, you can't make this stuff up. What might have surprised her even more was the incident which occurred with her daughter, Tara, a couple of years later.

I met Tara at a dance music awards ceremony at the Royal Albert Hall. After we'd been chatting for about twenty minutes, she grabbed a bottle of champagne with one hand, my arm with the other and before I knew what had hit me, I found myself sitting next to her in a taxi, which had been hailed by somebody else. Talk about family entertainment...

JEAN-JACQUES BURNEL

With the exception of local lads, Buzzcocks, The Stranglers were the first punk band I ever saw live. It was the day after Her Majesty The Queen's Silver Jubilee celebrations during the tour which took the band from the pub circuit to mainstream punk. Their debut album, *Rattus Norvegicus*, had just been released and would stay in the album charts for more than a year. Later that same month, May 1977, they would make the first of many appearances on *Top of the Pops*. However, you would never have guessed from this classic show at Manchester's Electric Circus. In a word, it was complete mayhem. The place was packed with wildly pogoing punks and punkettes. Although the tabloid press was hell-bent on associating punk with violence, the tightly-packed gyrating crowd gave off more than a whiff of sex. Right in front of me a guy started stripping his friend off until she was down to her knickers. He ended up covering her in his rubber mac.

After the show I slithered sweatily to the dressing-room and instantly felt at home. The band were cheerfully chatting to fans and photographer Pennie Smith was there shooting a cover for the *NME*. If this was a snapshot of the rock 'n' roll lifestyle, I thought, count me in! Having discussed keyboard influences with Dave Greenfield, who preferred not to be drawn on whether he was a big Doors fan, I got talking to Jean-Jacques Burnel, the athletic bassist who appeared to be the main visual focus on stage. He immediately offered me a drink and admitted that he himself really liked The Doors.

'There was lots of stuff I liked when I was growing up,' he added. 'I actually started playing classical guitar at the age of eleven, but suddenly a lot of other things were happening from the British pop scene to the late 60s blues boom.' Being music fans proved invaluable when it came to joining the punk scene. 'It was a struggle at first because the only places we could play were either youth clubs or pubs. We desperately wanted to play support on the university circuit, but no-one would have us. We often had the plug pulled on us in pubs, or the police would arrive and there would be a stand-off. If you thought tonight was a bit of a riot, you should have seen some of the gigs in the early days!' Like Dr Feelgood, The Stranglers were not originally a punk band but they found themselves falling in with the same audiences, kids that demanded something more basic than the over-egged instrumental jerking off by the prevailing prog bands.

I went to see The Stranglers regularly over the next couple of years watching them progress from clubs like the Electric Circus through to the Manchester Apollo and the cavernous New Bingley Hall in Stafford. This was actually a county showground that, until recently, had only attracted established acts like Genesis and Pink Floyd.

In 1979, Jean-Jacques put out a solo album based on the theme of European unity. Entitled *Euroman Cometh*, the sleeve featured him standing in front of the Pompidou Centre in Paris. 'I was always interested in the idea of a united Europe,' he told me when he took the project on the road, in the spring of that year. 'It seemed to be right because I associated synthesised electronic music with Europe, especially electro groups like Kraftwerk and Can.'

At the Manchester Apollo fans were offered free tickets because sales were so low. Yet within twelve months, electro was all the rage in hip London clubs like Blitz in Covent Garden. In a backstage conversation, I mentioned how my prediction of the success of Dire Straits had been proved correct by that band's recent Stateside success. Jean-Jacques was not too impressed snorting, 'I can't understand why a guy from Barnsley needs to sound like J.J. Cale.'

Later that year, I saw the band in less familiar settings. Firstly, on the set for the 'Duchess' video, where they all appeared dressed as choristers, and then a charity cricket match in Maida Vale. Participants in the latter involved likely lads Rat Scabies of The Damned and Motorhead's Lemmy. We ran a picture of The Stranglers' guitarist Hugh Cornwell adorning the following week's cover of *Record Mirror*. 'How Hugh Lost His Bails' was the headline and inside the paper I interviewed the band about their new album *The Raven*.

Soon afterwards, the group's name became synonymous with trouble, from appearing on stage with strippers when they played their hit 'Nice and Sleazy' to being locked up for causing a riot at a gig in Nice. They also had all their equipment stolen during an American tour. They fared rather better in Japan where Burnel completed his black belt training in karate. These days, he's a seventh dan.

'The three-week course included five-mile barefoot runs through the snow,' he told me at New York club Privates the following year. We had both come to see English post-punk band The Members who shared management with The Stranglers. 'Exchanging kicks and punches left me with four broken ribs,' he went on, before giving me a sample of his fancy footwork. A sharp kick to my thigh had me staggering for a while but fortunately no breakages. The blow was partly in response to a less-than-enthusiastic review of one of their shows a few months earlier. Jean-Jacques showed more tact to his Japanese fans, especially the girls. 'Everywhere we went we received the same hysterical reaction,' he enthused. 'When we arrived in a town, the girls would be waiting for us at a station. When we got to the hotel, they were there. We couldn't get rid of them. They even slept in the hotel corridors outside our rooms.'

In Lille, in northern France, Burnel enjoyed a lower profile. Being French, he'd been asked to produce a local band, so I flew over on a tiny plane from Stansted with, incongruously, a party of surveyors who were scoping Lille out for possible development. At the time, the city boasted much impressive ancient architecture, so I hope they didn't make a mess of it. 'It's part Flemish, because we're on the border with Belgium,' the bassist explained. The rest of the evening was taken up with an elegant meal and a gig attended by young Polish kids whose parents were earning money mining in Africa. Rock 'n' roll, like travel in general, certainly has the capacity to offer experience and broaden the mind.

The last time I saw Jean-Jacques was when he was touring his one man show at the Queen Elizabeth Hall on London's South Bank in the autumn of 1999. In total contrast to The Stranglers, this was an evening of acoustic punk interwoven with amusing anecdotes. It was spontaneous but obviously well-rehearsed. We shared wine in the green room beforehand – decent stuff, not like the usual plonk you get back stage. We discussed the possibility of a booze cruise and tour. If you are reading this, Jean-Jacques, there's been a slight change of plan. You might as well be a guest at my villa near Grasse, in Alpes-Maritimes. The local restaurants are as good as in Lille and we're not too close to Nice.

JEFF BECK

Guitar legend Jeff Beck keeps a six-stringed instrument in every room of his house. 'It reminds me of what I should be doing,' explained the musician idolised by all his contemporaries. These included fellow virtuosos, many of whom have also been stars since the 1960s. 'He's a maverick, an unsung hero to the masses,' reckons David Gilmour of Pink Floyd. 'He was the favourite guitarist of our keyboard player Rick Wright, much to my chagrin.' Beatles producer George Martin went a step further. 'He uses his guitar as his voice, and I don't know any other player like it.'

It was Beck who replaced Eric Clapton in The Yardbirds in 1965, making his instrument sound like a sitar on the classic 'Heart Full of Soul'. Soon afterwards Jeff scored a solo hit with the regularly re-released 'Hi Ho Silver Lining' but confessed to being a reluctant pop star, even if the song made a lot of people happy. Jeff's introduction to the rock world was exemplary. One night he went to see an up-and-coming guitarist at the classic swinging London club, The Cromwellian in Kensington. His name was Jimi Hendrix. In the audience were Rod Stewart and Ronnie Wood, knocked out by Jimi's sensational show. They were in the process of putting their own band together and realised they needed a five-star guitarist of their own. There and then, Beck agreed that the three of them should work together and the result was *Truth*, Jeff's first solo album.

As heavy rock records go, *Truth* was years ahead of its time, even pre-dating the Led Zeppelin debut. Following another LP, the equally lauded *Beck-ola*, friends and associates alike were reminded of his unpredictable behaviour when Beck decided not to play a certain rock festival – Woodstock. 'Some little bird whispered in my ear that it wasn't in my best interests,' he apologised, referring to the historic festival which attracted half a million people. 'Thank God for my integrity.'

In the 1970s, albums like *Blow By Blow* and *Wired* showed the guitarist moving in a jazzier direction, although on stage the emphasis was still on that heady brew of aggression, spirit and melody, Beck wowing his fans with his ability to bend notes with one hand while using a tremolo arm to detonate original sound effects with the other. Never one to stay in the same place too long, recent years have seen him record operatic specials like the Three Tenors' 'Nessun Dorma' and work with a new generation of female singers like Joss Stone and Beth Hart. This came as no surprise to me, since the first time we met he was watching a gig by the all-female Girlschool at the Electric Ballroom in the summer of 1980. Despite having a reputation for not liking journalists, he was happy to chat with me and trade anecdotes, as shown by the picture craftily snapped by one of my colleagues.

We talked about his blood brother, Cozy Powell, who was about to headline the first Monsters of Rock festival with Rainbow. 'I spoke to Cozy earlier and he was supposed to come here tonight but never mind, there's no shortage of blokes here,' he quipped. Jeff also talked about working with Stevie Wonder on the epic *Talking Book* album which yielded a great studio story. 'Stevie popped out for some lunch, so I started messing with the drum part and came up with the beat for 'Superstition'. When he came back I was caught in the act, but Stevie told me to keep playing. I protested that I wasn't a drummer and he said, "You are now!" as he started joining in on keyboards.'

When not creating infectious riffs, Beck's idea of relaxation is restoring classic cars. He likes to rebuild both the exteriors and the engines of hot rods in his professional workshop at his home in Sussex. He believes he was inspired by the Gene Vincent film, *The Girl Can't Help It*, which Jeff describes as 'the best rock 'n' roll film ever'.

The next time we met was in Molly Moggs, a small bar on Charing Cross Road in 1990. Chris Pope of The Chords and I were *en route* to the Marquee to see Icicle Works featuring Ringo Starr's son on drums. I asked Jeff what he had been up to since our last meeting. It had been a relatively quiet period for him compared with the previous decades. 'I didn't think it was my time,' he confided. 'It was all push-button music, wasn't it? No place for me, so I buried myself in my workshop and guested for others – Mick Jagger, Tina Turner, Stevie Wonder, Stanley Clarke and, of course, Rod again with our hit 'People Get Ready'.' In the 1990s and 2000s, Beck shared stage and studio time with everyone from Kate Bush and Morrissey to Guns N' Roses and Roger Waters on whose *Amused to Death* concept album, Jeff played on every track.

Meanwhile, on this particular night, Jeff was with Brian May of Queen and TV producer Peter Richardson of Comic Strip fame. They were all off to The Astoria to catch Bad News, the spoof heavy metal outfit featuring characters like The Young Ones' Ade Edmondson. 'I'm going on a consultancy basis,' explained Jeff. 'They want me to show them all the guitar hero clichés,' said the man who is one of the few guitarists who has managed to exclude such things in his auspicious career.

JEFF LYNNE

An unashamed Beatles fan who co-founded Electric Light Orchestra, Jeff Lynne was one of the first rock musicians to blend light classical music with melodic pop. It was not a combination achieved overnight. Despite hit singles like '10538 Overture', 'Livin' Thing' and the sublime 'Telephone Line', it took the best part of a decade for ELO to reach critical mass. In contrast, Lynne's next band, the Traveling Wilburys enjoyed a vertical take-off, which might have had something to do with the personnel. By 1987, Jeff was not simply an aficionado of The Beatles but also the producer of George Harrison's solo album, *Cloud Nine*. 'After we finished that, we had a few beers and started inventing this fantasy game with all our favourite people. Then one day in LA, George came up with this idea for a song and he decided to include his friend Bob Dylan. Soon afterwards we all went to see a Roy Orbison show together and we invited him to join the Wilburys.'

Jeff told me this amazing story when I interviewed him for *The Times* in 1990. In ordinary circumstances, I would have taken all this with a pinch of salt. It sounded like the sort of tale some drug-crazed PR would off-load to a tabloid. But this was Jeff, a down-to-earth Brummie with the level of talent which was bound to attract the cream of the crop. It didn't end there, however. 'One day I was driving through Beverley Hills,' Jeff continued, 'and this beautiful red Corvette pulled up next to me at the traffic lights. The driver wound down his window and asked, "Do you fancy doing some work with me?" It was Tom Petty who was a big fan of The Beatles, so I invited him to join our dream band, too.'

Soon Messrs Harrison, Dylan, Lynne, Orbison and Petty wrote a song called 'Handle with Care', named after a label on a box in Dylan's garage. The album, *Traveling Wilburys Volume 1*, was recorded in less than a fortnight, mainly because Dylan was about to go on the road. By the time Bob's tour reached Britain, Tom Petty and the Heartbreakers were his backing band. In the meantime, Jeff was eager to describe the no-nonsense means by which the album was recorded. 'We just sat around in a circle with microphones and acoustic guitars and wrote the songs, just as groups used to do in the 1960s. No computers, gadgets or sampling,' he emphasised. 'It was like a workshop, making noises from scratch in old fashioned analogue.'

My interview appeared under the headline 'Alternative House Music', pointing out how different this approach was from the other 99 per cent of records then being made. 'Sometimes we worked in Tom's garage using the bedroom as the control room, or Roy's house. We really enjoyed playing in a number of different rooms since, unlike a studio, every room has a different ambience which is conducive to creating different sounds. Plus, you can imagine what fun it was to be working with all your favourite people.'

Considering ELO was one of the most technologically advanced bands of their day, it was marvellous to hear Lynne championing this back-to-basics approach. 'I don't believe in technology for the sake of it,' he argued, 'I think it feeds on itself. The more gadgets some bands use, the more they think they need. In my case, I decided I didn't like the sound of sampling. Samplers just make a collection of second-hand sounds so why not use, say, a real piano? Nothing can match that and, of course, you have a great time vibing off each other and making what is essentially a live recording. It's even better when it's a record made by people who have been doing it for many years and listening to their fellow musicians for almost as long. George was also no big fan of machines and although younger than us, Tom was perfectly happy with guitars, keyboards and drums just like the Heartbreakers.

'For the second Wilburys' album we brought in Jim Keltner on drums whose name is not credited on the sleeve. Jim has played with everybody from The Bee Gees and Ry Cooder to Randy Newman and the Rolling Stones. He has also been known to team up with Charlie Watts for a double drummer project.' With three-fifths of the Traveling Wilburys no longer with us, we can't expect any more albums to materialise, but Jeff has been back on the road with ELO recording a live album in front of 60,000 people entitled *Wembley or Bust*. Not quite the same as making music live in a garage with some of the greatest rockers ever, but they've still got songs for fans who have been listening for a long time.

JOE STRUMMER

In August 1977, I was staying with friends in Paris when I had the urge to travel south west to Mont de Marsan to see the second annual punk festival. After being heavily fined for inadvertently taking a fast train, hitching a lift on the back of a motorbike and drinking some terrible table wine, I finally got to the site of an ancient amphitheatre. There, I ran into the guy who had managed the tour for Television and Blondie a couple of months earlier. Following the minimum amount of blagging, he furnished me with a backstage pass enabling me to catch Eddie and the Hot Rods, and Friday night's bill-toppers, Dr Feelgood.

The following morning, having crashed out in a field overnight, I found myself in a typical French open-air bar. Above it was a number of rooms where the bands and a couple of journalists were staying. The idea was to try and find the chap from *Melody Maker* who I had once spoken to on the telephone to help me purloin another pass for that night's bands: The Jam, The Damned, The Police and headliners The Clash. At the end of a tiny corridor which became part of a bedroom, I bumped into Joe Strummer. He seemed relieved that I spoke English and there began a relationship that went on for more than twenty years.

On discovering I was from Manchester, Joe asked me if I knew a cartoonist called Ray Lowry. As it happened, I had met Ray in the offices of the *New Manchester Review* to which we were both contributors. This put Joe in a good mood so we went down to the bar where he bought me a beer, a forerunner to a character on the London Calling song, 'Rudi Can't Fail', who used to drink Brew for breakfast. Being practically penniless from the previous day's fine, I reciprocated by finding a shop which sold me a litre bottle of mineral water. Years later, a friend told me that he had seen a photograph of me sharing this water with members of The Clash when he visited an exhibition at the Barbican Centre – a far cry from the beverages being consumed when the picture on the cover of this book was taken.

That night The Clash mainly played material from their recently released debut album plus a couple of new songs, including 'Complete Control' with matching graffiti artwork announcing 'This is Joe Public Speaking' as part of the stage set. They also played 'White Man in Hammersmith Palais', which was not released as a single until the following June.

By the end of the year, I had seen The Clash again at the Manchester Apollo – a great leap forward from their previous gig in the city which was at the Electric Circus during the White Riot tour earlier in the spring. After the Apollo gig, in what was by now becoming my second home, the dressing room, Joe informed me there was another aftershow party at Manchester Airport's Excelsior Hotel some fifteen miles away. He wondered if I could give a lift to a couple of his friends. They were members of Liverpool band The Spitfire Boys, so it seemed quite apt to cram them into my sporty two-seater Triumph Spitfire, soft top down all the way. Why four punks were never pulled up by the Old Bill for overcrowding with the roof down in the middle of winter remains an urban myth. Another event, however, of greater historical importance was about to unfold.

Present at The Excelsior was Tony Wilson, Granada TV celebrity and future Factory Records boss. Back then he was mainly famous for being the first television producer to put the Sex Pistols on air. In recent weeks the popular *So It Goes* series had featured everybody from Iggy Pop to Mink DeVille, two or three acts appearing per show. I introduced him to Clash manager Bernie Rhodes whom I had spent some time with at Mont de Marsan. By the end of the evening, they had planned a Clash *So It Goes* special from Manchester's 5,000 capacity Belle Vue theatre. The concert took place the following week – but not without incident. As a result of jobsworths keeping the excited fans waiting, the crowd surged forward and demolished the venue's glass doors, a local television news item usefully publicising the programme itself.

The next legendary Clash gig was the Rock Against Racism bash in London's Victoria Park in April 1978. Getting backstage was a breeze, what with Clash roadie Roadent and the rest of the crew accepting me as one of the gang. Velvet Underground and Andy Warhol icon Nico was there and asked me if I was Indian. Ditto Jimmy Pursey of Sham 69 who ended up jamming with The Clash on 'White Riot'. By the time I next saw The Clash we had all been to America but not together. This was towards the end of 1978 on the Sort It Out tour promoting the second album *Give 'Em Enough Rope*. Once again, The Apollo was involved but for a few nervous moments it looked as if it could be for the last time. Joe came offstage and literally collapsed under a table in the dressing room. He lay there motionless, prompting concern from the rest of the band. After what seemed like an age, he gradually winched himself up admitting exhaustion coupled with an excessive amount of boozing and other substances. He offered me a brief homily on the downside of speed and cocaine, both of which had been available in abundance Stateside.

I was rapidly discovering that interviewing artists was not a one-way activity. They soon got fed up of answering the same questions and often welcomed an anecdote or two in return, so I thought I'd mention how when I was in the States, I had borrowed a brand new car and driven it from LA to San Francisco for free. The idea was that if someone bought a car in one city and lived in another, they could have it delivered to where they wanted. Joe said he hated the former hippie stronghold, reckoning Texas his favourite part of America. There was no answer to that because I had not been to Texas so, instead, I told him I had been to see Neil Young at the LA Forum. 'Did he play burnt out basement?' he asked quirkily, referring to the song by his favourite lyric rather than the actual title. Generally speaking he enjoyed visiting America and it was no surprise that when The Clash performed their first live dates in the USA the following year, they hit the ground running. This was in marked contrast to contemporaries such as The Jam and Elvis Costello who for some years would struggle to gain popularity over there.

On planet Clash, the most important event of 1979 was the release of their third album, *London Calling*. Produced by ska and rock legend Guy Stevens, it represented a massive musical leap forward for the band combining punk, reggae and rockabilly with classic rock 'n' roll. Even lyrically it was ahead of its time, the title track presaging nuclear disaster while with 'Guns of Brixton', life really did imitate art when the riots broke out in the spring of 1981. A couple of weeks after this I went on the road with them to Spain, the start of a world tour which took in more than a dozen nights in New York, major American festivals and shows in the then emerging rock 'n' roll countries such as Portugal, Poland, Yugoslavia and Thailand. The idea, according to manager Rhodes, was to abandon Britain for a while because the country had reverted to its 'pre-punk jaded self'. This conversation took place in Barcelona airport as the rest of the band were recovering from the night before. The gig at Pavillion Juventual had been attended by a boisterous gang of Joe's Spanish friends who he had met while hitch-hiking around Spain just before The Clash took off.

The picture on the cover of this book should give some idea of the aftershow party which gave every indication of being sponsored by a certain brand of tequila. The band were not expecting to see me; I was actually on the road with another act but obviously wanted to drop by and pay my respects. The band responded with bear-like hugs and other demonstrations of masculine affection. My reaction was to rain a series of blows on the makeshift bar holding all the booze. It promptly collapsed causing a selection of bottles to rattle their way to the floor. Fortunately, the main casualties were sticky 'from concentrate' products although the mishap certainly helped set the scene for several hours of mayhem which did not conclude until about five a.m.

On the flight to Madrid later that day, I caught up with Joe and our conversation covered the roots of *Sandinista!*, their triple album which had attracted a mixed reaction when released six months earlier. Extending the group's repertoire into areas such as rap, dub and even calypso, it nevertheless contained its fair share of rock tunes such as 'Somebody Got Murdered' and 'Police on My Back'. The title referred to the Sandinista rebels in Nicaragua who had overthrown the ruling family oligarchy – not that it was front page news anywhere else in the world. 'There was a total media blackout at the time, so the title is useful inasmuch as we were able to tell people about it,' Joe explained. 'We felt sympathy with what they were doing, not that we are preaching even if we are committed. Politics is something which concerns every individual so in raising people's awareness, they have the opportunity to investigate for themselves. As for ourselves, we don't have any political ideology other than human rights.'

This represented something of a shift in Clash geopolitics, especially when viewed alongside previous sympathy for Red Brigade terrorists whose colours Strummer sported around the time of the Rock Against Racism gigs. Plus, on the current tour there were photographic images projected onto the stage backdrop featuring Right to Work marches in Detroit, devastation in Cambodia and so on. 'I don't want myself or anyone else to go round killing people,' Strummer declared. 'I'd rather walk around with the sun on my back and my hands in my pockets. That's why we're here, for the sun, the wine and the women. Five years ago, I went out with a great Spanish girl in Madrid and still have a love of the country. 'Spanish Bombs' isn't just about the civil war, it's also a love song dedicated to myself and my father. We never saw eye-to-eye on a lot of things but one night after a few drinks, he admitted that in the late 1930s he had had half a mind to fight for the Republican cause in the Spanish civil war.'

It was illuminating to see this compassionate, concerned side of Joe, not that anyone could ever doubt his sincerity. Onstage he flogged himself into the ground to the point where he was once described as looking as though he was about to have an epileptic fit. Releasing multiple albums such as the double LP, *London Calling,* for little more than the price of a single disc and the triple set, *Sandinista!,* for the price of a double LP, showed further generosity towards his audience. It was authority figures he took issue with, including hotel managers who were happy to rake in a small fortune from the band's entourage and then complained when they played the radio at little more than television volume. After that night's show – another cracker starring red hot renditions of 'Bank Robber', 'Hammersmith Palais', 'Armagideon Time', 'Jimmy Jazz' and about twenty other all-time greatest hits – this is exactly what occurred in Madrid. In fact, the manager called the local *caribineri* who kicked the door open with such ferocity that a bookcase collapsed sending rows of bottles, tapes and other personal effects crashing to the floor. They were so embarrassed by this unintentional demolition job that they could not leave fast enough. Neither could Joe. 'C'mon man, let's go and find some action and something to eat. I'm starving... I can feel the pangs of hunger. Let's hit the streets!' So much for the cossetted life of a rock star, I thought, as dawn broke while we searched for a café serving whatever the local market traders ate for breakfast in this part of town.

The early 1980s saw The Clash break America big time and become one of the most revered bands in the history of rock 'n' roll. Then things started to go wrong. Guitarist and co-songwriter Mick Jones was sacked in 1983 for reasons explored in the chapter about him, and a lacklustre album with a makeshift line-up slipped out two years later, before The Clash officially called it a day. Along with The Pogues, Joe got involved in amusing film projects like Alex Cox's *Straight to Hell,* scored some film soundtracks and worked with new bands in different countries. Towards the end of the decade, I saw him play the Electric Ballroom with his brief band Latino Rockabilly War. He also performed an Amnesty International benefit at the Milton Keynes Bowl where he ran into Jean-Jacques Burnel of The Stranglers. I'm not sure that the early rivals of the nascent punk scene had really met before, but Joe admired JJ's latest gleaming Harley Davidson motorcycle. I felt I had witnessed another piece of history when they met. 'I thought you were a Triumph man,' I chided Jean-Jacques. 'Ah, but its engine design follows that of the classic 750 Bonneville,' came the rejoinder. Joe then introduced me to Gabby, his long-standing girlfriend and mother of his children. We had originally met in early 1980 at the start of the London Calling tour at fabled rock venue Friars in Aylesbury. She was now Joe's acting manager, trying to persuade his record company to stump up some money for studio time. After the huge success of The Clash, especially in

America, you would think it was the least they could do. Joe clearly agreed. 'They keep saying: "Well, give us a demo," and I say: "Why the fuck should I?" For the price of a bit more studio time, we could go straight in and record a whole new album. In one take. And if we don't like something, we'll play it again. The whole studio system has got ridiculous, teams of technicians watching a wave form on a screen and agonising over whether a note needs flattening or not. It's time these people realised that music is about getting up and playing.'

We had a couple of drinks one afternoon shortly afterwards at The Windsor Castle on Portobello Road, then quite a few more at the launch party for a Pogues' album at the Boston Arms ballroom in Tufnell Park. It was our longest, most rambling, putting-the-world-to-rights dialogue to date, much to the annoyance of other journalists present. Matters were not helped by the fact that I was with my attractive blonde girlfriend who was about to qualify as a rock 'n' roll lawyer. Joe decided that he would like to be one of her clients, possibly encouraged by her bee-stung lips.

Then came Glastonbury 1999 when he appeared in the afternoon with his latest band, The Mescaleros. I had hardly spoken to him since the start of the decade, family and work commitments in Manchester, Belfast and east (as opposed to west) London keeping me estranged form the usual rock 'n' roll haunts. So, it was with a certain amount of euphoria that I learned, when I bumped into early rock pal and Clash photographer Pennie Smith, that Joe was lighting a bonfire in the backstage campsite a few metres away.

Armed with cans of Special Brew and other essentials, I went to join Joe. He looked pleased and introduced me to his new wife Lucinda. They had been together for a while and now lived near Taunton in Somerset. Good Lord! So, it was not only my family life that was keeping us apart on the streets of Camden, Soho and Notting Hill. Well, we all have to grow up sometime. But not necessarily at Glasto where veteran Clash associate Trish Ronane was guarding the kids' tent and Joe rolling the herbals.

Conversation flowed deep into the night and we really did drink Brew for breakfast. It's just a shame that Joe barely saw out his forties, but at least there are the music and the memories. Not to mention that cracking photo of me and Joe tearing up Spain on the front cover.

JOHN CALE

John Cale was a music student from a remote part of Wales who won a scholarship to a top American conservatory. Having studied electronic music and joined an *avant-garde* ensemble in New York, he met the equally left-field songwriter Lou Reed. Together they formed The Velvet Underground who, over the course of only two albums, became one of the most influential bands in the history of rock 'n' roll.

Following the release of the second of these records, *White Light / White Heat*, Cale left The Velvets to pursue experimental projects of his own. These included early 1970s LPs such as *The Academy in Peril* and *Paris 1919*, whose haunting refrains came to the attention of future collaborators like Brian Eno and Patti Smith. Cale produced Smith's *Horses*, arguably the first ever new wave recording in 1976. This was shortly after the release of John's solo album, *Fear,* which highlighted the multi-instrumentalist's melodic sensibility. I noticed this when reviewing the LP for the University of Warwick students' newspaper – the first time I saw any of my work published.

Cale's commercial streak continued when he produced an EP for Squeeze in the early days of punk. I didn't get to meet him until 1981 when he was promoting *Honi Soit*, as in the French motto *Honi soit qui mal y pense* (Shame on he who thinks evil of it). Despite its menacing title, the record enjoyed a mild flirtation with pop, especially on cuts like 'Dead or Alive'. 'That's about a former lover who didn't care whether she was dead or alive,' he explained bluntly. If that seems rather a curt reply, at least it was a complete sentence. Most of his responses elicited fewer words.

When he opened the door of his room in a West London hotel, I thought I had just met someone with an almighty hangover. Lugubrious is probably the best description. My attempts to gain information were akin to drawing teeth. In fact, I will reproduce some of his answers as evidence:

Musically, Honi Soit seems closer to Fear than some of your other LPs?
'Certainly, they both occupy the same sort of musical position.'

Are you hoping to play any dates in the UK?
'I think that would be in my best interests.'

How do you feel about having been described in the past as an 'honourable psychotic'?
'It's okay if it helps to sell papers.'

Where are you mainly based these days?
'I've been living in New York for the past fifteen years.'

Room service then arrived with tea. Hopefully it would revive his spirits, I thought.

Although a producer yourself, I understand you have been working with Mike Thorne, as did acclaimed weird act, Wire?
'He's a conservative person. It's nice to have some stability in the studio.'

Are the lyrics as important to you as the music? They seem quite impenetrable to me at times. Are there any running themes?

'What? Like a rash?'

On noting my incipient lack of patience, he added, 'My favourite track on the new album is 'Fighter Pilot'. That's based on Biggles, y'know.'

Have you heard any other interesting artists of late?
'Yes.'

Living in New York, do you get out to see bands very often?
'Well I live in Manhattan, but I try not to go to too many clubs there. I'd rather stay in and read books, they're more likely to influence my lyrics. For example, that line in 'Fear', "fear is a man's best friend", is a parody of John Le Carré's *Tinker, Tailor, Soldier, Spy*. I see a lot of films, too. I like Sam Peckinpah movies, the way he makes moral judgements between right and wrong.'

Is that what you do yourself?
'I suppose I must, but I don't like to sound too pious.'

I remember in the mid-1970s seeing your band on stage and you were wearing a fencing mask. Was that to express some kind of fear of the audience?
'No, it was more about changing persona from song to song.'

What was Paris 1919 all about?
'Nostalgia.'

You've made quite a few albums since leaving The Velvet Underground, yet your name is still synonymous with them. Do you find that annoying?

'Not really. Just mystifying. What other people see in the Velvets is not what I saw. I'm still friendly with Andy Warhol, he's been a good friend over the years. I wouldn't know about him making a comeback, I don't think he ever went away.'

The same could be said about John Cale and, indeed, the rest of The Velvet Underground who briefly reformed in the mid-1990s. Since then, like Warhol, the remaining members have all passed away making them even more of a legend, something which Cale must really find 'mystifying'.

JOHN COOPER CLARKE

By the spring of 1977 it was obvious there was more to punk than three-chord thrashes and a 'street credible' working-class attitude. Bands like Talking Heads and XTC were waiting in the wings and there was an art college vibe in the air, so it should have come as no surprise when a poet arrived on the scene.

One evening in May, I went to the Band on the Wall on the edge of Manchester's city centre to see the Buzzcocks. A renowned jazz venue, like London's 100 Club, Monday evenings saw the place taken over by local listings magazine the *New Manchester Review*. While chatting to some of the young punks in the queue, one of the spiky-haired chaps informed me that the support act, John Cooper Clarke, was a poet. Like many Mancunians in the thriving local extended family, the next year saw John popping up all over the city reciting his unique poems from a battered notebook. Some of his verse was transferred to vinyl, courtesy of a few different record companies. His ode to Hell's Angels, 'Psycle Sluts', was released on Didsbury's own Rabid label while Virgin records copped the rights to a couple of his tracks on the *Short Circuit: Live at The Electric Circus* 10-inch LP.

By 1979, JCC had a major record deal and *Record Mirror* was allowing me to write features as well as submitting live reviews. So, it came to pass that John and I met in an official interview situation not in our native comfort zone of Salford but in one of Notting Hill's more refined cafés, a *pâtisserie* just off

Westbourne Grove. We met outside, John obviously excited by the enticing window display. 'Look at them, hey? Edible jewels!' he exclaimed pointing to the miniature strawberry tarts glistening provocatively. 'Are you going to be able to decipher what he's saying while he's eating?' asked Judy, his solicitous PR. 'Course he is!' remonstrated Mr Clarke, nodding in my direction. 'He's from Manchester. He knows what eating Mancunians sound like.'

John's capacity for dispatching sweetmeats without appearing to put on weight was reflected in poems such as 'Health Fanatic' and 'Tracksuit' which mock the exercising classes. 'It's an urban phenomenon, you never see people jogging in the countryside,' Clarke observed. 'It's a neurosis, you know, because the people doing it are always real thrombosis cases, tricking themselves into thinking they're doing something good breathing in more pollution than anybody else.'

'Middle-class guilt?' I asked. 'Yeah. Christian Barnard, the godfather of heart transplants, bears that one out. The other week he was saying that running fulfils the same need as flagellation. It's a bit like these people who think artists should suffer for their art and live in poverty. All this talk about street credibility... I like to keep off the streets as much as I can, actually.' Why? 'Because it's fucking cold! Why should people demand that people who entertain them suffer? It doesn't give rise to any kind of eloquence, just turns them into articulate grumblers.

'There's that story about Humphrey Lyttleton giving up his music to go and live in a bedsit because he thought it would help him play jazz better. I tell you what: I've written three very long poems in the last couple of weeks from a four-star hotel room with colour TV and room service. I didn't need to go out and didn't see a warm room as being unstimulating or sterile.' Here the poet was talking about the short break he took after spending much of the winter of 1979, one of the coldest in living memory, on the road with Elvis Costello. 'It's like anything else,' he went on, 'if you're working you deserve decent conditions. Miners, engineers, everyone is always looking for a better standard of living. There's a middle-class attitude to poverty being conducive to creativity. It's not. Poverty turns people into fucking criminals, murderers, wife-beaters, child-molesters… all the ugly things. It's very rare that beautiful poems or architecture or anything nice comes out of poverty.'

By the time we did our next interview the following year, John's debut album, *Disguise in Love*, was hovering around the Top 20, yet it did not seem to have improved his own standard of living. He was still residing in a bedsit, or as he put it 'sharing a cupboard with a vacuum cleaner for twenty-five quid a week. I was doing me yoga exercises the other day when somebody tried to grab my feet and sweep the stairs with me. In my bedsit you can watch TV and eat a meal without getting out of bed. In fact, you've got no choice in the matter!'

So not up to speed with all the latest gadgets then? 'Well the only one I really want is one of those things that toasts sandwiches and presses the sides down so that all the contents are sealed inside. Then I could make lentil soup sandwiches and curry sachets 'cos that's what I eat.' Not quite the celebrity lifestyle but it was better than sharing with the likes of a previous flatmate. 'Bit of a psychopath,' he recalled. 'Looked a bit like the boxer, Henry Cooper. I remember there was a knife fight on the stairs one night. Mind you, you never know who you're gonna live next to.'

It was this kind of circumstance which inspired one of his most popular and enduring poems, the dystopic 'Beasley Street'. 'Based on somewhere I knew, even though it's not its real name. It had flop houses, knocking shops, people saving up for sex change operations… there'd always be accidents, ceilings caving in and faulty wiring, that sort of thing. The weird thing is that it's such a long street. If you were driving down it and listening to the poem, you wouldn't be able to get to the end of it before the track finished.'

Not that John drives or even accepts lifts from strangers any more. 'Some lads stopped once to give me a lift, but it ended up a disaster. We got chased by the police and it turned out the car was nicked. When the driver eventually stopped, he and the other guy in the front scarpered. That left me facing five charges and I got put inside for thirty hours. But they had to let me go because no one claimed the car so there was no proof it was stolen.'

Fast forward to more recent years and this type of incident is unlikely to be repeated. These days John is back on the road and he has a driver. Enter Johnny Green, gentleman companion and chauffeur. He's also famous in his own right as the author of *A Riot of Our Own*, the autobiography based on his exploits as tour manager with The Clash. We've known one another since the dawn of punk but the last time we met up was in a café-bar in Catford, south east London, where John Cooper Clarke was performing. It was a freezing night during the winter of 2012, and I was lucky to be wearing a fur hat. 'It's rabbit,' announced John, a word often associated with himself.

There was no need for rabbit skins when I saw John at The Quay Theatre in Sudbury, Suffolk, in the sweltering summer of 2018. The poet was wearing a silver silk suit, white shirt, battered snakeskin ankle boots and a classy polka dot scarf to combat the highly efficient air-conditioning. I opted for a genuine Hawaiian shirt inherited from my father-in-law who lived in New Jersey which, coincidentally, matched the theme of some of the evening's new material. There were lots of references to *The Sopranos* and gangsters in East London, Essex and Manchester. Each anecdote came with matching accent and there was a crazy limerick about another Mafia stronghold for his forthcoming book. John explained how this was designed to appeal to the under-elevens market, 'the progeny of *Guardian*-reading single mothers who can be relied upon to make remarks like, "Tarquin swears a lot but at least he's reading something instead of looking at his phone all the time."' Then there was a relentless assault on aspects of modern life in quick-fire, dead-pan one-liners:

Obesity: 'There are special cells for fat guys in Chelmsford prison – bars five feet apart.'

Marriage: 'She steals the chips off my plate. No wonder I'm losing weight.'

... and random musings such as, 'If Jesus was Jewish, how come he's got a Spanish name?', which revealed his own religion, as did anecdotes about his adolescence. 'I learned to play snooker in the Manchester Jewish hospital in 1962. It's the only sport that isn't good for you. Remember the cocaine riots of the 1980s and 1990s with players like Jimmy White and Alex Higgins?'

In contrast to most artists appealing to the middle-aged nostalgia market, only a fraction of his set comprised old material. 'Beasley Street' became 'Beasley Boulevard' as part of his rage against current architecture, which also mocked the East Anglian 'model village' of Jaywick and regeneration company Urban Splash. The show might have taken place in the middle of a heat-wave but it was John who was truly on fire. We had a non-stop roller-coaster catch-up afterwards in the theatre bar that embraced everything from mutual Manchester low-life acquaintances to why he thought Stalin had suffered a bad press. 'It was Trotsky who was the real villain of communism,' he suggested. 'The evidence lies in heirs such as Jeremy Corbyn and Diane Abbot whereas

Stalin at least respected engineers, rewarding them with holidays in resorts like Odessa on the Black Sea.'

Johnny's father was an engineer which ties in with his principle that the proper use of language has the same integrity as a decent, sympathetic environment: teaching your children well and an appreciation of vocabulary are the key to modern life not being rubbish. As John approaches his eighth decade, holding to this belief hasn't done him any harm.

JOHN LYDON

These days the former Johnny Rotten may be considered a national treasure but this was not always the case. More than forty years ago, following the Sex Pistols' appearance on a teatime news show, he became Public Enemy No. 1. Provoked by the programme's presenter, Bill Grundy, the Pistols used 'bad language' which would today be considered pretty tame. The incident led to the band being sacked by not one but two record companies before the release of 'God Save The Queen' on a third label. It topped the charts during the Queen's Silver Jubilee celebrations in May 1977 and led to vicious attacks on two of the band for allegedly calling Her Majesty a 'moron'. It didn't help matters that their previous single had been entitled 'Anarchy in the UK'. With the exception of the release of their only album and a few secret gigs the following Christmas, this effectively ended the Sex Pistols' career in Britain.

The following year saw the launch of John Lydon's new band Public Image Ltd (PiL) and the rush release of their debut album *First Issue*. I had already become acquainted with The Clash, Stranglers and Buzzcocks, and I finally got to meet Johnny or John as he now called himself. There was no big introduction or standing on ceremony, it was just a chance meeting at a preview for a documentary film about the reggae poet Linton Kwesi Johnson. I remember telling John that I liked most of *First Issue* despite its experimental nature being slightly outside my comfort zone. I was even more impressed on seeing PiL live at Manchester's Belle Vue theatre in early 1979. The sneering singer with the maniacal glare had evolved into a dignified frontman dancing along to the dub-wise sounds with a certain dramatic grace. I wrote this in my review for *Record Mirror*, which proved a useful ice-breaker when it came to interviewing him at his home the following July.

The house, a mid-Victorian terrace on the border of Fulham and Chelsea, had clearly seen better days. It was an astute investment, however, by someone who had no reason to renovate it; he had no need to turn it into an enticing palace when there was a constant stream of rehearsing musos, friends and hangers-on already beating a path to his door. We settled down on a comfy if battered sofa opposite a very large television, the volume turned down and bad reception causing garish images to flash across the room. PiL guitarist Keith Levene padded in and out, and various other characters swanned around like extras in a Derek Jarman film. It was almost like he was running a guest house, I ventured. 'I quite like having people around, I'm getting used to being a piece of public property,' said the chap about my own age, decked out in a bright red tartan jacket, green slacks and slip-on shoes, but no shirt or socks. He might have been about to go on stage. If there had been a balcony, he would probably have gone out to wave to the assembled masses.

So, who were the fans these days – punk diehards or followers of the new sound? 'Fucking hell,' he replied ingloriously, 'I've no idea. It could be curiosity, which I don't like. I'm not a showpiece but I do enjoy performing live because all the songs take on the meaning they should have on vinyl. Really, before you can appreciate any song by a group, it's best to see it live then at least you can get an idea about our attitude.' So how come you haven't toured in the year or so since PiL have been together? 'I couldn't take it,' he emoted with self-parody. 'That would be terrible – like working nine to five. That's the worst thing about this business, expecting bands to go on the road. It's like a prison sentence. Now all these supposed *revolutionaries*,' he sneered, 'if they're gonna try changing things, how come they're still doing fifty-date tours?

What would you prefer then? Just the odd gig? 'Exactly. I'd rather just get in a van and say, "Oooh, let's go to Edinburgh tomorrow," or Manchester like we did the other week. See what we can get up there. So much more fun, cheaper as well and you don't wear yourself out or get too *excited*,' he grinned, mad expression restored. 'Most bands don't give a thought about playing their songs in the same order night after night. They're really robotised. Outside London you're not dealing with the usual arty-farty intellectuals or big-mouthed goons grunting "it better be good". Northern audiences are much more open-minded.'

Unfortunately, John doesn't feel the same way about the press or the fact that these gigs are likely to be reviewed. 'There's not one music paper you can open and feel happy about, you just pile through a load of drivel. If journalists enjoy music so much, how come you only read about depression and gloom?' So why talk to them? 'I suppose I must be a masochist... no, I talk to them because I don't want to fade into oblivion and never be heard of again,' he replied candidly. 'All forms of communication are important, even *Top of the Pops*. There's no point hanging on to morals and principles if nobody in the world can hear you.' Following Radio One's ban on the Sex Pistols at the time of 'God Save The Queen', John realised that he had to have a Plan B. That is why he and the Pistols agreed to perform their subsequent single, 'Pretty Vacant', on *Top of the Pops*.

'Now, they don't play PiL records on the radio except in the chart countdowns on a Sunday afternoon and I'd like the new record to be heard.' Here John was referring to 'Death Disco', hardly Top 40 material, especially since it was about his mother who had recently died. 'I had thought of telling people but I'd rather they put some brain-power into it. But yes, it's about how I felt when I watched someone die. It was vile.' If the lyrics weren't exactly radio-friendly, where did that leave the music or, to be honest, lack of it? 'Death Disco' wasn't exactly the catchy verse, chorus, verse, chorus stuff expected by daytime audiences. 'At least it isn't cliché-ridden garbage, loaded with slogans,' he retorted. 'If you're talking about the hollowness of the sound, that's because we cut out all the mid-range. Everything else around is mid-range and I don't like it. Records are made that way, so they come over nice on the radio. Now I listen to my records at home on this,' he explained, pointing to an unusually large sound system, 'and middle of the road records don't sound *naice* on it. They sound muffled and watered down instead of outspoken.'

Another way in which John was rewriting the rule book was by no longer bothering to have a manager. 'They serve no purpose. If you keep on shelling out 25 per cent to them, you end up in debt yourself. It's the same with the record company, we try not to depend on anybody, we just need to check that they're doing their bit.' As it happens there was one person at their record company, Virgin, to whom John was close – Head of International, Lisa Anderson. In the early 1980s, before decamping to New York, Lydon was a regular visitor to her mews residence near Hyde Park in Kensington. I know this because my then girlfriend was a lodger there. In the spring of 1981, Johnny bowled up to Lisa's birthday supper and amused the dozen or so guests by going to town on a handsome joint of roast beef. Since then he's given up red meat, but it was an education seeing him in relaxed mode fuelled by a few glasses of wine.

The following year at Virgin's local, The Earl of Lonsdale pub on Portobello Road, lagers were the order of the day. It was something of a farewell evening, PiL having decided to relocate to New York for a number of reasons. These included constant police harassment, especially at John's house which had become an easy target for minor drug busts. The most memorable part of the afternoon was the singer startling everyone present by pulling out a rolled-up wad of cash the size of a baked bean can, this being the era before credit cards were dished out to all and sundry.

It was another eighteen months before he returned to the UK heralded by a memorable press conference at the Royal Lancaster Hotel in London's Bayswater. Representing the *Evening Standard's* Ad Lib column, I asked John if he thought the city had changed since his sojourn abroad. 'With all the coloured hair and fake punk clothes, it's like being surrounded by a non-stop fashion parade,' he blurted out with exemplary disgust. Despite taking notes I have no record that John said anything else of consequence that day because the questions posed were so facile. For example, one hack asked if he had ever thought of giving money to anyone less fortunate than himself. 'I don't know anyone less fortunate than myself!' John replied.

By this point in my career, I had gained a reputation for asking most of the questions at rock 'n' roll press conferences, the rest of the journos being either too nervous or unimaginative to open their mouths. Of course, this never stopped them from using the answers to my questions in their articles, so I learned to keep my powder dry. Over Bloody Marys with John and his PR at the bar after the event, I flagged up the idea of doing another one-to-one interview for one of the music magazines I was writing for at the time. This was *International Musician*, a publication ostensibly about musical instruments and equipment but not without an element of celebrity chat to smooth the proceedings.

The interview took place at some hotel in Bristol during a short UK tour promoting PiL's *Live in Tokyo* album. There had been a recent Top 5 single with 'This Is Not A Love Song' but as regards touring, Johnny was still living up to what he had said at our earlier *Record Mirror* meeting. Following their move to America, PiL's first ever tour comprised a mere ten dates over six weeks, slightly less than the sixteen shows in their current UK tour. In between, they played ten gigs in Japan in the summer of 1983, hence the *Tokyo* LP which, with the exception of two new tracks, only consisted of previously released material. 'There was no way we were going to let Japan's version of Joe Bloggs tape it and sell it to his friends,' John explained, with reference to the proliferation of bootlegs around. 'But the record company over there had some amazing engineers who were more like laboratory assistants, wearing white coats as if they were scientists.'

In contrast, John was wearing a puce jumpsuit and a baseball hat worn back to front – not a common sight back then. This caused a few of the hotel's older residents to polish their spectacles as John enthused about the Far East in the lounge bar. 'It was nice to be impressed by somewhere, but the thrill soon wore off,' he complained. 'Too many kimonos and chopsticks. They've got a strange attitude towards drugs, too. Even Vicks inhalers are illegal because they're considered a stimulant but it's okay for businessmen to fall over and throw up in the street. It's considered a marvellous achievement to get drunk very quickly,' he continued, 'and if you're too drunk to get home, they'll hire a cubicle where you can crash out for the night and even inform your wife.'

John did not approve of the Bristol venue, The Studio, particularly the rows of seats facing away from the stage. 'Look at those chairs pointing the wrong way! I suppose some people are going to act really cool and spend the whole gig with their backs to me.' The hotel service rated even lower on the Lydon amenity monitor. 'The fucking cleaner came and woke me up at eight o'clock this morning saying, "I've come to do the room,"' he said, impersonating a West County accent. 'So, I told her that if she didn't get that Hoover out of here pronto, I'd wrap it round her neck.' The backstage rider also came in for criticism; processed cheese and white bread sarnies were not exactly what Lydon had become accustomed to of late. He had recently been in Rome filming *Order of Death* with movie gangster and future insurance salesman Harvey Keitel. 'They don't even have fridges in some of the restaurants,' he went on. 'They serve the food the same day that they kill it. Mind you, it can be a bit off-putting seeing some mackerel with big sad eyes staring up at you.'

It was another three years before Johnny and I stared at each other again and what a great night out it was. His PR man, Keith, also looked after Martyn Ware of Heaven 17, producer of the first Terence Trent D'Arby album. Terence had just played the Marquee in Wardour Street and his record company were throwing an aftershow party upstairs at The Groucho Club in the next street. Back then, the downstairs bar at The Groucho was my home from home and I saw Johnny and company enter the building. He was with his elegant wife, Nora, and I felt it would be remiss of me not to gatecrash the party.

Sure enough, John came over and greeted me like a long-lost brother. This impressed my artist pal, Fred Ingrams, son of Richard the then editor of *Private Eye*. '*He* came over to *you*,' Fred exclaimed excitedly. Introductions completed, John then hatched a plan to upstage our host, Terence Trent D'Arby. Grabbing a chair, he ordered Nora to sit on it while the rest of us stood around wondering what would happen next. 'This way we'll be the centre of attention and everyone will come over to us,' Lydon predicted. No sooner said than done, Mr D'Arby being the first to bite, swiftly followed by photographer Terry Lott who snapped the three principles. We were then joined by Rolling Stone Ronnie Wood who had just jammed onstage with Terence. There had been a recent At Home interview with Ronnie in one of the Sunday supplements which hinted that he was completely out of it. Referring to the article, John challenged Ron like an anxious parent, 'You're still on drugs, aren't you?' Ron gave an embarrassed grin. The remainder of the evening saw the rest of us enjoy equally free speech fuelled by copious amounts of champagne.

We must now leap forward to March 1996 and the announcement of the Sex Pistols' reunion Filthy Lucre tour at the 100 Club. This was exactly twenty years after the original punk band had played the original punk festival there. Another press conference with the original line-up of the band on the stage facing a full complement of London's Fourth Estate. Grabbing a seat up front, I set about doing what by now had become expected of me – asking all the questions, some more serious than others.

Johnny – are you on any prescribed medication we should know about? 'The only thing I'm on is ego and I've got more than enough to go around.' How much money are you getting? 'More than The Beatles and fucking right and all. We're the people who wrote the songs and now we'd like to be paid for it. Every fucker has lived off us and we've not seen one penny, or respect. If you want to complain about people getting money, then look at all those trashy little pop stars you've got out there like Oasis. Through the years we've all gone off and done different things and left it to others to make waves, but nobody out there has done bollocks. So here we are again. The Sex Pistols never finished properly so now we're putting a full stop on it. We don't give a shit what we look like and there's nothing wrong with getting old. Like a fine wine I've matured with age.'

Would you like to appear in *Hello!* magazine with Nora? 'We could make a threesome with Lady Di but not Fergie. That tart in a tent can stay where she is. She's like The Clash of the Royal Family, always one step behind.'

Well, those were the highlights and three months later came the crowning glory of the Filthy Lucre tour, the gig in Finsbury Park, a stone's throw from where John grew up. Suffice to say it was a great gig, enhanced by receiving a VIP pass which enabled me to watch the band from the wings. This came courtesy of Pete Shelley of the Buzzcocks, one of the support bands on the bill. He even offered to open the band's rider bottle of champagne but for once I declined; it was a hot day and a can of Red Stripe sufficed. Besides, there was work to do. Also in the VIP area were Kate Moss and her then squeeze Johnny Depp. At first, I didn't recognise Kate when she came over and wondered if the empty chair next to me was free. She had a beautiful smile and looked much prettier in the flesh than in her trademark sultry photographs.

At the end of the evening, I was invited to the Sex Pistols' private party, John giving the nod to his skinhead mate who was in charge of security. I believe I was also anointed an honorary Gooner, or Arsenal supporter. As well as being loyal to his fellow Sex Pistols, John is still an Arsenal fan after all these years. I also met Mr Lydon Senior, John's dad, who offered me a slice of his birthday cake. It was decorated with a toy crane, a reference to his job as a crane driver. The date was 23 June 1996, which also happened to be my birthday too. I believe it's still one of the best I've ever had.

JOHN MARTYN

A musical trailblazer and a boozy hell-raiser, John Martyn also happened to be one of the most versatile artists in modern music. His first album, the folksy *London Conversation*, was released when he was still in his teens, on Island Records, by far the hippest UK record company of the 1960s and 70s.

In fact, it was on that label's legendary compilation album entitled *You Can All Join In* – also featuring Traffic, Fairport Convention, Spooky Tooth and other innovators – that I discovered John courtesy of the haunting 'Dusty' from his second LP, *The Tumbler*. This showed a gradual shift towards jazz while future classics like *Bless the Weather* and *Solid Air* introduced us to Echoplexed guitars and wah-wah pedals, key tools of later generations of rock guitarists. Jimi Hendrix might have been an early influence but so were pop-soul stars like The Isley Brothers whose 'Summer Breeze' also boasted these special effects. One should also appreciate the underlying reggae sound of 'Johnny Too Bad' and the straightforward sentimentality of 'May You Never', which could best be described as 'words to the wise'.

I eventually met John in 1991 at the Chelsea Arts Club, his London pad when not living at home in Scotland with his second wife. While the members' list contained numerous lords and ladies, John's attraction to the elegant establishment was its 'faded splendour, extensive gardens and pub prices'. An infamous drinker, he conceded to taking the bibulous life a little easier these days but insisted he was not on the wagon. 'It's more a case of realising you must not step over a certain line,' he specified. 'It wasn't so much that my liver was in bad shape, though it was, but after a couple of bottles of rum I tended to pass out. There are some amazing characters here. One of the old boys isn't in the best of health but he still manages to drink a bottle of Scotch a day. We're trying to get him elected to the club's council, which should make for some interesting AGMs!'

I mentioned that I first saw him onstage at Warwick University in 1973 on the Inside Out tour. 'Ah yes, *that* album,' he laughed. 'The crazy one. But I had a licence to do it because the one before (*Solid Air*) had done so well.' Then there was *Grace and Danger* which I reviewed for *Record Mirror* and rated my favourite LP of 1980, even if it was produced by Phil Collins. 'That was the divorce album,' he admitted ruefully, referring to his first wife, singer-songwriter Beverley Martyn. A decade earlier they had recorded *Stormbringer* together, but the record company weren't impressed by her contribution. 'She was short of songs so I wrote quite a few of them and she accused me of stealing what should have been her solo album. In fact, I think she still believes I hijacked her career but it's all under the bridge now. I don't even play any of those old songs any more unless I get drunk at parties.' The latter could well have occurred when John was in the company of the similarly unhinged Danny Thompson, the virtuoso double bassist he teamed up with onstage for many years. There is a great story that Danny once marched into a pub, slapped a whole lot of cash on to the bar and said, 'That's for the damage.' When the confused bartender replied there wasn't any damage, Thompson retorted, 'There will be.'

'I think we both have the same insecurities,' John suggested. 'My parents divorced when I was about five.' This explained a lot, family issues being common in the history of rock 'n' roll.

During the 1980s, Martyn's usual prolific output – twenty-two studio albums alone in forty years – was disrupted by record company problems. These were finally resolved when his manager formed his own record label, Permanent, which released LPs like 1990's *The Apprentice*. 'That took a long time to surface but I'm really pleased it came out on an indie. I don't really have anything to do with the business side but I'm against the multinationals. I was with Warner's for a few albums and they seemed to be run by lawyers and accountants. I think that shows a great depth of dishonesty.'

There is a case for stating that the teenage John was spoiled by originally signing to Island by the label's owner, Chris Blackwell, who started out by recording ska and reggae musicians in Jamaica and selling their records to the Caribbean community in Britain from the back of his car. Blackwell, who I interviewed for BBC Radio 4 when he sold Island to Polygram in 1989, was responsible for discovering Bob Marley, Grace Jones, U2 and many other rock bands during one of the most illustrious careers in the music industry ever. 'I met Lee "Scratch" Perry through Chris,' Martyn reflects, referring to the eccentric reggae producer, 'and for me reggae died with Marley, a former student of the Perry school of sound. He was the one who put it all together and no one else has been big enough to fill his shoes. These days I mainly listen to jazz and I'm sorry Miles Davies never got to do an album with Prince. The high register trumpet and Prince's voice would have gone together brilliantly. Just about the only pop music I listen to is rap, which makes me want to laugh and dance. Otherwise most black soul singers appear fake to me and nine times out of ten, white guys don't cut it,' he says with a glint in his eyes. 'I think I'll always remain jazzy. For me, things work off one sweet chord which is the key to improvisation. I'd hate to do exactly the same set every night, it would be sheer drudgery like a nine-to-five job. It would also betray a great lack of imagination and a large capacity for greed. I can't stand formula music and besides, there's never been any shortage of work. Eric Clapton has even covered one of my songs but best of all,' he cracked, 'I'm able to be a member here. Fancy another?'

CHAPTER 48

JOHNNY THUNDERS

I had only been at university for a few weeks when the New York Dolls came to town. There had been some sensational stories about them in the music press and an eccentric appearance on BBC2's *The Old Grey Whistle Test*. Now my new circle of rock 'n' roll chums enjoyed speculating about these guys who were being hailed as the new Rolling Stones. One way or another it seemed worth paying sixty pence to wander upstairs from the students' union bar to the hall where they would shortly take the stage.

The Dolls' gig at Warwick was one of only a handful they were playing in the UK, including the better publicised shows at the Biba boutique in London. With the benefit of hindsight, it was a memorable event, a combination of gutsy power chords, louche exhibitionism and all-round trashy excess. A lethal blast of rock 'n' roll slithering out of the college circuit swamp, generally inhabited by self-pitying singer-songwriters and prog rock bores. The Dolls were extrovert in their unmistakable American way. One of their entourage even gave me a unique pin badge featuring a Polaroid of three of the band. Despite a major label releasing two albums, the New York Dolls never really transcended cult status. American music fans were in the process of lapping up dozens of more melodic acts with images less likely to scare the horses, while in the UK those in thrall to Bowie and Roxy Music had yet to discover punk. There was, of course, a vital connection between the Dolls and punk, for who had presided over the last vestiges of their career but Malcolm McLaren, future manager of the Sex Pistols.

It came to pass that when McLaren put the Pistols' Anarchy tour together, he included Johnny Thunders & The Heartbreakers featuring two former Dolls. The fact that the Sex Pistols had been fans of the New Yorkers sealed the deal and the real 'special relationship' between England and America began in earnest. Within a year Johnny's band had completed a few tours of duty in the UK. In late 1977 I saw them at Manchester Polytechnic, one of many punk venues in the city within walking distance of each other. I showed Johnny my treasured badge and wondered if he'd want it back since he was pictured on it. He generously turned the offer down after proudly showing it to the rest of the band.

The next time I saw Thunders he was equally hospitable, this time on his home turf. I was in New York City with Midge Ure who had just joined Ultravox. We went to see The Spectres featuring Midge's fellow ex-Rich Kid *compadre*, Glen Matlock. Having toured with former Pistol Matlock on the Anarchy tour, Thunders joined our merry throng and afterwards took us all to the Mud Club in Tribeca – quite an honour as it was then one of the most famous clubs in the world. Beer was the stimulant of choice, notwithstanding Johnny's taste for the hard stuff. Although he was to spend much of the 1980s in London and Europe with his Swedish wife, Thunders was extremely proud to be a New Yorker and happy to talk about his East Coast roots. 'I was brought up in Queens, a middle-class area of Manhattan, but only in a two-room apartment with my mother and sister. She was older than me, so I got to listen to a wide range of music, mainly 1960s girl bands like The Shangri-Las, The Ronettes and The Crystals.'

A particular hero was Gene Vincent whose 1950s look was clearly an influence on Johnny's rock 'n' roll style. He met former Dolls' singer David Johansen, another rocker with a singular image, at a New York club called Nobody's, the irony of whose name was not lost on anybody. Virtually everyone who went there went on to form a band, a bit like all the Mancunians who would go on to be stars after the original Sex Pistols gig at the Lesser Free Trade Hall. 'In the beginning, the New York Dolls had a lot of fun,' Thunders recalled. 'Gigs then were in big hotels like the Waldorf Astoria with all these weird kids in dresses and make-up coming to see us. Then we got a deal with a major label but were unlucky with our choice of producers.'

The Dolls' eponymous debut album, containing classics such as 'Personality Crisis', 'Lonely Planet Boy' and 'Looking for a Kiss', was produced by the then hip Todd Rundgren. It was practically a waste of good tunes. 'What we thought we needed was a simple approach, but it ended up sounding like a blanket had been dropped over the music. We wanted a sound like something from the 1950s combined with our own magic approach, sort of loud and full like we were live but... ' The next album, *Too Much Too Soon*, was even more of a disappointment, particularly as it was produced by Shadow Morton who had masterminded the records of classic girl bands of whom Johnny was so in awe. 'The trouble there was he had a serious accident which was supposed to have ended his career. As it happens, he was off the scene for a long time and by the time he came back it was all over for him.'

With The Heartbreakers, Johnny made *L.A.M.F* followed by the solo *So Alone*, famous for its slower songs and one of the outstanding releases of the post-punk genre. Throughout the 1980s Thunders continued to appeal to a hard-core audience all over Europe, releasing albums on indie labels while being continuously ripped off by bootleggers. The quality was in direct proportion to his drug intake, an inability to quit narcotics leading to ongoing isolation from the mainstream record industry.

It is believed Johnny was murdered in 1991 in a hotel room from which all his worldly possessions had been stolen. Sadly, the incident took place in the French quarter of New Orleans, generally regarded as the birthplace of rock 'n' roll. Still, he was adored which is more than many can claim.

JULIAN COPE

Julian Cope was brought up in the Midlands but will always be associated with Liverpool where his career took off. This is partly because like predecessors and contemporaries, The Beatles and Ian Broudie, he had a particular facility for songwriting and melody. With both The Teardrop Explodes and his own 1980s solo albums, he wrote great catchy songs at a time when other chart stars tended to be controlled by one-trick pony record producers.

I first met Julian six months after the success of 'Reward', the Teardrop's first Top 10 hit which looked set to make him a star as well as the face of 1981. We met at Nottingham's Rock City on a press trip where journalists were invited to hear material proposed for the band's second album. One of the best PRs of the day, Colin Bell, who went on to become Elton John's manager, had the bright idea of using journalists in a consultative capacity. The working title for the LP was *The Great Dominions* which in my subsequent review for *Record Mirror*, I suggested was the outstanding track. The album actually ended up being entitled *Wilder*, which was not unreasonable; from its psychedelia for beginners to its tales of childhood longing and betrayal in love, the record might not have been the most comfortable of rides but represented the then-current pop of Britain.

Julian appreciated my review and often mentioned it in conversation in years to come. A few months later, I went up to Liverpool for an interview and to check out his Club Zoo concept, a musical evening starring himself and various associates past and present. We met at what can best be described as a rock 'n' roll guest house whose walls were adorned with signed photographs of previous pop visitors going back to the days of Helen Shapiro and Cilla Black. Julian was beginning to have a reputation for ingesting hallucinogenics and you could say our conversation bore testimony to this. He was accompanied by future rock biz legend, Dave Balfe, the man behind Blur and at the time of writing a recently elected councillor for Sussex. 'Balfie', who had been in the original line-up of Teardrop Explodes, was sacked and had now been reinstated to co-write 'simple songs that are less abstract and personal than those on *Wilder*'. From this we can deduce that the *Wilder* album was not an overwhelming commercial success even if, over the decades, it has been declared a cult classic after the fashion of Love's *Forever Changes* or Neil Young's *On The Beach*.

During my interview with him, Julian started scratching away at a 12-string guitar, assembling a new song provisionally entitled 'Log Cabin', 'a sequel to the film *The Shining*, set in the snowy wastes of Montana or some American place like that.' He offered me the opportunity to contribute to the lyrics in return for a songwriting credit. Meanwhile Balfie had just noticed the singer's mug on the cover of a recent magazine. 'Have you seen that Billy Idol picture here?' he asked cheekily. 'I remember someone once saying that any haircut Billy Idol ever had, two weeks later Julian had it.'

Pop star adulation had not agreed with Julian Cope. 'I can't keep it up,' he admitted, 'it was accidental in the first place that I became "a face". There hadn't been anyone like me before and I like to try and be spontaneous. If we'd been Duran Duran or Spandau Ballet, we would have had follow-up images planned. But I'm not the sort to start changing clothes every three months or going to a designer. I never wanted to be a pop star in the first place.

The only thing I wanted to have in common with The Beatles or Bowie was to keep changing musically regardless of the tastes of the nation.' He then inhaled deeply on a tightly-packed blended cigarette and started talking about Kevin Stapleton, his alter ego. 'It was the name,' he explained. 'There's a lot of Kevin in me. He doesn't quite cut it and I associate that person with myself. There are a lot of sides to Kevin and he's evolving all the time.'

With the benefit of hindsight, we know that Julian's career has seen him spread his wings as an author, writing books about archaeology as well as specialist guides to Krautrock and underground music in general. So, whereas other stars of the early 1980s like Adam Ant may have been solely focussed on becoming celebrities, Julian always had other things on his mind. Meanwhile the Cope-Balfe banter continued. 'He kind of forced his way back into Teardrop Explodes,' Julian claimed. 'I was so vehemently against it that it had to happen. But Dave is the only person in the world I know that I would have every confidence in being able to write a tune for one of my songs. Plus he's into intricate arrangements with cellos and stuff. We're now crossing over as writers instead of pitting ourselves against each other. He's a creative partner instead of an irritant generating musical friction.'

Well, that's as maybe, but a third Teardrop Explodes album was never released and by 1984 Julian had gone solo. His first album was entitled *World, Shut Your Mouth* and contained 'An Elegant Chaos', one of my favourite songs of the decade. Apart from the wonderfully catchy tune, it contains the haunting words, 'I was happy for a while, but the joke is over'. A timeless warning for us all.

KATE BUSH

The things we do for love. In March 1979, *Record Mirror* contacted me about a special assignment. This was unusual because, although I had been freelancing for the magazine for almost a year, it was me who was expected to come up with the ideas for any story I wished to write. Kate Bush was playing her first ever gig in Liverpool the following month and I was commissioned to review it for that week's issue. This entailed phoning the report directly to the printer after the show in order for the article to be in the edition of the magazine hitting the streets the following day. The show was sold out and the record company wouldn't give me a ticket in case there was some onstage mishap on the first night, however, having asked around I discovered this geezer at the *Liverpool Echo* newspaper who could supply me with a ticket for a price. As part of the deal, he offered to let me use his office to file the copy.

The things we do for career opportunities. I sussed that if everything went according to plan, I would secure the next staff job at *Record Mirror*, just as the editor had hinted. Well, everything went swimmingly – those were the days: the uncomplicated 1970s! – and the concert was unbelievable. In fact, it was an historic occasion. Not only, ahem, a world exclusive but what turned out to be Kate's first and last tour. Last but not least, it was an event unique in modern rock. Kate interpreted each song as a theatrical performance in its own right, to the extent that I went on to describe the whole show in my review as 'the ultimate rock 'n' roll extravaganza'.

Kate remembered my description, too, when I went backstage to meet her at the Manchester Apollo the following week. It was the start of a special relationship which went on well into the 1990s when I interviewed her about the duet she had just recorded with octogenarian harmonica maestro Larry Adler.

Meanwhile, back in 1980, Kate was voted No. 1 female singer in the annual *Record Mirror* readers' poll. This called for an interview, even though she was currently holed up in Abbey Road Studios recording her third album, *Never Forever*. Sixteen hours a day in a windowless room: it was just like the Victorian Factory Acts had never happened. 'Yeah, but it's standard in studios,' Kate reasoned. 'We try and stop by midnight otherwise it gets crazy. You start looking like a drained flower that hasn't seen any sunshine.' Fans of Kate Bush may well imagine she talks like this all the time, however, the artist is quick to add, 'But I love the studio. It's No. 2, where The Beatles did a lot of their stuff. The vibes are incredible. It's as if the walls have held them for years. No wonder Paul McCartney got such good sounds.'

The only difference, of course, was that McCartney was not The Beatles' producer whereas Kate was taking on this role, too, as well as writing and arranging all her own material. 'I don't like to be told what to do with my songs because they're mine,' she explained. 'It's your own creation that you're sharing with the audience, so you don't want any conflict or restrictions.' As well as being voted top singer, Kate was runner-up in another category – sex symbol. How did she feel about that? 'Well,' she replied with controlled professionalism, 'I get two angles on this which I find fascinating. Sometimes the press says I'm not a sex symbol, yet I encourage it, and at other times they say I don't want to be one, which encourages them all the more. Now, I don't say "I am a sex symbol" because that's a label the public puts on you. If you went around saying you were one, no one would take any notice. The only thing that worried me when it first started happening was that it would interfere with my music, that people would treat me as a body instead of a musician... and one day my body's going to go. It's incredibly flattering for me to think that people do regard me like that because I think all females feel insecure about their sexuality and it's such a buzz that people get off on it. But if people appreciate the music as well as the way I look, what more can I ask for?' Well, that's that one sorted out!

Bearing in mind that this conversation took place within two years of Kate having shot to fame with her No. 1 hit, the iconic 'Wuthering Heights', a remarkable number of myths had already built up around the singer. Story had it that she'd picked up a recording contract while still at school, thanks to Pink Floyd's David Gilmour paying for recording sessions and making sure the tapes went to the right people. 'I've hardly ever seen him,' she revealed. 'It's strange that, for someone I know so little about, he's probably done the biggest thing for me that anyone could.'

Is he one of 'them heavy people' you sing about on your first album? 'He is. Sometimes I think, "Why did he do it?", 'cos he didn't need to. But if he hadn't given me that money and the odd phone call here and there, I'd have had a hard time I'm sure. I mean I was still at school at the time. It was suggested that it wasn't a good idea to throw myself into the music business at such an early age. But there wasn't anything else I wanted to do apart from music. I was supposed to be studying for my O-levels, but I wasn't doing any revision because I was in the studio. I couldn't really tell my teachers that I was missing exams for that reason. Anyway, David got EMI to hear my tapes, but I don't think they knew what to do with me because I was such a freak. I mean there's this little girl, just sixteen, tiny, still at school, walking into their office with her dad and hundreds of songs.'

EMI was reluctant to take a gamble on Kate and it was another three years before they advanced her the money to record an LP. 'I got very frustrated waiting for someone to phone me and say, "Come and do your album". So, I got into disciplining my days, dancing, writing songs and practising at the piano. You should always be aware of what an honour it is to be in this business because everybody wants to be, don't they?' Indeed, they do.

There were also a fair number knocking on our door wanting to come to the *Record Mirror* 25th Anniversary party a month or two later (the paper had been going since 1955). I didn't realise that Kate had been invited until she phoned me up at the office expressing regret that she wouldn't be able to make it. She was still tied up in the studio. I tried to convince her to take a break, offering to collect her from Abbey Road myself. That would have been some entrance: swanning into the office bash with Kate Bush on my arm! Alas, to no avail. Still, I had no shortage of female company that night – or the following morning if I remember rightly.

When *Never Forever* came out the following summer, Kate and I reconvened in the private garden outside EMI's offices in Manchester Square, London W1. She apologised for not having been able to make the party, adding, 'I don't go to parties very often, only if I've got the time or if there's someone there I want to meet.' I suggested that it's probably best to be a studio perfectionist rather than a party animal. 'I actually don't think I'm a perfectionist and it's imperfection which makes me want to do more,' she replied. 'I think all my paranoias, all my doubts and all my vulnerabilities are what I depend on to keep my songs happening.'

A key theme in this woman is belief. Whereas John Lennon's notion of God was as 'a concept by which we measure our pain', Kate's idea of God was 'something you believe in'. One of the best tracks on *Never Forever* is 'All We Ever Look For', which analyses this subject. 'Belief is motivation and without that you wouldn't do anything,' she asserted. 'I mean, if your God is to have a husband and children, then it's fine to be fulfilled by that. Many people don't see the thing they love and believe in as God. Most people aren't even happy and that's because their God isn't complete. My work is my God. Everything in my life goes into my music. If I did become perfect and was no longer vulnerable, perhaps I wouldn't get the same shocks of emotion that make me want to write.'

Perhaps this explains why at this stage in Kate's life, one of her greatest influences was the Armenian philosopher and mystic, Gurdjieff who said, 'We had better torture our own spirit rather than suffer the inanities of calm. Any unusual effort has the effect of shaking the mind awake.' There was to be no husband or children for the singer at this time, nor by the next album, *The Dreaming*, in 1982. Once again, we met at Abbey Road, only this time in the bar where Kate, still as skinny as ever, showed a wholly unnatural ability to knock back brandy with Holsten Pils chasers. Even more impressive, she drank continuously without needing to use the facilities. I happened to have got married a few months earlier and so part of our conversation returned to spouses and children.

Kate reckoned she couldn't be doing with it. 'I don't fancy it myself. I'm very happy at the moment so why ruin it? I have no urge for commitment because right now I can still work and have a lovely relationship (with one of her musicians Del Palmer) and don't see how marriage would help in the slightest. There's not much difference between living together and being married unless you're going to have children which I don't want to do yet. My brain is only in work mode which makes me far too selfish. Some women spend every minute from the age of twelve just looking forward to getting married and having children. I'm not one of them. I know lots of guys who don't want to get married and I think I'm a bit like them. A fear of getting trapped and having to make compromises when faced with the responsibilities which the lines of the marriage document are all about. Right now, I feel I've got something to share and if my music helps people and they can identify with the songs, that's good.' It was another sixteen years before Kate decided to have a baby, by which time she was knocking forty on the door. His name is Bertie McIntosh, sharing the surname with his father, Dan.

Long before then, in 1985, Kate released what is widely regarded as the best album of her career, *Hounds of Love*. By then I was a full-time, freelance journalist and had come to the attention of *The Times* newspaper. Kate had also moved on, building her own studio in an outhouse in her parents' back garden in Kent. It was a cost-effective option compared with paying a grand a day at Abbey Road. 'Although I can work under a certain amount of pressure, it got to be too much. It also meant having to travel into London every day, which can be pretty exhausting.'

The album was preceded by the single 'Running Up That Hill', a song about the inability of a man to see things from a woman's point of view, and vice versa, as a result of fundamental biological differences. 'It seems that the more you get to know a person, the greater the scope there is for misunderstanding. Sometimes you can hurt somebody purely accidentally or be afraid to tell them something because you think they might be hurt when really, they'll understand. So, what the song is about,' she went on, 'is making a deal with God to let two people swap places so they will be able to see things from one another's perspective.'

The other main theme of the album is alienation. It is the basis of the second side of the record which comprises a suite of seven songs about 'someone drowning or rather, trying not to drown'. One track in particular, 'Watching You Without Me', portrays a man with nothing but a lifejacket to keep him afloat, becoming quite delirious after being in the sea for a while. He imagines his spirit returning home to tell his wife, but she cannot hear him because he is only a ghost. 'Let's face it,' Kate tried to rationalise, 'it's going to get pretty weird in the water after a couple of hours. But I suppose the specific message of the song is the horrific thought of being away from the person you love most and there's no way you can communicate. A parallel situation could exist if it was about divorce. You know, a husband coming back home to see his children but he's no longer a part of the home. Instead he's just an observer who isn't being seen by the people there because his role has become so different.'

Hounds of Love topped the album charts for four weeks and there was a gap of four years before the next LP. Then just three collections of new material over the next three decades. 'My God is the force that rules our lives,' she told me during one of our philosophical sessions. On Planet Kate that is as good an explanation as we're likely to receive.

KEITH RICHARDS

'When you've got three thousand chicks ripping off their panties and throwing them at you, you realise what an awesome power you have unleashed. Everything they'd been brought up not to do, they could do at a rock 'n' roll show.'

This observation was made by Keith Richards in the Rolling Stone's autobiography, *Life* (Weidenfeld & Nicholson). He is referring to that period in the mid-1960s when something called the generation gap kicked in and the bad old days disappeared for good. Which meant the Keiths of this world became household names and, in his case, collected nicknames like 'the walking laboratory' and 'the human riff'. For many of us Mr Richards is the living definition of rock 'n' roll. A childhood friend of partner-in-crime Mick Jagger, the duo clicked musically more than sixty years ago when they became re-acquainted on a train. Jagger was carrying a handful of imported American blues albums and Keith a guitar. Within a couple of years they were part of the Rolling Stones with a bad-boy image which persists to this day. Timing was of paramount importance, as the guitarist succinctly notes: 'Jerry Lee Lewis had been disgraced, Elvis was in the army, Buddy Holly and Eddie Cochran had taken the dive and Chuck Berry was in jail.'

I first met Keith when I was on the road with the Stones in America. It was 1981, backstage at some enormodome in Cedar Falls, Iowa, deep in the Midwest. I was reporting for *Record Mirror* and had flown in from Chicago where the previous night the guitarist had found himself jamming with some local blues musicians. He had always been a disciple of R&B, eschewing technical prowess in favour of pure rhythms and licks. The combination of Charlie Watts' snare drum and Keith's crunching chords has always been at the heart of the Stones' sound. At the venue I was invited into the band's inner sanctum somewhere inside a labyrinth of hospitality rooms. Keith and Ronnie Wood sprung out of their chairs to extend warm fraternal greetings. Not entirely anticipating such a sudden welcome, I was momentarily lost for words before blurting out something along the lines of first having seen the band on the *Out of Our Heads* tour. A small reservoir of Jack Daniel's and Coke soon put paid to my understandable anxiety and we started to talk about music. I mentioned that my favourite Stones' album was probably *Let It Bleed*.

'That's a good example of how we put songs together,' Keith enthused. 'The track 'Country Honk', which eventually became the single 'Honky Tonk Women', started off as my particular riff and was then taken up by the rest of the band. I wrote it as a real Hank Williams country song and it eventually evolved into the finished cut. Songs tend to come together or not at all. We like to record live in the studio which now is apparently a bit of a novelty. These days technology seems to be taking over which is a shame since for me one of the most essential things about making a rock 'n' roll record is the spontaneity.'

I went on to add that I was hugely impressed with *Some Girls*, the Stones' late 1970s album. It contained the classic 'Shattered' whose unforgettable line 'love and sex and dreams are still surviving on the streets' acknowledged the challenge of punk. 'Many of the English punk records sound like our early records,' he replied. 'We recorded them on a two-track tape machine in rooms insulated with egg cartons. Today the new bands are having to work against advances like 24-track studios.

So you end up with someone like Glen Matlock from the original Sex Pistols bringing Ian McLagan from the Small Faces (and playing keyboards on this Stones tour) into his next band the Rich Kids. You could say the Stones are a punk band! We might make more money but it's still the attitude which counts.'

This was a timely gateway into a more infamous side of Keith's career, Class A drugs. I broached the subject by quoting one of my all-time favourite Richards remarks: 'I have no problem with drugs, just policemen.' A few years earlier he had been busted by The Mounties in Canada and it was rumoured he was on the wagon. Had this had any effect on his creative juices? 'Well,' he responded easily, 'it's like all the jazz players who took heroin because they thought it would make them as good as Charlie Parker. But all drugs are different, and I would say I got a lot more out of cocaine. It made me concentrate more but that doesn't mean to say you're going to come up with something better. I originally got into drugs because it was part of the job,' he continued candidly. 'When you're working 350 days a year and are on the road for months on end, you sometimes need help to make it through the next gig because you are so knackered. It was never a big deal at first, but it is now because it's being pushed on kids which is obviously an absolute disgrace.'

The last time I saw Keith he wasn't even chugging down half a lager; he was swigging Evian water while his patient manager, Jane, was offering his guests something a little stronger. The occasion was a gig by the X-Pensive Winos, the guitarist's occasional band with whom he had recently recorded his second solo album, *Main Offender*. The venue was the dressing room in the Town & Country Club, Kentish Town, north London. We talked about my favourite track, 'Hate It When You Leave', and other key issues of the day before being joined by Chrissie Hynde of The Pretenders. A life-long fan of Keith's, she was gobsmacked, too tongue-tied to even talk about her own latest exploits. For a few moments there was absolute silence before the three of us cracked up and all started talking at once. It was a bit like a Stones song, really, waiting for Keith to hit the first chord before everyone else joined in. As a rock 'n' roll person, Keith Richards has been leading the way for several decades now – but he would be the last person to boast about it.

Picture by Brian Aris.

To Mike
Fondest
Jackie

ROCK 'N' ROLL AUTHOR, JACKIE COLLINS — GREATLY MISSED.

MAY 3, 1980 25p

RECORD MIRROR

WIN
MUSIC CENTRE/
RADIO RECORDER/
CAR RADIO CASSETTE
DETAILS COMPETITION PAGE 16

**Q-TIPS
10cc
CURE**

**JOHN
COOPER CLARKE**

Subterranean bedsit blues

**TYGERS
OF PAN
TANG**

**DETROIT
SPINNERS**

POLI

PETE TOWNSHEND
THE RUTS
SONGWORDS

JOHN COOPER CLARK PIC BY TERRY LOTT

by Howard Barlow.

Picture by Terry Lott.

NORA AND JOHN LYDON WITH
TERENCE TRENT D'ARBY.
THE GROUCHO CLUB. LONDON. 1987.

Story: Mike Nicholls
Pics: Adrian Boot

MY RECORD MIRROR EXCLUSIVE WITH KEVIN ROWLAND OF DEXYS MIDNIGHT RUNNERS. SUMMER, 1982.

The girl who reached Wuthering Heights

'The more you know a person, the more scope for misunderstanding'
Kate Bush

'Making a deal with God . . .'

Mike Nicholls

THE RAVISHING KATE
BUSH ON TOUR, 1979.

Love Kim Wilde X

DESPERATELY SEEKING SANCTUARY WITH KIM WILDE AT THE SANCTUARY, COVENT GARDEN, 1983.

Picture by John Rogers.

ANOTHER TOUR
OF DUTY WITH
THE STONES,
EUROPE, 1982.

MICK JAGGER IN HIS PRIME.

Picture by Jane Bown.

WITH PETER HOOK OF JOY DIVISION AND NEW ORDER, UTRECHT, 2018.

GUITAR HERO:
MICK RONSON
PLAYING WITH
SANDY DILLON,
DINGWALLS,
1985.

CHAPTER 52

KEVIN ROWLAND

I first heard about Kevin Rowland's band, Dexys Midnight Runners from The Clash's management in 1979. Then I gave a good review to 'Dance Stance' for *Record Mirror* when the single came out towards the end of that year. Dexys was nothing if not a controversial band, musicians constantly leaving or getting fired. At one point their record company was blackmailed into increasing their royalty rate when the band stole the master tapes for their first album. On the other hand there was no doubting DMR's musical talent, this debut, *Searching for the Young Soul Rebels*, being one of the musical highlights of 1980.

The following year they played three nights at London's Old Vic theatre and were in a class of their own. In my appraisal for the same magazine I described their show, dubbed 'The Projected Passion Revue', as 'an exciting event of solid commitment, soaring brass and devastating athletics... dispensing authentic R&B and soul.' After another year there was a new sound and look. The *On the Waterfront* donkey jackets and woolly hats had given way to a gypsy vibe of dungarees and leather waistcoats, soundtracked by matching Celtic strings. Rowland had never been keen on talking to the press but with a colourful new project to promote, the *Too-Rye-Ay* LP, he agreed to meet me in a West End café.

'However good you thought we were at the Old Vic, we were really just warming up for this year,' he began. 'We were tunnelling underground but now's the time to burst up for air. I

215

think we're going to be big now, really successful.' Indeed. A fortnight later they were top of the singles charts with 'Come On Eileen'. A first proper headlining tour would follow. 'Theatres only,' he had promised that day. 'I don't mind people dancing – wherever we play there's always space to dance if you want to – but the main thing is that when the fans come in, they will be entertained. I don't like dance halls where you just end up playing to the people at the front. We want to project to everybody and give them the show of their life.'

This was a far cry from Rowland's original belligerence to both the media and Dexys' first record company. 'In the beginning, I had a totally different approach from the one I have now', he agreed. 'I wanted DMR not only to be successful, but also a band which people would never forget. I had ridiculous ideas which contributed to the group splitting up. The first year we would have hit singles and make a successful LP; the second year we would make a film (not a pop film) with me writing the script and all of us acting in it; then in the third we'd do something totally different like blowing up the Houses of Parliament. Then we'd all go to jail for ten years and it would be a crazy story. But it really freaked some of the band out.' As did another incident which left Rowland with a suspended sentence. It's such an unusual story that we'd better leave it to Kevin to relate in his own words.

'There was a quiet section in the middle of one of the songs and I wanted some tramps for the video,' he began. 'So I went down to the local police station and they recommended this churchyard. On the way there two blokes followed me, then another four. I didn't know who the hell they were, but they started kicking my heels and generally trying to provoke me. So I picked up this iron bar and started swinging it at them. Then suddenly a copper appeared and all he could see was me looking threatening. I decided to leg it and was losing him until I saw this other one waiting for me with his truncheon. He said, "Do you want some of this?" and I replied, "No thanks," and got arrested. I received a nine-month sentence, suspended for two years. It turned out these other people were some nowhere band seeking publicity.'

Did Kevin feel he'd mellowed at all since then? 'No, but I've changed and got something different to say.' He explained this with the phrase 'Too-Rye-Ay', its musical definition being the way in which he recruited fiddle player Helen O'Hara. 'I used to see her waiting at the same bus stop as me outside Birmingham. One day I noticed her carrying a violin case and asked her if she would be interested in playing with the band. I'd already had the idea of using strings and she looked great too! Unfortunately she gave me the cold shoulder, saying she wasn't interested in pop music, only traditional stuff which she was studying at college. Anyway, I asked her again and went as far as following her home and putting a tape through her door. Within the hour she'd phoned me back and we've been inseparable ever since!'

Around this time some colleagues of mine had started up the Bizarre pop page on *The Sun* newspaper. As a daily column it required a lot of feeding and since it was staffed by tabloid hacks rather than music aficionados, they didn't always have access to rock stars and stories. I told my contacts Kevin's tale about Helen and they scooped it up without missing a beat. The article was then repeated on Radio One's highly-rated *Rock On* magazine programme the following Saturday, which had the unintended consequence of effectively launching the promotional campaign for both single and album. Trebles all round, to coin a phrase. Kevin was obviously pleased with the publicity but as an artist it was the music that mattered, which he described 'as neither specifically folk nor Celtic. It's a combination of lots of things, transforming a range of influences into a completely new and fresh sound. I want DMR to be an always changing, ever-challenging force.' This ambition was certainly realised with the next album, *Don't Stand Me Down*, complete with a dramatic change of image. Gone were the rustic dungarees in favour of Ivy League suits and ties. Despite combining some great catchy rock with unusual spoken-word anecdotes, it proved to be their least successful LP to date, commercially if not artistically. Then more than a decade later, at the height of Britpop, Alan McGee, who discovered and signed Oasis, re-released it on his Creation label.

Rowland then followed this record with an album of cover versions and another change of image – lingerie and ladies' make-up. A showcase gig at the Scala in King's Cross left a lot of fans scratching their heads. I think the least we can say is that this blip in Kevin's career is perhaps best forgotten. On a more positive note, in the twenty years which followed his initial success, I used to see him quite often out and about in London. He tended to frequent Soho media clubs like the Groucho and Fred's, and one night joined a crowd of us for my rowdy thirty-second birthday party.

Then, in the early 2000s, he spotted me buying a dining table from a second-hand store in Islington. I explained it was for a buy-to-let house I was setting up in Walthamstow, to encourage my single tenants to get to know one another by eating their convenience food together. The next time Kevin and I bumped into each other he enquired whether the tenants were getting to know one another. I had to admit that multiple dining hadn't worked, each of the saddoes tending to scamper off to their individual bedrooms to chomp their over-priced pizzas. He laughed and exclaimed, 'Kids, eh?' Taking into account the adventurousness of our own careers and generation, it was a profound remark.

KIM WILDE

Talk about a family affair. Barely out of her teens, Kim Wilde was in a recording studio singing backing vocals for her brother and then suddenly became a singer in her own right. The studio belonged to Mickie Most who in the 1960s and 70s had produced a variety of rock and pop acts ranging from Jeff Beck and Donovan to The Animals and Hot Chocolate. Also the owner of the RAK record label, he only had to hear a couple of verses of Kim's 'Kids in America' before practically signing her on the spot. In early 1981 the song reached No. 2 in the charts, Kim being managed by both Most and her mother, the wife of 1950s rocker Marty Wilde.

Kim told me all this the following year when we met for a cover story for *Record Mirror*. 'Ricky had tried to be a singer since the age of eleven,' she revealed about her older brother. 'The idea was to adopt the persona of a teen rebel, as in Alice Cooper's 'School's Out'. Now he's happy being my producer. He comes up with the ideas and Dad helps him with the music. I tend to keep out of the way because they don't need me – and I'm very pleased with what they're coming up with. There's no point in limiting myself quality-wise so I can fulfil some selfish ambition. You can't automatically become a songwriter. You've got to write twenty shit songs before coming up with anything that's any good.

'It's good working with the family,' she went on, 'if it occasionally gets stifling, I just go out to dinner with some friends. I was surprised to read in an interview with a certain star that he felt all his friends had changed and he couldn't talk to them anymore. I mean what kind of relationships did he have?' A perk of the job, she felt, was meeting fellow pop people in TV studios and radio stations. 'The only person I don't want to meet is Elvis Costello,' Kim smiled. 'I admire him so much I'd probably make an arsehole of myself telling him so! He's had an influence on my musical taste and really enhanced my direction. I also like Adam Ant very much. He's pure quality entertainment and I like to be entertained. I understand the situation he is in, although obviously he's a far bigger star.' And, like Kim, regarded as a sex symbol. In the 1982 *Record Mirror* readers' poll, Kim did even better than Kate Bush the previous year by being voted No. 1 sex symbol. 'Was I?' she enquired innocently. 'I don't think much about these things; I read them and laugh.' Did she like to be talked about in terms of sex and glamour, I pushed. 'I love glamour,' she swerved sneakily. 'I wish I could be a bit more glamorous myself, one of those girls who can wear an off-the-shoulder dress instead of a leather jacket and monkey boots.'

By the time of our next interview Kim had started touring and later in the 1980s found herself opening for Michael Jackson on a series of UK and European dates. 'It takes something to sing in front of 75,000 people,' she exclaimed, 'but I can't have been that bad or I wouldn't have been invited to continue with the second part of the tour. I didn't stage or choreograph anything, I try to be spontaneous.' By this time the singer was writing her own material, having composed most of the songs on her latest album, *Close*. 'I wrote all the lyrics whereas I hadn't written any on the first three LPs. The change came when I switched record companies to MCA and requested they identify me as an artist who could develop, as opposed to the teen queen I had appeared to be during the previous few years. I've also worked hard at being a more musical person in the family studio. I came to the conclusion that if I didn't address technology I'd get left behind.'

The studio is near Knebworth, Hertfordshire, not far from the stately home of rock which has seen major gigs by the Rolling Stones, Led Zeppelin and Oasis. It is also close to Kim's barn conversion where she now lives with her husband and children. Back in 1990, the singer was using her parents' flat in St John's Wood, near central London, which was where we met for our next rendezvous. Like a lot of citizens, Kim was starting to fall out of love with living in the city. 'Not just because of the traffic but the whole vibe. I don't find it particularly safe anymore. It's been ten years and I'm ready to move on.' Her boyfriend at the time was Mickie Most's son, Calvin Hayes, drummer with the pop group Johnny Hates Jazz. He'd previously played with Original Mirrors' singer Steve Allen in a band called Hot Club.

Though loath to discuss her private life, Calvin's name kept slipping into the conversation. She'd been on holiday with him to the Grenadines in the Caribbean and he proved 'very useful for sorting things out'. Indeed. The previous year he had usefully organised a foursome for dinner which included myself and my then girlfriend. The four of us also double-dated at Odette's in Primrose Hill, much to the surprise of fellow diners who knew me from the numerous watering holes in the area. So their relationship was hardly top secret, even though she liked to 'keep my personal life slightly enshrouded in mystery'. This was partly for security reasons. 'I was hounded out of one flat when people found out where I lived,' she revealed. 'There were break-ins and it wouldn't have been safe for me to stay there whether I wanted to or not. Calvin's flat is on the fourth floor and he's been burgled, whereas in Hertfordshire you don't even have to lock the door.'

Not that wedding bells were on the cards. 'It's not as if I'm under pressure from my parents, like someone my age might have been once upon a time. I don't feel I have to worry about having children, in fact having them late runs in the family. My younger sister Roxanne wasn't born until I was in my late teens. But I wouldn't want to get married just to have children anyway. I'd rather get married because I want to, and you have to make sure it's the right person before you even think of having kids. Without a good marriage the child will be at a disadvantage in life. Not that there's anything wrong with being a single parent if that's what works for you, but I'd rather have a balanced family life.'

Armed with these opinions, our next meeting possessed a fine sense of the absurd. It took place at the annual Midem conference in the South of France, at a press conference where Kim was promoting her mid-1990s *Greatest Hits* album. I crash-landed amidst all the gormless Euro-trash journos and their asinine queries, demanding to know when the singer was going to eschew all this rock 'n' roll malarkey and settle down and have children. She was ready for me. 'Ladies and gentlemen, this man has fancied me for many years and...' The rest of her reply was drowned in laughter as everybody realised the rock media didn't need to be taken too seriously. I guess the same applies to Kim who continues to enjoy a life in music, touring, interior design and gardening, not to mention finally raising a family of her own.

LEMMY

When rookie musicians airily boast about having been there and done that, eyebrows should be raised. Especially when you've had regular conversations with Lemmy and still only skated over the surface of his extraordinary career. The singer and bass player with Motorhead moved down to London from the Midlands in 1967 and shared a flat with Noel Redding of the Jimi Hendrix Experience. Soon afterwards he became the band's roadie. 'I used to score acid for Hendrix every now and then,' he told me in his suite at the Westbury Hotel on Conduit Street in Mayfair. 'Then I went on the road with him and support acts which included Pink Floyd, The Nice and Amen Corner. Good tour, that was,' he reflected. 'You'll never see the likes of that again.'

Lemmy next joined Hawkwind, the psychedelic rockers who reached No. 3 in the singles charts with 'Silver Machine'. He was the lead vocalist but was sacked after being charged with possession of drugs in Canada. His next step was to form Motorhead, arguably the only pre-thrash metal band to court a punk following. Whatever one's musical taste, many of us would agree that their terrific death-head biker logo was one of the most striking emblems in the history of rock 'n' roll, a huge mural of it overlooking the Westway near the Shepherd's Bush roundabout. When I first met Lemmy he lived nearby in Colville Houses, one block away from Portobello Road. I lived in the next street, in Colville Gardens, in a period building which had once been a refuge for reformed hookers. There was this running gag that when Lemmy moved in, our lawn died. I can confirm that this never happened, although he did manage to do a fair amount of damage to the one-arm bandit slot machines in the neighbourhood pubs.

The musician could also be seen all over Camden and Soho, forever seeking adventure at London's rock 'n' roll landmarks. On one occasion, I remember being at a party upstairs at the Intrepid Fox in Wardour Street. I saw him loitering around below and ushered him into the bash. The host, the editor of a new I.T. magazine, was made up, as were the legions of rock journalists who had all checked in for the free booze. Another guest was TV Smith of The Adverts who many years earlier had opened for Motorhead at the Roundhouse. The two singers hadn't seen each other since, so I had inadvertently organised a reunion. This, I mused, is how our business operates, while they reminisced about how fans of each band had hurled bottles at one another.

The first time I undertook a proper sit-down interview with Lemmy (born Ian Fraser Kilmister but duly nicknamed for habitually cadging cash for slot machines) was in January 1991 when Motorhead were about to release their *1914* album. Unlike such previous outings as *Ace of Spades* and *No Sleep 'til Hammersmith*, the LP had a serious historical theme. '1914 was inspired by a documentary I watched about the battle of the Somme,' he began. 'Nineteen thousand British soldiers were killed before midday, instructed by the generals to walk into the teeth of machine gun fire. Whole towns in the north of England lost a generation. For nothing. They didn't even get to the first objective. Meanwhile the Germans were in their underground bunkers with electric lighting and other home comforts. Great diggers, the Germans.'

Lemmy's next unexpected verbal onslaught was the revelation that, notwithstanding his obvious patriotism, he had

Lemmy

Lemmy

just relocated to LA. Why? 'I've always toyed with the idea of living there and I think I'll stay,' he considered. 'People say how healthy I look with a tan which is probably because the bars close an hour earlier... but the drinks are bigger!' Naturally, Lemmy was not living in some carbon-copy suburb of the city. He had acquired an apartment just off Sunset Boulevard, opposite the Roxy venue and his new local, the Rainbow Bar & Grill. Remarkably, he was paying a mere $70 a week for the honour. 'Two rooms, a swimming pool out back, great looking women and the same price as a box-sized flat-share in London. What's more I've been seeing everyone in Hollywood,' he went on. 'I meet more English people there than over here. They all go down to the cricket club and to the Cat & Fiddle for the warm beer. When other bands stop by on tour, it really pisses them off that I'm staying put and their next stop is Canada or somewhere in the snow belt.

'Most people who slag off LA have never even been there. I like Americans, they're keen. The attitude is, the customer has paid and therefore you must look after him, so he'll come back and give us more money. The English,' he continued, 'are resentful when you're staying in a hotel. It's always "you can't check in for another two hours" or "the bar's closed."' The ex-pat then compared the American way with our current predicament. 'Six quid for a bourbon and Coke and it's not even that good a bar,' he complained. 'They look at you as if you've just crawled out from under a rock. They're smug, self-satisfied fucking robbers! Just because you're wearing a suit doesn't mean you're not a thief. You will never teach the English anything, determined to go down with all flags flying. The trouble is the flags are all full of holes!'

I recalled the notice at the Hyatt House in Hollywood: 'Treat this man with respect, he might have just sold a million

225
225

records.' Lemmy grunted his approval before moving on to his next contentious anecdote – the sacking of his manager of fifteen years in a high-profile court case. 'You try to preserve some things in your life which are important and that includes friends,' he explained. 'I wanted to believe that he had not been ripping us off but in the end the evidence was overwhelming. Now I've got the same manager who acts for Yes and Bad Company and used to work for Led Zeppelin.' It transpired that the singer has many A-list connections. Although he has never been married – 'I've never found a woman I wanted an exclusive relationship with and if I got married it would have to be the real thing. I wouldn't fool around, you know.' – he has two sons. One, a certain Paul Inder, aged twenty-four at the time, was once in the habit of taking the stage at rock festivals, in between the other acts. The other, he has never seen as he was adopted at birth. 'I was eighteen and the mother was fifteen,' he revealed. 'She was taking GCEs at the same time as she was in maternity class. Paul's mother used to screw John Lennon but really wanted to sleep with McCartney. I was going to form a band with Julian Lennon. That would have been even more incestuous, right?'

Having been around since the 1960s and still going strong in the 1990s, Lemmy enjoyed a non-executive role as an elder statesman of rock. Apart from appearing in numerous rockumentaries, including a self-titled one featuring dozens of fellow stars paying tribute, he also spoke at conferences like the New Music Seminar in New York. 'It would be fun to do a lecture tour of the States for a couple of months,' he remarked, 'that way you wouldn't have to go on tour. It would be a break from the corporate world of major record companies and promoters. I prefer small independent lunatics. That's what it was like when I first came to London. Acid, speed… everything was available and cheap, so it wasn't surprising the place was swinging. The city was positively rebounding! Life was a lot easier, a lot more relaxed. Then people started dying because they didn't have any sense. In the late 70s they started going down like flies: Elvis, Marc Bolan, Sid Vicious...'

With vicious irony a longer succession of rock stars fell during an even shorter period of time just a few years ago. Lemmy himself died of cancer at the end of 2015. The following year saw the demise of David Bowie, Prince, George Michael and Rick Parfitt of Status Quo – all before reaching the relatively modest age of three score and ten. Lemmy just about made it to seventy but didn't go down like a fly. He was more of a blackbird, or even a golden eagle.

LEONARD COHEN

Leonard Cohen was widely regarded as the ultimate merchant of gloom. A poet and author who came to realise music would be more marketable, he could be described as a clown in reverse. However, whereas jokers and comedians are often funny on the outside and tragic within, Cohen had a mordant sense of humour. He might have flaunted the hang-dog expression of a depressive, but he could also be profoundly dry and droll.

I met him at the New Music Seminar in New York in 1988, a Midem-style week of conferences and workshops in a mid-town Manhattan hotel. Cohen hosted an artists' panel of speakers having recently released *I'm Your Man*, the singer's best album since those masterpieces of the 1960s, *Songs of Leonard Cohen* and *Songs from a Room*. I asked him about the changes in the record industry, how musicians were now gaining a fairer percentage of royalties. 'The marriage between music and money is very dangerous,' he gravely replied. 'Many manage to transcend this spectre and sing good songs. We need to discover an alternative.' This proved to be one of the most ironic remarks I'd ever heard, for in 2004 Cohen discovered that his manager had been ripping him off for almost a decade. Having somewhat naively granted her power of attorney over his finances, she proceeded to embezzle millions of dollars from his bank accounts. Most of the money came from selling the rights to his music publishing and recorded music. Large tax bills had remained unpaid and at the age of seventy-five, Leonard was obliged to embark on a world tour to recoup the money.

Anyone who has seen Cohen live will appreciate the facetiousness of his banter between songs. In conversation it's not always easy to decode whether he's being serious or funny. Take the subject of being a writer: 'Writing is terrible work!' he exclaimed over a chilled white wine in the hotel bar. 'Coming up with the words can drive you mad. But I'm not complaining. You have to come to terms with your own predicament. On the bright side, as you get older you become accustomed to the ups and downs inherent in your craft. The more expressive you are, the easier it is to shake off any writer's block.'

Apart from *I'm Your Man* being a classic, I'd always been enthralled at seeing Leonard onstage, especially when he performed at the Hammersmith Odeon in 1979. Apart from as well as working with an excellent band, his friend and lover Jennifer Warnes was on backing vocals. Cohen wasn't having any of it. 'My life,' he intoned, 'is a mess. I have no opinions about anything of any depth. I feel my head is surrounded by a swarm of bees and I just try and move with dignity from one step to another.' It transpired, notwithstanding the artistic and commercial success of his latest opus, 'it was made under dismal conditions'. Roughly translated, this meant he was still suffering from the fall-out of the demise of his most recent relationship. Also, still on his mind was the split from Suzanne, yes, that Suzanne, the legend from his debut LP who 'feeds you tea and oranges that come all the way from China.' But surely all this was grist to the mill? His work had always been fuelled by anxiety and depression, which also inspired many of his songs about women.

I saw Leonard again five years later when he was in London to play some excellent shows at the Royal Albert Hall. He happened to be in Fred's, the stylish Soho members' club situated next door to the *Private Eye* offices in Carlisle Street. I was with a female friend who was entertaining me with a blow-by-blow account of the break-up of her marriage. This was surely a story for Lenny who was standing less than two feet away, chatting up a girl about one-third of his age. Eventually catching his eye, I re-introduced myself to this man of impeccable bearing and manners. During our conversation I mentioned I was a big fan of the Greek islands – he'd owned a house on Hydra for many years – but as far as I knew, he was still living in LA where there had been race riots the previous year. Would he not be better off in Europe, especially since he had a huge following over here?

'LA is a risky place to live,' he agreed, 'and I can say that because I was right in the middle of the trouble. The local shops where I buy my groceries and electrical goods were burned to the ground. Yet there's something compelling about a place which is falling apart geographically as well as socially. The future is grim, and Los Angeles is at the centre of it. Then again it's the sort of place I want to write from because it's where things are really going on.' This explained why he called his next album *The Future* – one of the tracks, 'Democracy' proclaiming the words 'democracy is coming to the USA'. Leonard Cohen might never have been a stand-up comic but there's no mistaking the gallows humour, as persistent as the forest fires which annually threaten his favourite city.

The great and gracious Lenny, R. I. P.

CHAPTER 56

LOU REED

It was a passport to another world, an invitation to join one of the most rarefied cliques: *White Light/White Heat* by The Velvet Underground in its original black sleeve. At the end of the 1960s and his first term at university, my brother came home with a copy. Soon afterwards David Bowie recorded 'Queen Bitch', referencing 'VU' on the sleeve of *Hunky Dory*. It remains one of the greatest homages in the history of rock 'n' roll, while a whole genre of music inspired by Lou Reed changed the lives of many of us forever.

By 1972 Bowie was the brightest star in the firmament and one of his first subsidiary projects was to resurrect the career of the almost forgotten Reed. In conjunction with Mick Ronson, David produced Lou's *Transformer*, his second solo album, the one containing 'Walk on the Wild Side' and 'Perfect Day'. These songs enabled The Velvets' legend to become mainstream while Lou still hung on to his cult status, a privilege reserved for the finest. Meanwhile I'd been raving about him for three years, a long time when you're in your mid-teens.

The first time I saw Lou Reed live was at the large open-air gig at Charlton Athletic FC in 1974 when he played down-bill to The Who and Humble Pie. It wasn't his best era, swastikas highlighting a bleached barnet and a stage show which included shooting up like the junkie he had always professed to have been. It was a preview of *Sally Can't Dance*, an album inexplicably aimed at the gay disco market. Much better was his headlining performance at the Mont de Marsan punk festival in 1977. It was a heady mixture of classic Velvets' cuts plus some of his best solo material including 'Leave Me Alone' which would appear on the following year's *Street Hassle*, Lou's best LP since 1973's *Berlin*. With their own reporter unable to attend the gig, I reviewed it for *Melody Maker*, my first article for the music press. Unfortunately, I wasn't able to shimmy backstage for an interview, ditto the next couple of times I saw him live, at the Hammersmith Odeon in 1979 and at The Bottom Line in New York the following year. After The Bottom Line show I pleaded with an executive from his record company for an interview for *Record Mirror*. There was no chance but then what could one realistically expect from an obese obsequious creep in a blue satin jacket? I trudged back to my digs reassuring myself about being careful what you wish for, the potential disappointment of meeting your heroes, and so on. It was a full decade before this theory was finally put to the test.

In the summer of 1990, the year after the watershed *New York* album, there was a press conference at the Institute of Contemporary Arts. The occasion was the release of *Songs for Drella*, a tribute to the late Andy Warhol, the artist who had originally made it happen for The Velvet Underground. The LP was made with Lou's co-founder of The Velvets, John Cale. The Q&A section of the event was typically mediocre, Reed fielding most of the questions with his usual acerbic one-liners. Afterwards, drinks were served in a spacious reception room, one end occupied by Lou, standing by himself, none of the journos seemingly having the wit or gall to go and talk to him. Stepping into the breach, I wandered over and started asking questions about his recent work. I remarked that, despite his career-long contempt for journalists, he had incorporated a certain amount of reportage on the *New York* platter, especially on tracks like 'Last Great American Whale' and 'Good Evening Mr Waldheim'. Remarkably, he agreed with my assessment and it became apparent that, for him, keeping abreast of current affairs was as important as lending an ear to whatever new music was being made.

With that day's affair being about Andy Warhol, I thought I might as well bring up the fact that I was one of the last people in London to talk to him when he was in town for his self-portrait exhibition. A reasonable gambit, as it happens. Looking back, how would Lou describe their relationship? 'When we worked together,' he confided, 'we were very close. We were working towards something in common, but approaching it from different angles. He was about film, art and performance and we were a rock 'n' roll group. Andy worked very hard. It was no coincidence that he called his studio The Factory. One thing I learned from him was that whatever you do, you should work very, very hard otherwise nothing will happen. Andy worked as hard as anybody I ever knew. Once he asked me how many songs I'd written that day and, whatever I said, he replied, "Oh, you should do more." I had to learn certain things the hard way but working with him was really fantastic. People always said he was strange, but they probably didn't know him or understand him. He was actually a very good, honest person who was enormously talented. So *Songs For Drella* is our way of doing something in honour of him.'

Lou himself was no stranger to work, having released sixteen solo albums in the previous twenty years. His first job after graduating from Syracuse University with a degree in English was as a factory songwriter. This entailed spewing out quickie albums for a record company specialising in cashing in on popular trends. It was similar to working at Broadway's Brill Building where songwriters like Neil Diamond and Carole King learned their craft. 'There were literally four of us locked in a room writing songs,' he recalled. 'We would be told "write ten California songs" or "invent a new dance craze", then we'd go to a studio for a couple of hours and cut three or four albums really quickly. That came in useful later when it was necessary to know my way around a studio.'

Then in 1964, at the age of twenty-two, Reed met Cale, the viola virtuoso and together they formed the most important and influential band since The Beatles and the Rolling Stones. You don't get many CVs like that these days.

MADONNA

On a cold and rainy evening in November 1983, Madonna made her live London debut at the Camden Palace. The former BBC TV theatre was sparsely attended, the mixed crowd of week-night regulars not noticing any shortage of elbow room over the three floors of the old building. Her record company had invited me along, hoping I'd write a feature for *Penthouse*. Paradoxically, a year or so later the magazine became embroiled in a legal dispute with the singer for publishing compromising pictures taken at a photo-session in the late 1970s.

Madonna lip-synched to three songs in a short but well-choreographed performance with two dancers. One of the tracks, 'Holiday', became her first hit but what was most memorable was the physicality of the dancing. Considering this was the decadent and drug-addled 1980s, it showed remarkable discipline. 'That's what years of dancing achieve,' the singer explained after the show. 'The training forces you to do things that you don't really want to do but which you know are good for you. A lot of people in the record industry are self-destructive and burn themselves out, but my lifestyle is very different. Of course, just because you go to bed early and don't do drugs doesn't mean you can't exude sexuality onstage. We might not wear sexy clothes, but you can get the audience worked up by the way you sing and dance.'

By the following year Madonna was on the way to becoming the biggest-selling female artist of all time. The *Like a Virgin* album sold more than 20 million copies and in 1991 she appeared at the Cannes Film Festival promoting her film *In Bed with Madonna*; it was a far cry from her earlier rom-com movie *Desperately Seeking Susan*. A compilation of live performance and embarrassing backstage footage, *In Bed...* confirmed her as arguably the biggest star in the world. At the press conference she didn't fall into the obvious trap of talking about sex but divulged information about her tough upbringing. 'My mother died when I two and my father was a real disciplinarian,' she revealed. 'He's Italian and I went to Catholic school, which meant getting up early every morning to go to church. It was a very regimented life but gave me the discipline necessary to become a good dancer.'

Madonna did well at school and was offered a scholarship at the University of Michigan near her native Detroit. Instead she relocated to New York, played in some bands, studied ballet and started writing songs. She described her early apartments as being '...squalid but good for inspiration. In New York there are always elements of danger, but I've never felt scared as there are always people out on the street.'

By the time of *In Bed...* Madonna had homes in LA, Florida and the UK. Following the provocative documentary came an album entitled *Erotica,* plus an expensive yet best-selling coffee table book, *Sex*. In 1993 she rolled up at the Brit Awards, not to receive one but to publicise her next movie, the ultimately unsuccessful *Body of Evidence*. On this occasion Madonna had no qualms about talking about sex. 'Children are very aware of it and it's a mistake not to teach them about sex,' she told a chosen few of us. 'That's why AIDS has spread through the heterosexual community, because people think they can't get it. A lack of sex education has also led to a great number of teenage pregnancies because nobody wants to talk about it. Even in our so-called enlightened times sex remains a taboo subject.'

Now in her sixties, it will be interesting to hear what one of the most famous sex symbols of modern times has to say about the menopause.

CHAPTER 58

MALCOLM McLAREN

Malcolm McLaren rescued the 1970s from its post-hippie malaise by managing the Sex Pistols and sowing the seeds of punk. The fact that their boisterous relationship ended up in the High Court proved to be a tiny blot on the McLaren landscape as he breathlessly proceeded to his next anarchic project – dragging Adam Ant out of obscurity only to steal his backing band, The Ants, a few months later. You would have expected Adam to have been somewhat put out by this sudden turn of events, but this is what he actually said about the heist: 'I paid Malcolm a grand to work with me for four weeks. He sorted me out but he's an artist, really, even though as a manager he's on a par with someone like Colonel Tom Parker, Elvis Presley's manager. And he's still the best-dressed man in town.'

McLaren was a lot of things to many people. Some thought he'd turned popular culture into a cheap marketing gimmick, others felt he was a self-publicist addicted to shock tactics. As if the whole Pistols imbroglio hadn't been enough, he went on to launch the career of fourteen-year-old Annabella Lwin, poaching Adam's Ants to provide her with a backing band. As part of the marketing, Malcolm published a magazine called *Chicken* which celebrated the idea of sex between individuals below the age of consent – from the offices of EMI, the first record company to have fired the Sex Pistols.

Soon after this episode I interviewed him for *Penthouse*. Part of the profile included his wayward upbringing which would appear to have had some connection with a future career in controversy. 'I had little to do with my mother and after the Second World War my parents broke up, so I never got around to meeting my father. I was brought up by my grandmother who had nine sisters. They would come around to the house and talk late into the night while I was falling asleep on the settee. They would discuss everything from the government to the beginning of rock 'n' roll but perhaps most importantly, style. I picked up many useful things as a result of these nocturnal conversations. Around this time I was expelled from primary school for crawling under tables and looking up girls' skirts. My grandmother would talk to me about sex and there were no boundaries at home, no structure. It was total anarchy. When I did return to school, I became aggressive in the face of discipline and never stopped misbehaving. I guess I was a delinquent, my upbringing provoking an ability in me to be anarchic without feeling self-conscious about it. That attitude has remained and made me what can be termed a very unorthodox person.'

Rock 'n' roll people will hardly argue with this assessment, especially when McLaren decided to become an artist in his own right. Inspired by the black community in the South Bronx, he recorded an album entitled *Duck Rock*, influenced by New York DJs who added the sound of scratching to hip hop and R&B. 'I suppose I undertook that project in order to step out of the closet as a manager,' he told me during the *Penthouse* interview in 1983. 'I didn't want to get shunted into any one particular drawer by the pigeonhole conscious English. I guess I'm just someone who goes out of my way to be provocative and who likes messing around with ideas. It was also a means of getting a different perspective out there on the street, away from running a production line of teddy bears, you know, pin-up pop stars. I also wanted to catch the mood of the time which has a lot to do with technology.

'In New York I discovered DJs making their own mixes from other records. That trend spread from clubs to the street where kids were mixing one racket with another and then talking over the top with a microphone. I saw that as a way of the culture being in control as opposed to the record industry. I suppose to some extent I do create images, the ten-gallon hat, the ghetto blasters accessorised with bull-horns, but I simply put everything together from the raw materials around me. Most people in the music industry are neither intelligent nor creative which makes them easy to manipulate.'

Alongside this was the growing interest and awareness on both sides of the Atlantic in ethnic music. 'People are looking for the roots of their culture and seeing what they belong to. The barriers to communication are breaking down and as people receive information, they can use it for themselves. The blacks in the South Bronx were cut off from their culture for so long, it was only a matter of time before they became aware of it. The development of the ghetto blaster made it possible technologically to meet in the street and do their breakdancing. No matter how poor they are, the one thing they own is their body and being able to demonstrate their physical prowess engenders a sense of achievement which makes them feel powerful within their own culture. In control.

'When I made *Duck Rock*,' he continued at breakneck speed, 'I had the enjoyment of going and finding out what all this dance stuff was about. Learning to think with my hips rather than my head and making myself aware of what it was that originally made me so excited about rock 'n' roll. Songwriting no longer had to be verse/chorus, verse/chorus. Techniques like scratching have made it more of an adventure, wondering what sounds are going to come next. It could be the sound of machines in an amusement arcade or a record blasting out of a bedroom window or a car horn. You can cut and mix all these sounds together, press a button to create a mechanical dance-beat and suddenly you're no longer restricted to a three-minute packaged tune but have got something you've made yourself. Suddenly everyone is involved and not just a teddy bear star. That,' he concluded on this particular occasion, 'is the most rock 'n' roll thing happening now.'

This, of course, was a good decade before the global romance of downloading from the internet and three decades prior to the communal affair with smart phones. I continued to fraternise with Malcolm throughout the remainder of the 1980s. He was a regular at The Groucho Club, on sparkling form at the Fashion Aid party there in 1985. He laughed like a drain when I introduced the editor of *Penthouse* to Sandie Shaw, the first British winner of the Eurovision Song Contest back in the 1960s. The singer, renowned for performing in stockinged feet, started arguing with my boss, convinced he was too young to be editor of such a publication. McLaren clearly enjoyed the set-to, presumably amused by the probability of confrontation.

Rifling through some memorabilia, I found a bill from the following year bearing his name and phone number. It was an LA number, which shouldn't have come as a surprise since he was prone to changing countries and offices as regularly as most people take vacations. By 1991 Malcolm had added movies to his CV, narrating *The Ghosts of Oxford Street*, a TV film broadcast by Channel 4 on Christmas Day. Billed as a 'variety show', it was a history of London's most popular shopping street going back to the days of Tyburn gallows, prostitutes, highwaymen and other miscreants of an age appropriately inhabited by McLaren's ancestors. The stars of the show were an interesting bunch too, including Tom Jones and early 1990s faces like Shaun Ryder of the Happy Mondays and chart-toppers from the previous

Christmas, Kirsty MacColl and Shane McGowan. Sinead O' Connor looked stunning in a shoulder-length platinum blonde wig and the rapping community was represented by Rebel MC.

A couple of weeks before the screening there was a launch party at, believe it or not, the Next cafeteria in the Oxford Street branch of the retail chain. I hadn't seen Malcolm since starting work for *Hello!* in 1988 and when I told him who I was writing for he replied, 'So why haven't you brought Juan Carlos with you?', a reference to the King of Spain, the country where the magazine was founded.

The last time I saw Malcolm was in 1995, after the David Bowie exhibition in Cork Street. He was hanging around with some guys in the art game who all seemed quite a bit taller than him. Nevertheless he performed an impressive sheep dog routine, rounding them all up and deciding which restaurant they should go on to. You don't suppose he picked up the tab, do you?

MARC ALMOND

Nottingham Rock City, 3 June 1981. The name of the venue may suggest the usual guitar-crunching gang of Nazareth or Iron Maiden but the entertainers that night were a little different: a tinny-sounding synth duo called Soft Cell, who not many people knew about. Still, they were smart enough to have enlisted the services of Stevo Pearce as manager. He, in turn, was smart enough to have organised a coachload of fans to come down from Leeds to bulk out the 2,000-capacity venue.

The resourceful, if eccentric, then-teenage entrepreneur had recently released a compilation album on his Some Bizzare label, featuring a collection of acts attached to the new electro-futurist sound. The movement included rising stars like Duran Duran, Depeche Mode and The The. Soon after the gig, Stevo announced he was shooting off back to Yorkshire for a sunrise photo session with The The. As a result, when it came to interviewing Soft Cell, there was no one to prevent all the fans piling backstage after me. It was hard enough coping with motor-mouth singer Marc Almond. Having to handle scores of excitable attention-seekers dressed to the nines in their New Romantic finery increased the mayhem factor exponentially. At times I felt like I was being interviewed: it was like a press conference in reverse. In fact, it was practically a rally, many of these followers having evolved from soul boys and soul girls belonging to the cultish Warehouse club in Leeds into fans of the new electro sound. It was at the Warehouse that Marc first became acquainted with the

60s Northern Soul classic 'Tainted Love', sung by Gloria Jones. Within two months of the Rock City gig, Soft Cell released their own version of this track which topped the charts for weeks.

With the benefit of hindsight, it's understandable why all the fans were in such a hyperactive condition. Sounding and not looking unlike *Carry On* actor Kenneth Williams, Marc assumed the role of guru, slagging off the rest of the music scene for being 'about as decadent as a packet of crisps' while extolling the joys of clubs and sleaze. When 'Tainted Love' reached No. 1, I thought I'd better sneak into *Top of the Pops* to gain further and better particulars of this whole phenomenon of dirt and eroticism. 'What Soft Cell is about,' Marc explained, 'is the whole nightclubbing scene: the sex, the smokiness, the jazz and the wet streets. There's a lot of filth in the things we do, not in a blatant way, more tongue-in-cheek. We always laugh at ourselves and our shortcomings,' he went on, 'laughing at things which are said about your appearance or vanity is necessary, especially in the pop business, where everybody is full of their own self-importance.'

The duo's career continued to proceed at quite a pace. Soft Cell's debut album, *Non-Stop Erotic Cabaret*, was released in time for Christmas 1981, yielding more great singles such as 'Bedsitter' and the epic 'Say Hello, Wave Goodbye'. Meanwhile 'Tainted Love' went on to enjoy the then longest-ever stay in the American Hot 100, leading to many a promotional trip to the States as well as other parts of the world. The downside of this success was the fate of the next album, 1982's *The Art of Falling Apart*. Containing less commercial, if more artistic material, it led to problems with their record company Phonogram.

Marc, however, was unperturbed and enjoyed talking about its creative concept – the exquisite agony of those living on the edge. 'You see some people whose lives are a complete mess, who've just finished with their boyfriend or girlfriend and who are down to their last few pounds,' he explained, one booze-fuelled night at The Columbia Hotel, 'but who at the last minute get themselves together. They'll do okay again for a while before the whole cycle starts again. I really admire those kinds of people and yes, in a sense that's what we're doing. The record company is only interested in us being commercial and selling zillions of records, but we don't want all that. I mean, what have we got to prove? Nothing to ourselves, at any rate. We've already had a No. 1, so we know we can do that. The main thing to me is the quality of the music and the development of ourselves as artists. Not whether we go mega-platinum in Outer Mongolia.'

Matters came to a head just before the release of *Torment and Toreros* the following year. It was so 'out there' it was credited to Marc and the Mambas, as opposed to Soft Cell. The Mambas were a mini-orchestra with saxophone, guitar, bass, and even a string quartet. Furthermore, Marc had so many songs, the LP came out as a double album. Phonogram only agreed to it providing they didn't have to pay the musicians or any royalties. 'I wanted a double as we'd done all the recording, plus a nice fold-out sleeve, which we took a long time over. There have been loads of sleepless nights and I've almost made myself ill at times, now they want me and the band to renounce all royalties. But for the fans it's real value for money. I felt all these ideas pouring out and there were too many for a single album to contain. There are ninety minutes of music in all.'

The sound had clearly come a long way from the catchy synth-pop of the recent past. Flamenco guitars, castanets, everything you'd expect from the album's title. 'It's raw, Spanish gypsy music,' Marc enthused, 'like another type of soul music. It's very sad sounding but there's also a lot of cruelty in it, harking back to the treatment of the Spanish gypsies, which is why the music is so sad. The imagery is fiery. I've got more to offer than being part of a disposable pop band. I've started writing a lot of tunes myself, influenced by travelling around so much.'

In 1983, I saw quite a lot of Marc and Stevo. Having left *Record Mirror* the year before I was free to roam, wandering around Soho bumping into friends and acquaintances and finding stories for the tabloids. Never one to shy away from fellow party animals, Stevo invited me to the Some Bizzare offices above the famous Trident recording studio in St Anne's Court, where Marc was pursuing his creative endeavours. One day, photographer Peter Ashworth turned up to play the drums. He had recently completed a Mari Wilson photoshoot in the flat my then wife Jo and I were renting in Hampstead Garden Suburb. It was pure Art Deco and perfect for the sleeves of the 7-inch and 12-inch singles of 'Just What I Always Wanted'. The song includes the words, 'A song from Teddy, an Ashworth snap' while each of the sleeves bear the legend, 'A location from Mike and Jo Nicholls'. Danny Baker, then a Radio 1 DJ, described the sleeve picture of our flat as 'a chic little film set. Very in, very in indeed.'

Another visitor to the Trident studio was Leonard Cohen's first manager, Marty Machat. Stevo enthusiastically introduced him to me, pointing out that Marty was also the lawyer retained by himself for his own American affairs. Too bad Marty was no longer with us when Lenny had problems with his embezzling fraudster of a manager some twenty years later.

We should now turn to Marc Almond's autobiography, *Tainted Life* (Sidgwick & Jackson), where he describes a Siouxsie and The Banshees' party at Camden Palace. Steve Severin of the Banshees and Robert Smith of The Cure had both contributed to *Torment and Toreros*, but neither were happy with the way the record had come out. 'So I staggered around depressed,' wrote Marc in his book, 'trying to avoid Mariella Frostrup, my record company PR. A journalist, Mike Nicholls, had been talking to me and afterwards Mariella slithered up to me saying, "What does he want? I hate him." Unfortunately for Mariella, Mike's wife overheard her and said in a loud voice, "Mike, Mariella says she hates you." Mariella could have sunk into the floor. No PR points there.'

The delicious irony here is that the year before, Mariella and my then-wife Jo, had been friends and colleagues, Jo working in the promotions department of Polydor records. In fact, Rick Sky, at the time one of the main Fleet Street columnists, used to tell the pair of them they were his favourite girls in the whole music industry. Anyway, Miss Frostrup's hatred didn't last for long. The following year she was having trouble arousing press interest in an act to which she had been assigned. I knew more about them than she did, having been tipped off by John Taylor of Duran Duran, who had recently toured with them in Australia. The band's name? INXS.

Their UK debut was at the Astoria in Charing Cross road. Along with 2,000 diehard Aussie fans, I reckon my companion and I were the only English people in the place. INXS were promoting an album called *The Swing*, which featured 'Original Sin', one of their best-ever songs. It goes without saying that there was a Swing party afterwards at the One-Legged Goose, a restaurant in the as yet ungentrified Primrose Hill area. It was a breezy summer evening. Basement doors opened on to a colourful garden where you could take the air, along with your bottles of beer. What more could you ask for?

The guests were mainly record company people who hadn't attended the show, and the band themselves. I spent most of the evening chatting to Little Steven, who was enjoying a sabbatical from his day-job as guitarist Miami Steve Van Zandt of Bruce Springsteen's East Street band. I'd already interviewed him the year before, on the release of his solo album *Men Without Women*. Both conversations were cryptic, to say the least, the two of us eye-balling one another as I attempted to decode what on earth he was on about. It seemed of little consequence that I was a major fan of a track called 'Daddy's Come Home', one of the tracks on *Dedication*, the 1981 album released by Steve's hero, Gary U.S. Bonds. Apart from writing the song, Steve had played guitar and bass and produced and arranged it, in conjunction with Springsteen. My enthusiasm seemed to cut no ice. I guess it was a New Jersey mob scenario, a matter which became clearer towards the end of the century when Steve took on an acting role in the celebrated TV series, *The Sopranos*. Nevertheless, the ineffable 'Daddy's Come Home' remains one of my favourite songs of the 80s.

Meanwhile, going back to Marc Almond, in *Tainted Life* he went on to admit, 'I'd lost it. I was having a psychotic episode, so I wrote a letter of retirement to every paper and magazine. "The New Soft Cell album currently being recorded will probably be my last. I'm grateful to those who have supported me."' I took this as a cue to pop round to his flat in Soho's Brewer Street, taking a present, as you would, in such circumstances. It was a large, lurid liquorice allsorts sofa cushion from Woolworths, suitably kitsch, perhaps. I sympathised with his situation; retired at twenty-seven, exactly the way I felt the year before when I was fired from *Record Mirror*. At the same time, Marc was receiving offers of all sorts of new projects – but I'll let him tell the story himself. 'Journalist Mike Nicholls, working at *Penthouse*, offered me the strangest job of all: answering people's sexual problems, a kind of agony aunt. At first I thought it might be amusing but on reflection it was I who needed to talk to someone about mine.' Well, you can't blame a guy for trying...

The last time we met was when I interviewed him for the

Evening Standard on the release of an album entitled *Fantastic Star* in 1996. It was co-written with Neal Whitmore, formerly Neal X of Sigue Sigue Sputnik. Neal would go on to join the ranks of Chris Pope, members of Spandau Ballet, Fergal Sharkey and even local folk queen Maddy Prior in washing down lukewarm grub with cold drinks at my house in Summerlee Gardens.

CHAPTER 60

MARIANNE FAITHFULL

'It was actually a Curly Wurly,' I muttered, returning to the *Record Mirror* office after interviewing Marianne Faithfull. In the 1960s the singer had a lot to answer for, making constant newspaper headlines with stories that provided us prepubescents with an alternative sex education. First of all there was the incident which took place at Rolling Stone Keith Richards' country home in Sussex. Apparently, the police busted the place looking for drugs but had to settle with Marianne wearing nothing but a fireplace rug. Apparently, she'd just had a bath and couldn't locate a towel. Then came the urban myth about the Mars bar or more specifically the unusual orifice where her boyfriend Mick Jagger chose to insert it. A bit of a porky, as it happens, but there was never any denying that Marianne was drop-dead gorgeous, boasting the sort of eyes, lips and body which could cause unsuspecting motorists to crash. Ms Faithfull also possessed a gentle, poignant voice as Stones' manager Andrew Loog Oldham discovered after meeting her at a party. Once again identifying star potential, he encouraged her to record a Jagger-Richards song, 'As Tears Go By'. It was a hit, as were 'Come and Stay With Me' and 'This Little Bird', all charting while Marianne was still in her teens.

This success came in the mid-1960s when PR, promotion, marketing and image did not inhabit the minefield they do today. Recently out of convent school, the singer was the epitome of louche, aristocratic cool. Though raised in an ordinary terrace house in Reading in the home counties, there was nothing ordinary about the Faithfull background. Her father, Glynn, was the son of a sexologist while her mother was an Austro-Hungarian countess, the great-niece of Baron Leopold von Sacher-Masoch. He wrote the novel *Venus In Furs* which influenced the Velvet Underground song and a few generations of bohemian lifestyles. His other world-class legacy was the label sado-masochism.

At the age of eighteen, Marianne fell pregnant by the upmarket art dealer John Dunbar. Their subsequent marriage did not last long and he won custody of their son, Nicholas. This would have suited most of the Stones; Ms Faithfull enjoyed brief liaisons with Brian Jones and Keith Richards before embarking on a four-year odyssey with Mick. In her autobiography, *Faithfull* (Little, Brown), she claims their affair finished for two reasons: Jagger's growing infatuation with aristocracy – 'he would attend events given by anyone with a title and castle' – and drugs. With her upbringing, Marianne was susceptible to the notion of Romantic decadence; from de Quincy and Baudelaire to Burroughs and the late 1960s rock scene, she became the classic junkie trainspotter.

The inevitable downward spiral reached its nadir in 1969 when Jagger was shooting the film *Ned Kelly* in Australia. He was asleep in their hotel room overlooking Sydney Harbour when she tried to commit suicide. 'I attempted to open a window and would have jumped if I'd been able to. I had also taken fifteen Tuinal tablets but they were taking ages to kick in. When I eventually woke up, I couldn't remember who I was. There was a complete identity crisis, so I thought I'd better go and look in the mirror. The problem was I didn't see me, but Brian Jones who had drowned in his swimming pool two weeks earlier. So I reasoned that since he was dead, I ought to be, too.'

This led her to take the rest of the sleeping pills and fall into a coma for six days. I remember reading all this in the news at the time, one report concluding with Faithfull announcing to the world's media: 'I was virtually dead.'

Yet there was to be no happy ending for a while. After splitting up with Mick, Marianne spent two years on the streets and sleeping in squats, amazingly avoiding recognition. Then Island Records boss Chris Blackwell persuaded her to go into rehab which was shortly before the release of *Broken English*, the singer's startling album of vengeance and redemption. It was at this point that I conducted what was obviously a difficult interview, not helped by the fact that she had recently sustained an injury, as indicated by the plaster covering part of her face.

Marianne was accompanied by her next husband, Ben Brierly, who tactfully let her do most of the talking and didn't tell me he was a musician in early punk band The Vibrators. His wife's voice suited the new wave era, those pure 1960s notes replaced by a husky drawl which hinted at a surfeit of whiskey and cigarettes. Great dirges like 'The Ballad of Lucy Jordan' and 'Why D'ya Do It?' sounded more like Tom Waits than the Marianne I knew.

I didn't see Marianne again until the launch party of *Faithfull* in the mid-1990s. Like most of the press conferences I went to, there were very few journalists asking questions, so as usual I steamed in. By then her seven-year marriage to Brierly had ended, ditto a third, shorter union in the late 1980s. So I asked her one question about married life and another about drugs. 'Going into rehab was an immense relief to me,' she replied in front of all her guests, 'I didn't want to die yet I didn't want to live that way either. As for marriage, I don't seem to be the marrying kind. For me the romance seems to go out of the window once you're married.'

Those in agreement should form an orderly queue.

CHAPTER 61

MARK KNOPFLER

It was an early lesson in the machinations of the media and the importance of striking while the iron is hot. One winter evening I received a phone call from a stranger inviting me to a Dire Straits gig in Sheffield the following night. It was 1978, I was still living in Manchester and it would involve a potentially hazardous drive over the snow-capped Pennines. The caller was a PR for the band's record company who had just spoken to one of the editors of *Record Mirror* about the gig being reviewed. My colleague, who I had never actually met, informed the PR that I was the magazine's Northern correspondent and since time was getting on, why not contact me himself? It wasn't the usual way of doing things but what the hell. At least I wouldn't have to drive back after the show since a local hotel was part of the deal.

As it turned out, the snow wasn't a problem, it was the fog. The journey ground to a halt at a Road Closed barrier which I was obliged to open before risking the rest of the trip. Otherwise everything went according to plan. The band, led by singer-songwriter and guitarist Mark Knopfler, proved as skilful onstage as on their debut album while the Sheffield University students seemed impressed with the post-prog guitar solos. After the show, I was invited back to the band's hotel for beer and sandwiches, Knopfler bribing the night porter to reopen the kitchen and bar. 'I'd rather do things straight up,' he rationalised, 'but this is England, after all.' We ended up chatting till four a.m. which was a bit of a coup; within weeks Dire Straits were to take off all over the world with *Sultans of Swing* and there would be little need for interviews thereafter. At the same time, however, the band hadn't been around for that long so there wasn't a great deal to discuss. Fortunately, Mark was interested in the fact that I was a local newspaper reporter, partly because he had been one himself.

'When I was seventeen, I went to a journalists' college in Essex and then got a job in Leeds on the *Yorkshire Evening Post*. But two years of muck-raking and character assassination was about as much as I could stand. A healthy dose of cynicism is good for you but there's no point in doing something just because you are good at it. I had to do a lot of court reporting and it was quite illuminating, the nastiness of some of the cases. Like the pathetic kid who'd killed someone and then fainted when the charge was read out.

'Another case which really pissed me off was when a Pakistani had stabbed a white lad. Someone claimed Leeds was a "seething volcano of racial hatred" so that was the headline. I'd never realised how powerful the press could be in their ability to distort. But the final nail in the coffin occurred when a famous musician died. One of the bosses came up to me and demanded, "Now lad, this Jimmy Henderson who has just been found dead from a drugs overdose... do you know 'owt about him?" It was, of course, Jimi Hendrix and it was a Friday afternoon. I didn't even bother going back to the office after the weekend.'

Over the next few years Mark's career developed exponentially: Dire Straits achieved multi-platinum-selling albums and sold-out stadium shows; Knopfler even worked with Bob Dylan. By 1984 he had still only participated in relatively few interviews, but his PR talked him into speaking to me for *Penthouse*. So it was down to Air Studios in London's Oxford Street where Mark was working on the soundtrack for the Helen Mirren film, *Cal*, having previously scored the music for the popular comedy drama *Local Hero*.

Success had also enabled him to record with some of his favourite artists: Walter Becker and Donald Fagen on Steely Dan's *Gaucho*, Van Morrison (*Beautiful Vision*), Scott Walker (*Climate of Hunter*) and of course, The Zim (*Infidels*). How did the Bob gig come about, I wondered? 'We originally met in early 1979 on our first American tour,' he explained. 'Bob came to see Dire Straits at the Roxy in LA. There was this club upstairs where all the stars congregated after a show and he asked me to join him for a drink. It was very funny; there were about twenty photographers there, but not for us. They were there to take pictures of Linda Ronstadt and Rod Stewart, those kinds of people.'

Some years later Mark also got to play with his all-time heroes, The Everly Brothers, and through them, top session guitarist Chet Atkins. Fast forward to 1991 and I was invited to a mini-press conference in a hotel suite in central London. Present were a handful of national newspaper journalists to hear the announcement of the next Dire Straits album and tour, their first since the release of *Brothers in Arms* in 1985, still one of the biggest-selling LPs in UK chart history. Mark immediately recognised me – 'We've met before, haven't we?' – wonderfully winding up Fleet Street's finest. More to the point, sitting next to him was Chet Atkins, creator of what has become known as 'the Nashville Sound' and producer of every country stylist from Elvis Presley to Willie Nelson. Knopfler introduced him as his 'guitar teacher', not a bad title since he himself had sold more than 120 million albums. The best question was about Mark's voice, that unmistakable mid-Atlantic vocal mumble. Was he able to sing any other way?

'Well,' he blushed, 'I can't sing like Andy Williams, although I've often wondered what it would be like to have a vibrato and all that. But I can get a good impersonation of Harry Secombe going in the shower. Then again so can anyone if there's nobody listening.'

MARTYN WARE

Martyn Ware was an original member of The Human League, who I first saw at The Factory in Manchester in 1979. The singer, Phil Oakey, had a unique asymmetrical haircut, shoulder-length tresses framing one side of his angular face; the other two guys, Ian Craig Marsh and Martyn Ware, were former computer operators. They were a pioneering combination of synthetic sound and visual kitsch, with 'visual director' Adrian Wright projecting onto a screen what amounted to a scrapbook of his favourite images, from Motown to glam.

When I met them in the bar after the show, I was surprised to find that I got on best with Ware; I'd never been remotely tech and, to this day, steer clear of stuff like apps and smartphones. We chatted till chucking-out time. He might have been a fellow northerner but he was from the other side of the Pennines, Sheffield to be precise. Still, being an educated fellow, he didn't have any discernible sign of that notorious Yorkshire chippiness. Indeed, over the decades he proved to be something of a charming party animal.

Following two wonderfully left-field albums and a colourfully-dressed double EP, the League sensationally split up. There was the usual gossip about ego problems and artistic differences but to my mind there was simply too much creativity in one quartet. This was duly confirmed the following year when the two couples in the group separated from one another and went on to find success elsewhere.

In late 1981, The Human League (Mark II) enjoyed a string of hits culminating with 'Don't You Want Me', a harmonious call-and-response Christmas No. 1 featuring two girls who had joined Oakey and Wright. Their LP, *Dare*, was voted album of the year in the annual *Record Mirror* readers' poll. Meanwhile, Ware and Marsh had formed the British Electric Foundation, an umbrella organisation overseeing different projects. The first of these was *Music for Stowaways*, a cassette-only collection of experimental tracks. It was a haphazard affair boasting only one stand-out cut, 'Gates of the West'.

Their next release was equally pioneering, a compilation album featuring an unlikely collection of faces. Entitled *Music of Quality and Distinction* (Volume One), it was the epitome of diversity. Songs included The Associates' Billy Mackenzie tackling Roy Orbison's 'It's Over' and my dear colleague Paula Yates warbling 'These Boots Were Made for Walking', a one-time hit for Frank Sinatra's daughter, Nancy. Paula turned up to the *Record Mirror* office in an attempt to cajole her way on to the cover of our august publication. In fact she sat on the desk facing me, throwing a leg over each of my shoulders while opening her sales pitch. I had to admire her ingenuity but was unwilling to face charges of corruption.

Alongside these releases the BEF production company launched Heaven 17, named after the fictional band mentioned in the film *A Clockwork Orange*. Like that controversial movie, their first single, '(We Don't Need This) Fascist Groove Thang', was banned, at least by the BBC. Personally, I was rather fond of its infectious backing track with its reference to the forthcoming occupier of America's White House ('Reagan is President-Elect'), and ended up making it my single of the year.

The singer in Heaven 17 was Glenn Gregory and as the band's profile rose both he and Martyn Ware started to spend more time in London. Their debut album, *Penthouse and Pavement*, with its witty sleeve parodying emerging corporate culture, was a revelation, yielding catchy singles like 'Play to Win' and 'The Height of the Fighting'. More to the point, the duo became fixtures of the London rock 'n' roll scene, frequenting The Columbia Hotel in Bayswater along with fellow out-of-towners Soft Cell, ABC, Simple Minds, Julian Cope and many others. The Columbia sported a spacious lounge reeking of faded elegance and a late bar which was easily reopened once the elderly night porter fell asleep. As far as I know there has never been anywhere like it since, a combination of pub prices and haughty women contributing to the air of decadence. Many of the new generation of stars were in town to play on *Top of the Pops* and once they had appeared on the programme their female followers would descend upon the hotel like moths to a flame.

Another fine night out with Martyn attracted American record industry legend Clive Davis who would then have been about fifty, twice the age of the rest of our posse which included John McGeoch of Magazine and Siouxsie and the Banshees plus Spizz of Spizz Energi fame. The venue was Club for Heroes in the West End, the hub of the New Romantic scene before Steve Strange and Rusty Egan opened the Camden Palace.

Clive had been an important A&R boss at CBS Records in the States, in charge of signing the record company's first generation of major rock acts such as Bruce Springsteen, Santana and Aerosmith who graciously namechecked him in one of their songs. Then, in the late 1970s, he founded Arista, swiftly snapping up Lou Reed, Iggy Pop and Patti Smith. The London A&R boss was Simon Potts, an ebullient chap who became part of my rock 'n' roll family, turning up to any old social whether it was relevant to his own role or not. Since Davis was in town, Potts felt it necessary to take him to the latest happening place, proudly introducing Clive to us all with the words, 'This is my boss'. The ice-cool Clive was a veritable role model: polite, urbane and generally drinking in the whole scene while saying very little. In contrast, the rest of us were drinking too much alcohol and talking a prodigious amount of rubbish.

Martyn's penchant for party animalism continued when he bought a home in Notting Hill, long before the yuppies, politicians and all the other Johnny-come-latelies who colonised what had been one of the most brilliant villages in Britain. This was in the mid-1980s, soon before he received the call to produce the first Terence Trent D'Arby album. Some of the soirees there, involving guests such as D'Arby and my old chum Paula Yates became part of tabloid history. However, it is a good, sensible story about property to which we must now turn our attention.

At the beginning of the current century I had this wheeze about combining rock 'n' roll people and their houses for the Home section of *The Sunday Times*. It was a sequel to my consumer-friendly features about the record industry which I'd written for *The Times* in the 1980s and 90s. In addition, I had been writing about property for the *Evening Standard*, having become involved in the buy-to-let market in Walthamstow. One way or another, rock stars and their habitats seemed to be the way forward, as the editor of *The Sunday Times* property section readily agreed. It was time to call up a few of the old gang.

Fortunately, Martyn had sold his Notting Hill pad when the market peaked, replacing it with a four-bedroom house in Primrose Hill some time before this other exceptional London village became celebrity central. He invited me to visit the residence he shared with his second wife, Landsley, and their children, then aged five and seven. The Hill of Primrose is ingeniously situated between Belsize Park and Camden Town, yet it was the actual location of the house which was truly impressive, being a mere stroll from three of my favourite haunts in the area: the Princess of Wales, The Engineer and the Greek restaurant Lemonia where I courted *my* second wife, Kira.

Picking up where we'd left off, a pub crawl had to be in order while Martyn updated me about his adventures in property. He had paid £357,000 for the three-storey terrace in 1994. By 2003 it was valued at £1.4 million, pretty good for somewhere originally built as social housing. There was more to come. The Wares had also picked up an apartment on the island of Giudecca, a fifteen-minute boat ride from Venice. 'That was in 1989 when the royalties came through from producing the Terence Trent D'Arby album,' he revealed. 'At the time it wasn't a smart part of the city, but it had great views over the lagoon and shops selling fresh produce. The island has no cars, which means the air is clean and we were welcomed as part of the family...'

The plot thickened... 'This hospitality probably has something to do with the fact that Venice has always been a magnet for foreigners. Ever since the fifth century, in fact, when Attila the Hun invaded the mainland and the smarter locals scarpered to the hundreds of islands, nearby. There's also a feelgood atmosphere caused by most of the people visiting the city intent on having a great time.' This could explain why one of his neighbours is Sir Elton John, whose husband David Furnish followed in Martyn's footsteps by acquiring a two-bedroom bolt-hole carved out of a seventeenth-century palazzo. The couple subsequently turned it into an art gallery to house a collection that includes works by Andy Warhol, Damien Hirst and other rock-related riff-raff.

In contrast, canny Yorkshireman Ware bought 'in an area of local authority housing comparable to London's Docklands, only a lot smaller. There are about 50,000 full-time residents on Giudecca, many of whom rent out during the tourist season.' This applied to the musician who, at the time of our interview in 2003, had placed it on the market for up to thirty weeks of the year at £600 per week. Considering he only paid £135,000, it meant he was achieving a yield of 14 per cent, well in excess of what investors in London properties have been earning throughout the past couple of decades. Furthermore, Martyn spent hardly any money doing the place up. 'We just painted the place white to highlight the designer Italian furniture we bought nearby.' For a song, naturally. 'I originally discovered Venice with my first wife, Karen, on the Orient Express,' he continued. 'She was a dancer on a cruise ship and had been everywhere. We stayed at all the ridiculously expensive hotels like the Cipriani and the Gritti Palace. That was a result of the royalties I earned working with Tina Turner.' ...Someone you should be reading about before very long.

CHAPTER 63

MEAT LOAF

While 1976 and '77 signalled the years of the punk revolution, one shouldn't underestimate the contribution of 1978. As the new wave rolled in, it swept ashore some of the great albums of the era: Costello's *This Year's Model*, Blondie's *Plastic Letters*, the debuts of both the Buzzcocks and Magazine, and many more. In the midst of all this modern endeavour, who should come galumphing onstage like a pantomime baddie but Meat Loaf. His sound and style were so dissimilar that it was almost like turning up to the wrong venue. He might have been American but he hardly had anything in common with The Dickies or Dead Kennedys. No, Meat Loaf, aptly nicknamed by a college sports coach, was unique and enjoyed a fascinating backstory.

Unlike most American bands, his apprenticeship didn't involve entertaining drunks in redneck bars but performing in top musicals such as *Hair* and *The Rocky Horror Show*. Then he worked in Todd Rundgren's Bearsville Studios with Jim Steinman, the musician who brought life to the singer's florid theatrical vision. The duo would go on to form one of the most successful symbiotic relationships in rock. Steinman was an exceptional songwriter and producer who fancied himself as a latter-day Jim Morrison until he realised he didn't have the larger-than-life presence of Mr Loaf.

Meat, born Marvin Lee Aday but sensibly changing his name to Michael, could never have fired on all cylinders without Jim. In fact, at one point, Meat Loaf stormed off to do his own thing without Steinman and ended up having a nervous breakdown. Lawsuits followed in hot pursuit and the big guy must have felt a right fool turning down one of Jim's songs. It was *Total Eclipse of the Heart* which became a huge hit worldwide for Bonnie Tyler. Not that Meat Loaf ever lacked when it came to selling records. *Bat Out of Hell*, his debut album, which crashed the scene in 1978, notched up sales of 7 million copies in just ten weeks. In the UK it has been in the Top 200 album charts for the past forty years.

None of this was apparent when Meat Loaf landed in Manchester on Sunday, 4 June 1978, for his first-ever gig in this country. The local record company representative organised a lunch-time meet 'n' greet at the Piccadilly Plaza hotel. This being a Sunday in the pre-opening time Rainy City, hardly anybody turned up. There were so few of us – a chap from the evening paper in Leeds, another from the university rag – that the event took place in Meat Loaf's suite. In those days the singer weighed in at around twenty stones but was a typical gentle giant. He came out with some interesting remarks, particularly by today's PR-driven standards. 'Anything I attempt, I do intensively,' he said. 'However nuts someone tells me I am, I'll fight until I prove I'm right. When people said that if I wanted to make it as a star, I'd have to begin by playing Top 40 hits in a bar, I ignored them and went into theatre instead.'

Appearing in several Shakespeare plays increased the performer's clout with record companies and he persuaded Epic ('How could I not sign to a label with a name like that?') to make videos for the proposed singles culled from *Bat Out of Hell*. These included 'Paradise by the Dashboard Light', a romantic duet with rising star Ellen Foley about riding a motorcycle into hell (see subsequent chapters on Mick Jones and Mick Ronson). 'I'd describe all my work as fun, heroic, violent, theatrical and romantic.' The singer could have added soft-pornographic. The alluring Ms Foley didn't appear that night, replaced by a certain Karla DeVito. Meat Loaf and Karla became embroiled in a right old dance, lurching and gesticulating across the stage, the large fellow swapping his gentlemanly persona for that of a depraved lecher, pawing away at her ample bosom.

At the micro-press conference the performer was very much a gent, which was probably why I had no qualms about posing the question which would go on to haunt my entire career, although sooner or later someone was bound to grab the tusks of the elephant in the room. At school we had a gym teacher who was a similar size to Meat Loaf. Legend had it that he was an Olympian athlete who sustained an injury that damaged his glands, effectively blowing him up like a balloon. What else could a poor journo do except ask the question which should have been on everybody's lips... 'How come you are of such impressive bulk? Is it glandular?'

It might have been a typically humid Manchester day but one could sense a certain *froideur* in the room. Meat Loaf didn't look angry, more shy and embarrassed. It was like he'd been caught doing something not entirely legal. I didn't feel so great myself, consumed with guilt for asking a question which was genuine if tactless. Then, bang on cue, room service arrived with four plates of bacon and eggs and four portions of ice cream – all ordered exclusively for our host. So that explained his size. 'Would you like some ice cream?' he offered. But the damage was done, in more ways than one. All interviews were cancelled for the rest of the tour. Soon afterwards I moved down to London in a cloud of notoriety. The powers that be at *Record Mirror* were delighted, having heard the whole story chapter and verse via the media grapevine.

The next time I met Meat Loaf bordered on the absurd. It

was fifteen years later with the release of *Bat Out of Hell II: Back into Hell*, a new record deal and a standing room only press conference in a big London hotel. By this stage I'd been working with the paparazzi on *Hello!,* the tabloids, the broadsheets and everyone else you can think of. Within minutes I'd been whisked on stage to be photographed with the man who, in all fairness, had lost a little weight. When I interviewed him for the *Evening Standard* the following day it was obvious why. Not only did a portion of fish arrive without chips but he proceeded to remove every scrap of batter from it. Some might say he was no longer creating a rod for his own back.

CHAPTER 64

MICHAEL JACKSON

There was never any doubt that the Jackson 5 were hugely talented, exploding on the scene with an irresistible combination of dance-pop and rock 'n' roll guitars. Yet something niggled when Michael sang, 'Sit down girl, I think I love you... show me what you can do!', especially when he was only eleven years old. It didn't help that at the time I was getting into proper, out-of-this-world guitar music, my hero *de jour* being Jimi Hendrix. By the 1980s he was a half-forgotten virtuoso whereas Jacko had become the biggest star in the world. If *Off the Wall* was his *Revolver*, then *Thriller* was the equivalent to The Beatles' *Sgt. Pepper*, topping the charts in territories most of his fans had probably never heard of.

It came to pass that in 1984 Michael flew over to London to unveil a sculpture of himself at the famous Madame Tussauds wax museum. Word got around and Marylebone Road, a main artery between west and central London, was besieged by screaming school girls, remarkably unsupervised by police, security guards or indeed any species of jobsworths in hi-viz jackets. Access to the museum's main entrance was out of the question yet with eye-popping disbelief I saw him, in head-to-toe glittering finery, walking towards a small doorway round the back. If he was accompanied by a single aide then that person was maintaining an unusually low profile because there, in broad daylight, was one of the biggest celebrities of modern times completely exposed to the world. This was no time to be nervous or get cold feet. Running would have attracted too much attention so it was a matter of speed-walking to this back door and trying to make eye contact before it closed.

Having achieved my goal, I posed a couple of questions in time-honoured style: how did Michael feel about this uproarious reception? Was it intimidating? He blinked, almost in a cartoon fashion, and those gentle yet hard eyes looked straight into mine. 'I love to see kids have a good time, always have,' he responded. 'It was the same with the music. You see them enjoying themselves and find out which sounds they like best, which singles to release. I've always gone to places where the fans go, it's much better than sitting in some office.' This tied in with the very early days of the Jackson 5 when the group would perform in shopping malls in the brothers' native Gary, Indiana: no point bothering with market research and other forms of Chinese whispers when you can get out there yourself. However much you hear about stars cocooned in their gilded palaces, the major success stories have always hung out, from Dylan and the Stones to Jack Nicholson and Joan Collins. However famous you are, there really is no place to hide.

The next time I saw Michael Jackson wasn't in London, Liverpool, Manchester, New York or LA, but in a park in a bleak suburb of Bucharest, the capital of Romania. He was there to open an adventure playground for deprived kids. In my day they were called swings and slides and, to be perfectly honest, you would probably see a better class of climbing frame in remote corners of Hackney Marshes. But what the hell, Jacko was in town and the grub was better than the average gastropub. This was extraordinary for at least two reasons. First of all, Michael was hardly renowned for shoving his face in the old trough. In fact, his dietary needs were practically non-existent which probably explains why he was such a good dancer. Secondly, within the last couple of years there had been a bloody revolution in Romania resulting in the execution of the President Ceaușescu and his wife. Before then the local youth weren't allowed to talk to Westerners, let alone listen to popular beat music. Then the tide turned into a *tsunami* and the whole city became awash with arty haircuts and baggy leisurewear. So who was paying for all this sudden luxury amidst the grim tower blocks and badly pollarded lime trees? Not our problem. A sprinkling of journalists were there to see Jacko indulge in his latest act of charity and patronise local officials who, like communists everywhere, were very efficient when it came to spending other people's money.

I had never had the pleasure of sampling red caviar and other exotic types of party food, but it would have been bad manners not to have joined in the consumption thereof. While wondering what flavour of vodka to knock back next, I noticed a familiar figure frolicking towards me: Andy Coulson from *The Sun*'s Bizarre column. Raving and drooling as one does when arriving late at a party in a strange city, he seemed suspiciously pleased to see me. 'Come on, shake hands like a man!', he beamed. Fortunately this was a good decade before the current mode for attention-seeking hugging. The reason for his arch display of conviviality soon became clear: he had missed the press conference and was gagging for a few choice morsels. This put me in a difficult situation; I had been despatched to Romania on behalf of *Hello!* which was, of course, a weekly magazine. Divulging any information would have amounted to shooting myself in the foot.

I had already encountered this problem in the conference when some work experience ex-public schoolboy from a broadsheet had purloined all the quotes I had eventually managed to extract from Jacko. Not that the song-and-dance man was being difficult, the issue was with the array of flunkies and all-purpose hangers-on surrounding him. Every time I was about to ask a question, I was reproached for addressing Michael directly; we were supposed to go through *them*. Yeah, well maybe that's how the press works in America... So while the other alleged members of the Fourth Estate maintained their disposition towards being tongue-tied, I got on with it. If anything the singer seemed relieved, his usual intense expression barely disguising a conspiratorial smile. How did he feel about engaging in these kinds of situations? Meeting the press but not actually being allowed to talk to us? 'Well, I'm here on behalf of the local children,' he sympathised. 'I'm not as comfortable as I would be onstage but then that's what's normal for me. As you know, I was raised onstage and that for me is the safest place in the world.'

And what do you think of Eastern Europe, not generally a popular destination for Americans?'It's all about the kids and giving them something they don't already know. I love music but I also love children – crazy about them.'

Without wishing to put too fine a point on it, sentiments like these would come back to haunt him.

MICK FLEETWOOD

As far as superlatives are concerned, Mick Fleetwood has cornered the market in a few categories. Apart from leading one of the longest surviving bands in rock – the current line-up alone dates back to 1974 – Fleetwood Mac have sold more than 100 million albums. The best part of two metres tall, Mick is also the loftiest drummer of his generation and has the most educated accent. Matching his stately demeanour, the musician is also polite and charming.

On a beautiful summer's day in 1990, I met him in an elegant Mayfair hotel near St James's Park in central London. A resident of California for many years, I wondered what had brought him back to the UK. 'Well, first of all, I haven't seen my elderly mother for a while and, secondly, to be interviewed by you for *Hello!* magazine,' he replied enthusiastically. His mother would be a hard act to follow. 'You know, last night I went to visit her in Salisbury and somehow she had got hold of this video of Spinal Tap. She turned to me and said, "This is all about you, isn't it?" '

Despite Mick's air of aristocratic understatement, there was no disguising his delight at the latest round of Fleetwood Mac's success. 'We're playing Wembley Stadium in a couple of months,' he twinkled, '40,000 tickets sold so far without any advertising. I suppose it helps that we get a real cross-section of people at our gigs from young kids up to seventy-year-olds, three generations, which is great.' The first generation found ample stories to tell their grandchildren. In the 1960s, Fleetwood Mac built their following at tiny clubs like Klooks Kleek, a backroom attached to a pub in West Hampstead. By 1980 it had become The Moonlight Club, a fashionable venue for the likes of U2 and Joy Division. 'I remember that place,' Mick recalled, 'it was just down the road from the Decca studio. For a short while John McVie, Peter Green and myself were all in John Mayall's Bluesbreakers. It was Peter's birthday, so Mayall gave him some free studio time and he recorded an instrumental called 'Fleetwood Mac'. That's where the band's name came from, me and McVie. Peter flatly refused to include his name. I guess it was a precursor of times ahead.'

Here Mick was referring to one of the most admired guitarists of his day. He shared hero status with the likes of Eric Clapton and Jeff Beck, but as an introvert from the East End, Green didn't want anything to do with fame and adulation. He just wanted to be a team player and to this end recruited two other fine young guitarists, Jeremy Spencer and Danny Kirwan. 'From the start we were very lucky. Our first show was at the Windsor Jazz Festival where we attracted a large following without even having a record deal. So we never actually struggled, progressing from clubs and colleges to town halls. It was only after the release of our debut album that we put out the single 'Albatross'.'

In the winter of 1968, this shot to the top of the charts and was followed into the Top 10 by 'Man of the World', 'Oh Well' / 'The Green Manalishi' and 'Dragonfly'. 'Unfortunately, those hits led to accusations that we'd sold out,' confessed Mick, 'but our audience must have been huge because each album we put out sold really well, too.' Interested parties may wish to track down *Mr Wonderful, Then Play On* and *The Pious Bird of Good Omen*. 'But I suppose our core fans felt they were losing us,' he continued. 'With the benefit of hindsight I guess the band was undergoing a metamorphosis, especially with so many members coming and going.'

The first departure was one of the saddest in rock – that of Peter Green himself. Whether the cause was the result of drug abuse, religion, Green's personal insecurities or a combination of all three remains open to conjecture. However, some weird stories surrounding the next stage of his life have circulated ever since. One of these is that he returned to his previous occupation as a gravedigger. Another is that he tried to shoot the accountant who arrived at his home to give him a royalty cheque. Mick remains as confused as everyone else. 'Peter did start playing again a few years later. He made a solo album which did very well in Germany and other places where he toured. I saw him in 1983 when he played on a song on my solo record, but it wasn't the Peter that I knew. His life is no longer part of mine but I was very close to him and, I would like to think, vice-versa. He chooses not to be part of any rock business structure and keeps himself to himself. I'm of the opinion that if he played more it would make him feel better but you never know, he could always change his mind.'

Indeed later in the 1990s and earlier this century Green did re-emerge to join other musicians onstage every now and then, but there were too few appearances to constitute a fully-fledged comeback. Meanwhile, he had not been the only member of the original line-up to drop out while Mac was riding high. Guitarist Jeremy Spencer disappeared during an American tour to join religious sect the Children of God, while Danny Kirwan also left. Eventually they were replaced by the musicians who took Fleetwood Mac to its next level as one of the biggest bands in the world. One was Christine Perfect, later McVie, formerly the singer in Chicken Shack, another product of the 1960s blues boom. Stevie Nicks and Lindsey Buckingham also joined Mick's band and it was their songwriting skills which introduced the new line-up to a vastly increased audience.

In 1975, their eponymous album sold five million copies.

However, not even this amount of success could have prepared the band for the following year's *Rumours* which over the next few years sold 14 million LPs. 'It was so far above anybody's expectations that the only question interviewers used to ask was how much money we were making,' Mick recalled. 'At the time it was the biggest-selling record ever, including *Sgt. Pepper*. It was also ahead of Michael Jackson's *Thriller*. *Tusk*, our next album, did 6 million and that was a double.

'We were criticised at the time for being self-indulgent but we needed to do it. I wanted to record in Ghana and Stevie was, and always has been, a prolific writer which is why she has maintained a separate career as a solo artist. Lindsey is also a very intense character whose contributions allowed him to release a lot of pressure creatively. He's left and rejoined the group a few times but we're still very much together in one form or another.'

A conversation with Mick could hardly exclude his role at the Brit Awards when he was asked to co-present with Page Three girl Sam Fox, the busty blonde who measured some eighteen inches shorter than his lanky self. My boss at *The Times* described the event as 'a national disgrace'. I wondered how the drummer managed to get roped into the situation. 'Roped in?' he exclaimed. 'That's one way of putting it! I was roped in and thoroughly lashed in public. I was asked to do it and thought it would be fun, but it turned out to be hell. It was beyond our control and everything that could go wrong did – in front of millions of people. Give me making albums and going out on tour for a living any day of the week. It might get exhausting but I'd rather be doing that than clocking in at an office every morning.

'I love being in the rock business and wouldn't like to do anything else. I still consider myself to be very lucky doing a job I enjoy so much,' he concluded with typical grace.

MICK JAGGER

On their classic *Some Girls* album, the Rolling Stones performed a cover of The Temptations' song 'Just My Imagination' in which the protagonist deludes himself about winning the girl of his dreams. Of all the guys in New York, Mick Jagger fantasises she belongs to him. In contrast, it wasn't just my imagination when I saw him in the city's East Village. In fact we were both looking in the same window of Trash and Vaudeville, 'clothiers to celebrity rockers'. Our eyes met for a second and then he vanished, gone like a thief in the night.

A few days later he didn't find it so easy to escape my attention. An English band, The Selecter, were playing Hurrah's, a medium-sized nightclub near Central Park. I thought I'd give them a surprise by nipping into the soundcheck. One of the band, after introducing me to his long-lost auntie, pointed out the club's DJ. He offered me a pass to watch the gig from the vantage point of his bijou booth. Shortly before showtime some jobsworth tried to shoo me back on the dance floor to join the rest of the great unwashed. 'Can't you see what I'm dealing with here?' he whined. As it happened, the functionary had nothing to deal with. That honour belonged to someone else, this Mr Jagger who had come out for a bit of a lark with his girlfriend, Jerry Hall. They also fancied spectating from the DJ booth, giving me all the more reason to stay.

So I gave jobsworth the usual, 'I've come all the way from London, I'm with the band,' routine then swiftly turned to Mick, wondering what to ask him first. In the event, he got in the first question: what kind of music were we about to receive and had I seen The Selecter before? This being 1980, I informed him there was a ska revival going on in Britain and that I'd been on the road with them the previous autumn, along with The Specials and Madness, on what I believe I had christened the 2-Tone Tonic Tour. I thought it best to hint that I was a journalist in case a formal interview was mooted at some later date. No point blowing any future opportunity by pretending to be an ordinary civilian.

When The Selecter took the stage Mick's memory went into overdrive. 'I remember seeing bands like them in Soho in the early 1960s,' he recalled. 'There was that club Georgie Fame used to go to where everyone looked really cool at the bar. Not the Marquee... The Flamingo, that's it!' The music was too loud to continue any conversation and the club too crowded to reach the bar. This would explain why my new best gig buddy sneaked a crafty swig of my rapidly warming lager. I pretended not to notice, and he asked me who wrote most of the songs. I told him it was Neol Davies, the white guy in the band. 'That's rich!' he responded.

With Jerry Hall expressing understandable discomfort about the venue and the heat, they left before the end. I didn't mention that to singer Pauline Black in the cab on our way back to the band's hotel after the gig. However, she was well chuffed Mick was there and judging by the way he was bopping in the tiny enclosure, he had a good time too.

The following year, I actually got to go on the road with the Rolling Stones, flying out to Chicago before joining them for gigs in Cedar Falls, Iowa and Minneapolis-Saint Paul. Since none of the band were doing interviews, I hung out with opening act the Stray Cats, a useful way to gain access all areas. Young, hip and handsome, the support group were casually tuning up in their dressing room when who should bound in with his minder but Mick. Laughing and joking about Midwest audiences, he behaved like some proud older brother, advising the Stray Cats not to be afraid of the size of the stage and to 'move around a bit. I mean this is fucking Iowa,' he declared, 'they'll take anything that's thrown at them. So just give it some stick. I mean, what else have they got round here? They probably work in factories making farm machinery. I know they grow a lot of corn!'

The remarks were directed as much to me as any of the band. Jagger wouldn't have recognised me from the year before and probably thought I was the guitar tech or something. He kept chatting away, talking about American audiences, how fans his age have brought their kids to the concerts and how extra dates kept getting added to the tour. For example, the Stones ended up playing five extra shows in the New York area after there were 4 million applications for 100,000 tickets. Life on the road obviously suited Mick. He looked fitter and less haggard than the last time I'd seen him, hair shining and muscles rippling as he swanned around the dressing room, looking as much like a boxer as a rock star. Then he invited us all to the Stones' dressing room.

Situated about 200 metres from the Stray Cats' quarters were the headliners' suite of rooms. Yes sir, the Rolling Stones' backstage circus was everything it's cracked up to be. It looked like Royal Ascot: parasol-covered tables loaded with lobster, caviar and some of the smarter marques of champagne. Then there were the belly dancers and other more dubious ladies of the night. And this was just the vestibule. Ambling into the inner sanctum we encountered Keith Richards and Ronnie Wood. Both shot out of their seats with welcoming enthusiasm; Keith in fine fettle, the serried ranks of lines on his face turning into a concertina every time he laughed.

Much of the humour could be attributed to the hyperactive

antics of Ian McLagan, the former member of The Faces and Small Faces, who had been enlisted to play keyboards on this tour. Counter-pointing his faux camp merriment was the more Zen-like Charlie Watts, greying, world-weary and looking old enough to be the father of pranksters McLagan and Wood. He giggled politely when I enquired whether he was missing his Sunday lunchtime jams with jazz bands at Dingwalls in Camden. They would certainly be a lot less strenuous than the show about to take place. Highlights of the performance included Jagger alternately looming over the crowd in a cherry picker and running through the audience, leaving many fans gasping with disbelief. Thanks to being pals with Stones' head of security, Mike Callaghan, I was able to observe all this from the side of the stage.

Well, that was my first tour of duty with the Rolling Stones. Roll on summer of '82 for the sequel in England and mainland Europe. As an appetiser, a secret gig was announced for the 300-odd capacity 100 Club in Oxford Street. I duly collected a pair of tickets from a secret address. The 'dressing room' was round the corner at the Berners Hotel. Security was tight but I managed to collar Mick for a few minutes in the lobby. He gave the nod to his minder indicating preferential treatment for this cheeky young pirate. So how did the rest of the American tour go? 'Well, we were expecting to play for a million fans but ended up performing for 2.5 million, which was quite gratifying,' he grinned with understatement. I mentioned the forthcoming couple of concerts at Wembley Stadium and wondered why they hadn't booked themselves in for the week. 'We thought two was pretty ambitious,' he replied, 'nobody's ever played that many. Then there's Wales and Scotland and about five or six other stadiums dotted around the country.' With that, the entourage trotted off round the corner to the type of venue they had played twenty years earlier.

Next stop, Paris, to a hotel suite high above the Champs-Elysees. The arranged interview nearly didn't happen; in fact I was lucky not to end up on the guillotine. Let's hear the start of the story from Mick, as he waxed anecdotal about an incident the night before: 'Yeah, so we're all sitting in Maxim's (one of the most famous restaurants in the world) and we've all got suits on because it's Maxim's and this bloke in a T-shirt steams in and says, "I'm from *The Mirror*". So I says, "Congratulations, you can fuck off." Then the word got round and someone said, "No, he was from *Record Mirror*" and I thought that's odd, that's not the behaviour of someone from *Record Mirror* because they don't need to go to that trouble, y'know.'

Absolutely, Mick, except there's always an exception to the rule and we all have our own standards. Apart from which I'd been hanging around Paris for three days, wondering whether I'd ever get to do the interview. Then that afternoon, Bill Wyman came into the hotel bar and spilled the beans about some party going on at Maxim's. I had no idea it was actually an exclusive seated *soirée* for about a dozen people, including maverick film director Roman Polanski.

When interview time came around the following afternoon, Jagger fixed me with a baleful stare trying to work out if I was the gatecrasher from the night before. He couldn't decide, so he asked Jerry Hall who clearly looked fed up sitting around with an endless stream of gents from the press. 'Gee, I dunno,' she drawled indifferently, provoking some choice language from Mick. Spying a row of recent singles next to the stereo, I urgently changed the subject, asking him what he had been listening to of late. 'There aren't many new bands inspiring me this year,' he replied frankly, 'I still go out a lot but haven't got a favourite act at the moment. Last year was pretty good, so was 1977.' Aha! That explains the fine line on *Some Girls'* – 'Shattered':

'Love and sex and dreams are still surviving on the street... I've been battered!' Punk might have stolen your thunder but it was soon regained. 'Well music is inspired by whatever you hear,' he reasoned. 'Charlie will be able to tell you more about the English scene, and Bill, because they spend more time there.'

So where exactly do you live these days, I asked the man with homes in France, America and the Caribbean, to name but a few. 'Most of the time I'm in the States, but I also spend part of the year in those other places. It's not a bad life,' he smirked, sounding like Del Boy from *Only Fools and Horses*, 'but the New York winter is a bastard, so I like to spend those months around South America. I was in the middle of doing a film there with Werner Herzog, but there were delays and then the American tour started.' When filming was eventually resumed, Jagger's role was replaced by another actor but you can still see him preparing for it in *Fitzcarraldo – The Director's Cut*.

How about appearing in a Roman Polanski film? I ventured, isn't he a mate of yours? 'Well I'd like to, but he hasn't made me any offers... apart from which, as you say, he's more of a mate. I've known Roman since he first came to London during the, er, Swinging Sixties.' Did Mick miss the London of that era? Do you think there's a big difference between how it was then and what it's like now? 'Bleedin' hell, I hope there is,' he ejaculated, 'otherwise it would be moribund. But I quite like the current London club scene, Camden Palace and all that, although we're only in London for a few weeks and I need that time to get my voice in shape. Playing these big stadium gigs requires a lot of preparation.'

Were there still signs of original fans bringing their kids along? 'Yeah, it's called brainwashing,' he cracked, 'but it's also about the age of rock 'n' roll. It's been around so long now you can't expect old people not to like it as well as young. It's the same as it was with jazz. When that came out it was seen as something only young, crazy people liked.' I'd heard that during these stadium gigs, Mick ran around the stage for about ten or twelve miles, the same as the average footballer. Did this mean the more successful you got, the harder you had to train? 'Well, I don't find it harder except from the point of view that we now play a much longer show. When we were kids it would just be for about twenty minutes and it was a doddle. Even in the late 1960s, we'd only be onstage for about an hour whereas now it's about three times that. So vocally it's more difficult and there's more physical strain because the stage is bigger. Then there's the so-called days off,' he went on. 'I've got five interviews to do today and I only woke up an hour ago! Then I'll have to train later today – my usual five-mile run round the Bois de Boulogne.'

How about recording? Do you find songwriting more of a task these days? 'Not when I put my mind to it, it's all about the regularity with which we go into the studio. If we don't feel like it, we don't do it. That's the benefit of being wealthy,' he grinned, 'you no longer have that pressure of, "I need the money, I'll have to go and make a record." ' So work is no longer a major part of your life? 'Work?' he echoed incredulously, 'music is not just work. It's *play*. That's where the word comes from. You *play* music. I'm not just a journeyman musician, I still get a lot of excitement out of it all. As you can imagine, there's an incredible rush when I go onstage. Then if you've written the song as well, there's a double buzz because there's twice the amount of fulfilment.'

At this point he got up and crossed the room to the mini-bar, pulling out two bottles of beer. He gave one of them a quick shake to verify it was my beverage of choice. I didn't mention that the last time I'd seen him with a beer in his hand it had been mine. Instead I asked him about his role as a man about town, a face, an arbiter of style and all the rest of it. 'That,' he responded with a degree of resignation, 'is my own bloody fault. It was something I did in the 1960s and I now find it a bit of a bore, to be honest. It's for the kids, really, something I've grown out of. But I love watching the kids do it wherever I am and seeing it all on TV. It's one of the things which livens up your life. If you're not such a good band you can always dress up funny and maybe become a good musician later on. That,' he announced in time-honoured fashion, 'is rock 'n' roll.'

Since that interview, which I believe holds its own alongside many of the more routine ones I've read since, I've met Mick on several times. One notable occasion was when he came down to Soho's Borderline club to see a little-known alt-country band called The Red Devils. I was standing near the stage with another journalist when he came over for a quick chat. Another time, there was an aftershow at Walkabout following a Dave Stewart gig at the Shepherd's Bush Empire. It was just before the Stones' 1996 Wembley dates and he was standing near the bar on his tod – a Stone alone. I wandered over and asked him what he thought about the room we were in, particularly the high stage. Would he fancy doing a secret warm-up show here, *à la* 100 Club? Taking a few seconds to recover from this unexpected intrusion, he replied, 'It would be fun, wouldn't it?', although in the end the band chose another venue for the same purpose, the Brixton Academy.

Since then there have been more big tours, more children, grandchildren, paramours and even a knighthood. On one of the Stones' most famous album tracks, 'Street Fighting Man', Mick posed the question 'What can a poor boy do, but play in a rock 'n' roll band'. The answer remains as simple as ever – plenty.

CHAPTER 67

MICK JONES

Although we would meet whenever The Clash was on tour, I didn't really get to know Mick Jones until he moved into a flat across the road from me in Notting Hill Gate. We didn't celebrate becoming neighbours over cups of sugar or even cans of lager, it was more of a celluloid situation. One evening I noticed arc lights transforming our cul-de-sac into a mini Blackpool Illuminations. The presence of punk film-maker Don Letts suggested a movie being shot. In fact, it was a promotional video for Mick's then girlfriend Ellen Foley, described by *Record Mirror* as 'the female Bruce Springsteen'. Don would go on to direct all The Clash videos before joining Mick's next band, Big Audio Dynamite.

Being more of a private person than myself, Mick had net curtains across his bay window. This enabled him to see whether I was in residence without me being able to do the same. Sometimes he'd call me over when I was on my way to the shops and we'd head off to the mini-mart or somewhere equally banal. It was all very *EastEnders*, except we were based in what Don called 'the Wild West'.

For most of 1982, Mick was travelling the world with The Clash but I'd usually catch him between continents on account of his telltale trips to the dry-cleaners. Sometimes, I'd be summoned for a walk around the block to hear enthusiastic tales about Thailand or the number of wood-trimmed VW shooting brakes still on the road in New Zealand. Then I was forced to leave Notting Hill when I married a girl who found the

West a little too wild; but not before Mick's band enjoyed their legendary tour supporting The Who in North America. 'It was really good for us,' he told me in late 1982, the year of *Combat Rock* when its hit 'Rock the Casbah' made The Clash the most popular act on the planet. 'The Who's audience might have been different from ours, but they treated us well and we sold lots of records. I think America believes in music more than they do in this country. It's their way of life and they've got more stadiums in one state than we have in the entire country.'

The following year, Mick was sacked from The Clash for 'ideological differences' but he was soon back in the saddle with Big Audio Dynamite (BAD). This resulted in an emotional return to Notting Hill for an interview with *The Street Scene*, a new magazine I was editing. It was more involved with dance music and hip hop than rock'n' roll, which suited the theme of our conversation. 'I like the whole idea of hip hop,' he asserted, 'the fact that the scratching and the rapping belongs to the kids. You won't get people in bow ties and tuxedos trying to get involved because it's too tough for them. It's independent and not under major record company control,' Mick added, echoing the thoughts of Malcolm McLaren.

'Hip hop is a product of its environment, as is BAD. We like the concept of taking what affects us and making it our own, whether it's the way you wear a baseball hat or the way you lace up your sneakers. Personally, I prefer London to New York because whereas over there cultures are somewhat separate as in Spanish Harlem or South Bronx, in this part of town everything is mixed. People of all races and tastes bump into each other all the time and it becomes a shared experience. Everything is continually changing which helps keep you on your toes. You're only as good as your last idea, never mind your last record.'

Mick was on a roll here. The first BAD album is very dense,

lyrically, because at the time he wrote the words, he felt he had a lot to say. 'It was my chance to speak to the world,' he declared, referring to the fact that in The Clash it was Joe Strummer who wrote most of the words. 'It was like I'd climbed a mountain, rolled up my sleeves and let it all out. It was a good release and I'm looking forward to repeating the process onstage.' The first single, 'The Bottom Line', was about disentangling himself from his Clash legacy, whereas the more abstract 'Medicine Show' was an altogether weightier affair. 'It concerns the gullibility of the human condition and how people these days swallow any old rubbish, bludgeoned by the media into talking the media's language. *The Sun's* language.'

At this point, we were joined by Don Letts who had a theory of his own – the living language. 'In Jamaica, words evolve and change their meaning,' said the Rasta who had started growing his locks in 1970. 'Black people were really rocking long before the white man ever existed,' he claimed. 'There were empires and art and civilisations like Egypt and Ethiopia: you only have to look at the pyramids. Black people don't realise how great we are. I'm just fulfilling my heritage and there's plenty more to come.' Both Jones and Letts are mainly self-educated: Don received a present of a Super 8 camera 'from a posh lady' at the start of punk. 'My film school was The Roxy club,' he laughed, referring to the original punk venue where he shot much of *The Punk Rock Movie.* 'Instead of picking up an instrument, I got a camera and went off on that one.'

'He's the only Rasta in society who gets invitations to debs' balls,' added Mick. Sure enough, the next time I saw them both together was at the rock 'n' roll bash of the 2016 season, held on a private island in the Thames Estuary and sponsored by champagne house Krug. Mick was in charge of 'curating' the music – several up-and-coming artists played live, including

Hollie Cook, daughter of Sex Pistol Paul. That in itself was a pleasant reunion, Paul giving me the lowdown on mutual chums in LA such as Mick Rossi, formerly of Slaughter & the Dogs who played on the 1976 Anarchy tour. Cook also revealed how he was still in touch with former Pistols guitarist Steve Jones, who had become one of the hottest guitarists on the West Coast.

The fizz-fuelled reception was followed by a banquet cooked by Michelin-starred chef Michael O'Hare. I'm more of a liver, bacon, egg and chips man myself so I had no idea what I was eating, but it certainly soaked up the bubbly. I sat opposite Don and his wife of some decades who reminded me of Debbie Harry. Sitting next to me was Jaime Winstone, daughter of actor Ray whom I'd originally met in the 1970s when he appeared in *Quadrophenia*. Jaime almost stole the show by announcing her engagement to a certain James Suckling, a milliner of Shoreditch renown.

Mick proved to be a more than adequate host, frequently popping over to check we were enjoying ourselves. We'd all moved on since the early days of Big Audio. Mick had recently been interviewed by a top travel magazine about his taste in holidays – he said he was looking forward to spending a fortnight on the moon – and Don had a regular DJ spot on the estimable BBC 6 digital radio station. I freaked them both out by mentioning my latest wife and I were keeping chickens at our home in the countryside between Manchester and Liverpool, and that my main source of income was the rent from a buy-to-let house in Walthamstow in London's Wild East, as opposed to the Wild West.

A year later, I was invited to interview Don in front of a live audience at a black punk festival in Nottingham. 'You still livin' on a farm, man?' he growled before we commenced a roller-coaster drive down punk memory lane. I suggested to those packed in the room above the Rough Trade record shop that they were welcome to interrupt the proceedings with questions if they so desired, and the whole event was a riot of anecdotes and non-stop banter. The next day we had breakfast together at the boutique hotel where we had both been billeted. Then my daughter Grace, at twenty-four, younger than most of Don's children, walked him to the railway station in time for his next gig in Liverpool. I, in turn, drove up to Manchester to see my ninety-three-year-old mother. All in a weekend's work for rock 'n' roll people.

MICK RONSON

Nineteen seventy-two saw the release of *Transformer*, the Lou Reed album adored by future generations of punks and the link between glam-rock and new wave. It was co-produced by Mick Ronson who also performed lead guitar, piano and backing vocals. When Reed died in October 2013 sales tripled, especially digital downloads of tracks like 'Walk on the Wild Side', 'Perfect Day' and 'Satellite of Love'. Mick also played on five key David Bowie albums, including *Hunky Dory*, for which he also arranged the strings, *Ziggy Stardust* and *Aladdin Sane*. Bowie and Ronson were also infamous for their onstage double act, Bowie simulating fellatio on Ronno's guitar. 'Ziggy and Mick were the ultimate rock 'n' roll duellists,' said Bowie some years later. 'I thought we were every bit as good as Mick and Keith.'

How unfortunate, therefore, that the hugely venerated Ronson never received any royalties for his sterling services. 'I never saw a penny for that stuff,' he said when I interviewed him for *The Times* in 1990. He had just released *YUI Orta* (as in why you... I ought to...) in conjunction with Mott The Hoople's Ian Hunter, the duo having worked together intermittently since the early 1970s. Both were still extremely popular. 'Considering the number of musicians who like us, neither of us have made a fortune,' Mick went on, 'then again, if it wasn't for the people in important positions who have mentioned our names over the years, we probably wouldn't still be around.'

Here he is referring to everybody from Bob Dylan, with

whom he played on the legendary Rolling Thunder Revue tour in 1975, to Guns N' Roses, still one of the hottest metal acts in the world. It was appropriate that the first time I met Mick was in Germany when he played the Rockpalast TV show with Hunter (see Ian Hunter chapter). Soon afterwards, I went on the road with their band in America and found Ronson to be a fine fellow traveller. He spent as much time as possible with the fans and ensured there was always plenty of champagne in the tour bus fridge. There were great anecdotes about the Bowie years and his own early days in his native Yorkshire. For example, he once worked part-time as a gardener at a girls' school in Hull. One hot day he took off his shirt and practically caused a hormone-fuelled riot. The headmistress reacted with something like, 'Very funny, but don't bother coming back tomorrow'. When Ronno revealed Hunter's age (he was forty at the time, older than Dylan, McCartney or Jagger) Ian got his own back by nicknaming Mick 'The Bat out of Hull'.

The offstage highlight of the trip was the LA aftershow party at On The Rox, the private club above the Roxy theatre on Sunset Boulevard. Ever the *ingenu*, I found myself sitting on a sofa flanked by Ellen Foley, the beautiful blonde rock singer, and Bebe Buell. Apart from being a gorgeous leggy model who would later be the mother of actress Liv Tyler, Bebe was famous in rock 'n' roll circles for dating every eligible Englishman who came to town. In the early 1980s, these chaps included Elvis Costello and John Taylor of Duran Duran. Ms Buell was also chummy with Bob Geldof and my gossip column colleague Paula Yates. We were soon swapping stories, her ample bosom flirtatiously pressing against my over-excited ticker. As I was making a mental note to remember all this, who should come gliding towards us with a tray of cocktails but a beaming Mick Ronson. 'Fuck me!' I thought, 'I've arrived. Twenty-four and so much more,' to quote another hero.

The next time I saw Mick was on the streets of an equally important part of the rock 'n' roll world – Wardour Street, Soho. He had just been to see a band at the Marquee and accepted my invitation for a few liveners at the latest hip bar in town, the Soho Brasserie. I told him I'd seen him on TV the previous week with regard to a story about him going on the road with Midge Ure's new band. Mick told me he had dropped out, 'for not being able to play how I want even though I was being hired for the way I play.' The next day I reported this morsel to the *Daily Mirror* who made it the page lead in their White Hot Club gossip column. That lunchtime Mick phoned me up to offer generous thanks and to arrange another rendezvous. We started the evening at a party in Knightsbridge and gradually proceeded across town for a medicinal brandy at The Groucho Club. *En route* he started talking about this new musician he was working with and wondered if I fancied doing PR for them both.

The following morning a motorcycle courier arrived with a package containing a single, publicity shots and other paraphernalia. It was from the London office of Mainman, once David Bowie's label. A few phone calls later I was on the Mainman payroll, organising interviews with national and music press. That evening Mick came over to my house in East Finchley. For ongoing entertainment, a couple of girlfriends were put on the guest list and some fizzy stuff on ice. As we were getting the party started, a pretty blonde in a mini-skirt suddenly appeared in the drive. Mick seemed to recognise her and I thought, 'Crikey, when did he meet her, I was with him till two a.m.?' It so happened she was his sister Maggi, with whom I remain in touch to this day.

The subject of the single and press shots was Sandy Dillon, a singer, keyboard player and songwriter, who the owner of Mainman discovered performing in a musical off Broadway.

Her soulful eyes and *gamine* shape reminded me of Édith Piaf, although musically she had more in common with Suzanne Vega or a latter-day Marianne Faithful. Sandy's management had booked her a couple of gigs with a three-piece band, including Mick on guitar: one was at The Fridge in Brixton, the other at Dingwalls in Camden. To these, I added a solo show at Ronnie Scott's of Sandy playing just a baby grand piano. Gaining column inches in magazines was easier than expected; *Sounds* and *Kerrang!* stepping up to the mark. The Ad Lib column in London's *Evening Standard* also did the decent thing, ditto the city's listings publications.

One day, I took Mick and Sandy over to *Record Mirror* from where I had been fired in 1982 and against whom I'd recently won an industrial tribunal claim. No way would they allow us into the office but my old colleague Robin Smith welcomed us at reception with the immortal words, 'Mike Nicholls – a legend returns.' A story duly appeared with yours truly *in* a gossip column for once.

On another occasion, I took Mick on a press trip. Chrysalis, the label who had signed heavy rock band UFO, were running a coach to the band's studio in Surrey. It was a sly way of introducing Ronno to more journos and once we got to the studio, they couldn't get enough of him. As he was busy shaking hands and signing autographs, UFO guitarist Pete Way sat slumped in a chair feeling forlornly unloved.

Returning to London, we got chatting to the record company's head of A&R. Mick and I ended up securing a production deal for him with Kiss This, a new group featuring Karen Ware, wife of Heaven 17's Martyn. Ronno received forty grand for an album which never came out. This was lucky since the Sandy project never took off either. Everyone agreed she operated better as a solo artist, the delicacy of her songs coming across more effectively without a band. She has subsequently released a number of albums on different labels.

At the end of 1985, Mick went back to his home in Woodstock, New York state, returning a few years later to play a couple of shows at London's Dominion Theatre with Ian Hunter. Backstage, I met his mother for the first time, entering her good books by saying she looked more like an elder sister. Mick Jones of Big Audio Dynamite and his pal Tony James (ex-Gen X) also dropped by to pay tribute.

The release of *YUI Orta* at the beginning of the new decade was a mixed blessing. The executive at the major label who signed the duo had subsequently been sacked, leaving the two of them in potential limbo. It was the same man who had given Mott The Hoople the deal which brought about their eventual success. 'Record companies take the least line of resistance nowadays,' declared Hunter. 'Nobody works as hard as they used to and it's far more corporate. They don't really employ people who love music as much as those with the right connections. We didn't realise how exciting the 1970s were until we got to the back end of the 1980s, we just took it for granted.'

'We'd be better off with you at the head of a major record company,' Mick complimented me, 'but I think we've had enough of that side of it. Our strength is going out on the road where we've still got a big following. From now on, I think we'll concentrate on building up our audiences in each town by returning on successive tours, which new bands are unable to do because they can no longer count on record company support. We've got a fanatical following in major cities, such as Birmingham, Glasgow and Newcastle. Last time we played Liverpool it was chaos. There were so many fans outside the venue we couldn't get back to the coach.'

The next time I saw the guys was at a Freddie Mercury

tribute concert in April 1992. Mott had given Queen a live break by taking them out as an opening act in the early 1970s and both camps had remained friends ever since. Ian and Mick joined Bowie onstage for 'All the Young Dudes' and then Ronno played the solo of a lifetime on 'Heroes'. A year later, Mick died of liver cancer. At his memorial service in St Martin-in-the-Fields, Hunter spoke with emotion and dignity. 'Mick never made a fortune but he was rich in life,' he said. 'His thing was always about working and improving, and he was so kind to everybody. As a musician he will stand up after many stars have been forgotten.'

A quarter of a century after his death, Mick still appears high in the lists of greatest ever guitarists. He was also no slouch as a sweet-natured friend, mentor and substitute older brother either.

NEIL YOUNG

Twenty years after releasing the landmark album *After the Goldrush,* Neil Young made a tempestuous return to form. Apart from making two dazzling albums in the form of *Freedom* and *Ragged Glory,* he grabbed the attention of a new generation by inspiring grunge; those one-string, feedback-framed guitar solos from Nirvana and Pearl Jam didn't just appear out of thin air. In 1990, I finally got to interview Neil while he was rehearsing with his historic band, Crazy Horse. Some of my questions were referred to his cohorts, Messrs Sampedro, Molina and Talbot, the songwriter asking, 'What do you think of that, you guys?' with the sort of ramshackle improvisation that characterises much of his music.

Neil's commercial success began in the early 1970s with 'Heart of Gold', the worldwide hit from the *Harvest* album. That record also contains the darker 'The Needle and the Damage Done', a harrowing dedication to two of his colleagues. When Neil sings, 'I hit the city and I lost my band, I watched the needle take another man', he is referring to Danny Whitten, original guitarist in Crazy Horse, and Bruce Berry, a close friend and roadie. Both died as a result of heroin abuse which Neil agreed led to a major change in direction on the next couple of albums. '*Time Fades Away* was an angry, bitter LP,' he admitted, 'but it was a reflection of what I was going through at the time. Then the next record, *Tonight's the Night,* was like a wake for those two friends and all the others who never pulled through. It was an extreme time and the only way to get it out of my system was to go straight ahead and confront it.'

The next album of that era, *On the Beach*, sounds depressed and detached; most of the songs were inspired by the celebrity status Neil had inadvertently acquired. One track, 'Revolution Blues', is positively homicidal with Young adopting the persona of a Charles Manson character, living on the edge of Hollywood and planning to murder some of its famous residents. He was, as it happens, an acquaintance of the murderer. 'I was fascinated by his intensity and creative force,' claimed the artist. 'I usually like those kinds of people but it was an uneasy feeling being around Charles. I attributed this to the fact that he'd been in jail a lot and wasn't used to being out on the street.'

Towards the end of the 1970s, the singer was back on track with two sensational rock albums, *Zuma* and *Rust Never Sleeps*. Then came the coruscating *Live Rust* recorded at the LA Forum: I was lucky enough to catch the concert, which I reviewed for *Record Mirror* during my first-ever trip to America. This was followed by *Trans*, a strange record drenched with synthesisers and vocoders. It was only when its composer explained what it was about that I felt motivated to give it another chance.

Young's two children, by different wives, both suffer from cerebral palsy. Neil has spent a long time trying to come to terms with their disability and raising funds for a special school in California. Some of his fans, artists who felt they owed him a musical debt, contributed to a compilation album, *The Bridge*, whose profits went to the school. Acts like The Pixies and Sonic Youth each covered one of Neil's songs.

'I was very flattered by their efforts and spend quite a lot of time at the school,' he told me. 'It was painful at first and I almost became a recluse. Then I realised the best way to deal with it was to let it all out, sing about it just as I had when my friends died. The vocoders on *Trans* are me trying to communicate with my younger son Ben, who is unable to talk. He can understand what people are saying to him but can't reply, a bit like someone who has suffered a stroke. I tend to refer to the whole situation as a condition of life. It will never be easy to reconcile myself, but the more I understand and the more I am able to communicate with Ben, the less of an ordeal it is.

'I recorded *Trans* when he was two years old. I was still in shock about the way he was affected, so it was an incredibly personal record. The scene is a hospital where there are all these bionic people, half-man, half-machine. They are trying to communicate with this baby and teaching him how to communicate with them. Vocoders seemed to be a way of reaching someone who couldn't understand anything. As far as people listening to the album were concerned, the vocoders meant it was impossible to listen to the words. That was the whole point – making people aware how difficult it can be to do something which we all take for granted – communicate.'

At the time of our conversation, Neil's elder son, Zeke, was well enough to live at his family ranch near Redwood. 'There's a 48-track studio in the yard and although I don't always play with Crazy Horse, I know when I need to, which is why they are on *Ragged Glory*. Half the band had never heard the material before playing it,' Young pointed out, underlining the importance for long-term musical empathy. 'The rest of the time they do recordings of their own or go out on the road.'

Indeed, in 1995 I enjoyed meeting one of rock's most celebrated backing bands at the aftershow for their gig at the London School of Economics, which happened to coincide with my fortieth birthday celebrations. Two years later, I saw them again when they played with Neil at the Phoenix festival in the Midlands, a veritable feast of guitar-fired rock 'n' roll. Talk turned to Young's albums of the 1980s, some of which sold so badly he was almost sued by his record company for being deliberately uncommercial. One of these was *Everybody's Rockin'*. 'That was my early rock 'n' roll project,' he explained. 'I thought it would be a good idea to explore its origins, both for my own benefit as a musician as well as the people listening. Rock 'n' roll came out of Philadelphia, New York, LA and Nashville. That's not to be confused with rockabilly which has its roots in the South. But it's weird that people don't like most of the stuff I did in the 1980s although, thankfully, I don't think that includes 'Rockin' in the Free World',' he said, referring to the song from *Freedom* which became an anthem for all those involved in the liberation of Eastern Europe.

'Obviously, it was a coincidence that the Berlin Wall came down the same month as the album came out, but freedom has big problems, too. Those Eastern Bloc countries used to condemn capitalism, claiming Westerners were degenerates whose streets were alive with drugs and murderers. That is part of freedom now which is why the notion is a double-edged sword.' As double-edged as most of the Neil Young songbook, in fact, a never-ending combination of compassionate ballads and instrumental aggression.

CHAPTER 70

NILS LOFGREN

For an artist who is not quite a household name, Nils Lofgren has nevertheless enjoyed the kind of career on which rockumentaries are based. As a teenager the American made a prominent contribution to Neil Young's *After the Gold Rush* album, and since the mid-1980s he has been the regular guitarist in Bruce Springsteen's E-Street Band. In between, Nils has written enough songs to fill more than two dozen solo albums and he continues to headline gigs across the world.

I first saw Lofgren on his 1977 UK tour when he was promoting the *I Came to Dance* LP, the one whose title track boasted the unforgettable words, 'I'm not Bob Dylan but I never miss a beat, I ain't no philosopher, I dance in the street.' His special guests were Tom Petty and the Heartbreakers which, looking back, must have been one of the best double bills in rock history. Nils later recorded a couple of albums for Petty's Backstreet label but not before releasing his 1979 classic, *Nils*. I drove up to Sheffield to interview him during another popular British jaunt.

I originally remembered his unusual name (his father was Swedish) from the Gold Rush sleeve notes which seemed like a useful way to start our chat. 'When I was seventeen, I went to a Neil Young gig in Washington and sneaked backstage to give him a tape of some songs. The next year I got a call to come down to his studio to play piano. Although I'd learned to play classical and jazz music as a result of having an accordion as a child, I wasn't a professional piano player. One day when the others went out to lunch I stayed behind in the studio and experimented with the track 'Southern Man'. I ended up changing the whole song by giving it a polka beat which I believe clinched my career with Neil.' Meanwhile Nils was attracting a following of his own. He recorded a cover of Carole King's 'Goin' Back' and wrote 'Keith Don't Go (Ode to the Glimmer Twin)', a tribute to Keith Richards which was coincidentally released around the same time as the Stones' guitarist's notorious drugs bust.

As a high school student Nils had been a top gymnast, which explained his back somersaults when he appeared on BBC TV's *The Old Grey Whistle Test*. There was a discreet trampoline onstage and he suddenly performed his party piece, still playing guitar. It became a regular part of his stage act until the 1990s when its novelty value expired. 'It got to the point where I would spend the whole set worrying about the backwards flip which meant it was time to stop doing it. The trampoline is now part of the memorabilia collection at the Hard Rock Cafe in Acapulco.' This conversation took place at The Grand in Clapham in 1995 following Lofgren's double hip replacement, the result of years of flipping. Fortunately it never affected his work rate, not even when playing with Bruce Springsteen for three or four hours a night.

'On the last tour (2016-17) we played 270 different songs,' he told me the following year, 'and it's not easy to second-guess Bruce. So on top of that I used to arrive at the venue before anyone else to get in some extra rehearsal time.' Compared to this kind of routine his own tours were a walk in the park, especially as he had now bought his own tour bus. 'After fifty years on the road I'm tired of airports and since the bus has all the traditional tour comforts, I can bring Amy, my wife. She's in charge of selling the merchandise which takes place every night after a gig. We have all the new T-shirts and records on sale and fans are encouraged to bring all their own souvenirs if they want them autographed. I'll sign anything!'

Talking about records, Nils' favourite recent acquisition is a vinyl-based stereo system. 'It's great to hear a side of an album again, just like I used to do as a kid. I'm not sure if it's nostalgia or a case of never really having grown up.' The latter, I trust, not growing up remaining the prerogative of those who have relinquished adulthood for a life of rock 'n' roll.

NOEL GALLAGHER

Apart from being a prolific writer of memorable rock and pop songs, Noel Gallagher has other qualities which established Oasis as the top band of their generation: he is a very sharp listener and an enthusiastic networker, something which is not always the case with rock 'n' roll people. I discovered this when first introduced to him in the summer of 1993, long before his band became famous. He was with his old photographer friend, Paul Slattery, whose routine was to ingratiate himself with promising acts before they got big, thereby ensuring free trips around the world once the band could afford it. Sure enough, old Slatters spent most of the next two years on the road with Oasis, producing a book about their various exploits in the USA, Japan, backstage at *Top of the Pops*, trashing The Fleece in Bristol and so on.

The introduction took place at a Who party at The Half Moon, Putney, a historic pub venue on a par with, say, the Hope & Anchor in Islington. As Noel was twenty-six at the time and The Who were at their peak when he was about five, I wondered how he came to be a fan. It transpired he knew a lot about that era. 'The Beatles, The Who, Neil Young... I even listened to the Bee Gees. I always thought that Saturday Night Fever stuff was shite and then someone gave me a tape of their early hits which I thought were much better. There's so much music, so many great bands and I want to hear them all,' he went on, adding cheekily, 'You've got to check out the competition, haven't you?' Slattery then informed him that I, too, was from Manchester. I suggested that Oasis might have been named after the club in the city centre where the Rolling Stones had once played. He neither admitted nor denied the possibility but said he had heard of the venue.

I told him I had been the Northern correspondent for *Record Mirror* when punk happened and his eyes widened. 'Well you know the Sex Pistols were a big influence on Oasis,' he said. 'I always wanted us to have that same "fuck you" attitude. We plan to do what they did, make records which blow your head off. There's nothing complicated about us. It's just guitar and words, the essence of all the best records.'

It was more than a year later before I saw Noel again, by which time his band had enjoyed a couple of hits, been involved in a few lifestyle incidents and turned their hands to mayhem in old stamping grounds of my own such as the Columbia Hotel in Bayswater and the New Music Seminar in New York. More to the point, the first Oasis album *Definitely Maybe* had come out in the summer selling 150,000 copies in three days, making it the fastest-selling debut album ever in the UK. So within months of our first meeting and his remark about checking out the competition Noel had lived up to his words.

The next time I saw Gallagher was at a Polygram Christmas Party. Oasis were signed to rival major label Sony via Creation yet here was Noel sleeping, or rather drinking, with the enemy. Also present was an old associate of mine, Dave Massey, a senior executive for Sony America. Noel was prowling around, building up contacts, including people such as Dave. Like everyone else at the bash, he could have been laying into the free booze with a vengeance yet was content to sip ordinary lager, keeping a clear head to assist networking. We exchanged Manchester stories and he told me his family were from County Mayo. I told him I had family in Belfast which he credited with being a 'top place'.

During the next two years Oasis toured continually but by this stage Noel had moved to London and was a man about town. He regularly attended small gigs, accompanied by low profile minders. One night he was at The Borderline in Soho and during our conversation I asked him about Swampy, a character then in the news for disrupting the construction of an extra runway at Manchester Airport. The guitarist dismissed him as 'a middle-class twat', a fact which so impressed the *Daily Mirror* they ran a story about it.

On another occasion there was a party at Madame Jojo's, a transvestite club in Soho where songwriter Burt Bacharach was launching his latest album. Noel was there with his long-suffering PR guy, trying to arrange an introduction to the ageing legend. Having said he was a big fan of the Sex Pistols, it was no surprise to see him turn up for their London reunion show in Finsbury Park on 23 June 1996. Either he couldn't find a decent class of networker in the VIP area or he was just pleased to see me, and while I was talking to Mary McCartney, daughter of Paul and an ambitious photographer, he came over to join the conversation. This illustrious clique was then enlarged by the presence of another snapper, New York veteran Bob Gruen who had worked prolifically with Noel's heroes The Beatles. Noel was almost speechless.

The Pistols' Filthy Lucre tour marked the twentieth anniversary of the events of 1976 which included the release of *Anarchy in the UK* and the band's dismissal from EMI. What did Noel think his own band would be doing twenty years from now? 'Everyone's going to remember us for recording some great rock 'n' roll songs,' he replied, 'not some indie band responsible for making a noise.' True.

CHAPTER 72

PAUL CARRACK

Summarising the long and labyrinthine career of Paul Carrack is a complex task requiring mainly chronological analysis. In 1972, when he was twenty-one years old, Paul was involved with a band called Warm Dust. Their album, *And It Came to Pass*, had an interesting sleeve featuring the names of cultish jazz-rock musicians. As a fusion fan who was getting into the likes of Miles Davis and John McLaughlin, I felt I'd better investigate this LP and its wonderkid multi-instrumentalist Paul Carrack.

There can't be many people around now who still have this record, yet at the same time everybody knows Paul's voice if only from 'How Long', the worldwide hit he enjoyed with Ace a year or two later. Paul also sang on 'Over My Shoulder' and 'The Living Years' when he was with Genesis-offshoot Mike and the Mechanics in the 1980s and 1990s. Followers of Squeeze will recognise him as the keyboard player who replaced future TV personality Jools Holland in that particular band. In fact, Carrack contributed to their best album *East Side Story* and the highly-underrated *Some Fantastic Place*. Amidst all this activity the musician found time to play with Roxy Music, Roger Waters after he left Pink Floyd, ex-Beatle Ringo Starr and original rock god Eric Clapton. All the more surprising, then, that this plain-speaking Yorkshireman found time to invite me to his Grade II listed country house so that he could appear in the Home section of *The Sunday Times*.

Apart from being a top session musician, Paul also proved to

303

be a keen historian. The house, thirty miles from central London in the Chiltern Hills, hosted the wedding of William Penn, the Quaker whose family gave their name to the American state of Pennsylvania. The Quakers, for all you rock 'n' roll people deprived of decent history teachers, were a non-conformist religious group which rejected the priesthood and all the dogma of the established church. They followed in the tradition of the Pilgrim Fathers who fled across the Atlantic in the Mayflower to found the first New England settlements. 'There was actually a barn here built out of the remnants of the Mayflower,' said my host, showing me around the grounds. 'Those holes in the garden wall were made for musket fire during the English Civil War. By then the house would have been established as an anti-royalist, anti-Catholic stronghold and there's still a functioning Quaker meeting house in one of the local villages.'

Paul and his wife, Kathy, moved to their half-timbered pile in the mid-1980s as the size of the family increased. 'The kids needed a garden to play in and we thought it would be nice to bring them up in the countryside,' Carrack explained during the visit in 2003. 'At the time I was working in a studio close to where we are now, and I realised we could find somewhere well away from the hassle of London yet close enough for anything connected with work. The local schools proved a winner and through the kids we've made a lot of friends.' Things almost went pear-shaped when the sale of the house they were selling in London fell through. 'I was supposed to be going on tour with Roger Waters and we'd already paid for this place. There was only one solution – Roger had to give me a bridging loan and he charged for it. A couple of per cent over base rate!'

Paul has clearly invested almost as much time into his property as he has into his work. When not touring he's busy at home overseeing the building of extra rooms, including a recording studio. Grade II projects come with their own set of problems. 'We weren't allowed to point and plaster in case we couldn't get a matching finish,' he admitted through gritted teeth. 'Instead we had to source a variety of old bricks with English Heritage and the local planning committee decided which types we could use. The same applied to the roof tiles and the joinery. They eventually decided we had to have oak window frames.' More issues followed. 'English Heritage then inspected the ground to check there was no buried treasure of historical importance, charging us thousands to tell us there was nothing there.'

The cost of the renovations came to half of the original price of the house but since then the value of the property had almost tripled. 'When Kathy and I started going out in the early 1970s, we had a bedsit in a house in Camden which we had to share with four steelworkers,' he recalled with some amazement, 'which only goes to show that at the end of the day whatever problems you have, everything is relative.

Or, one might say, the blues had a baby, they called it rock 'n' roll. When rock 'n' roll had a baby they called it... property development.

PAUL McCARTNEY

Talk about an offer you can't refuse. I had only been on the staff of *Record Mirror* for a few months when I was invited to go up to Liverpool to catch Paul McCartney on the first night of Wings' tour in November 1979. Not only that, but there was an opportunity to interview the self-styled 'cute one' in The Beatles too. I'd been a fan since the age of eight when I bought *With The Beatles*, scraping together pocket money, birthday money, car-cleaning money and any other money. So, basically, this offer was definitely... on the money.

Taking no chances, I drove up to Manchester on the weekend, pausing only to drop into my local pub to alert everybody as to what I was doing there. The gig was on the Sunday at the Royal Court Theatre, scene of the young McCartney's school-age speech days. It was a fair old show cramming in Fab Four favourites and better-known material from his solo and Wings albums. The encore was a mighty 'Mull of Kintyre' which developed into a raucous sing-along. It was like a Friday night pub session except with 1,500-odd people joining in, apparently standard practice in Merseyside. The interview afterwards was officially a press conference but there were only six of us present. The other journos were tongue-tied so I got to ask all the questions and ended up with enough copy for a full-page feature. I decided to carry on like this for the next forty years.

Sitting with Paul on the other side of a table were the rest of Wings, including his wife Linda. Paul was as relaxed as he had been on stage, good-humoured and happily cracking the odd joke. Linda made frequent interjections and although sometimes annoying, they also had the advantage of allowing Macca to raise the level of banter. As with Mick Jagger earlier in this book, when you've been a fan for most of your life, hoping to meet that person, where are you supposed to start? Well, there hadn't been time for a bevvy, so it was left to the adrenalin to kick in.

'How come you are suddenly speaking to the press again,' I blurted out. 'Well, it's alright, you know,' Paul replied. 'When you're working you get quite into the swing of things. It's when you're not, that you don't bother. If you're confident, you don't mind talking to people. When you feel bad about what you're doing and people start pulling it apart, that's where it all goes wrong because you might secretly agree with them.'

By 'working', McCartney really meant playing. This was Wings' first tour for three years and their debut with the current line-up. In addition to the McCartneys and Denny Laine, this included new boys Steve Holley (drums) and Laurence Juber (guitar). How were they recruited? Linda: 'The army!' Paul: 'Actually, these two are Denny's fault. He lives near Steve.' Steve: 'I was doing a TV show with David Essex and Denny was one of the guests.' Denny: 'And he just hounded me!'

Are the new guys going to be able to contribute to the next album?

'Depends what they come up with, really,' Paul replied. 'Anyone with anything good can contribute as much as they like. Unless they come up with a whole album which is out of the question!'

Will the material be written in the studio or are most of the songs prepared beforehand?

'Again, it depends,' said the Mac, 'Some of it is written in advance and other stuff just comes up on the day. You can't say when you write; it just comes if you're lucky or depending on what mood you are in. We usually book a studio, I've got a few songs, Denny's got a couple and we just run through them all and see which ones we feel like playing that day,' he continued, giving some insight into the rock 'n' roll song-writing process. Linda: 'I've got this one in my pocket, Paul.' Paul: 'And Linda's got a few which I always reject.' 'Absolutely,' his wife replied, the chatter proceeding apace.

Do you and Denny actually write the songs together, or does one do the lyrics and the other does the tune?
'Well, 'Mull of Kintyre' – our biggest seller – was jointly written. Denny wrote the words.' 'And he had the tune. He needed me, but he won't own up to it,' claimed Laine. 'It's true,' agreed Paul. 'I hadn't finished it and one good thing about writing with someone is that if you are stuck for an idea, or you have got a couple of gaps, the other person can fill them in. I had the chorus and we didn't have any verses, so we just sat down in a field in Scotland that day, got our guitars out with a bit of paper and a pen, started mapping it out and just kind of did it.' 'You get inspired by your environment,' Denny added. Paul: 'Talking of which, I love the UK. We've travelled a lot between us and wouldn't want to live anywhere else. I don't like LA because of the earthquakes and in Nashville there are always tornado warnings on the telly. Of course, when you get back to England, it might be pissing rain all the time but the people are great. You can walk up to some copper and ask him the way to somewhere and he doesn't hit you.'

No, but these days they probably wouldn't know the way either, even if you could find one.
'I think there's more sense of humour.'

Some of my bessies describe me as 'an honorary Liverpudlian' and, speaking as one, I can only concur that this is certainly the case in Liverpool. They're a cheeky bunch, too.

So, did you feel nervous tonight in front of the home crowd?
'No, less nervous and I enjoyed it more. Last night was a preview for my old school so I thought tonight was a genuine audience from the point of view that there were people who queued and paid for tickets. So, it felt nice, yeah. I enjoyed the general informality of playing in a small theatre and chatting to the audience. One of the reasons we played here is because they're closing down these kinds of places and turning them into bingo halls as they make more money. This fellow from the Royal Court wrote a letter and said this might happen, informing me that Ken Dodd was doing pantomime to try and save it. So, we said we'd play this place instead of the much bigger Liverpool Empire. It's a shame we can't play these size places every night, but you have to be realistic. Unless you play somewhere like Wembley as well, it's like doing a job and not getting paid for it. I can't really say to the band, "Sorry chaps, I've given all your money to charity.". It wouldn't feel the same,' he smiled, as the band laughed nervously.

In terms of personal satisfaction, does what you've done as a solo artist compare to what you achieved in The Beatles?
'The thing is, obviously, after a group like The Beatles breaks up, you think, "How are you ever gonna follow that?", 'cos they did pretty well, you know. Surprisingly enough, I never thought we'd be anywhere as near as good or I'd derive anything like the same amount of pleasure. But it's every bit as good now. I mean, you're either going to give up, rest on your laurels and say, "Okay, I did all that, thank you and good night," or you actually like doing it.'

*Was that a veiled criticism of the other Beatles who haven't
been as productive in the last few years?*
'I don't know really; I can't speak for them. They haven't done
that little, actually, because John has had some good solo albums
and so has George. Ringo's first was good, too, though he
hasn't done much since. They're neither writing as much nor as
obviously up front as we are, but I can't knock them. They're
doing what they want to do and it's not for me to be saying that
they should be doing something else.'

*Absolutely. Last question on this occasion – any unfulfilled
ambitions?*
'Not specifically. I mean we've travelled everywhere and done
almost everything we want... To tell you the truth, my ambition
is just the same as it always has been, to play better music. Each
time you make an album you want to make a better one than
last time. That's what keeps you going – and the simple fact of
enjoying playing together. That's the secret.'

Of course, what Paul hadn't taken into account was, in his
own words, the long and winding road. As he continued working
throughout the 1980s, quality control slipped into a downward
spiral reaching a nadir with his solo album, *Off the Ground*. It
was launched at a press conference at London Docklands Arena
on 5 February 1993 and a sorry affair it was, too. Some of the
songs were the first new ones he'd written for years, including
a couple with Elvis Costello. Moreover, the album was co-
produced by Julian Mendelsohn who had provided sterling
service for the Pet Shop Boys on classic cuts, like 'It's a Sin',
'Rent' and 'Always on My Mind'. But all to no avail.
    At the press conference, most of the journos seemed
embarrassed, never mind tongue-tied. I asked Macca if he, as

Picture by Linda McCartney.

PAUL McCARTNEY
RETURNS TO LIVERPOOL.
1979.

Linda McCartney
& Ross Young's
invite

Mr. Mike Nicholls

to attend a Press Conference in the
Abraham Lincoln Room,
The Savoy Hotel, The Strand WC2
on Tuesday, 30th April 1991
at 11.30 am for 12.00 noon

R.S.V.P.
Liz Cardrew Tim Shaw
Tel: 071 887 1475

Please enter via the
River Entrance

WITH THE
SENSATIONALLY
TACTILE RONNIE
SPECTOR, 1991.

ABOUT THE
YOUNG IDEA
THE STORY OF THE JAM 1972-1982

MIKE NICHOLLS

THE BOOK THAT
INSPIRED THE NAME
OF THE EXHIBITION!

STALKING ROGER DALTREY AT THE WHO'S END-OF-TOUR PARTY. THE TROCADERO CENTRE, LONDON, 1988.

Pictures by Richard Young.

MIDEM '90
PRESS
MIKE NICHOLLS
THE TIMES/HELLO MAGAZINE
U.K.

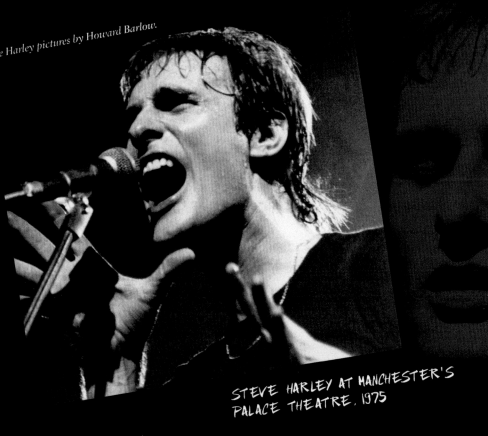

...e Harley pictures by Howard Barlow.

STEVE HARLEY AT MANCHESTER'S PALACE THEATRE, 1975

Picture by Andy Phillips.

WITH STEWART COPELAND AT RECORD MIRROR EDITORIAL MEETING, 1980.

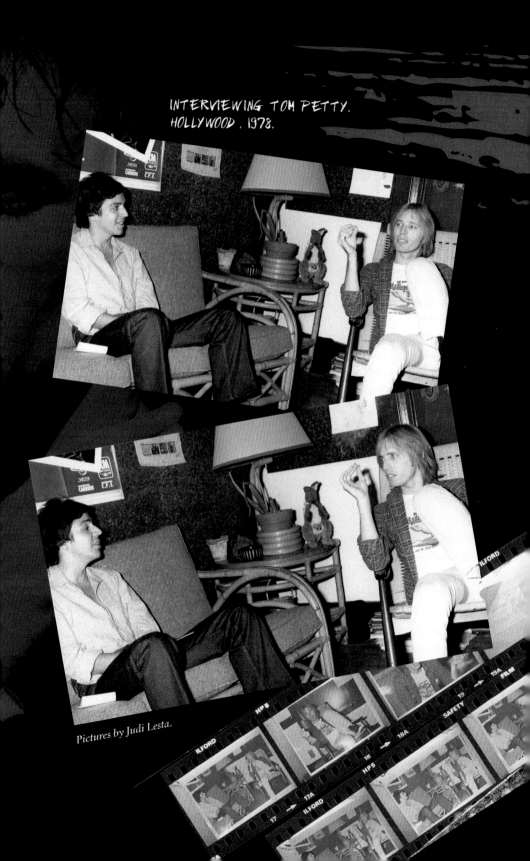

INTERVIEWING TOM PETTY.
HOLLYWOOD, 1978.

Pictures by Judi Lesta.

TOM VERLAINE.
MANCHESTER FREE
TRADE HALL, 1977.

Picture by Howard Barlow.

THE CITY

NAME

Mike
Nicholls
BBC Online

COMPANY

Pictures by Andy Earle.

Picture by Royston.

HOMAGE TO
LOU REED'S STREET
HASSLE. IBIZA, 1987.

Picture by Howard Barlow.

WILLY DeVILLE. MIDDLETON TOWN HALL. 1977.

Picture by Nick Ballantine.

SOHO, 1986.

a celebrity, felt he had been sidelined by Linda who had recently gone stratospheric with her own extra-curricular activities. The previous Christmas she had upstaged her husband in the seasonal TV stakes with a Boxing Day screening of *Behind the Lens*, a prestigious *Arena* documentary about her photographic career. After years of speculation we actually got to see her portraits of everyone, from Jimi Hendrix and Otis Redding to the Stones and, something of a surprise here, The Beatles. The year before that, in 1991, the missus had enjoyed an even higher profile when, in conjunction with frozen food company, Ross Young, she launched a range of dehydrated, textured vegetarian products, which included such dainty dishes as Golden Nuggets and Italian Toppers. At the 1991 press conference, held at the Savoy, I caused something of a furore by asking Linda when I could bring round a *Hello!* photographer *chez* McCartney (any of their homes would do) to create the usual mayhem in her kitchen. The answer was not in the affirmative but my question certainly broke the ice.

Following the presentation, I saw a bunch of Fleet Street hacks buzzing around a younger brunette. Since I knew all the others, I asked her if she was from the *Daily Star*. In actual fact, she owned up to being a member of the 'Family Firm'. Her name? Mary, the twenty-year-old daughter of Paul and Linda, originally seen as a baby on the cover of the first McCartney solo album. As we chatted, it became clear that, like her mother, she wanted to be a photographer. In fact, a few years earlier she'd undertaken work experience with a leading book publishing company who shared offices with Shinko music, owner of *Music Life* Magazine, whom I worked for around this time.

Two months later, on 20 June 1991, Linda invited me to a party at the Hard Rock Café for the launch of her veggie burgers. Obviously, Paul and Mary McCartney were present, so was an eclectic crowd of other famous people. I shared a table with Victor Spinetti, Mary Hopkin and Jim Capaldi. Victor, with his incomparable Welsh lilt, was hilarious company as you would expect from an actor who not only appeared in The Beatles' films, *A Hard Day's Night* and *Help!*, but also co-wrote *In His Own Write* with John Lennon, the play adapted from Lennon's book of the same name. According to Spinetti, the play was written one winter in John's flat overlooking the Thames. Loathing the cold damp weather, Lennon suggested they go somewhere warm. 'I thought he meant into the room next door,' cracked Spinetti. 'The next day we set off for Morocco!'

Mary Hopkin, another Welsh person, remains most famous for 'Those Were the Days', her No.1 single produced by McCartney for The Beatles' Apple label. When I first met Mary, she lived by herself in a small house in the home counties following her divorce from David Bowie's producer, Tony Visconti. She was promoting an album called *Spirit* and was obviously rather lonely. I was reporting for *Hello!* magazine, so she showed me around her home and then insisted on paying for lunch in the local pub. We parted company after a couple of hours, but not before an affectionate exchange. She asked me to come back anytime. I would have taken her up on the offer but I already had enough on my plate, what with the *Hello!* column and being editor of *For the Record*. There was also the small matter of having two birds on the go, one of who was living in my house in East Finchley. By the time of Linda's veggie party a year or two later, I was officially single and would have quite cheerfully gone out with Mary Hopkin but... timing, eh?

I'd already known Jim Capaldi, the excellent drummer and songwriter in Traffic, since 1983. At the time, I was writing for *Sound Maker*, a Northern & Shell weekly newspaper. Jim had just released a solo album entitled *Fierce Heart* and rather than going through the motions of just another let's-promote-the-album-scenario, I had a more agreeable wheeze. Why not get this proper musician to review singles? His record company pledged an empty office and a serviceable stereo so we spent a lively hour or two exchanging scathing words about most of the rubbish before us. Jim's single of the week by some measure was Paul Young's brooding take on Marvin Gaye's 'Wherever I Lay My Hat (That's My Home)'. Despite having cemented his reputation in the Q-Tips, this was early in Young's solo career, so it was an astute choice by Capaldi. When we met at the Hard Rock, he remembered our first date, so we mooted the possibility of an at-home feature for *Hello!* The only problem was he was mainly living in Brazil at the time and nobody seemed too enthusiastic about paying the plane fair.

Earlier this century, I was out with PR Judy Totton of John Cooper Clarke fame when she mentioned that Jim had bought a monastery somewhere in Sussex. Could I secure an article for the Home section of *The Sunday Times*. After the usual hurdle of trying to negotiate with commissioning editors who didn't really know what they were talking about, I finally got the go-ahead. Then, sadly, Jim died in early 2005, only a few months after his sixtieth birthday. Almost as catastrophic is the fact that he remains best-known for his chart-topping cover of The Everly Brothers 'Love Hurts'. Yes, for a drummer he did have a great voice, but let's not forget he also performed with stars such as Jimi Hendrix, Eric Clapton and George Harrison.

Considering it was primarily a burger joint, vegetarian Mary McCartney seemed to spend a lot of time at the Hard Rock Café. Another occasion was the aftershow party at something called The Third Annual International Rock Awards at London Arena, eighteen months before the fraught *Off the Ground* affair. The event was positively barking, with artists like Ben E. King, The

Doobie Brothers and ZZ Top emerging out of the woodwork to receive awards for reasons largely unexplained. What I remember most vividly was not being able to watch the awards but being trapped in a press pen with some of Fleet Street's finest and being obliged to interview these acts as they came off stage. The upside was sweet revenge. We also got humongously drunk and asked questions which betrayed an inexcusable lack of manners. I confronted one of the Doobies with a request for forgiveness for not having brought my mother, who belonged closer to his age group than mine. He responded with something equally rude about my grandmother. And you should have seen the look on poor Ben E. King's face when yours truly opined that although he might be well known for the song 'Stand by Me', it didn't hold a candle to John Lennon's searing rendition on his *Rock 'n' Roll* album.

A future *Daily Mirror* editor, actually wearing a grubby raincoat, got so smashed he was incapable of speech. Meanwhile Rick Sky, another denizen of the tabloids, was also there and he and I resumed our occasional series of double-acts. When squeaky clean Swedish duo, Roxette, minced onto the platform in front of us, we started firing questions at them about how they sorted out their laundry on tour. Did they trust the hotel to have it ready by the following day's check-out time? Or did they take the independent route of finding a local laundrette? What was their choice of detergent? Washing powder or those ludicrous plastic balls you put the liquid stuff in? And on and on.

A casual glance at the invitation indicated that one of the sponsors of the event was the Hard Rock Café Foundation and you'll never guess the location of the aftershow; right on the other side of town from London's Docklands, at the Hard Rock near Hyde Park. I gave a lift to a mate from the Style section of *The Sunday Times* and her photographer. We'd all been drinking, we needed food and started jabbering on about our blood sugar levels – that was pretty *avant-garde* in 1991. The three of us were crammed into Spitfire Two, a reprise of that evening with the Clash fans, except this was mid-summer, a bright evening and even more provocative in terms of attracting the attention of the Old Bill. As we were getting parked up near the Hard Rock, I inadvertently nicked the space earmarked by Mary McCartney. She cursed me with relish, which was rather rude for someone fourteen years my junior, I thought.

After consuming just enough veggie burger to reset my blood sugar levels, it was time to contemplate dancing. Now being a shy kind of guy, it wasn't really in my nature to ask a girl to dance. What would happen if she said, 'No'? And you thought today's kids were a bunch of snowflakes. In the event, I felt someone take me by the hand and haul me onto the dancefloor, right into the centre, no less. Yes, Ms McCartney had clearly forgiven me and all was well with the world. Then again, the DJ was spinning 'Blue Suede Shoes' by Carl Perkins, who'd always been one of Mr McCartney's premier faves, so I suppose any old partner would do. Bo Diddley was there, too. Not to mention, Michael Ontkean, the actor who played the sheriff in *Twin Peaks*. Isn't it remarkable who turns up at these dos?

The last time I saw Mary was at an Annie Leibovitz photographic retrospective at Dave Stewart's Hospital complex in Covent Garden, in February 2004. She was with her husband at that time, Alistair, who seemed a nice enough guy. At least he seemed amused when I told him about my Liverpool connections, and how I had relatives on the council in the 1970s who voted against all the terrace housing being demolished. 'So, you're the one to blame,' he exclaimed with polite irrelevance. Six months later, I met wife No. 2. Sorry Mary.

Unless suffering from congenital dementia, you may remember that about halfway into this chapter Paul McCartney reckoned Ringo hadn't done much of late. Well, more than a decade later, it appeared the feeling was mutual. In 1992, Mr Starr released an album *Time Takes Time* featuring a stellar (get it?) cast of musicians and producers. Take a bow, Jeff Lynne, Peter Asher and Don Was. Mr Lynne needs no introduction but, back in the 1960s, Asher was half of Peter and Gordon. Their hit, 'A World Without Love', fought a bitter chart battle with The Beatles' 'Can't Buy Me Love'. Macca wrote both songs... clever, these Scousers. It didn't do any harm that, at the time, Paul was going out with Peter's sister Jane. This should give you some understanding of the term Swinging Sixties.

Asher went on to sign James Taylor to The Beatles' Apple label, where Taylor recorded his debut album which included the haunting 'Carolina in My Mind', his best-ever song in a brilliant if roller-coaster career. Then Asher went to LA and became one of the biggest moguls in the history of the record industry. Don Was exploded onto the scene with the duo Was (Not Was) whose single 'Out Come the Freaks' was one of the most original and fascinating dance classics of the early 1980s. Don went on to produce the B-52's 'Love Shack' and albums for Bob Dylan, Iggy Pop and Glenn Frey of the Eagles. Another Eagle, Joe Walsh, came on board for the tour which supported *Time Takes Time*, as did fellow established virtuosos like Todd Rundgren, Dave Edmunds and Nils Lofgren. Yet conspicuous by their absence were former Beatles McCartney and George Harrison, despite the fact George's Traveling Wilburys, Tom Petty and Jeff Lynne, were both involved with the album.

I managed to pull off a short but not terribly sweet interview with Ringo. 'How come there's no sign of the old muckers who made you fab?', I demanded. 'I didn't ask them,' he retorted. 'Paul half-wrote a song which didn't pass quality control and, no, there will never be a Beatles reunion. Every time Paul goes on tour, a rumour goes around that I've always said, "No". Actually, it's time people stopped talking about a come-back,' he went on. 'After all, we haven't existed for more than twenty-two years, which is three times as long as we were together.' Very succinct. But then the drummer-turned singer always tended towards the laconic. When The Beatles were first asked how they found America, it was Ringo, who was brought up in The Dingle – one of the toughest parts of Liverpool – who cracked, 'Turn left at Greenland!'.

He could also be a bit of a grumpy individual as I discovered when meeting him at the Marquee, towards the end of the previous year. He was there to see his son Zak drum with The Icicle Works, another bunch of Merseysiders from, it has to be said, Mossley Hill, one of the posher suburbs. Ringo's sharpness might have something to do with the fact that he'd recently given up the demon hooch, although he claimed to be happy enough. 'The All-Starr Band have been touring on and off for about three years now and although there was a bit of stage fright at first, that's not a bad thing. It means I always have to run on stage, you'll never catch me strolling. But within a few moments the panic is over and suddenly all I'm aware of is that love coming across from the audience. It's addictive, which is why I'm still doing it.'

At the time, home for Ringo was Monte Carlo. 'Of course, there are tax advantages, but do you know a more beautiful coastline than the Côte d'Azur?' No, which is why I went to buy a place in the area. You can still buy decent wine, forage wild strawberries and find the kind of luscious pears you forgot existed. But fast-forward to this thing called Brexit and for the Brits, it's more a case of things going pear-shaped. Rather like some of the post-Beatles' musical legacy.

CHAPTER 74

PAUL WELLER, BRUCE FOXTON & RICK BUCKLER

Apart from a brief introduction at the Mont de Marsan punk festival, the first time I spoke to Paul Weller was when the single 'Strange Town' was released in the spring of 1979. He was accompanied by fellow Jam members Bruce Foxton and Rick Buckler for a lengthy *Record Mirror* interview at their record company's HQ in central London. In the previous twelve months The Jam's fortunes had changed dramatically. Following a disappointing second album, their third, *All Mod Cons*, boasted some of their best songs to date, including 'Down in the Tube Station at Midnight' and their infectious cover of the long-forgotten Kinks song, 'David Watts'. This set the scene for 'Strange Town' finding its way half way up the Top 40 within a week of release. The Jam were no longer one of the first generation of punk acts but a successful outfit in their own right. I asked them what the new single was about and whether they still considered themselves a mod band. Weller, still only twenty years old yet a prolific songwriter, chose his words carefully but seemed happy enough to answer these and other questions. At least as happy as could be expected from such an infamously moody fellow.

'The basis of the song is the ideals and principles everyone had in 1976 and how so few of them have followed through. Now it's back to the old 'group and fans' type of situation. Everyone's scared about becoming inaccessible when, really, it's not so much about a physical inaccessibility but a mental one. There's no way we're going to live the same lives as the kids who come to see us,' he elaborated, 'but we can live similar lives and still stay in touch. We don't float around clubs with Mick Ronson or the rest of the cats you're supposed to hang out with,' he practically spat out, a pointed reference to Mick Jones of The Clash. Let us not forget that The Jam had not only pulled out of playing Mont de Marsan with this band but failed to finish supporting them on the White Riot tour in 1977.

As for that mod image, so different from the early looks of the Sex Pistols and The Clash, 'I think it has been a bit blown-up, really,' claimed Paul, notwithstanding the Union Jack backdrops, sharp suits and other artefacts of that age, 'it's just a sort of look we got into, specifically myself, a few years ago. When I first heard 'My Generation' by The Who I thought, "What's all this about?" It may be nostalgia for some but for me it was a total innovation, guitars slashing through the mix and that whole wild production. It still reeks of youth or, in the words of our first single, 'In the City', about the young ideas. Mod seemed to be the last youth movement which promised a good time. Although I had a scooter and made trips to the coast with other guys, it wasn't a case of jumping on bandwagons. Obviously, I was too young to remember the early 1960s.'

Bruce Foxton, aged twenty-three at the time, agreed. 'We found we liked playing this kind of music and we certainly liked the manner of dress so the whole thing grew from there. We didn't just say, "This is a good image", it developed naturally. Image goes hand-in-hand with music and having got into songs like 'In the Midnight Hour' and 'Sweet Soul Music' (both staples of early Jam gigs) and the clothes, it seemed logical to be in a mod band.' 'But,' added the ever-changing Weller, 'I don't think it's fair to say we're still a mod band, we're much more than that.'

Talk turned to Jam tracks and Paul's songwriting. I suggested that the subjects of their songs fell into definable categories like violence (''A'-Bomb in Wardour Street'), the need to escape ('In the Crowd') and righteous anger ('Mr. Clean').

'I'm not too keen on categorising songs as simply as that,' he replied, 'but if you must use headings then the one I like best is emotional music. 'In the Crowd' is about the love/hate relationship with people in general, while 'A'-Bomb is about The Vortex club which was heavy. Not in terms of physical fighting but people's attitudes.' You mean like all the back-biting? 'Great fucking chunks of flesh being bitten out of your back, more like!' As with many an artist, Weller preferred to express these emotions through his work rather than indulge in actual violence. I'm thinking of the way he smashed up his guitar onstage at the previous year's Reading Festival. 'There was no sort of showbiz stigma attached to doing that,' he replied, once again defending himself, 'it was just one of those unfortunate incidents when things got too much. But I'd sooner do that than go out and bash someone. I learned early on in life that instead of setting fire to a police station I could let off steam as a musician.'

In those days, nine months was a long time in rock 'n' roll and by November The Jam had released their fourth, and best, album *Setting Sons*. By this time I had joined the staff of *Record Mirror* and been promoted to Reviews Editor. This meant I was able give myself this album to review, which I did with style. Awarding it the maximum five stars, yours truly speculated it would be regarded as 'the last great LP of the 1970s'. My reward, as it were, was to be invited on the road with the band the following month.

There was a right old gang of us billeted at Manchester's Piccadilly Plaza Hotel, including record company personnel, music journos, radio folk, some of Paul's street-poet mates and so on. Having to share Weller with this crew meant being able to spend more time with his father and manager, John Weller, and Bruce and Rick, the other members of the trio. Their relationship with Paul dated back to schooldays at Sheerwater Secondary Modern near Guildford in Surrey. As well as being a drummer of some dexterity Rick Buckler proved to be something of a fashion aficionado. In the subsequent report, the following week's cover story, he talked in detail about how he customised his own jackets, and clothes in general. 'We're living in the 1970s and people are discovering new ways of combining the past with the present. Twenty years ago if you didn't dress a certain way you weren't hip. These days you can walk down the street and see fashion from all eras. I don't think rules apply anymore.'

A trickier subject was a veritable elephant in the hotel lobby – The Jam and the USA. Following poor sales of their second album, *This is the Modern World*, which was released too soon after their *In The City* debut in 1977, the band decided to lay low and undertake a promotional tour of America. It involved playing small clubs in Boston, LA and New York. San Francisco was abandoned as a result of sound problems. The trip also meant engaging with a less than sympathetic record industry and media.

On being tapped for further and particular details, all Bruce could do was roll his eyes while Rick recalled a couple of sad anecdotes. 'There was this guy, a right brickhead DJ, who didn't have a clue what was going on. All he kept saying was "punk" as in "the weather is really punk here in this punk city in punkland" which didn't make sense since the Americans seemed more into music than image. Then at a press conference in New York the only things the journalists asked about were spitting and safety pins while we sat there in our suits and ties.' Bruce at least enjoyed the show at the city's new wave mecca, CBGBs, mainly because other artists came over to check them out. 'Mind you, even that was a disaster. Patti Smith waltzed into our dressing room expecting to be greeted like royalty and then walked right out. Dee Dee and Joey of The Ramones also dropped into see us along with some of Blondie. They all seemed well out of their heads.'

In March 1978, The Jam had another attempt at the States, which went on longer and proved even worse. Deciding it would take an entire career to crack it in the clubs, John Weller went to the other extreme and secured the band gigs in 20,000-seater auditoriums supporting heavy metal bands like Angel and Blue Öyster Cult. From Bridgeport, Connecticut, where the tour kicked off in a blizzard and the trio weren't even billed, the word travesty springs to mind. 'The boys were really pissed off about it,' confessed John, 'but we needed to do it otherwise we would have been completely unknown over there. Yet playing to 23,000 jeering kids in Chicago wasn't the answer. A lot of it was due to my inexperience,' added the former boxing promoter who had also worked in the building trade. The last word about America goes to Rick: 'Over there the record companies sell their bands like soap powders. In this country the clubs are a lot smaller so that when a band starts off fans identify and grow up with it. Plus, in order to break the States, you have to tour endlessly. We're not prepared to do that when we've got such a loyal audience at home.'

Indeed, the two nights at the Manchester Apollo rocked and there was some fine networking in between. I arrived the day before the first show and, with it being my old patch, I recommended we go to The Millionaire Club, owned by Peter Stringfellow who later moved to London himself. Like his eponymous joint in Covent Garden, The Millionaire was essentially a glittery disco with restaurant attached. I took the boys mainly for amusement value, to give them a glimpse of the Mancunian *nouveau riche* in all their finery. With his customary style and generosity, Stringfellow insisted we stay for a champagne supper. Bruce and Rick tucked into steaks the size of skateboards whilst Paul opted for a seafood pie loaded with lobster. The following night's post-gig bash saw the tour bus pitch up at The Sandpiper, a rock 'n' roll club on the edge of the city, near where I went to school. Amongst the revellers was actor Ray Winstone, one of the stars of *Quadrophenia*, the popular mod movie which had come out earlier that year.

During the course of the following decade The Jam's career continued to advance, the single 'Going Underground' entering the charts at No. 1, a feat unequalled since the heady days of Beatlemania. Two more quality albums followed and the band earned a lot of money playing some big European festivals. Then suddenly Weller announced he was splitting up the band. 'It's best to quit while you're on top,' Paul later explained, 'we've really achieved a lot in six years and the idea of going on for another ten terrified me. I can understand if Rick and Bruce are pissed off.' I should coco. Having written almost all the songs, Weller was the one earning the royalties. The others felt they had been left in the lurch although there was a wildly successful UK tour to follow.

Afterwards, Paul formed The Style Council before continuing with a creatively mixed solo career. Rick went into business as a French polisher and Bruce eventually joined Irish punk band Stiff Little Fingers. In 1997, both Bruce and Rick turned up to Soho's Wag Club to celebrate the twentieth anniversary of *In the City*, and both thanked me for their inclusion in *About the Young Idea*, my Jam biography which was published the year after they split up.

For me, the new millennium was accompanied by a lightbulb

moment – writing about rock stars and their properties for the Home section of *The Sunday Times*. I hit the ground running with a cover story about Spandau Ballet's Steve Norman and his home in Ibiza. On meeting Bruce at some London gig I wondered if he fancied following suit. The following week he called me up to suggest featuring his cottage on the southern coast of Cornwall. It's worth acknowledging that during the previous twenty years Bruce and his wife Pat had shown themselves to be astute players of the property market. They bought their first home in Surrey for sixty grand, gradually moving upmarket to Wonersh Park on the south side of Guildford. They sold this for £800,000 in the year 2000, prior to buying a house with 'more potential for considerably less.'

'We've had fifteen months of building hell but it was well worth it,' Bruce told me. 'Apart from having five bedrooms and a walk-in wardrobe, it is just across the road from our previous house and the neighbours are great. We hardly needed a removal van, we were even able to move the jukebox on a trolley.' I should point out that this jukebox was the star prize in the raffle at *Record Mirror*'s 25th Anniversary party – the one Kate Bush was unable to attend.

Our conversation took place in the summer of 2003 when I was invited to visit Haven Cottage in Polperro, a picture-postcard fishing village built around the harbour. It was once part of a pilchard-canning factory which the Foxtons discovered in 1987, on the way back from celebrating their third wedding anniversary in St Ives. They paid £40,000 for the cottage which had already been converted into a two-bedroom home arranged over three floors. 'It didn't need any structural work, just new kitchen units,' Bruce enthused. 'Seventeenth century cottages weren't designed for fridge-freezers. The work cost about £2,500 with another £1,500 to find and fit the lounge fireplace with its

Victorian tiles and nice surround. It was definitely worth it, you can't beat an open fire when there's a gale blowing.' Nevertheless, the couple found they were not using it as often as planned; the 500-mile round trip too long for weekend jaunts, not to mention the increase in heavy traffic. 'So within a year it became a rental operation,' he continued, 'which was necessary in order to keep it in good condition.' Then tragedy struck when Bruce's father died. 'Every year he used to come down here on his birthday but last year he passed away just before we were about to leave. We now associate the place with his death so have decided to draw a line under the great times we had here and sell up.'

Which indeed they did, putting it on the market for £225,000. *The Sunday Times* article entitled 'Living: Anarchy on Sea – Bruce Foxton swapped punk rebellion with The Jam for the property rental market in Cornwall' appeared towards the end of the summer. A month later Bruce phoned with the news that it had gone for a quarter of a million. Trebles, or indeed Sea Breezes, all round!

The last time I saw Rick Buckler was in Liverpool in 2016. He was there for the launch of *About the Young Idea* at the Cunard Building on the historic banks of the River Mersey. It was an exhibition charting the rise and influence of The Jam, mainly curated by Paul Weller's sister, Nicky. Bet you can't guess whose book with the same title sat enthroned in a glittering showcase of its own…

CHAPTER 75

PAULINE BLACK

If one may paraphrase the 'Theme from Shaft' by Isaac Hayes, Pauline Black is a complicated girl and no-one understands her except her husband, Terry. They have been together since 1972, when they were both in their teens. Of all the characters in this book Pauline, born Belinda, has probably had the most disrupted life. Her journey, from being adopted by white parents and embracing Black Power to eventual self-discovery, is almost beyond credibility. She hit the ground struggling and has been trying to catch her breath ever since.

Our first encounter took place on a train leaving Exeter and continued in New York and LA. Thirty-five years later we reconvened in London where we had both escaped to join the metaphorical circus. Even then, at a party in newly-gentrified Shoreditch, she claimed not to recognise me, something which did not impress my daughter Grace. At the time Grace was serving her apprenticeship as a party animal and had spotted her dad's name in Black's autobiography. The non-recognition proved rather confusing.

The train ride was an early journey on the 2-Tone Tour, that historic excursion starring The Specials, Madness and The Selecter in the autumn of 1979. Hypnotised by The Specials' debut single, 'Gangsters', I then chanced upon Madness opening for The Pretenders on one of those classic Sunday night bills at The Lyceum. With the exception of a small nucleus of fans, no one at this stage knew about Madness and it was fascinating to see Chas Smash dominate the proceedings without actually singing or playing an instrument.

The following day, not realising I'd seen them the night before, *Sounds* journalist Garry Bushell presented Chas and fellow frontman Suggs to the *Record Mirror* office. I told my colleagues that these guys were going to be big, a tip not missed by Paula Yates who was a journalist on *Record Mirror* and chronicled the event in her Natural Blonde column. Soon afterwards the organisers of the 2-Tone Tour suggested I join them on the road. It was a bit like offering a dehydrated man a couple of pints of lager.

Following gigs in Bournemouth and Exeter some of us were obliged to return to base to satisfy the voracious appetite of media demand. Pauline was looking pukka in ski pants with an elasticated waistband. In contrast I felt bloated from the awful sausages of a hotel breakfast, requiring the loosening of trouser belt. Ms Black muttered something about the curse of pot-bellies and I've been borderline anorexic ever since. With the benefit of hindsight and a perusal of Pauline's *Black by Design: A 2-Tone Memoir* (Serpent's Tail) none of this should have been surprising, non-stop banter being the side-effect of a difficult upbringing. Black was hardly starved or abused but often felt uncomfortable in her own skin. Adopted by stuffy English provincials, Pauline Vickers only discovered she was born Belinda Magnus a few years ago. Her unmarried mother was descended from Sephardic Jews, her father the son of a Nigerian tribal king. Talk about a crazy mixed-up kid!

As well as becoming the charismatic singer in The Selecter, Pauline has also been a successful actress. Prior to the band reforming in 2010 she won an award for playing the part of Billie Holiday in a London theatre which 'never descended into the mawkish sentimentality of the Hollywood version of her life,

Lady Sings the Blues, starring Diana Ross'. I'm not sure Ms Ross will thank her for that, nor the rest of us raised on Motown. Then again Pauline and I are roughly the same age and share the same primal influences – Dylan and the Stones. More of a coincidence is that her early songwriting partner, Lawton Brown, read the same course and was in the same year as me at the Warwick University. It was through him that I joined the West Indian Society, as it was known in those days, and enjoyed the infectious laughter and other attributes of numerous Caribbean queens, but you don't want to know about that. On the other hand, if there's any advice I can pass on to future generations it is to soak up the TV series *Death in Paradise,* and listen to Mick Jagger rhapsodising about the joys of 'Brown Sugar'.

It was great timing when *Record Mirror* sent me off to New York. I'd already been in the city a few days when The Selecter arrived and found myself acting like the mayor, rounding the band up after their show at Hurrah, the first nightclub in NYC to feature punk, and organising transport back to the hotel. This was the Gramercy Park, pleasantly sleazy in the 1980s, the staff turning a blind eye to the number of people sharing a room. Sitting next to Pauline in the cab, I told her about Mick Jagger attending the gig. She tried to play it cool, but I could almost feel her heart rate soaring in the slow traffic filtering down Broadway.

The following day saw us all pile into a record shop in what is now known as the West Village. The plan was for the group to sign copies of their album which fans were being encouraged to buy – the sort of caper I'll probably be indulging in order to sell this book. Meanwhile, in her autobiography, Pauline waxes nostalgic about my *Record Mirror* article from 14 June 1980 entitled 'How the West Was Won'. I'm grateful for this since part of my back catalogue drowned in a flood after the branch of a neighbour's tree smashed through the glass roof of my East Finchley storage facility. You might as well get the whole story, straight from the Serpent's Tail as it were (the publisher of her book).

Apparently, I described the venue as 'a swanky uptown club full of failed fashion victims'. You wouldn't get away with that these days, the podgy PC police would come wobbling into the office claiming hate crime from the bowels of their hi-viz vests. 'While trying to get a bird's eye view of the stage from the raised DJ podium, Nicholls was surprised to find himself in the company of Mick Jagger and Jerry Hall. He notes that Mick was dancing and, to all intents and purposes, enjoying himself.' Pauline also points out how I wasn't beyond delivering the odd lecture to Neol Davies, the austere leader of The Selecter. When he complained that American kids were 'a bunch of idiots, posers not interested in our music but just thinking they ought to be there', I replied that if this was how the scene operated in New York, they should just try and make the most of it, especially as his band were selling plenty of albums and concert tickets.

'Nicholls,' Pauline writes, 'muses that for someone in a group whose self-avowed purpose is to get people dancing, he is perhaps taking everything too seriously, including himself. Bored with Neol he tests out Desmond who eagerly tells him about his visit to a local hospital's ER department that morning with a rash on his arm. There he was made to wait in line for ages while white patients were seen ahead of him. Nicholls continues: 'Pausing only to raise the keyboard player's spirits with a few shots of duty free, we went for a stroll around the East Village while Desmond related a typically daft anecdote. "I tell you, when we got into town, I asked this guy where there was a park to go and have a walk around. So he directed me to a car park, the foolish bastard." '

For all their bitching and bickering, The Selecter were doing much better in the States than a lot of British bands. After arriving in LA with The Hunter Ronson band, I discovered The

Selecter had been invited back to Sunset Boulevard for a further week of sold-out shows at the Whiskey a Go Go, Hollywood's equivalent to London's Marquee, only with better seating and sightlines. Once again, we found ourselves staying at the same rock 'n' roll hotel, the legendary Tropicana... on Route 66. Ha!

Earlier, its larger rooms and apartments had been home to Jim Morrison of The Doors and, later, Tom Waits. Another regular guest, before he could afford to move to the more upmarket Sunset Marquis, was Bruce Springsteen. He wasn't in LA that week but his ex-girlfriend, the photographer Lynn Goldsmith, rocked up to take pictures of Pauline. These tactfully excluded the cute young fellow the singer had spent time with the night before.

If memory serves, that was the last time I saw Pauline as a member of The Selecter. In 1981, following an album somewhat tactlessly entitled *Celebrate the Bullet*, they were forced to disband due to musical and personal differences on a large scale, and a record company which had its eye on the next big thing (New Romanticism, since you ask). Over succeeding decades, history would keep on repeating itself until the entire record industry started to implode. Artists were forced to think for themselves, reuniting onstage and releasing music by other means. Only the strong survived and, inevitably, Pauline Black was one of them.

PETER HOOK

In November 2018, Peter Hook was extracting the final vestiges of pink flesh from the shell of a lobster when his phone rang. It was his daughter, Heather, with an update on her pregnancy. By the time you get to read this the former bass player in Joy Division and New Order should have become a grandfather. In his usual uniform of washed-out T-shirt and battered leather jacket, Mr Hook is not everybody's idea of a grandparent. I remember my own grandpa as a grey-haired, sober-suited gent who even wore a collar and tie on the beach. Times have changed and so has Peter Hook. Infamous for being one of the hardest-living rock stars of his generation, these days he doesn't even drink beer. 'I'm an alcoholic,' Hook admitted, enviously eyeing my second lunchtime pint. 'When you've got an addictive personality you have to give up everything,' declared the man who for many years also consumed a considerable amount of the old marching powder.

As a result, it was solids rather than liquids which were taking priority. He felt guilty about not visiting the gym but for Hook this was, after all, a holiday weekend, albeit one destined to rake in a considerable amount of money. We were in Utrecht, Holland, for Record Planet, a bi-annual record fair attracting buyers and collectors from all over the world. It takes place in a massive modern indoor market space which makes Earls Court look like a car-boot sale. The biggest stall, occupying a glass-walled room of its own, belonged to Omega Auctions. This company, which has grown exponentially over the past decade, had been entrusted with selling all Hook's memorabilia. This has included everything from vintage recording equipment to the biker jacket worn onstage with New Order for most of 1980s and 1990s. 'I can't wear it any more,' he explained when accused of lacking sentimentality. 'Since giving up booze I've taken up weightlifting and now have a 44-inch chest. It's too small so I might as well get rid of it along with all the other junk.'

This junk looked set to earn the musician hundreds of thousands of pounds. The catalogue alone cost fifteen euros and at the Omega stand, effectively the preliminary round of the main auction in 2019, Hook dutifully signed more than a thousand copies. These were snapped up by fans of all ages, most of whom were creating a long queue by demanding selfies. With remarkable patience the bass player accepted every request which meant that after a couple of hours he was ready for a break. When I suggested doing an interview for this book, he decided I should take him out for 'dinner'. Hook is, of course, from the Manchester area and up north 'dinner' means lunch. You can take the boy out of Salford but you can't…

I don't think he remembered but I first met Joy Division at their rehearsal studios in Central Manchester in 1978. Most of the local unsigned bands used the semi-derelict basement; what it lacked in home comforts, it made up for by being conveniently situated. I'd been attending JD gigs since the band was called Warsaw when they played on the bill at the last night of the Electric Circus the previous year. In November 1978, Joy Division headlined at the Check-Inn club in Altrincham, promoted by the owner of the local record shop. He asked me to DJ the gig and as well as writing a preview piece for the *Altrincham Guardian*, I reviewed the concert for *Record Mirror*.

The record shop, Streets Ahead, was owned by local chiropodist Bob Jefferson who was tickled pink when I marched around Altrincham referring to him as the 'punk chiropodist'. While I was entertaining Hook with his fat lunch, he claimed to have 'hated' the gig yet the club was rammed, mainly with teenagers, the surrounding streets filled with parents on taxi duty. Moreover, Bob's wife and Joy Division manager Rob Gretton got on famously, Rob arriving with a large box of expensive dark chocolates. In fact, I ate quite a few myself in an attempt to neutralise the effect of too many bottles of Special Brew.

The following year, I went to the rehearsal studios to interview another promising Manchester band, The Distractions, who sometimes opened for Joy Division. During the interview, JD's guitarist, Bernard Sumner, dropped by to give me a white label copy of their debut album, *Unknown Pleasures*. I duly reviewed it for *Record Mirror*, awarding it the maximum five stars.

In 1980, I was in New York looking forward to seeing Joy Division on their first American tour. Unfortunately, singer Ian Curtis committed suicide just before the band were about to leave Manchester. Soon afterwards the group changed its line-up and became New Order. 'We decided that since the members were no longer all the same, we had to alter the name,' Peter pointed out in Utrecht. 'I thought we would have had the same deal with New Order when I left several years ago, but the others seem to have forgotten and are still using that name,' added the bassist who is no longer in touch with his old comrades. These days Hook tours with his latest outfit, The Light, performing his previous bands' back catalogues. In 2015, I saw their show at an old church in Macclesfield, Cheshire, Peter singing as well as playing bass. His voice sounded eerily like that of Curtis's. 'Same register,' Peter agreed, 'but I always thought the world of Ian's words. He wrote all the lyrics to Joy Division's songs.'

While Hook was in New Order we met on a few occasions, which is more than can be said by most journalists as they participated in very few interviews. 'Our manager reckoned not speaking much would contribute to the band's mystique,' Peter confessed, 'and you can't really argue that the mystique hasn't grown over the past forty years. It's a great compliment that a new generation has come along with the same, if not more, enthusiasm as their parents. Being around for more than twenty years has meant New Order have sold more records, but Joy Division are catching up which is amazing when you consider we only made two albums when the band was still together. It's funny that when we came along at the time of punk the whole idea was to get rid of all the old farts but just look at me now. Still here at sixty-two... luckily.'

During the intervening decades Peter has crammed more into his life than the average chap. Apart from being a member of two bands which, he professes, 'changed the world', he has also occupied the chair of record producer, working with several former label-mates on Factory Records, the Manchester indie label set up by the late TV presenter Tony Wilson. Hook also helped establish The Hacienda, the Manchester super-club that evolved from a boat showroom. The roller-coaster history of The Hac is detailed in one of Peter's books, *The Hacienda: How Not to Run a Club*, packed with lurid tales of gangsters, guns and drugs. At one point the club was even closed down by the police. What made Factory Records and New Order open the 1,600-capacity disco? 'All the ex-punks and other Mancunian misfits needed somewhere to go out at night and although for a long time we didn't have a clue what we were doing, in the end it became a temple to rave and acid house. It was the centre of those scenes in the 1980s and by the following decade it was the focal point of Madchester, attracting clubbers to the city from all over the world,' he explained.

By the mid-1990s, the club's heyday had passed and Hook

formed Monaco, the second of his extra-curricular acts following Revenge. He turned up to the annual In The City conference in Manchester to drum up some publicity for Monaco and we ended up having a right old time, getting drunk and asking cheeky questions in the various seminars and workshops. The high point was listening to Bill Drummond of KLF who presented a film of him burning a million pounds of legal tender banknotes, cash earned from records like 'Dr Who' and 'The Justified and the Ancient' starring Tammy Wynette.

It was only later Hook realised that, between them, Factory and New Order had lost far more money on The Hacienda. The ongoing legacy of Joy Division and New Order is still helping recoup the lost funds, not to mention a career's worth of memorabilia. Until then it will be left to hapless writers to pick up the tab for the occasional succulent lobster.

PETE WYLIE

In 2018, a month before his sixtieth birthday, Pete Wylie decided to address a rally in Walthamstow, an outer suburb of East London. It took place at a venue called Mirth, Marvel and Maud, originally built in 1930 to be a 2,697-seat cinema. By the 1960s, it was an integral part of the rock'n'roll circuit. Little Richard and Gene Vincent played there, as did Mr Wylie's hometown heroes The Beatles. Pete was there to talk to his fans and his wife, Kate, did a great job of drawing him out, as one would expect. The event was advertised as 'Pete Wylie talks… and talks… and talks and talks', as indeed he does and always has done.

I originally met him in 1978 in Probe Records, a celebrated record shop in Liverpool. I used to go to the city every week, supposedly to attend a day-release course as part of my training to be a journalist with the *Altrincham Guardian*. Now, forty years later, a whole gang of us from the punk days planned to reconvene in the former cinema, much of which had recently been converted into a fashionable café/bar. In fact there were a couple of bars so where would I find Wylie? A no-brainer – his voice was audible all the way from the Tube station. He was surrounded by the usual suspects, a *bona fide* musical family represented by dons from London, Liverpool, Manchester, Glasgow and other outposts which could best be described as 'rockist' – an adjective coined by Pete many years ago.

Pete greeted me warmly with his customary exuberance, introducing me to new faces as sponsored beers were swigged and glory days recalled. When it came to him taking the stage at the old movie theatre, it can't have been easy to know where to start. So he began with a warm-up gag: 'This is going to be a game of two halves, but a pint is more economical.' Then came his life-story. 'I was born two days after Buddy Holly played Walton (a Liverpool suburb) where the fascist Oswald Mosley was hit by a brick and where Everton FC got their ground.'

Wylie discovered The Beatles when older cousins brought records round to his parents' house – not being a spoilt brat, he could not afford to buy his first single until he was twelve years old. This was the ineffable Elvis ballad, 'The Wonder of You', which topped the UK charts for six weeks in the summer of 1970. Two years later, 'Bowie became an obsession. I saw him play live towards the end of 1972, nothing else was happening in Liverpool at the time. I'd been to see Free and The Who and got my first guitar in 1971, the year Arsenal beat Liverpool in the FA Cup final.' As an Everton fan this last piece of information came with a slight whiff of Wylie *schadenfreude* which was not as surprising as the next stage of his timeline. 'At school I was shy and a bit of a swot. I loved being clever and at the time of punk got into Liverpool University. I applied to Manchester University so I suppose I could have ended up in Joy Division. But I was on the full grant of £1,076 pounds and went to more parties than I can remember. Then when Roger Eagle started Eric's, the whole world opened up...'

This is quite accurate, so what we should do now is let Pete pause for breath, take a sip of red wine (he was becoming awfully bloated on beer) and examine the life and work of Mr Eagle who had landed in the music business a generation earlier. Roger's initial power base was as a Northern Soul DJ, but he also promoted rock bands at The Twisted Wheel in Manchester where Jimi Hendrix had a residency. Then in 1976, in the early days of punk, he opened Eric's with Pete Fulwell, my Friday afternoon drinking buddy – when I should have been at college studying journalism. True, it might have been beneficial to master the secretarial skill of shorthand, but if I hadn't used a cassette-recorder to tape interviews then you would have had to settle for a far slimmer volume than the one you are reading.

'Roger Eagle,' Pete resumed, 'wanted to educate you. I saw the Sex Pistols at Eric's but they weren't very good that night. Then on 5 May 1977, I went to see The Clash with Ian McCulloch (from Chapter 36) on his eighteenth birthday. There was a queue which blocked the street. All the future stars of Liverpool bands were there: Julian Cope, Holly Johnson, Bill Drummond, Pete Burns (of Nightmares In Wax, then Dead Or Alive who actually worked at Probe). I argued with Joe Strummer about The Clash's policy of not playing *Top of the Pops* and when Sham 69 played we got battered by skinheads, but everything was intense and exciting, and I still feel sentimental about it all. At Eric's, we'd meet all the bands in the bar and I remember Mark E. Smith roadie-ing for The Clash. I took their security guy Steve English to a curry house in Toxteth. During the filming of the documentary *Rude Boy*, Mick Jones said me and Paul Rutherford (who went on to front Frankie Goes to Hollywood with Holly Johnson) that we would be stars and he gave me his 1959 Gibson Les Paul saying, "Pay me back when you're famous." '

This is where Roger Eagle's educational role becomes relevant. 'He said, "You've got to form a band of your own or you won't be let into this club. I'll even pay for you to record a demo." ' And so it came to pass that Pete Wylie became the post-punk version of a proper rock star. Naturally, it wasn't all plain sailing. His first attempt, the Crucial Three with Cope and McCulloch, only lasted a month. Then he joined The Spitfire Boys which must have been just after that *al fresco* Spitfire ride to

The Clash aftershow (see the Joe Strummer chapter) because he wasn't at the Excelsior that night. The Spitfire Boys split up the following month. Next, he joined local act Crash Course after seeing them support Big in Japan. They disbanded in January 1979 after recording the promised demo for Eric's label which never made it on to vinyl, the tape mysteriously vanishing.

With the new decade came a change of luck. Pete formed Wah! Heat, who released two exhilarating singles, 'Better Scream' and 'Seven Minutes to Midnight'. Their cult success led to a deal with Warner Bros. and an even better single, 'The Story of the Blues', reached No. 3 in the charts at the beginning of 1983. 'That song,' Wylie continued at the Mirth, Marvel and Maud lecture, 'was about the mess made by politicians and how my education came as a result of listening to The Clash, Dylan, Springsteen, The Who and others. Rock stars help people's lives.'

This would be a convenient conclusion to the chapter but we're not finished yet. 'I never thought about being a singer in careerist terms,' he claimed, 'but then John Peel made it his single of the year. Then I met him at a Fall gig and he called me the Mighty Wah! So that became the name of the next band.' By this time, Warners' had dropped Wah! because of poor album sales, only for the new group to have another hit with 'Come Back', another song with a message. 'That was my appeal to get people to come back to Liverpool after the economic crisis of the early 1980s. It's all there in Alan Bleasdale's *Boys from the Blackstuff*,' he went on, referring to the TV drama series which had such an effect on the public it was, uniquely, repeated only a few weeks later.

I remember a Wah! gig in Brixton and going backstage afterwards. Mick Jones was there and Pete was brandishing the Les Paul Mick had given him. I can't remember what we had consumed that night but there was a serious amount of gibbering which went on all the way across town to the Columbia Hotel where there were a few more excitable hours of booze, dialogue and song. I believe the author Jack Kerouac would have been in his element.

Then in 1991, Pete nearly died after a fall which left him with a fractured spine. Following a long period of rehab he signed a recording contract with Dave Balfe, The Teardrop Explodes co-founder, who by this time was head of A&R at Sony in the UK. Unfortunately, the resulting album, *Songs of Strength & Heartbreak*, was rejected by the global corporation even though it cost the best part of a £1 million pounds to make in both Memphis and Abbey Road. Being Wylie, at Mirth, Marvel and so on, he managed to produce an anecdote from the wreckage of this terrible situation. Mike Joyce, former drummer with The Smiths, turned up to a session 'because he thought I was Elvis Costello!' recalled Pete, still incredulous. To add more insult to injury, another of his records, 'Heart as Big as Liverpool', 'didn't even sell in Liverpool although it still gets played at Liverpool games.' And Pete, as we have already discovered, is an Everton fan.

The Walthamstow shindig could have doubled as a crowd-funding exercise for an autobiography, but don't hold your breath. I think this report is exhausting enough for the time being.

CHAPTER 78

PHIL LYNOTT &
GARY MOORE

Thin Lizzy are one of the most popular bands the British Isles have ever produced. A guitar-based group who refrained from self-indulgent solos, they combined crunching power chords with accessible catchy songs. On the one hand they enjoyed such raunchy hits as 'The Boys are Back in Town' while on the other, they produced solid rock albums like *Jailbreak* and *Bad Reputation*. Singer and bass player Phil Lynott also had a way with words, producing two books of poetry while still in his twenties.

The son of an Irish mother and a father from British Guyana, Phil cut a charismatic figure, a mane of dark curls framing a handsome face and come-hither smile. Oddly enough we didn't meet in some Wild West type of bar on the outskirts of Dublin but at his mother's 'showbiz' hotel near Moss Side in Manchester. He was staying there during Lizzy's UK tour in late 1977. Although this was at a time when punk was gathering pace, it was also the era of the street poet. Bruce Springsteen's *Born to Run* was still high on my playlist while LA bohemian Tom Waits had recently visited England. 'I'm very proud of my anthologies but I'd prefer to be acknowledged as a musician rather than a poet,' he told me in the glitzy bar of Mrs Lynott's refuge for itinerant showpeople. A disco ball overhung a bijou dancefloor and a myriad of coloured lights twinkled on our Irish coffees. 'I work in music and music has lyrics. A lot of those are based on personal experience, something which I feel the need to share with fans. After our first hit, 'Whiskey in the Jar', we didn't have any success for three years. The only place where we seemed to be happening was on the street.'

With the exception of his hero, Jimi Hendrix, there have been relatively few black rock stars. Did Phil think this had affected his career in any way? 'I'm proud to be Irish and black,' he declared. 'People in Ireland aren't that bothered about the colour of your skin, they're just as likely to refer to you as "the guy with the cowboy hat and leather jacket". The hardest time I ever had being black was when I came over here for the first time and tried to find somewhere to live. Being Irish was bad enough without being black as well.'

Needless to say, racism had become less of an issue by the 1980s and Phil enjoyed living in England, becoming a regular fixture on the London social scene. Unfortunately his lifestyle led to a downward spiral of drug abuse and at the age of thirty-six he died of heart failure. 'He was too young and unstable to handle success, and so adopted that whole romantic myth of living fast and dying young,' said Gary Moore, one of the guitarists in Thin Lizzy. Moore expressed this opinion in 1992 when I interviewed him following the release of his solo album *After Hours*. He had been a member of the band on and off since 1974. 'I left Lizzy three times because of the chemicals,' he revealed. 'I've been in groups since I was a teenager and now, at the age of forty, I'm only just gaining a degree of emotional stability. That's why I live in Henley-on-Thames, near enough to London to go in for meetings but not so close that I'm out caning it every night.'

Most rock fans will be familiar with Moore's melodic guitar playing as a result of his Top 10 single 'Parisienne Walkways' during one of his breaks with Thin Lizzy in 1979. However, his main musical infatuation was the blues, *After Hours* featuring guest appearances from legends of a previous generation like Albert Collins and B.B. King. 'When B.B. King suggested singing a duet with me on 'Since I Met You Baby' it was like a dream come true,' Moore exclaimed. 'For me, he's the most important blues veteran of all time. I've been a fan since the age of twelve.'

Gary's talent was originally spotted by Fleetwood Mac founder Peter Green when he saw him play in Belfast with early UK blues busters Skid Row. 'He liked what he saw and persuaded his management to give us a support slot. It was through Peter that I first came to London,' he said, paying tribute to one of the most emotionally intelligent guitarists Britain has ever produced.

Following a career in heavy rock, Moore decided he should devote more time to playing his first love and found a record company prepared to pledge support. 'So I cut an album called *Still Got the Blues*. It was a labour of love, but we thought if it sold a couple of hundred thousand copies, fine, everybody's happy.' In fact, it sold 3 million copies, while touring the album was an even bigger thrill. 'I thought the gigs would be attended by my regular metal audience plus a sprinkling of blues fans who might want to check things out,' Gary remarked, 'but the actual audience ranged from young kids with their parents to other people old enough to be grandparents.'

Another classic case of family entertainment.

CHAPTER 79

PHIL &
RONNIE SPECTOR

A fundamental rule taught to eager young journos is always to answer a phone – especially someone else's. During the summer of 1989, I was installed in an empty office at EMI Records to interview, of all people, Leo Sayer. The phone rang so I picked it up. I immediately recognised the voice from the caller's album, *A Christmas Gift for You*. It was Phil Spector, the same voice as the one introducing 'Silent Night' on the same record as 'Christmas (Baby Please Come Home)' by Darlene Love, perhaps the greatest Christmas song ever.

Struggling with nerves, I prattled on awhile about how I was a lifelong fan, who would have thought Phil's Wall of Sound would still be sounding so timeless thirty years later, and so on. The notoriously mercurial Mr Spector, who was clearly in a good mood, thanked me for the compliment and asked me about myself. This animated conversation continued for what seemed an age until a large gentleman of a certain age strode into the office. He looked like a bit of cartoon gangster and it transpired he was Leo Sayer's manager. I passed him the phone, he had a brief chat with Phil and then he turned to me. The manager then told me what they had been talking about, finishing with the words, 'and Phil enjoyed speaking with you and wishes you luck in your career.' I went to some restaurant opening that night and told everybody about my new best friend, Phil Spector.

Two years later, I interviewed Phil's former wife, Ronnie

Spector, on the occasion of the publication of her autobiography *Be My Baby*. As a kid I adored The Ronettes and there's a case for stating that the early influence of singers like Ronnie and Tina Turner gave me a preference for brunettes. In the fullness of time it became apparent that this was due to the downright sexiness of these women's smiles, voices and devastatingly good looks. Ronnie was forty-seven at the time and still ravishing, hardly a wrinkle in sight. 'You know why?' she confessed, 'For years I didn't do much. I was in a mansion with servants and whenever I went into the kitchen Phil would scream, "It's not your job!" He'd scold me for emptying an ashtray.'

The couple were married in 1968, five years after he wrote and produced Ronettes' classics like 'Baby I Love You' and 'Be My Baby'. Phil's originality, talent and business acumen were such that he'd been a millionaire since the age of twenty-one. Not that this was of any consequence to Ronnie. 'We had an affection for one another as soon as we made eye contact,' she revealed. 'All those songs were like love letters to me except for 'You've Lost that Lovin' Feeling'. That was about his first wife, although I didn't know he was married at the time. I was young and naïve and had never been in a limousine or expensive hotel. I remember a couple of nights after I met Phil, we went to dinner at a restaurant in Park Avenue and it cost more than my mother earned in a week as a waitress.'

The Ronettes were more popular in the UK than America so in 1963 they came over to tour, going on the road with the Rolling Stones. 'They were our opening act,' Ronnie exclaimed. 'The first night I was in London I was taken to the Ad Lib club by John Lennon who had a crush on me. Paul was there too with his girlfriend Jane Asher. Up until then I was just plain Veronica. It was The Beatles who decided to call me Ronnie Spector.'

By the late 1960s, Phil's career was starting to wane. Ike and

Tina Turner's 'River Deep – Mountain High' wasn't even a hit in the States and, with the benefit of hindsight, Ronnie realised this is why Phil decided to marry her and keep her as a virtual prisoner in their Beverly Hills mansion. 'He had a fatal attraction to me and when he felt his career was slipping, Phil shut us both in his library and played my records night and day – records which he would not release because he said they were just made for him. He couldn't deal with me being successful any more. When I'd ask him about my career he'd say, "What do you mean? I'm a busy man!" Within three months of moving into his mansion he'd put up barbed wire fences and had guard dogs roaming around the grounds. It was like a maximum-security jail except it was this lavish twenty-room home. I never got to go out as he kept it locked from the inside. Of course, all this happened gradually, Phil was very clever like that. I loved the way the place looked, the fountain out front and all the rest of it. I had everything but was miserable because I wasn't allowed out to see anybody.'

At the time of our interview Ronnie had remarried and produced two sons, something she was told she wouldn't be able to do while she was with Phil. 'Every doctor told me I couldn't have children, but I guess they weren't real doctors. Eventually my mother came over from New York and helped me plan my escape. I left without any shoes so Phil would think I was just taking a walk in the grounds. But I missed rock 'n' roll, I missed singing and performing. My new husband is from a wealthy family and we've got a nice house outside Connecticut, but money can't buy you the vibe or the love you get from the audience. I get orgasms onstage and I love orgasms! Then again, I love my life now, especially having young boys. It would all make a good movie but I wouldn't be able to play the part of myself in The Ronettes days. I'd have to let the movie people figure that out.'

By the mid-1970s Phil was back on top, producing albums

for John Lennon and Leonard Cohen. This was when the rumours began to circulate about Spector taking guns into the studio and threatening all and sundry. 'He started to believe everything he read about himself and decided he was a genius – a mad genius,' Ronnie disclosed. 'During the recording of Lennon's *Rock 'n' Roll* LP, John went to the bathroom and Phil followed him into the next cubicle and started firing a gun. John said, "Man, don't do that, you'll screw up my hearing," but he told me afterwards he was totally devastated.' Ronnie reckons this extreme behaviour was the result of their divorce in 1974.

The following year she recorded Billy Joel's classic 'Say Goodbye to Hollywood' and went out on the road to sing it with Bruce Springsteen and the E Street Band. A couple of years later she performed it in the UK with Bruce's friends Southside Johnny and the Asbury Dukes, but her revival was cut short. 'Phil threatened to sue anybody who tried to offer me a recording contract and so no one wanted to have anything to do with me. In our business people envy you when you're on top and then when you're not, breathe a sigh of relief that one of the competition has been removed.' Ronnie said all this without any discernible rancour, adding, 'But I loved Phil and would still want to be friends today if it wasn't for the fact that he'd want to control me. About a year ago he actually sent me a six-figure recording contract which was frightening. He still has that fatal attraction.'

As luck would have it these nightmares have come to an end. Earlier this century Spector was jailed for being found guilty of second-degree murder. His first parole hearing isn't likely to take place until he's in his late eighties. Meanwhile, Ronnie isn't too impressed with the current music scene and the way would-be stars behave. 'When most of our generation started out in the clubs, it wasn't to be discovered but because we loved it. Today there's all this choreography and over-the-top stage sets because the artists haven't got enough talent. They should just be going with their feelings because that's the basic value of rock 'n' roll. The business side of the industry never sees that,' she went on. 'It always falls for the hype whereas the audience don't bother with that, which is why bands like the Stones keep going. They're still hungry, hungry for what they're doing even if they are rich. So many acts have lost that. If you don't still love it, give it up.'

So where does that leave Ronnie and the rest of her career, I wondered. 'If I knew what was going to happen every day for the next ten years it would be very boring,' she replied, 'that's why I love rock 'n' roll... but you're smart, you got in there. You didn't ask basic questions and I like that. Now, do I get a kiss?'

I thought that could be arranged.

CHAPTER 80

RAY DAVIES

Unusually for a future rock star, Ray Davies enjoyed a very happy upbringing. He described his family as 'closely-knit' and was doted on by six older sisters and a younger brother, Dave, with whom he would form The Kinks. Whereas most mothers hope their sons secure steady jobs, Mrs Davies encouraged Ray to attend art college which is where he dreamed of becoming an artist or film-maker. As it happens, he channelled his creativity into music to become one of the best songwriters this country has ever produced.

Between 1964 and 1967, The Kinks scored eleven Top 10 hits before Ray went on to pioneer the concept of writing rock operas. More recently, he has written and directed TV plays and movies. In the early1990s, he directed *Weird Nightmare*, a Channel 4 documentary about the jazz musician Charlie Mingus which featured Elvis Costello, American saxophonist Bobby Keys, Chuck Leavell of The Allman Brothers Band and guitarist-songwriter Vernon Reid. During this period Ray and I met a few times, notably at Konk, his North London studio, for an interview for the *Daily Mail*. A composer, bandleader and double bass player, Mingus, who died in 1979, had an extraordinary private life. Davies discovered this when collaborating with Sue, the third of Mingus's five wives and the curator of his equally extensive musical legacy.

'The film was a labour of love,' explained Ray. 'It took two years and I probably won't make any money out of it, which is fine because I think people of my generation owe something to people like Mingus. Along with many black American jazz musicians he hardly received any royalties, but he was an artist and composer of some value. He crossed over from mainstream and modern jazz to blues and R&B, a sound less intimidating to a young white guy like me living in the suburbs. Charlie was also a big influence on musicians on the UK scene like Alexis Korner, who he hung out with when he visited London in 1962. That was the same year I left college and formed the band which became The Kinks. My earliest memory of his name was when our bass player Peter Quaife said, "Let's play one of those big riffs like Charlie Mingus." You probably remember that the first Kinks hits, 'You Really Got Me' and 'All Day and All of the Night' were based on big riffs.' Indeed, and in years to come, critics would claim those singles formed the basis of punk.

There was another reason why Mingus appealed to Davies: he was able to identify with his non-stop creativity and its incompatibility with family life. Despite his own cheerful childhood and adolescence – 'my dad played the banjo and danced, my mum sang at parties and where I grew up in Muswell Hill there were great woods and parks' – Ray was unable to continue the tradition with his own kids. In fact, it emerged that he never saw the three daughters fathered by one of the wives and a girlfriend.

The most recent of these to arrive was Natalie, the result of his volatile relationship with Chrissie Hynde of The Pretenders. She had never even met her two half-sisters, Louise and Victoria, then in their mid-twenties, from the singer's marriage to Rasa, his notorious gymslip bride. 'Like a lot of parents these days, I wouldn't know how to find them either,' he confessed. 'I don't interfere and although I worry about them, why should I track them down? That would be being a boring parent. The last thing they said when I saw them was, "Why can't you be a dad who wears slippers and watches television?" I answered that it wasn't the sort of thing expected of a sex symbol.'

The artist did see his elder daughters for a while after the marriage broke up but felt there was something intrinsically wrong with being a Sunday father. 'We used to go to places like Regent's Park where you'd see all these other sad cases getting expensive gifts but no real affection. When you are in that position, your children are soon turned off. I could have been a weekend parent to Natalie but I think that would have been damaging. However much it is accepted in today's world, you can't change a little girl's natural instincts. So I thought it better not to see her at all, not that it makes me any happier. When we're on tour and the other guys in the band are buying clothes for their kids, I could almost cry. Being a parent is not only the biggest thing in anyone's life but also a major duty. Most people treat it far too lightly. I should know.'

The reason for this abrogation of responsibility boils down to one excuse – work. Whilst contemporaries like The Beatles and the Stones made the most of the Swinging Sixties and envied the sharp satire of Kinks songs like 'Dedicated Follower of Fashion', Davies was alone in his room writing about this world and its people. 'At art school I was inspired by train stations, people in cafes and couples like Terry and Julie,' he said, referring to the heroes of 'Waterloo Sunset', my all-time favourite single. 'I was so busy writing about other people my own life was put on hold. That stopped me developing as a proper person, an adult. I preferred to look out on the world and not become too introspective. They're the subjects of 'A Well Respected Man' and 'Autumn Almanac' which was influenced by my gardener; he'd talk about sweeping up the leaves and I thought I could write something along those lines, a part of ordinary everyday life.'

Overlapping the fabulous run of hits, which continued with the wistful 'Days' and the droll sexual ambiguity of 'Lola', were the rock operas. *The Village Green Preservation Society* stood up for a world increasingly ruled by faceless corporations while *Arthur*, released before The Who's *Tommy*, was based on Ray's brother-in-law, a war-time fighter pilot who became so disillusioned with Britain that he and his wife emigrated to Australia.

During the mid-1970s, The Kinks started to carve out a successful career in the USA, another reason why Ray lost touch with his children. 'It was American music which caused me to be a musician in the first place,' he pointed out, 'hearing guitarists like Big Bill Broonzy and Hank Williams when I was a kid. But it cut both ways. Americans are fascinated by English culture and they couldn't get enough of albums like *Muswell Hillbillies* and *Schoolboys in Disgrace*. We started to gain stadium-sized audiences while in England all the younger people seemed to be interested in punk.'

Fast forward a couple of decades and the wheel had come full circle; Britpop bands like Blur and Pulp suddenly revived notions of Englishness. Once again, The Kinks were in demand, recently headlining Glastonbury, yet having signed a major deal with Sony in America, where Ray was to be found most of the time. 'What's missing from my life is a conventional family,' he admitted, 'and so, at the moment, I have no reason to live in this country. My house is rented out so when I'm here I have to stay in hotels or with friends. I have friends... a few friends – but I find it difficult to maintain relationships, I think everybody does, it's one of the factors of modern life. In New York if you go into a restaurant alone, they give you what's called a widow's banquette – you've either got to be a widow or there's something wrong with you. There's a kind of stigma about people who eat or go out alone. I'm often asked to eat with people, and I accept because I don't want to be isolated. I suppose I like to be busy with work but it's nice to have somebody in the background for company. I guess it's all about finding a compromise but after all these years and relationships I haven't found it yet,' he concluded reflectively.

Towards the end of 1993, we spoke again in less melodramatic circumstances for a what-are-you-doing-for-Christmas celebrity round-up for *Hello!* magazine. He called me at home and heard three-month-old Grace crying in the background, as babies do. 'Ah, what a beautiful sound!' he exclaimed, perhaps enviously. Four years later his third wife Patricia presented him with Eva, another baby daughter of his own.

In 2017 he followed in the footsteps of veteran rivals Paul McCartney and Mick Jagger by receiving a knighthood. I haven't seen him since, but a former neighbour told me *she* had; he was sitting at a table next to her in the local Indian restaurant in East Finchley. He was dining alone.

CHAPTER 81

RICHARD THOMPSON

Richard might not be a household name, but he remains one of the most sophisticated musicians and songwriters to have emerged from these shores. Thompson must also be one of the most prolific, having released more than thirty solo albums as well as the records he made with Fairport Convention in the late 1960s.

Richard Thompson grew up listening to jazz musicians like Django Reinhardt, his guitar playing very much inspired by the genre. Then, at the age of eighteen, he joined the Fairports and helped create some of the most groundbreaking music of the era. Thompson effectively transformed a group specialising in covering traditional tunes into the first-ever folk-rock band. Combining the sound of the American underground with a more acoustic English sensibility he contributed original material like 'Meet on the Ledge'. More than half a century later it is still an acclaimed classic.

The singer-songwriter had the good fortune to play alongside Sandy Denny whose soaring, emotional vocals made her one of England's most cherished singers. She can be heard at her poignant, nostalgic best on 'Crazy Man Michael' on the historic *Liege & Leif* or 'Who Knows Where the Time Goes?' on the equally groundbreaking *Unhalfbricking*. This album also features 'Si Tu Dois Partir', the French version of Bob Dylan's 'If You Gotta Go, Go Now'. Fairport Convention covered another Dylan favourite, 'Lay Down Your Weary Tune', endorsed by the Zim as the best version of one of his early songs. Another fan was Jimi Hendrix who jammed with the Fairports at London venue Middle Earth. Thompson recalls him strolling on stage, borrowing his guitar and blasting straight into 'Like A Rolling Stone'.

Despite all this acclaim, Richard left the band in 1971 to concentrate on writing and playing more of his own songs. With his wife Linda he recorded 'I Want to See the Bright Lights Tonight', the first of several joint efforts before they divorced in the early 1980s. Then came a series of solo albums of increasing instrumental and lyrical intricacy. I caught up with him in 1993 on the release of *Mirror Blue*. 'It's named after a phrase in Tennyson's The Lady of Shalott,' he explained before describing one of its best tracks, 'Beeswing', as being '...a tale of this beautiful girl from the hippy era who declines the offer of a conventional lifestyle and eventually ends up a terrible old lush. No, it wasn't based on personal experience, purely my imagination. The idea of the song is to romanticise and fictionalise whatever that period was about.'

Relationships are a key part of Richard's songwriting whether involving humour, as in 'Taking My Business Elsewhere', or horror, such as 'I Can't Wake Up to Save My Life', about a nightmare. 'However, I don't focus on specific themes,' he pointed out, 'I just start writing and see what comes. That's the exciting part of creating anything. The final structure, plot and characterisation all fall into place along the way. It's something I've learned from books,' he confided, citing favourite novelists such as thriller writers Len Deighton and Ruth Rendell. 'I'm also a big fan of Balzac,' he added, referring to the nineteenth-century French author whose tragic life was capped by dying six months after marrying the love of his life.

Enjoying this educational conversation with someone so wise was in stark contrast to trying to get any sense out of the majority of the here-today-gone-tomorrow wannabes around at the time.

What did Richard think had caused the sudden proliferation of puppets who hadn't paid their dues? 'It's the way people arrive at music which is wrong,' he reckoned. 'Starting with a sequencer, form a band and then failing after one or two hits... the whole system is bound to collapse. Back in the 1960s, groups like The Searchers and The Animals had to struggle to win audiences before they eventually got better. But there has to be some raw creativity in the first place. Music often suffers because those trying to play it are not musicians.'

An accusation which could hardly be levelled at Thompson who is feted by numerous famous peers. His extraordinary musicianship has led to invitations to play on records by everyone from commercial rockers like Crowded House to such artists as Robert Plant and Suzanne Vega who already have distinct identities of their own. Elvis Costello went as far as to cover one of his songs, 'Withered and Died' – a fate hardly likely to befall Richard Thompson's adventures in music.

CHAPTER 82

RICKIE LEE JONES

The launch of Rickie Lee Jones' debut album in the late 1970s involved the type of marketing today's young hopefuls could only dream about. Her photograph on the cover said it all: a retro beret, long tousled hair and sleepy eyes completed an image of effortless bohemian cool, brought to life by the singer's light, jazzy vocals. Already a darling of the LA acoustic scene, Jones had been courted by most of the major record companies and found herself at the centre of a bidding war. Rickie selected Warner Bros., home of top musician and composer Randy Newman. He made a guest appearance on the self-titled album along with local heroes, Dr. John and Michael McDonald. The LP went on to sell 2 million copies, boosted by the relaxed, radio-friendly 'Chuck E's in Love', a hit with a real-life backstory; the lyric was about a *ménage-a-trois* comprising herself, former lover Tom Waits and Chuck E, and a shared West Hollywood apartment. It was quite a start to a career which has never really recaptured those highs. When I caught up with Rickie Lee Jones in the early 1990s she seemed extraordinarily down. Actually, it was one of the most depressing interviews I have ever conducted which, perversely, made it quite interesting.

The former 'Queen of Coolsville' appeared to be anything but. 'Most people know my name,' she began querulously, 'but wouldn't recognise my voice or music.' The situation wasn't helped by the fact that although the new album *Pop Pop* was her first for several years, she'd hardly written any of the songs herself. 'Some of the tunes are classic crooners from the 1950s, others Tin Pan Alley standards of the 1920s,' she said, not apparently aware that the road she had just mentioned, Denmark Street, was less than half-a-mile away from our hotel rendezvous. Another track was the Jimi Hendrix number, 'Up from the Skies', which along with all the others was backed by an acoustic trio.

' 'Bye Bye Blackbird' dates back to the Great Depression,' she continued and from then on, along with bad luck and trouble, depression seemed to be the operative word, clouding the Jones family for a few generations. 'My mother was raised in an orphanage because her father went to prison for stealing a chicken. He was Irish and fought in the Great War in France where he was incapacitated by nerve gas. His mind wasn't right afterwards, and he was caught cooking the chicken. While he was in jail all my grandmother's children were taken into custody because the authorities claimed he couldn't provide for them, so my ma was brought up in an orphanage during the Great Depression.'

Rickie's father didn't exactly have a great start in life, either. 'When he was young his mother killed herself, so he was brought up by his father who was Welsh and very mean. So my dad kept running away from the age of twelve, living on milk stolen from doorsteps and becoming a regular juvenile delinquent. He was from Chicago which is where he met my ma, in a drugstore.' The sob story didn't end there. When it came to her siblings, Jones described her brother and two sisters as 'social cripples for the most part, especially my brother. He was in a motorcycle accident at the age of sixteen and badly handicapped,' she went on, 'he lost a leg and suffered brain damage. His speech centre was affected so he talks really slowly. That wouldn't matter so much if it wasn't for the fact that his job is selling real estate where you have to be charming and fool people all the time.'

Mind you, it appeared that Rickie Lee Jones was not the full shilling herself, which perhaps explained why she'd been out of the picture for a while. 'I've been in France, chilling out after taking a lot of drugs,' she blundered on, throwing another curveball, 'getting rid of the person I was and trying to come to terms with the family tradition of rack and ruin. But who you are never changes,' she went on, 'the family inheritance is still a terrible millstone. There have also been suicides and drug addicts, and I was on cocaine for quite a long time. On reflection, coke is probably a bigger problem than heroin which is just a depressant. Cocaine is the worst drug of all because it affects you even if you don't have an addictive personality. To begin with you take it to feel good, then you go on to use it to relieve anxiety. Then you keep on using it because you crave that anxiety.'

Good lord! What should have been an interview about hip sounds and the politics of cool became a lecture on narcotics. 'Drugs have a life of their own,' she persisted. "You start out okay and then they take over. Coke is the worst because it leads to paranoid hallucinogenic psychotic behaviour. There have probably been more lives destroyed by cocaine than heroin which ultimately doesn't alter your character, it just puts you to sleep. But anyone who needs it isn't leading a well life.'

Now there's a thought. Best just to stick to multivitamins.

RICK WAKEMAN

For a quietly-spoken mild-mannered keyboard player Rick Wakeman has had an outstanding career. He left the Royal College of Music to work with David Bowie before joining Yes after they became one of the most successful bands of the early 1970s. At the same time, he enjoyed a parallel life as a solo artist creating concept albums about historic figures like Henry VIII and King Arthur. Along the way Rick managed to find time to compose soundtracks for maverick film-maker Ken Russell, marry four times, and build up and sell a luxury car dealership in order to finance his divorces and subsequent new homes.

In 1987, the *Sunday Express* magazine sent me to his latest house in Surrey to interview him about *The Gospels*, the live production he was about to stage at the Royal Albert Hall. A classical oratorio in four parts, it was based on the New Testament gospels of the apostles Matthew, Mark, Luke and John. It was to be narrated by actor Robert Powell and feature a choir from Eton school, with celebrated tenor Ramon Remedios flying in from Columbia to contribute operatic vocals. As well as producing the event, Wakeman planned to play most types of keyboard known to mankind, from the venue's grand piano and Hammond organ to the newer breed of digital Moog and Rhodes contraptions. Had he always fancied being a combination of both Tim Rice and Andrew Lloyd Webber?

'Well I thought it would be a lot of fun, but it has also been bloody complicated,' he confessed. 'Some of the keyboards will be amplified through the PA system, the choir will be miked up overhead, but Ram won't be using a microphone at all because opera singers don't. When Pavarotti played Wembley it was just the orchestra and him, no electronics or digital keyboards. There haven't been any guidelines at all, we've just had to solve each problem as it came along.'

Then again Wakeman has spent much of his life looking for solutions and making difficult decisions, like turning down David Bowie's Spiders from Mars in order to join Yes. How did that relationship come about? 'David decided he would like to structure the songs on his *Hunky Dory* album around the piano instead of guitar,' he explained. 'He had heard some of my work with the Strawbs – I was a member at the time – so I was invited round to his home in Beckenham, the place I went on to call Beckenham Palace. I was living in this tiny flat at the time where in order to sit in the dining room, I had to put my feet in the lounge.

'Next to that, David's place seemed huge with a minstrels' gallery and all sorts of things. David had the basis for the songs, he just needed someone to work out the arrangements for 'Changes', 'Life On Mars' and a couple of other tunes. What else can I tell you about him? Well, soon afterwards he started going through his identity changes. I remember joining him for a spot at Hampstead Arts Theatre when there was just him and his guitar. There were only about fifty or sixty people in the audience, but he romped onstage dressed like a transvestite pirate at a time when green flares were considered outrageous. Soon afterwards he asked me to put together the Spiders but I chose Yes instead. The main reason was, there would be room for my own writing and composing within their framework.

'It would have been nice to work with David, but I wouldn't have been able to pursue other routes. We remained on friendly terms. When I was living with my second wife in the late 1970s we saw each other quite a lot, our kids being friends and all that sort of thing. We spent some time together in my studio, too, where I learnt a lot from him. He had a great 'go for it' attitude – if you want to try something, give it a go, and if it doesn't work, don't worry. The next time I heard from David was a year or so ago when he wanted some help with the theme music for the film *Absolute Beginners* in which he appeared. He put in a request for some Rachmaninov piano.'

Rick moved out of London on the advice of wife No. 3, Nina Carter. This was connected to the demon brew; at one point Wakeman was putting away two bottles of brandy a day. 'During my twenties I suffered three heart attacks and the doctor told me if I didn't mend my ways, I'd be dead within two years. I was primarily a social drinker and wherever I went there was always someone to drink with, whether it was George Best or record company people. So we moved here which, after four years and £100,000 worth of refurbishment, still isn't modernised.' Nevertheless, one could do worse than a period property with high ceilings and extensive grounds. Nina, a former Page Three girl, proved to be an excellent hostess. In fact, it was the first and, so far, only time I have been served afternoon tea by an ex-topless model.

The drain on Rick's resources, however, was not only as a result of construction bills. Despite having sold more than 50 million albums at the time, he found life as a musician a costly affair. 'Everybody in this industry gets ripped off,' he said frankly. 'What happens with an artist is that his career hums along with peaks coming up at various points, then you check up on your affairs and suddenly realise you've been stitched up. Young bands today are getting wise to it quicker than our generation, but if you were to try managing yourself it would be detrimental to the music. There were incredible overheads with Yes. Apart from being talked into taking private jets all over the place, in hotels we'd opt for presidential suites. The Americans are very clever; in some places there are ten of those! Off the road can be even more expensive,' he continued, 'especially when you're spending seven months in a studio at a grand a day with twenty-five road crew on a retainer. With Yes I felt as though for every million pounds earned, I was spending 1 million and 100,000!' It's worth mentioning that between 1971 and 2014 Rick undertook five major tours of duty with Yes. No wonder he sold his collection of twenty-two Rolls Royces. 'These days,' he concluded, 'if I feel like letting off steam I'll play a round of golf, and make sure I steer well clear of the nineteenth hole.'

ROBERT PALMER

Robert Palmer was in a fine mood the day we met at the St James's Club in London during the summer of 1992. He had just completed a project many months in the making, an ITV special for the Des O'Connor Show. It involved working with a forty-piece orchestra produced by Teo Macero, the celebrated jazz musician who grew up in his father's speakeasy in Harlem. Teo also worked with premier league artists like Duke Ellington, Miles Davis and Tony Bennett. The arranger for the TV special was no slouch either. 'Clare Fisher, a German man who lives in America,' Robert disclosed, 'and a control freak, it comes with the territory.' The singer was delighted with the end result but something niggled – the contradiction between delegation and control. 'Delegation is a difficult thing,' observed the musician responsible for a string of popular albums including *Clues* and *Riptide*.

You probably know Palmer best for the sensational video of 'Addicted to Love' where he appeared surrounded by a brood of beautifully made-up, almost identically dressed pouting models. It was shot by Terence Donovan, a contemporary of fellow 1960s photographers David Bailey and Terry O'Neil. What all these creatives have in common is that they were a generation older than Palmer, who was forty-three when we did our interview. He had tremendous respect for all of them, which was why they were hired. On the other hand he seemed ambivalent: '...I'll do whatever they say because they know better than me, but it's really odd to lose control like that, because if you don't have that you can't fly.'

All this talk about control put me in mind of Hegel, the nineteenth-century German philosopher who influenced Karl Marx and his mate Engels. It transpired that Robert was a bit of a philosopher himself, not to mention a historian, and someone unusually knowledgeable about the key players in the global record industry. We had an extraordinary conversation with me doing my best to reciprocate when it came to sharing information. 'My tendency is not to do interviews,' he murmured before opening a whole cabinet of private files. 'It's very difficult because since the age of fifteen I've been doing rock 'n' roll, singing tenor and belting out R&B songs.' He could have added soul and reggae and being idolised for his good looks and impeccable clothes, but like a lot of artists Robert presented a modest streak. He seemed reluctant to dwell on such back-catalogue highlights as 'Some Guys Have All the Luck' and 'She Makes My Day', preferring to talk about how he had spent three years recording the vocals for his next album, *Ridin' High*. This was due to be released on the recently restructured EMI Records whose American boss, Charles Koppelman, I'd met a few months earlier at that year's Midem festival in Cannes. 'Really?' Robert asked, 'tell me about him.'

Well, I believe he worked for Clive Davis (see the Martyn Ware chapter) at CBS in the early 1970s when they were both involved with signing Billy Joel...

'Go on, go on!'

He was partly at Midem to oversee the release of Smokey Robinson's comeback album which hadn't sold very well in the States. The early Motown star, who had hits like 'The Tracks of My Tears' as well as writing a few classics for The Temptations, hadn't done himself any favours by letting the new label put out the record, particularly as he himself hadn't even written the best songs. I told Robert I'd gone to Midem to interview Robinson for the *Daily Telegraph*.

'Couple of things here,' he put forward. 'First of all, 1991 was their most successful financial year in the entire history of EMI, but I'm not being an advert for them. In the meantime, what did you make of Koppelman?'

I told him the whole story: how when Smokey postponed the interview Charles took me out to lunch with Gloria Estefan and about a dozen senior executives. We went to Tetou in Golfe-Juan, a cracking seafood joint in the hills overlooking the sea. Everyone was drinking water apart from me who required a few beers to wash down the toothsome lobster. There was no offer of wine which is what one is supposed to drink with crustacea, even PC Americans. However, the funniest part of the lunch was noting how the best table had been nabbed by Sire Records' boss Seymour Stein, an old Midem chum of mine who had signed The Ramones, Talking Heads and some bird called Madonna...

I thought Koppelman was rather full of himself, I continued. He hired a leading music industry PR and hosted a press conference where not even the trade press knew what he was talking about. My paparazzi pal, Richard Young, started to laugh loudly and ironically at one of his jokes but Koppelman didn't realise he was taking the piss. In fact, he clearly took it as a compliment and started looking even more chuffed.

'Yes,' Robert agreed, 'I thought he was that sort of person, but I also think he does love music and you've got to have someone at the top who cares. I just hope that with globalisation and everything he doesn't lose his heart.' Robert then drew an unusual comparison with the army: 'If you join the forces you have to accept the responsibility of using a gun. I don't claim to understand how to run a record company but he's as much part of my business as I am, so it's very important to me.

'The planet is in a weird state at the moment so we mustn't end up like we did towards the end of the 1970s before punk came along. Do you remember that however much you fiddled with the dial on the radio, all that came out was disco?' I replied that most of the music being played in 1992 was even worse and Robert agreed. In my opinion the problem was the torrent of old albums being re-released on CD which meant the record companies were living off the family heirlooms instead of getting behind something new. This was the theme of a number of articles I had written for *The Times* over the past couple of years. 'I wish you wouldn't encourage me in this type of conversation,' Robert sighed, 'but what's happening is like force-feeding the public. Personally, I don't mind stuff being reissued on CD, for example my Billie Holiday records are too crackly. But during a recession there's less money around and people are more discerning so there's more opportunity for a shakeout.'

Talking about the industry led to Palmer discussing his own situation. 'My manager, David Harper, started out with The Doors then went on to work with Traffic, Free, and Bob Marley and The Wailers, which is partly how I came to be signed to Island Records. I also knew the label's founder, Chris Blackwell, who signed Vinegar Joe to Island in 1971,' he went on, referring to the band he led with Elkie Brooks. Chris actually put that group together. I take it you know Chris...'

I related how I had originally met Blackwell in 1980 following a London gig by The Distractions (see Peter Hook chapter), having written about them a few times for *Record Mirror*. I also told him how Chris had invited me for dinner after the gig along with singer Judie Tzuke and BBC presenter Mike Read. During the meal, at chic central London club Legends, Chris had asked me about the state of the music industry in the UK. He was away a lot in Jamaica and New York and wondered which was the most successful record company at that point in time. My opinion was Chrysalis who were currently riding high with Blondie, the 2-Tone label and Ultravox, who had left Island to move to Chrysalis. Blackwell agreed with my assessment. In 1989, he sold his label to multinational Polygram for a breathtaking $200 million. I remember this because I sold the story to the *Mail on Sunday* for the most money I'd ever received from a publication. The sale was confirmed at a press conference the following week where I was interviewed by Radio 4 about Island and Blackwell; none of the other journos seemingly had a clue about why they were there.

The last time I saw Chris was in 1995 when he was the keynote speaker at Manchester's In The City conference. He had solved the problem of what to do with his millions by buying up dozens of hotels on South Beach, Miami, and restoring the once-beautiful art deco buildings. He sold two of them to singer Gloria Estefan who invited me to stay at one of them when I interviewed her for *Hello!* the following year.

Meanwhile, back to Robert Palmer and his thoughts on Chris Blackwell's nine-figure payday. 'Six months later he wouldn't have been able to do that deal,' he opined. 'A lot of stuff done then marked the end of that era. But you know what I was saying about CDs? I got some great new toy sent to me the other day.' This didn't come as any surprise. In 1980, he was seen wearing the first Sony Walkman and now he had an early Notepad 'where you write on the screen and it does everything else itself.' Talking about his taste for technology led us into details about Robert's personal life. Having lived on the island of Nassau in the Bahamas, word had got round that he had departed as a result of the rising crime rate. Apparently, he became particularly anxious after someone else's consignment of cocaine was washed up on to the beach at the bottom of his garden.

'That was true, but it was exaggerated by the media because it made an interesting story,' he replied. 'There were lots of reasons for leaving, including the corruption there and my children's education. I wanted them to be raised somewhere neutral where there were good facilities and they didn't have to attend an American school. So we moved to Lugano in Switzerland which is only about an hour from one of my favourite cities, Milan. It took four years to get into Switzerland, they only accept 200 new arrivals each year. I love the hills and the countryside, and you gain an incredible perspective living in that kind of environment. Your neighbours might be a mountain range away and speak a different language. The Swiss have got five languages. They also invented LSD and have never been to war, yet they make the most sophisticated weapons in the world. All they talk about is politics and religion because they have none of their own. I was there as a teenager when I was in my first group. I looked around and thought, "One day...".'

Robert's parents like it there, too. For a rock star he's remained remarkably close to them, partly because they're not jealous of his looks and success. This could be because they have led interesting lives themselves. Until his retirement his dad was employed by the wireless intelligence service in the Royal Navy. 'He's told me some incredible stories over the years,' the singer enthused. 'At the age of twenty-two he was sent to see the Forces' tailor. He went down with his colleague and they were kitted out with white suits and James Bond-style attaché cases with built-in secret radios. "You've got to go and live with the Kurds for three months," they were ordered. Everything was on a need-to-know basis and he wasn't told what part of the chain he was in. During World War II, there were certain codes which could launch a rocket bomb and when dad became involved with nuclear submarines, he couldn't tell anyone about it because he was bound by the Official Secrets Act.

'All the time I was growing up, finding out about what he

did was like pulling teeth. He knew all about the Cuban Missile Crisis before the event and our house was in uproar. Then it became public knowledge that the Russians were planning to test ballistic missiles in Cuba. It went on for two weeks and could have escalated into a full-scale nuclear war. My father knew the Americans were poised to retaliate but couldn't say a word. It cost a lot of people in his job their lives; they couldn't handle the secrecy, flipped out and committed suicide. Now,' he mused, 'compare that with the music business which is all about *having* to communicate. When you start off in a group you don't know what you're doing. You distance yourself from your parents having had the usual battles during puberty and then you get a better understanding of yourself, realising what it took to do what they did,' he added philosophically. 'Through this television show I've learned to try and be gentle and optimistic, which is where the delegation comes in. It's a matter of relinquishing control while still being able to fly.'

Roll over Beethoven and tell Herr Hegel the news.

CHAPTER 85

ROBERT PLANT

Like many great bands, Led Zeppelin appeared to come from nowhere. One minute there was an album in an unusual monochrome sleeve, the next they were the most powerful rock band in Britain. There was no record company hype and by the time the music press caught up with them they had released their second historic LP later that same year.

'We went out and worked hard,' guitarist Jimmy Page later explained, 'trying to move the boundaries of what music was.' Equally significantly, they did come from somewhere. Page was a member of The Yardbirds, one of the great rock and pop groups of the mid-1960s, while bassist John Paul Jones was an in-demand session musician who was finding studio work too claustrophobic. The other pair, John Bonham and Robert Plant, were in a relatively unknown Midlands outfit called Band of Joy with the latter setting the template for future generations of rock vocalists. Apart from possessing a voice whose range could flip from a gentle croon to a harrowing wail, Plant had the original sex-god looks of a conquering Viking – billowing hair, naked chest, menacing swagger, the lot. He loved American blues and interpreted the music with convincing belief. From early Zeppelin cuts like 'Dazed and Confused' to the mesmerising 'Since I've Been Loving You', here was a singer who could match the sound of Muddy Waters or Ray Charles.

Howling along with Page's huge riffs and possibly the most intense rhythm section ever, Led Zeppelin created a sound which hit the ground running. The band was particularly successful in America where during 1968 and 1969, the year of their first two albums, they gigged for a total of fifty weeks. 'We could have gone on longer,' reflected Plant, 'but if you stayed in the States for more than six months at that time you risked being drafted into the Vietnam War.'

Not that they were any less popular at home. The following year the group headlined the Bath Festival, riveting 150,000 fans for an unprecedented three hours. Despite specialising in discharging pulverising heavy rock, they could also do acoustic. For *Led Zeppelin III*, Page and Plant repaired to a remote Welsh cottage called Bron-Yr-Aur, name-checked in a song title on that LP. 'It was on the side of a hill with neither electricity nor running water,' Plant told me in vastly different surroundings, the VIP bar of the InterContinental Hotel on Hyde Park. Our conversation took place during the annual Nordoff-Robbins auction, the main music industry charity. 'My parents had taken me there for childhood holidays. There was an open fire, so we'd go out and collect wood. Jimmy had an acoustic guitar and I'd work on the lyrics. The whole trip was very inspiring and a complete break from the non-stop touring. We were partly influenced by the folk-rock sound of Fairport Convention and, of course, Sandy Denny would sing on our next album.'

Another acoustically-inclined Led Zeppelin song is 'Ramble On' which refers to characters from Tolkien's *Lord of the Rings*. 'The lyrics are about positivity and beauty triumphing over corruption and evil,' explained the singer, whose band had the worst reputation for rock 'n' roll misbehaviour. 'I'm proud of their naivety which is why I still include the song when playing solo gigs.'

Plant's solo career took off soon after Led Zeppelin split up following the death of John Bonham in 1980. He has released more than a dozen albums since then, all of which have displayed his ability to keep a keen eye on the contemporary scene. Over the years he has spotted the potential of future stars like Ry Cooder and Robert Palmer, while on the indie scene he was the first established artist to rave about acts as varied as the B-52's and This Mortal Coil. Plant still enjoys attending low-key gigs whether in London or at the international music markets like Midem where I once saw him share a duet with an unknown Asian musician.

Robert's down-to-earth attitude extends to regular visits to his native Worcestershire in the West Midlands. 'I never got the urge to buy a mansion in LA or Surrey or anywhere else where rock stars are supposed to be,' he said when I sounded him out about an at-home piece for *Hello!* or *The Sunday Times*. 'I'm still in touch with the same people I was hanging out with thirty years ago. I think that's what has kept me sane and free from drugs.'

ROBERT SMITH

Back in the day, every now and then, a record label did get something right. Chris Parry, the man in charge of The Jam's career, moved heaven and earth trying to get the band to break America but it never really happened. So when he left their record company to start his own indie label, he tried a different strategy: Europe first. Parry's first signing to Fiction was The Cure. Their early releases belonged very much to the late 1970s post-punk era: catchy, simple, quirky and slightly weird. Their image was similarly off-beat. Singer Robert Smith was clearly educated: The Cure's first single, 'Killing an Arab', was based on *The Outsider* (also known as *The Stranger*), a novel by French existentialist author Albert Camus.

During the course of the next decade The Cure built up a fanatical following in France, a country hardly renowned for rock 'n' roll credibility. During the summer of 1990, the band played thirteen major European rock festivals, topping the bill in front of up to 100,000 fans at each one. Only one of these was in England, at the Glastonbury Festival, where I interviewed Smith for *The Times*. 'The other week we headlined over Bob Dylan,' he told me backstage in his trailer in the VIP area. 'I don't think he was very amused. When we called him over for a beer at the hotel bar, he ignored us and walked the other way. We wouldn't have minded going on before him, but England were playing a World Cup match and we didn't want to miss it.'

With his backcombed hair, gothic black eye make-up and

taste for vividly-patterned blouses, Smith gradually cultivated a bizarre image. His CV took on a touch of originality, too. At one point, as well as leading The Cure he was the guitarist with Siouxsie and the Banshees. Other projects included The Glove, a collaborative recording project with the Banshees' Steven Severin, and contributing to some of Marc Almond's albums. 'That was a bit of a turning point in my career,' he acknowledged, 'getting involved creatively with other musicians. It led to Phil Thornalley joining the band after he was originally our producer.'

Thornalley, who had been an engineer for Duran Duran before going on to write songs for A-listers like Bryan Adams, went on the road with The Cure when they toured *The Top*, effectively their breakthrough album. I saw them at the Hammersmith Odeon in the spring of 1984 and noted the audience going berserk. 'That tour was the first time I realised how playing live could revolutionise the band,' he recalled. 'Phil was really in his element. He'd been playing since he was fourteen years old but only in pub bands. Suddenly appearing in front of thousands of people was a real turn-on for him and injected life into the rest of us.'

Another useful addition to The Cure camp was video director Tim Pope whose maverick style harmonised with Smith's lyrics, which occupied an imaginary world full of monsters and nightmares. The video for 'Love Cats' helped make it their biggest hit to date, paving the way for the following year's *The Head on the Door*. This album catapulted the group to becoming the country's leading alternative rock band, while in America they became the toast of increasingly important college radio. That LP boasted two more left-field yet appealing hits, 'In Between Days' and 'Close To Me'. The latter is probably best-known for another vitally useful video, the band singing in a wardrobe which slowly fills with water after it has been pushed off a cliff. I wondered what inspired the ideas that drove Smith's singular vision?

'Sometimes I don't write for ages and then suddenly everything spews out,' he smiled, 'often when I'm sitting at home watching TV. Usually the tune comes first, so I keep a tape recorder handy and sing into it. Once something takes shape, I'm happy with it. If you start trying too hard to make it perfect, you lose whatever it was which created it in the first place.' Or, to put it another way, too many hooks spoil the broth.

CHAPTER 87

ROD STEWART

My Rod Stewart story begins with a tale of two journos, two of Fleet Street's finest who were present but not correct at the party following the 1991 Brit Awards. The ceremony itself took place at London's Dominion Theatre where Rod stole the show with a fabulous rendition of 'Downtown Train', the Tom Waits masterpiece which boosted the careers of both artists. The aftershow was in the ballroom of Park Lane's Grosvenor House Hotel, a relaxed space affording easy access to all the celebs. I saw Rod chatting to an old colleague who had been my Glasgow correspondent at *Record Mirror*. They were discussing Celtic, Rod's favourite football team. The singer is also a huge fan of Dennis Law, the Manchester United striker who was in the same team as George Best, Bobby Charlton and Pat Crerand, another Scotsman with the same midfield skills as David Beckham but considerably more talented. I used to know all these players because at the age of fifteen I spent most of the summer holidays working for United's accountant. It was my first entry into the world of stardom, except in those days sportsmen behaved as such. They'd come in for a natter and a cup of coffee, inserting five pence into the vending machine like everybody else.

Observing Rod looking relaxed, it seemed natural to wander over and join the conversation, bringing along these teenage memories. The singer wondered if I still followed United, the dialogue remaining low-key and convivial, none of the usual repartee or banter you might expect if you've seen him on talk shows. In fact, bearing in mind his powerful performance earlier, he seemed somewhat reserved, depressed even. Furthermore, he was not accompanied by Kelly Emberg, his girlfriend of several years and the mother of one of his daughters. Surely she should be at his side on such an occasion? I didn't get the chance to enquire. Feeling a light tap on the shoulder, I turned around to see two fellow reporters practically having anxiety attacks: Piers Morgan and Andy Coulson of *The Sun*'s Bizarre column. I'd met them before and furnished the newspaper with the odd piece of tittle-tattle, off-cuts from *The Times* and *Hello!* which were too gossipy for those august publications.

'What did Rod have to say?' Morgan demanded. Well not a great deal, I murmured, he doesn't seem his usual self... I think he might have split up with Kelly. 'What? Are you sure? That could be a splash!' interjected Mr Coulson, the same chap who became a guest of Her Majesty earlier this century following another escapade with a newspaper. 'Well, I'm not *sure*,' I protested, 'it's just a hunch. But where is she?'

'But you're Mike Nicholls!' Coulson thundered, evidently trying to appeal to my vanity, 'the Mike Nicholls who writes for *The Times*. You must know!' Of course, part of being *moi* is knowing how far one can go. It's the same as being aware of one's capacity to drink. To date, I've never been arrested for being intoxicated nor sued for something I've written and the idea is to keep it that way. Everything calmed down, no front-page splash appeared and Rod duly *dis*appeared so I wasn't able to get an answer.

Later that year a story came up which I thought might be of some use to the Bizarre column. Unfortunately, Piers was on the defensive, claiming I'd tried to pull a fast one over Rod, '...so I won't be buying any more stuff from you, mate.' 'Really?' I countered. 'So how come you pinched that David

Bowie anecdote from my *Hello!* column last week?' 'Oh, that, well...' he backed down. Scenting blood, I went in for the kill, pointing out how, subsequently, it had been announced that Rod and Kelly had split up. 'Ah, but you can't have known that at the time,' he retorted. 'Never heard of journalistic instinct?' I pressed. Presumably not but, in any case, what was stopping him talking to Rod that night? In the years since then, we've seen Piers doing a lot of talking, often to A-list celebrities on TV. Whether he's any good at it, especially when compared to contemporaries like Jonathan Ross and Chris Evans, I'll leave to you to decide. I couldn't possibly comment.

The last time I saw Rod was at the annual Nordoff-Robbins charity auction lunch in 1996. He was sitting quietly with his then latest wife, Rachel Hunter, who during the intervening years had provided him with his fifth and sixth children. He would have enjoyed the high jinks in the VIP bar beforehand which involved a constellation of stars from different decades. These included the model Twiggy, Sting, Led Zeppelin's Robert Plant, actor Dennis Waterman of *Minder* fame, and funky Britpop couple Danny Goffey of the happening Supergrass and his girlfriend Pearl Lowe. Soon afterwards the couple became famous for being part of a new generation of Primrose Hill swingers and Pearl gave birth to Daisy, her generation's personification of someone who is famous for being famous.

In his riotous rollercoaster of a read, *Rod: The Autobiography* (Century), he namechecks both Sting and Plant, graciously recalling how the Led Zeppelin singer once helped him out of a tight spot. Rod was having a hard time winning over an inebriated Midlands audience so Robert bowled onstage for an impromptu duet. 'He saw I was in trouble and joined in on the R&B classic 'It's All Over Now'. Because he was a Midlander and local hero, his appearance saved us.' This event took place in the early 1970s when Rod was enjoying parallel careers: recording solo albums for one major record company and being lead singer with The Faces for another.

I first discovered him in 1969 when he released *An Old Raincoat Won't Ever Let You Down*, its unusual sleeve showing an old rustic character chasing what were, presumably, his granddaughters in a field. I was blown away by the song 'Handbags and Gladrags', both as a result of his voice and the fact that I'd never heard such melodic piano playing on a rock record. A year later he did it again with *Gasoline Alley*, cheekily recording the catchy 'Country Comfort' ahead of the song's actual writer, his friend Elton John.

During the following year I unearthed buried treasure: Jeff Beck's *Truth* featuring Rod as lead vocalist and *First Step*, the debut Faces album which boasted the superb 'Flying', a song Rod had co-written with the redoubtable Ronnie Wood and Ronnie Lane. By this stage, word had got around that Rod had been discovered by Long John Baldry, a former chart-topper who nicknamed him Rod The Mod.

All this information came in handy when one day our history teacher came bursting into class with an urgent enquiry: who was this Rod Stewart, the first artist to have topped both the singles and album charts on both sides of the Atlantic with 'Maggie May' and 'Every Picture Tells a Story'? I shared my knowledge provoking gasps of admiration from fellow pupils, henceforth being recognised as the rock scholar who could help them solve the problem of what record to buy with their birthday money. Rod would probably have enjoyed hearing this story and other things we had in common, like both of us owning Triumph Spitfires and buying our first houses in Muswell Hill. Perhaps one day we'll meet again and raise a glass to life's essentials: top birds, motors, music and one of his favourite phrases, 'excellent rock 'n' roll behaviour'.

CHAPTER 88

ROGER DALTREY

I ran into Roger Daltrey in the VIP Area at Wembley Stadium after one of Bruce Springsteen's shows in 1985. He seemed relieved to see a familiar face and I asked him what he thought of the gig. 'It was alright, I suppose,' he replied... 'but not as good as The 'Oo!' He had a point, I suppose. The first time I saw The Who was when I was a sixth former in 1971. The show climaxed with a massive flash of floodlit white light as Daltrey and Pete Townshend erupted into a frenzy of microphone hurling and windmilling guitar mayhem. I'd never seen anything like it, notwithstanding having attended concerts by David Bowie and the Rolling Stones.

The Who were touring with what remains their best album, *Who's Next*, the one featuring 'Baba O'Riley' and 'Won't Get Fooled Again'. The band had suddenly entered the big league having spent most of the 1960s as a Top 40 singles act. With early hits like 'My Generation' and 'Substitute' they were originally pigeonholed as a mod group although as Ray Davies told me with barely-disguised derision, they were not part of the original scene. The Who were closer to being an early example of a boy band, manufactured by ace face Peter Meaden, the famous mod publicist.

Around the time of the Springsteen gig, Daltrey released *Under a Raging Moon*, one of several solo albums. During an interview at his office, he threw light upon The Who's mod era and the role of Meaden. 'He sold us the look very well,' he recalled. 'We walked into a barber's shop looking like scruffy Rolling Stones clones and came out as mods, completing the look with button-down shirt collars, Italian suits and loafers.' The mod image saw a revival in the late 1970s with the release of the film *Quadrophenia* based on The Who's rock opera. Phil Daniels played the part of Jimmy, who Pete Townshend had based on himself in his teenage years. 'I feel closer to him than anybody,' he told a press conference at the time. 'In the story he could have had a relationship with a girl, but instead rows out to sea in a boat and sings 'Love, Reign O'er Me', an anthem to the rain. Because of his self-obsession he loses everything. There are a lot of people in rock 'n' roll like that.' It was left to Daltrey to sing Townshend's lyrics, a partnership which has lasted for more than half a century. 'I think my contribution to the character was giving him his vulnerability which stems from his sense of rage,' Roger told me. 'It manifests itself as a scream from the street which I recognised from my own working-class background. Pete might have always been the most brilliant songwriter but I was equally driven by the desire to be a singer. I was always clear about wanting to be in a band and still feel more comfortable as a team player.'

The first time I met the vocalist was in Leicester after the opening gig of a UK tour in early 1981. Despite being one of the most famous rock stars in the country, Roger was more than happy to join a crowd of us in the hotel bar, drinking and chatting until the early hours of the following morning. The conversation became quite philosophical, leading to speculation about the future world of work, machines taking over and all the rest of it. *He* would be okay, he decided, no computer could replace him as a singer. But what about me, Daltrey wondered, what did I do for a living? I confessed to being a journalist who had come up from London to write an early review of the tour. You could have parked a small vehicle in his dropped jaw. 'So now you tell me!' he joked. Since then we've met on several occasions, Daltrey always aware of my role in life. He wouldn't get fooled again.

ROGER WATERS

It's hard to believe that Roger Waters, the singer and principal songwriter of Pink Floyd, has been a solo artist for longer than a member of the groundbreaking band he co-founded. The conceptual impetus behind albums like *The Dark Side of the Moon* and *Wish You Were Here*, he left the group in 1984 following a period of creative friction. His next major project was to stage *The Wall* in Berlin, soon after the actual wall dividing both sides of the city came down.

Roger Waters has never been too fond of journalists. In fact, he's the sort of person for whom the expression 'doesn't suffer fools gladly' could have been specifically coined. Nevertheless he chose to grant me an exclusive interview for *The Times* shortly before the event took place in 1990. The original Pink Floyd album *The Wall* was Waters' autobiographical work about a bleak childhood during which he never met his father who was killed in action during World War II. It was only by chance that Berlin became the chosen venue for the event itself. 'I was thinking about the Grand Canyon, Wall Street or even the Gobi Desert,' he told me, 'but then in 1989 the wall came down, so I picked the former no man's land between the Brandenburg Gate and Potsdamer Platz which had once been the biggest public square in Europe. The plan is for it to be more like a film than a rock 'n' roll show, which is why there will be marching troops, helicopters and marionettes whose heads alone will be the size of a double-decker bus.'

The event, which proceeded more smoothly than could be expected, was attended by 200,000 people and the film itself has continued to be a steady seller on video and DVD. For some years, Waters was involved in litigation with his former colleagues over the use of the Pink Floyd name and brand, however by 2005 there was a reconciliation to the extent that Roger temporarily rejoined the group for Live 8, the twentieth anniversary of the original Live Aid performance.

In between, Waters recorded numerous solo albums, each as politically charged as The Wall which was essentially an anti-war affair. The best of these was *Radio K.A.O.S*, an attack on what the songwriter believed was a decline in the quality of America's pioneering rock radio. 'There are no longer any FM rock stations in LA,' he complained at the time. 'It's yet another example of the market economy going crazy. Like most of the record companies, the radio media has been taken over by lawyers and accountants who are only interested in the bottom line. Television is probably worse; even cartoons have been dumbed down. These days animated film is all about creating the cheapest possible format that people will accept, computer-generated jerky movement rubbish.'

Waters felt digital sound was also creating a rod for its own back. 'Hopefully, the dance music bubble will burst,' he declared while the phenomenon was enjoying one of its many peaks. 'Ninety per cent of releases seem to be dance tracks, compilations or remixes. Then again, there are some committed artists around like U2, although I'm not too impressed with the film industry. Eddie Murphy was almost a hero with films like *48 Hours* but then he started repeating himself with the *Beverly Hills Cop* series. Oliver Stone has made some great movies and he offered me the opportunity to compose the music for *Talk Radio*. I really liked the script but he wanted me to start work on it right away. I tried to explain that I was about to go on holiday with my kids but in the film business that doesn't wash. Everyone eats and sleeps work twenty-four hours a day whereas I prefer to develop projects slowly.

'Once upon a time, people in the entertainment industry were passionate about what they did, it wasn't just about the money. My main hope is that we get some decent people back at the top – men and women who know something about what they are dealing with.' Roger Waters, responsible for some of the most innovative rock music ever, expressed this wish almost thirty years ago. I think we can all agree that it hasn't exactly been fulfilled.

STEVE HARLEY

If ever there was an artist blessed with self-belief it was Steve Harley. As a child he suffered with polio, a long period of convalescence allowing him to acquaint himself with the works of T.S. Eliot, Ernest Hemingway and Bob Dylan. Apart from being inspired by some of the finest prose of the twentieth century, Steve inherited the musical talent of his mother who was a semi-professional jazz singer. It was no coincidence that by the end of his teens he'd made inroads into the singer-songwriter circuit, opening for the likes of John Martyn and Ralph McTell at such hip venues as The Troubadour and Bunjies folk cellar. Harley's ambitions exceeded the acoustic folk scene, however, and his timing was fortuitous. The early 1970s saw the rise of David Bowie and Roxy Music, artier acts who inadvertently paved the way for a maverick like Steve. In 1973, Harley's band, Cockney Rebel, released their debut album *The Human Menagerie*. It wasn't an overnight success, but it contained songs like 'Sebastian' which elevated the group to cult status and remains part of Steve's set today.

While satisfying the demand of an audience in search of experimentation, Cockney Rebel also appealed to the pop market. The following year they reached No. 5 in the charts with 'Judy Teen' which was followed by another hit, 'Mr Soft'. Then, in 1975, the band peaked with their third album *The Best Years of Our Lives*, its signature single 'Make Me Smile (Come Up and See Me)' making the No. 1 spot and, to this day, remaining one of the most played records on UK radio. By the time Cockney Rebel toured the album and single, they were the biggest name in Britain, Bowie having announced his retirement from the stage and Roxy having begun to go off the boil. I was still a student that year, when I wrote my first-ever live review for the *Altrincham Guardian*, describing Harley as '...stylish and charismatic, arms clasped across his chest in a quasi-religious display of melodramatic fervour. The devoted following matched his state of ecstasy.'

I didn't get to meet Steve for another four years, by which time the band had broken up and Steve had spent an artistically torrid time in LA, returning to London in need of fresh inspiration. In 1979, Harley released a musically ambitious solo album entitled *The Candidate* which failed to live up to its name. He was dropped by his record company, EMI, after being signed to them for almost a decade. Turning what could have been a disaster into something for his own advantage, he spent the next few years 'watching the kids grow up'. He told me this in 1986 when I invited him for a drink at The Groucho Club. He had just returned to the charts with *Phantom of the Opera*, a duet with Sarah Brightman, wife of its composer Andrew Lloyd Webber, from the musical of the same name. Apart from conducting the interview for the *Mail on Sunday*, I wanted him to listen to a tape of some musicians with whom I was working.

A few months earlier at Midem I had met Bob, a jazzy songwriter and bass player from New York and his keyboardist, Rick, an Essex boy. The duo were making a living playing the Riviera party circuit but deserved to be recording artists. As it happened, they were signed to a major publishing company which, in time-honoured music industry fashion, were doing nothing with their career except sitting on their contract preventing them from taking their talent elsewhere. I believed they would appeal to the same market as somebody like George Benson and suggested they use the name In Flight, the title of one of George's albums. I shopped the tape around my record company A&R contacts who mainly agreed that the guys had talent. The only problem was rap and hip-hop were in the process of going mainstream and the major labels were all looking for the next LL Cool J or Public Enemy.

The following week, however, I received a phone call from Steve Harley. He had been booked to appear on top TV show *The Tube* and needed a backing band. 'That tape you gave me... those guys can't half play... are they members of The Musicians' Union?' Unfortunately, they had been living abroad so you can guess where this is going – and there wasn't time to rectify the situation. Bob had learned everything he needed to know about the music industry and decided to go back to New York City; he believed he'd had enough.

Meanwhile, like the trouper he was and still is, Steve Harley put together another band and went back on the road where he seems to have been ever since. In 1993, 'Make Me Smile' returned to the charts thanks to a TV commercial, coinciding with the re-release of the Cockney Rebel back catalogue. Since I was writing for *Hello!* Steve took me out to an Italian restaurant for a damn good lunch. I had just become a father for the second time and was contemplating leaving London. At this point Steve was playing around 100 gigs a year in the UK and Europe so, as far as his career was concerned, he no longer needed to live in the capital. 'London's no good for children,' he advised. 'Mine will be starting secondary school soon, so we've moved out to a small town on the border of Essex and Suffolk. I know the area because I trained in Colchester for Essex County Newspapers before my musical career took off. Although I'm away a lot, my wife doesn't seem to mind. I think she's glad I'm out of the way!'

Never one to mince words, Steve had other reasons for choosing East Anglia. 'I don't like the M4 so the west wouldn't suit me and there are still a lot of status games being played in Berkshire and Surrey. Apart from which, I got a very good deal when I bought an old coaching inn – although not all the locals were impressed. A barmaid challenged me about being a newcomer, so I pointed out that my family were descended from French Huguenots and had lived in the villages surrounding Bury St Edmunds since the sixteenth century.' As a result of his family background he remains a devout Christian, occasionally reading the epistle in the parish church, a fine gesture in this godless age.

In addition to having sold out the forthcoming UK tour, Harley was looking forward to going back to Germany. 'We seem to do much bigger business in Europe,' he continued. 'In Dortmund the other week we played the same 10,000-seater which Simply Red were playing the following month. I could never do that in London. I think it's something to do with being an island race; nothing seems to last here very long, everything is subject to changing trends.' Indeed, as many an artist has discovered. Yet fast forward a few years and Harley's special brew of confidence, luck and sheer stamina was to serve him well. Guitarist Jim Cregan, who left Cockney Rebel in the 1970s to join Rod Stewart's band, reunited with the singer for some live dates. At the same time Rod boosted Steve's earnings by recording one of his compositions. What goes around comes around as they say.

CHAPTER 91

STEVE MARRIOTT

Few commercial pop groups have ever captured the spirit of rock 'n' roll as convincingly as the Small Faces. Led by former child actor Steve Marriott they enjoyed a series of brilliant hits during the late 1960s before moving on to more ambitious projects.

Steve came from an impoverished East End background yet won a place at a top theatrical school. He had barely entered his teens when he was selected for the role of Artful Dodger in Lionel Bart's musical of Charles Dickens's *Oliver Twist*. Then at the dawn of the mod movement he formed a group with Ronnie Lane and Kenney Jones. Their name was a play on the word 'face', mod-ernist speak for a well-known and respected man about town. Since clothes were important, their wages took the form of accounts at the best shops in London's Carnaby Street. Their manager also presented them with a shared rented house which soon became party central, visited by all the leading rock 'n' roll people of the day.

It was at the Sun & 13 Cantons, around the corner from many a West End landmark, that Steve suggested we meet for an interview in the late 1980s. He arrived with his new wife, Toni. Echoing the lyrics from their classic chart-topper 'Sha-La-La-La-Lee', I asked them about their wedding reception: had they invited 'just a few close friends'? He laughed and ordered half a pint of lager, his hedonistic days of cocaine-fuelled benders clearly behind him.

Drugs and financial mismanagement meant he had never

made as much money as most of his contemporaries, but regular gigs and the occasional recording were keeping him solvent. Steve was nothing if not candid when it came to discussing his earnings. 'It's true, the Small Faces were ripped off, but I've never really gone short. Look around and you can see too much money does more harm than good, it can get in the way of what you really want to do. At the moment I'm doing gigs around Essex and London, clearing about a grand a night, enough to keep anyone going.'

The Small Faces peaked in 1968 with the release of *Ogdens' Nut Gone Flake*, one of the first rock concept albums. Yet the following year the group disbanded. 'It was starting to get formulaic so I got bored with it,' Marriott explained, 'plus we had been together, literally living out of one another's pockets for about five years, a long time when you're in your late teens and early twenties. It's when you grow up and start to think about getting married. Another thing was that although Ronnie Lane and I wrote most of the songs, we didn't write together. Like Lennon and McCartney or Mick and Keith we tended to work alone and bring our ideas into the studio, so it wasn't like losing a partner.'

Something else Steve had in common with the Rolling Stones is that he almost joined them. 'After Mick Taylor left I auditioned for them,' he revealed. 'There was nobody I wanted to work with more than Keith Richards – but I think Mick realised I would also want to be the front man.' A decade earlier Steve also came close to working with David Bowie but felt better suited to his mates in the Small Faces. When the latter disbanded, he formed Humble Pie with Peter Frampton and David Bowie opened for them on their first tour. 'That was a bit of a coincidence,' Steve agreed, 'but you have to remember that in those days the music scene was a lot smaller so there was more likelihood of sharing a tour with someone you already knew. It was a bit like when Led Zeppelin recorded 'Whole Lotta Love'. I still think it was inspired by a song I wrote called 'You Need Loving' but, to be honest, both were based on an old Willie Dixon tune.'

In the early 1990s, Steve went to LA to record songs with Peter Frampton following a proposed reunion of the duo. On his return, jet-lagged and exhausted, he fell asleep while smoking a cigarette. It set his house ablaze and the following morning he was found dead from smoke inhalation. Although still in his early forties, even by rock 'n' roll standards Steve Marriott had made a lot of great music in a tragically truncated life.

STEVE WINWOOD

Considering Birmingham is Britain's second largest city, it has come up with surprisingly few rock 'n' roll people. Jeff Lynne and various members of Black Sabbath spring to mind but perhaps the Midlands' greatest talent has been Steve Winwood, one of my own personal heroes for more than fifty years.

I first spotted Steve when he was singing and playing keyboards with the Spencer Davis Group in 1965, supporting the Rolling Stones at the Manchester Odeon. He was still only seventeen years old when the band topped the charts with 'Keep On Running' the following year. Further hits like 'Somebody Help Me', 'Gimme Some Lovin'' and 'I'm A Man' followed before he formed Traffic in the early days of psychedelia. In this band he enjoyed a songwriting partnership with lyricist and drummer Jim Capaldi which lasted more than a decade, yielding classic albums like *Mr Fantasy*, *John Barleycorn Must Die* and *The Low Spark of High-Heeled Boys*. Much of the material was written while all four members of Traffic were living together in an isolated cottage on the Berkshire Downs. As well as collating an original combination of pop, rock and folk, the quartet pioneered the concept of 'getting it together in the countryside', away from the distractions of the music industry.

Famously shy and reluctant to be interviewed, I only met Steve a couple of times: once at the Bill Wyman Video Café party (see Chapter Four); the other on the street while I was talking to his brother, Muff, outside a party at Lennon's – a restaurant on the edge of Covent Garden which had been opened by Cynthia Lennon, ex-wife of Beatle John. Muff had also been a member of the Spencer Davis Group but went on to become a pillar of the record industry. Apart from being a senior A&R executive at Sony he had also produced the debut album of a then-unknown band, Dire Straits. I knew Muff as a result of various meetings in which I played him tapes of acts I was trying to manage and he was happy to introduce me to his brother. Steve had retained his youthful good looks, possibly on account of living a relatively quiet life. While most musicians went to every party going, back in the 1980s you would have been more likely to catch Steve playing the organ at his local church in Stroud, Gloucestershire on a Sunday morning.

On the other hand, Winwood was anything but a recluse as far as work was concerned, going on the road with everyone from Rod Stewart to Tom Petty and the Heartbreakers. Still, that image of Traffic, pictured at the cottage on their early record sleeves, lingered... 'Moving to the countryside was a means of avoiding unnecessary interruptions from record companies, A&R departments and all the rest of it,' Steve explained. 'The idea was to write together and be able to play and rehearse whenever we felt like it. Everything we created was born out of playing.'

Apart from having a distinctive soul voice, Steve was a masterly player of the Hammond organ. His urgent chords can be heard on the long version of 'Voodoo Chile' on the last Jimi Hendrix Experience classic, *Electric Ladyland*. Steve also played with the other leading guitar hero of the day, Eric Clapton, in Blind Faith. The two of them had known each other for years and decided to pool their talents after Cream disbanded and Winwood took a sabbatical from Traffic. Blind Faith only made one album but played for the first time in front of 100,000 fans at a free concert in London's Hyde Park. Steve could be seen at his peak performing 'Presence of the Lord' in a clip from the gig shown in the early 1970s rock 'n' roll TV film, *Season of the Witch*. 'I don't think that musically Eric and myself ever got round to completing what we set out to do,' the singer admitted that day outside Lennon's, 'mainly because we both enjoyed the independence of our individual solo careers.'

The upside to this scenario was that both artists were able to release a succession of fine albums of their own. Steve's include *Arc of a Diver*, *Refugees of the Heart* and *Back in the High Life*, inspired by his relocation to New York. It only goes to show you can take the boy out of hard-working industrial Birmingham, but you can't take the legacy of England's second city out of the boy.

CHAPTER 93

STEVEN MORRISSEY

The first time I met Steven Morrissey, as he then called himself, was at The Ritz Ballroom in Manchester in 1978. I had gone to see Magazine and John Cooper Clarke but arrived in time to see The Nosebleeds. Until recently they had been led by a highly-strung fellow called Ed Banger but he had left and been replaced by vocalist Steve Morrissey. His performance was memorable for the fact that he spent most of it shaking his head at the floor. With longish, straggly hair bouncing up and down you could hardly see his face. The one time he looked up was to announce the fact that the next song was a number by the New York Dolls. Having seen these glam-rock legends at Warwick University some years earlier, I went to have a chat with the singer after the show. He told me that the Dolls' song hadn't appeared on either of their two albums, only on a rare bootleg recording or private pressing, as they call them these days.

It transpired that young Steven, just eighteen years old at the time, was something of a character on the Manchester scene. At the age of fourteen he had started writing letters to the *NME* demanding the BBC should repeat the New York Dolls' appearance on *The Old Grey Whistle Test* in 1973. A petition duly followed but was largely ignored. Morrissey had also submitted scripts for *Coronation Street*, ITV's long-running soap opera, but to no avail. Steven had more luck when he decided to write for the music press – thanks to myself. In 1980, when I was back in Manchester to review a gig, I ran into him at a club called Rafters. We'd met a few times and he asked me straight off, 'Can I have your old job?' He was referring to the one I'd had as Manchester correspondent for *Record Mirror*. Since I was now the Reviews Editor of the magazine in London there was, presumably, a vacancy. I said I'd give him a try and during the next year or two he filed a few reviews. These tended to be of girl-led groups like The Photos and Altered Images. He also wrote about friends such as future Cult guitarist Billy Duffy who, at the time, was in a band called Lonesome No More. The pair of them were briefly in local punk band Slaughter & the Dogs.

Another friend of Morrissey's was Linder Sterling, former girlfriend of Magazine's Howard Devoto, who sang in a band called Ludus. Linder later became notorious for taking legal action against the producers of *24 Hour Party People*, the film about The Hacienda and Factory Records. Apparently, she didn't like the way she was depicted in the script and fought to have parts of it removed. Morrissey closed ranks with Sterling and refused to allow the early Smiths' single 'This Charming Man' to be used in the film. So far, so incestuous, but Steve didn't write exclusively about his chums. He penned a favourable piece about American swamp goths The Cramps although the up-and-coming Depeche Mode did not fare as well, being accused of 'resurrecting every murderously monotonous cliché known to modern man.'

The following year I didn't hear from him for a while, so I phoned him up at his mother's home. She took the call and sounded quite frantic, claiming her son had disappeared. When I finally got hold of him it turned out he had been visiting friends in America. We talked about his trip and he admitted he had not really liked New York. I was impressed by his honesty since most people who go there never stop raving about the place, especially to friends who have yet to visit the city.

The next time he got in touch was when he was about to publish a book about the New York Dolls. He might not have been able to persuade the BBC to show a repeat of their 1973 appearance but he was able to describe it in his slim volume. 'It was my first real emotional experience,' he wrote about the Whistle Test clip. 'I was fourteen and from then on my education was ruined. I was thrown off the athletics and football teams at school and I think the teachers expected me to turn up to maths in drag.' The book sold out its initial print run of 3,000.

Three years later, Morrissey was on the cusp of stardom, appearing on *Top of the Pops* where I was present in the TV studio to watch The Smiths go through the motions of 'Heaven Knows I'm Miserable Now'. For the first time Morrissey had his trademark bunch of gladioli hanging out of the back pocket of baggy jeans and was wearing an old-fashioned hearing aid. 'Johnnie Ray,' he whispered to me as he took the stage, referring to the lachrymose 1950s rock 'n' roll balladeer who had been deaf since a child.

As far as the title of the single was concerned, I suspected he had always been a depressive. 'I'm not an unhappy person at all,' he argued, 'I might have gone through periods of depression as a teenager but who didn't? I'm not really miserable, in fact I'm very happy to be here,' he said, drinking lukewarm tea in the badly-decorated canteen. One thing he was not pleased about was his record company trying to persuade The Smiths to make a video of the song. 'It's not going to happen,' he insisted, 'we would rather play on any TV show that wants us and I don't really approve of making a film to illustrate a song. I think fans would prefer to use their own imagination.'

It was an opinion echoed by Bruce Springsteen not long afterwards. Eventually both artists were encouraged to change their minds but neither have ever relied on the video format. Thirty-odd years later they are still playing live to huge crowds all over the world.

STEVIE NICKS

Stevie Nicks is one of the most creative and eccentric women in the history of rock, America's equivalent to Kate Bush. She is also a hugely successful musician, having played an integral part in the writing and recording of *Rumours*, Fleetwood Mac's first multi-platinum album. Among Stevie's compositions on that album was 'Dreams', their chart-topping single. Nicks also contributed tracks on subsequent major releases such as *Mirage* and *Tango in the Night*.

A parallel solo career has also seen the release of LPs like *The Other Side of the Mirror* which came out in 1989. It was while promoting this record that we met for an interview at London's Mayfair Hotel, a popular haunt of the high-end music fraternity. Since the feature was for *Hello!* magazine, home and relationships were very much on the agenda, yielding some extreme stories. For example, if you thought London property prices were exorbitant, back then Stevie's house in LA was costing her $80,000 to rent – per month. 'It's a Dutch castle at the top of a hill,' she revealed by way of explanation. 'It's usually used for parties or films, but I prefer to house my personal staff there. I have a lot of people to look after: musicians, make-up artists, costume designers... then there's my personal assistant, Ben, who's been with me for eight years. It's strictly platonic,' she added, anticipating my next question, 'he's been with me longer than any of the lovers who have come and gone during that time.'

Considering the amount of rent, the castle was not without

its drawbacks. 'The electrics are terrible, even a hairdresser is enough to fuse all the lights. When I tried turning the baronial dining hall into a rehearsal space it was a total disaster. Actually, it was probably a blessing in disguise since I'd probably have been charged a fortune for messing the place up.'

Luckily, the singer had another home in Phoenix, Arizona, a place Stevie owned which meant she was not answerable to anybody when she decided to turn it into a full-on creative space. 'My piano, recording equipment and paintings all live there,' she said. 'I was born in Phoenix and my house there is my sanctuary. LA is necessary for business and working with other musicians, but in Arizona I love the air. You can feel the desert as soon as you get off the plane. The house has a serene, sacred feel to it. I think it might once have been an Indian burial ground. It looks out on to a mountain which resembles some kind of creature, a camel or a monk praying, depending on the time of day. It's very sparsely furnished which is useful because most of the day it is too hot to go outside. In the afternoon the swimming pool feels hotter than the house. I bought it about ten years ago and, unlike the castle, it's wired for sound so it's my music place. Plus, my parents live nearby and we've always been close.'

Stevie added that she originally planned to be an English teacher but throughout her late teens and early twenties she had made a living playing in various bands. A few months before she got the call from Mick Fleetwood to join Fleetwood Mac her father suggested she went back to school for a course in teacher-training. 'He even offered to pay but then my life changed overnight. I don't say someone must have been watching over me because I'm not religious. In fact, as a result of the way I dress (lace shawls, flowing gowns) some people have called me a witch, but I do believe in a kind of god. I think there must be someone present in nature or at least some kind of presence amidst the mountains, trees and rivers, which is probably why I've always been attracted to the landscape around Phoenix.

'I don't really worry about dying,' she went on, 'because the women in my family tend to live beyond a hundred: I remember still having great-grandparents when I was sixteen years old. It's a good thing because there's a lot I want to do apart from travelling all over the world as a rock 'n' roll star. I like painting. Right now my speciality is hand-tinting black and white photographs with oil paints. I sometimes stay up for days if I get absorbed in something like that. I try to make time for watching movies or TV shows that people are talking about but I'm not very good at simply sitting down and relaxing in front of a screen. I always like to be doing something,' she concluded, hinting at that age-old adage about the key to success: 10 per cent inspiration, 90 per cent perspiration.

CHAPTER 95

STING, ANDY SUMMERS & STEWART COPELAND

Too young for the hippie generation and too old to be punks, few would have placed a bet on The Police becoming the most successful band of their generation. Yet a combination of musical know-how and sonic diversity enabled the trio to attract a mainstream audience without making any commercial compromise. Their striking image of bleached hair setting off craggy good looks didn't do them any harm, either.

The early Police didn't have any luck with the media. The music press slagged them off for trying to jump aboard the punk bandwagon while their first two singles were banned by Radio One; 'Roxanne' was about a prostitute while 'Can't Stand Losing You' involved suicide. On the other hand, they made up for lost time by touring constantly, rapidly gaining fans by word of mouth. They were sensational when I saw them at London's Rainbow Theatre towards the end of 1979, confidently rocking out and earning screams from female fans old enough to know better. Sting was clearly a sex symbol, but he knew how to play jazz and reggae as well as executing all the right dance moves.

By the following year, The Police had sold 7 million albums and were filling venues all over the world. This didn't seem to do much for Sting's disposition when he arrived at his publicist's office so I could interview him for *Record Mirror*. His natural moodiness was exacerbated by the fact that *Top of the Pops* had just announced their refusal to show the video for the band's latest single, 'Invisible Sun'. The song was about the Troubles in Northern Ireland, the citizens of Belfast having spent the last ten years or so caught in the crossfire of race and religion. The video contained newsreel-type footage of kids picking up sticks and stones, weighing up whether to throw them at British soldiers.

The singer and bass player denied it was a political song. 'In fact, just the opposite,' he claimed, 'it's anti-political in the same way as I'm anti-religious. The theme is hope, as in there must be some kind of invisible hope which keeps us going, relying on better times ahead. The sun is invisible because you can't see it. I'm coming to feel more and more that the only solution is spiritual,' said the former school teacher. 'Politics doesn't work unless people are treated like robots. I have no faith in it and place no value in leadership of any kind. People are far more complex than politicians think, no wonder there were angry riots all over the country earlier this year.'

As if all this wasn't a bit heavy for a music magazine, Sting went on to profess the extent of his responsibility as a successful musician. 'Shifting huge quantities of records puts you in an awkward position because of the number of jobs which become dependent upon you. Last year no one was selling records apart from us,' he reckoned, conveniently forgetting about Madness, the Jam, Blondie and The Clash, to name but a few. 'But at least the new music scene is more exciting here than it is in America,' he conceded.

At last something positive. So far, our conversation had been more like a lecture than an interview but any hint of optimism was clearly out of the question. 'I couldn't give a toss about the future of rock 'n' roll,' he went on. 'What are my worries? Neutron bombs and chemical warfare, and the miniscule chance of my son living a long and happy life.'

Sting would later have a hit with 'Russians', a song about that very subject. He would also record a number of accomplished albums with top jazz musicians. Where he never really scored was on the big screen despite looking cool in the mod film *Quadrophenia. Dune,* the sci-fi adventure, was dull while Dennis Potter's *Brimstone and Treacle* was a disaster. Then there was the small matter of a James Bond movie which never happened. Sting described the incident as 'appalling' although it's worth pointing out that as the sixty-year-old Bond franchise continues to flourish, Sting's film career has become extinct.

I wondered whether with all those millions in the bank he saw a future for himself in business, perhaps starting his own record company. 'I can't see myself in business,' he replied, 'I don't think I'd be terribly good at it and, actually, I'm not concerned with money. I live well below my means,' concluded the celebrity who some years later would sell a New York penthouse for $50 million.

Like Sting, Andy Summers was an experienced musician before joining The Police. After playing in Zoot Money's Big Roll Band he went to California where he studied classical guitar at music college. Despite this, Andy was able to describe with a refreshing lack of jargon what made The Police's sound so appealing. 'We all come from different backgrounds and have listened to lots of different things. It's that friction which creates our dynamic. We're unified in our diversity and there are spaces in the music which make it seductive and give it an ability to attract people's attention.'

He delivered this explanation at his eighteenth-century harbour-side home in Kinsale, near Cork in Ireland. It was home to Andy, his wife Kate and daughter Layla during a period of self-imposed tax exile. In 1980, Summers was only able to spend forty days a year in England – or else pay a whopping great 60 per cent in tax. He acknowledged that financially the band had come a long way from releasing indie singles as recently as the late 1970s. 'Yes,' he agreed, 'it doesn't seem that long ago since we were up all-night gluing sleeves together, but it was a useful training ground. We've had letters from kids praising us for changing their lives, inspired by the way we came up from nowhere.'

The next time I saw Andy was at his new mansion in 'the posh end of Putney' in south west London. Not that he got to spend much time there. While The Police were continuing to arrest sizeable numbers of fans – 'we recently pulled in 50,000 fans in Italy in one show' – Summers was pursuing other activities such as recording an album with King Crimson and David Bowie maestro Robert Fripp, and publishing a photographic memoir. He also seemed to spend a lot of time in the USA. 'On the whole, I prefer the American scene,' he admitted. 'Not necessarily bands like Foreigner but the whole attitude. They haven't got this intense pop hang-up. England is far too claustrophobic with too many magazines and too many people anxious to set trends. There are also too many videos. MTV has changed the whole market here as well as in America: Duran Duran wouldn't have stood a chance without their videos. Likewise, the whole film industry seems geared towards putting movies on tape but they'll never replace cinemas,' he predicted, successfully.

The third member of The Police, drummer Stewart Copeland, was the most sociable, often present and correct at gigs and clubs in London. One week, *Record Mirror* printed a Police special issue in which Stewart took over my job, pitching up at three or four venues a night. 'Thank God it was only for a week,' he groaned during our editorial meeting, 'it was more exhausting than going out on the road.'

Copeland happens to be from an interesting family. His father had been a director of operations for the CIA and his brother was the manager of The Police. His mother was an archaeologist while Stewart himself was married to Sonja Kristina, the stunning singer in 1970s rock band Curved Air. Like Sting, Stewart also became involved with film, working on Francis Ford Coppola's *Rumble Fish*. Sensibly, he drew the line at composing the soundtrack for the director, famous for epics like *The Godfather* and *Apocalypse Now*. His score for *Rumble Fish* remains one of the best scores in recent memory, a greater contribution to celluloid culture than most musicians have managed to achieve.

TINA TURNER

During the early 1980s, Tina Turner made one of the most sensational comebacks in the history of rock, at an age when many of her contemporaries would have been contemplating retirement. In a previous life she scored chart-topping singles like 'River Deep – Mountain High' and 'Nutbush City Limits' with husband Ike before their relationship disintegrated. A few years later the singer was invited to work with producer Martyn Ware, a former member of the Human League. She appeared on pop TV programme *The Tube* singing a version of the Al Green standard 'Let's Stay Together', Ware and fellow Heaven 17 member Glenn Gregory providing backing vocals. While at the television studio, Tina recorded an in-concert special, resurrecting her career as a mainstream R&B artist. A few weeks later 'Let's Stay Together' charted, making Tina the first female soloist to enjoy a Top 40 hit for six consecutive decades. After *The Tube* recordings, I dined with Tina in a Chinese restaurant, accompanied by Dave Stewart and Annie Lennox who had also appeared on the show. She wasn't reluctant to talk about the break-up with Ike.

'These days, I guess it would be called domestic abuse but you wouldn't believe the incidents which led to our divorce,' began the forty-three-year-old who still looked twenty-five. 'All our earnings went on his cocaine habit and he was so violent I lost count of the number of times my nose got broken. He also broke my jaw while I was applying make-up before a gig, mainly to disguise yet another black eye. I can still taste swallowing blood,' she went on, contemplating a jug of sweet and sour sauce. 'There were times when I felt suicidal, until several years ago I decided to escape, disappearing during the middle of a tour. It wouldn't have been so bad if it wasn't for the fact that we had four young children and there was constant intimidation all the time I was filing for divorce.'

Soon afterwards, Tina hooked up with Roger Davies, manager of Olivier Newton-John, one of the stars of *Grease*. With Davies pulling the strings, Tina's career accelerated from one landmark to the next, the album *Private Dancer* yielding such worldwide hits as 'What's Love Got To Do With It' and 'Better Be Good To Me'. Turner's rhythmic combination of soul, R&B and rock 'n' roll attracted a wide audience spanning several generations, the singer earning record attendances at major venues like Wembley Stadium. She also sang 'Golden Eye' for the eponymous James Bond film and captured the hearts of indie fans with her version of Massive Attack's 'Unfinished Sympathy'. The song was previewed at a press conference when she spontaneously produced a tape machine and played it to the assembled throng. As one of her biggest media fans, you don't suppose I had anything to do with it, do you?

CHAPTER 97

TOM PETTY

Tom Petty was the first rock star I interviewed on my maiden voyage to the United States in 1978. I'd been writing for *Record Mirror* for a few months and thought I'd better go to LA, to see how the other half rocked. I didn't really know anyone over there apart from cousin Lawrence who had recently moved to the West Coast to work as a tour manager. He was sharing a house in West Hollywood with my other cousin Judi, conveniently a photographer for the *NME*.

Judi had been doing the rounds and the week before had seen Tom in Madame Wong's, a Chinese restaurant-cum-rock venue. His record company, Shelter, was only a mile away from where I was staying at the Tropicana (see the Pauline Black chapter) so I wandered down and arranged an interview – just like that, none of the absurd PR and marketing red tape in those halcyon days. At the time, Tom and his Heartbreakers were rehearsing new material, Petty spending afternoons chilling out and writing the odd lyric. We hit it off from the word go which, naturally, had nothing to do with the sharing of combustibles. Cousin Judi dropped by with some courtesy pics she'd shot at Mrs Wong's and stayed around to take more photos of Tom with her long-lost rellie. It was three hours before I said goodbye to that part of Hollywood, during which time I learned quite a lot about the utterly cool star with the southern accent.

Petty had much to be pleased about, especially as he had recently enjoyed the honour of hearing his hero, Roger McGuinn, covering one of his own songs, 'American Girl', destined to become one of the most radio-friendly hits of the 1970s and beyond. 'We opened for Roger at the Bottom Line in New York and he invited me onstage to jam on the song. We did a real neat version of it,' he enthused, 'with Beach Boys harmonies.' It was bands like McGuinn's Byrds and the Beach Boys which drew Petty to California, bringing the Heartbreakers with him, in 1974. 'I came from this backwater in Florida called Gainesville, where you could only get gigs in bars and even then you were obliged to play the same stuff as all the boogie bands. Plus, I never got on with my father who was an abusive alcoholic, so it made perfect sense to come to LA and create our own rock 'n' roll family.'

Despite the endless summers and legendary California girls, many critics never missed a chance to slag off LA. How did Tom feel about that? 'What difference does it make living here or in Idaho?' he responded. 'Just because someone who has never lived here writes that it's screwed up, everybody wants to believe it. Trust me, I might not have sold a million records but I'm having a better time now than I had in my early twenties. Between gigs I used to work in a graveyard, cleaning up and loading trucks with garbage. It was a miserable life so what I'd do is take two uppers in the morning, mow the grass and then go and play five sets in a topless bar. During the third set I'd eat another pill, get two hours' sleep and then return to the graves. I got so run down I'm lucky I didn't end up in one myself!'

At the time of our interview Tom's main concern wasn't related to lifestyle or critics but something way beyond his control – the state of American radio. 'If there's too much guitar the jocks won't play it,' he complained, 'granddad would be shocked because it disrupts the format between Olivia Newton-John and Frankie Valli. We can fill auditoriums every night, people scream and go crazy and buy hundreds of thousands of records but the radio stations won't admit there's a market for us. American wireless has a very narrow vision,' he drawled over that charmingly old-fashioned expression. Although college radio would eventually break this deadlock, at that point in time many future stars were victims of the same problem. 'Springsteen and Costello are real good too, but none of us have had a single go higher than the Top 30. Car radio is my entire musical background because I never had a lot of bread, couldn't afford to buy many records and it's a shame for today's kids.'

Tom described himself as an Anglophile, his teenage years soundtracked by bands like The Searchers and the Animals as well as The Beatles and Stones, all of whom English fans grew up with on *Top of the Pops*. The previous year, when Tom had toured the UK with Nils Lofgren, he too appeared on the show, only to find it almost as disappointing as US radio. 'The silliest day of my life,' he simmered, 'we came on after Kermit the Frog and they tried to insist we were punk. It seemed anyone under the age of twenty-five got called that. Not that it bugged us but any time you put a label on something it gets ridiculous. The Ramones once said to me on an aeroplane, "What we're trying to do is beat this punk image". I thought that was absurd since it's what they are famous for but, whichever way you look at it, we're all just making music, so why bother with a label? Someone will only change it by the time of the next record.'

These words proved prophetic because by the next time I saw Tom Petty and the Heartbreakers on their 1980 UK tour, he was toying with the idea of them being a soul band. However significant the twin guitars of himself and Mike Campbell were to their sound, 'you can't underestimate the contribution of the keyboards. The organ underpinned all those great records by Sam & Dave, Solomon Burke, Wilson Pickett... and what about Percy Sledge? 'When a Man Loves a Woman' is one of the greatest songs of all time,' Tom enthused, decades before you could hear it destroyed on every so-called talent show. 'I grew up on a diet of R&B and it's the purest music I've ever heard. I think if you want to put a label on us, we're a soul band more than anything else. That's how we play guitar, it's not about virtuosity but feel and rhythm. I'm just a rhythm guitarist, couldn't play lead to save my life!'

This conversation took place in a hotel lounge in Birmingham after the band had opened their tour at the local Odeon. The third album, *Damn the Torpedoes*, had been Tom Petty and the Heartbreakers' most successful to date, selling more than two million copies in the first six months of release. Apart from boasting some of their best-ever songs – 'Refugee', 'Shadow of a Doubt' and 'Even the Losers' – the LP was produced by Jimmy Iovine, the man who had done the honours for Bruce Springsteen's monumental *Born to Run*. It came as no surprise when Tom told me that these two pillars of American rock were firm friends. 'I was walking down Sunset Boulevard with Bruce and he insisted we went into Tower Records to buy some discs. I was aghast but we did it anyway. It shows you can be a star without forgetting who you are. A lot of people in the music industry would be glad about you getting paranoid because it would give them more of a role. But if you get too far removed from the street, stuff builds up in your mind and you start to worry something bad is about to happen. Bruce's attitude is that it's dangerous to be treated like a god and give up that part of your life.'

The tour ended in London with a party at The Montcalm Hotel near Marble Arch. The hotel was about as high-end as rock 'n' roll hotels get with Lou Reed and Leonard Cohen being other examples of the clientele. On this particular night the establishment did not live up to its name. One of the waiters reprimanded drummer Stan Lynch for resting his foot on a coffee table. You don't mess with physically robust drummers at the best of times, especially when they are trying to unwind after a tour. Some fancy footwork followed and I had the privilege of a ring-side seat.

The next time I spoke to Tom was when he was in town to promote his 1982 opus *Long After Dark*. There had been some substantial changes in the music scene, but nothing so drastic as to erase Tom's sense of humour. 'We laugh amongst ourselves because we're one of the few bands left who play guitars,' he drawled, 'though I can't deny the appeal of groups like the Human League and Soft Cell. I don't mind drum machines and actually use one myself when demoing material. They are also useful in improving the rhythmic consciousness of all these acts, giving them something they didn't previously have.' Naturally, he had to admit the old ways were still the best, pulling out of the bag an old anecdote he'd never told me before. One of the reasons Tom got turned on to music was as a result of his uncle taking him to see Elvis Presley recording at Sam Phillips' Sun Studios in Memphis. The young Petty was barely knee-high to a speaker cabinet, but 'Elvis was very hospitable and generous with his time. Then came the British Invasion and everything else I grew up with, or maybe didn't. A musician's life doesn't really encourage growing up!'

Another year, another country. This time Holland for an over-the-top media festival involving Sting, Stevie Nicks, Duran Duran, *Billboard* magazine and the Paradiso, Amsterdam's most famous music club which was being used by some major record companies to ensnare journos to see acts they had absolutely no interest in. Tom rocked up to this five-day booze-fuelled beano to talk about his first solo album, *Full Moon Fever*. Somehow all the pre-release copies got lost in transit so we couldn't really talk about it, however, this being 1989 the Traveling Wilburys (see Jeff Lynne chapter) were still in vogue so we talked about them instead. 'We recorded our album while the Heartbreakers were on vacation,' Tom began. 'I wrote some of the songs with Jeff Lynne, the two of us playing face-to-face with our guitars. I'd never collaborated with anyone like that before but found it a really inspirational way to work with a song writing partner. When Jeff and I met it was like we'd known each other forever ... then we got engaged and married!'

Enjoying the atmosphere of one of the city's infamous 'coffee shops', Tom proceeded to embark on another masterpiece – a pen-and-ink cartoon of my good self. Trying to keep a straight face I asked the artist about rumours that the remaining Wilburys (Roy Orbison had died the previous year) were thinking of working with Del Shannon. Tom paused as he cracked a huge smile. 'Anyone could join the Wilburys,' he replied. '*You* could be a Traveling Wilbury!'

I've had worse offers.

CHAPTER 98

TOM VERLAINE

Few people leave their teens without being aware of that fascinating object, the tortured artist. A Van Gogh exhibition would normally do the trick or the sort of poetry book recommended at school; that slim anthology some of us never got round to reading on account of being too enamoured with gigs and record shops. From Janis Joplin to Leonard Cohen, rock 'n' roll has come up with a few contenders but there weren't too many tormented souls around at the dawn of punk. Not, that is, until Thomas Miller appeared on the scene, or Verlaine as he called himself. Apparently, he was named after a symbolist, whatever that was, but in any case the poet was name-checked on Dylan's *Blood On The Tracks*. The punk version of Verlaine had been a presence on Manhattan's Lower East Side since the days of the New York Dolls and now had a band called Television who would be visiting the UK in the spring of 1977. My photographer-in-crime, Howard Barlow, and I legged it to Manchester's Free Trade Hall to scoop up front row seats.

What made Tom Verlaine different was that at the age of twenty-seven he was a fully-qualified guitarist as opposed to a three-chord wonder making it up as he went along. The singer-songwriter also fitted the new wave image, gaunt, ascetic and intense rather than manic. He actually looked more like an actor, the kind of European you would see in a Bergman or Chabrol movie. We would later discover that he was of Russian descent. The show featured most of the tracks from the debut *Marquee*

Moon album with much guitar interplay between Verlaine and Richard Lloyd. The second encore was a surprising cover of the Stones's 'Satisfaction', something I was reminded of when reading my original review in the *Altrincham Guardian*. I also wandered backstage to secure an interview with Tom for the *New Manchester Review*. Word had it that he could be moody or difficult, as suggested by his occasionally whiney vocals, but in the event he was fine, greeting me with the words, 'Hi, are you in a band?'

We chatted about CBGBs, the club where Television had served their apprenticeship and which in those days of instant history had already become legendary. I also asked him about his record company, Elektra, and whether he had been influenced by the original acts on that label. 'Sure,' he replied, 'they were all pretty neat bands, especially Love when they made their first few albums and The Doors at the time of *Strange Days*. But my own taste in music goes back to classical stuff, like Wagner. Then came jazz and John Coltrane with all that improvising.' A far cry from The Ramones and Blondie, the opening group on the tour.

What did Tom think of another New Yorker, Lou Reed, who had apparently checked out Television a few times. 'The Velvet Underground had an *avant-garde* side but they sold themselves as a pop band,' he said intriguingly. How did he feel about the rising stars along the coast in New Jersey. Was there any empathy with Bruce Springsteen or Southside Johnny who had also recently visited England for the first time? Verlaine looked slightly puzzled before releasing his words as deftly as his guitar solos. 'Sure, there are some good bands playing in New Jersey but they're more into rhythm and blues. We play rock 'n' roll.' Or did. The following year's *Adventure* album received a lukewarm reception leading to Television switching themselves off.

There followed a series of Tom Verlaine LPs, the second of which, *Dreamtime*, I found pleasantly introspective, less cathartic and aggressive than its predecessor. In my review for *Record Mirror* I described it as 'the guitar album of 1981, notwithstanding the shuddering breaks of extensive angst'. That's how we wrote in those days, which didn't seem to trouble Tom when we met for our next rendezvous. However, he did describe the previous twelve months as 'the worst year of my life', which I felt was a little excessive considering that during that time David Bowie had covered Verlaine's 'Kingdom Come' on his *Scary Monsters (and Super Creeps)* album. Tom would later admit that he had earned more money from the royalties of the Bowie version than from the rest of his music combined.

The next formal interview took place three years later on the release of his fourth solo album, *Cover*. He had spent most of the year living in London. 'I like it better as a city than New York,' he explained. 'It's not so money-oriented and the record company seems to be as much into music as business. Perhaps, more importantly, record producers here are geared towards giving the artist what he wants as opposed to what they think.' By this stage Verlaine was signed to Virgin whose press officer, Mark Cooper, was a former colleague at *Record Mirror*. He suggested to the editor of *International Musician* that I conduct the interview since I was one of the few journalists responsive to Tom and his ever-changing moods. My patience was certainly tried that day.

The guitarist chose the venue, a popular *creperie* at that time called Obelix near Portobello Road in Notting Hill Gate. It was a fabulous summer afternoon and there was an enticing walled garden; Tom insisted we sit inside. He then decided to demolish the already hot and bothered waitress by demanding something more complicated than an ordinary coffee. Since the joint didn't do booze, I thought I'd go for a healthy fruit option. It turned out that the kitchen staff didn't like squeezing lemons, extraordinary when you think how women spend a fortune on citrusy scents. Exit waitress amidst a clatter of trays and crockery. 'I'm impressed,' quipped Verlaine, 'she really hates her job.' His next few ripostes weren't bad, either. 'What do I think of the current music scene? I didn't think there was one,' he replied disingenuously. Really? How about bands like Echo and the Bunnymen and Orange Juice who always seem eager to sing your praises? 'Yeah, I've heard those groups have said nice things about me but, to tell you the truth, I'm not over-familiar with their songs. Actually, I don't listen to very much at all because I'm working on quite a bit of stuff myself.'

Having wound up the waitress again by sending back an over-buttered jacket potato, he turned his attention to attacking the dessert, skilfully extricating chocolate mousse from its topping of synthetic cream. 'If I do make a point of listening to anything then I'll try and go to the source. So if I want to hear the sound of Himalayans in mountain villages, I'll go straight to that instead of bothering with plagiarised recordings. Of course, you can't help but hear pop music wherever you go,' he sniffed disparagingly, 'it's hard not to have an opinion about it.'

I asked him about a track on the current album entitled *O Foolish Heart*: catchier than usual, perhaps it had hit single potential. 'It's funny you should say that,' he enthused, finally agreeing about something. 'I thought it would make a nice summer single but I dunno, I don't make these decisions. I suppose it might come as too much of a shock to my usual audience.' Who are these people, I asked. 'Well, I guess they're rock fans. I mean my music could hardly be described as jazz or heavy metal.'

Despite Tom living in London, the *Cover* album was also made in New York and LA. Wasn't that an expensive process? 'Just the opposite,' he claimed. 'We actually spent two years recording it, only doing a few days here and there, which works out far cheaper than writing in the studio. At the time, the Power Station with its big drum sound was the fashionable place in New York which fooled a lot of people. It's one thing to have a live sound but in order for it to be vibrant it has to be controlled. So I used a factory space in the warehouse area of SoHo. Yes, I know that's now become trendy too but this was a big empty room with a fourteen-foot ceiling, brick walls and wooden floors – which probably means it's going to be turned into apartments. But it worked for me and, in any case, I've had enough of that big drum sound. A good drummer doesn't need to play extra loud, not if they play with subtlety like, say, Stewart Copeland of The Police.'

How about guitarists? Any particular favourites in that department? 'Well there aren't really any, are there?', he replied, trying to keep a straight face, 'certainly not any soloists who can play melodic breaks. Some have got the sensibility and the ideas but not their own style. And I don't think you can develop a style, you've either got it or you haven't. There's very little modern stuff I'm taken in by. Maybe Neil Young,' conceded Verlaine, 'I'm not so sure how good he is, but he's very committed to what he does. People have compared me to him in that respect so I started listening to his LPs. 'Cortez The Killer' on *Zuma* must be the best two guitars bass and drums track I've ever heard while Keith Richards has got the most incredible spirit of release. A sort of looseness which has an of-the-moment quality.'

Tom Verlaine was once definitely a man of the moment – but where is he now?

WILLY DeVILLE

Considering he emerged at the same time as punk, Willy DeVille carved out a niche as one of the most interesting characters of the late 1970s. Although best known for his Mink DeVille hit 'Spanish Stroll', he continued recording and touring until well into this century, working with top musicians and producers. These ranged from Jack Nitzsche of Phil Spector and Neil Young fame to Dire Straits guitarist Mark Knopfler with whom he shared management. Christened William Borsey of Basque, Irish and Native American descent, Willy was a true rock 'n' roll gypsy. Born in a nondescript part of New England, he pitched up in London at the age of twenty-one only to find the music scene trapped in the grip of progressive rock and its instrumental self-indulgence. So he went back west and headed to San Francisco where the lack of a club scene proved equally frustrating.

'After that I travelled around America for two years, looking for the right musicians,' he told me when Mink DeVille toured the UK in the late summer of 1977. 'When I arrived in New York I found myself playing CBGBs at the same time as all the punk bands, like The Ramones. But that's where the association ended. We never had anything to do with that kind of music although most of our songs are very New York, that's what inspired them.' This conversation took place, would you believe, at Middleton Town Hall in North Manchester where the band were recording a session for ITV's *So It Goes*. The incongruousness of a guy whose image was pure West Side Story playing in a municipal backwater was enhanced by the odd choice of opening acts – the Tom Robinson Band and XTC. You would be hard-pressed to find a greater contrast between the pared-down quirkiness of XTC and the operatic strains of The Immortals, Willy's black, male backing trio.

Mink DeVille's eclectic sound was informed by soul, blues, R&B, Latin and even a touch of zydeco. 'We like the original Chicago guys such as Muddy Waters and Bo Diddley. We're probably closer to the New Jersey bands like Southside Johnny and the Asbury Jukes or Jukebox Johnny and the Asbury Jokes, as I call them. Sure, they play well enough but they're trying to be too much like Otis Redding...

'Do you like Édith Piaf?' he suddenly enquired. 'All that CBGBs lot go on about the street but she was the street, actually born in the street,' he said, talking about the Parisienne chanteuse with one of the most emotional voices ever. 'I've been on the street since the age of fifteen when my parents separated but, oh man, someone just bought me this book of photographs taken of all those street life people in Paris in the 1930s. It was like that whole bohemian thing, y'know? Terrific, really good.' Who else was Willy fond of? 'Ben E. King, Pablo Picasso and Vincent van Gogh, they all fit together because they hurt real bad,' he declared. 'James Dean and Gene Vincent, too, both sensitive to the point of destruction. Then there was Nijinsky, the ballet dancer and choreographer, he was one of the first superstars. He also hurt really bad – it drove him mad in the end. All those people had something in common and I feel a lot for them. And I,' he added dramatically, 'feel a lot, too.'

I believe the phrase is tough 'n' tender, I cut in. 'Tough 'n' tender?' he echoed. 'Hey, that's great, it's where it's at! Because, like, I've got an open heart and carry around a lot of hurt. To do that you've got to be pretty tough because you get hurt all the time. But I would rather be hurt and feel than be numb and insensitive to pain.'

As well as Édith Piaf ('she had a great set of pipes, didn't she?') Willy also had a soft spot for gospel music. 'Anything sensual like Billie Holiday, which touches the heart. I'm tired of intellectuals, my head goes so fast that sometimes I like to turn off. It's better to be instinctive.'

Bruce Springsteen is often mentioned in the same breath as Mr DeVille, as is Phil Lynott of Thin Lizzy. 'I'm a lot better looking than both of them,' the singer claimed, 'I mean, for a long time Springsteen hid his face behind a beard. But Phil, now he's got mixed blood, too. We tinkers are coming up fast!'

CHAPTER 100

ZODIAC MINDWARP

Those of you familiar with the other ninety-nine chapters of this volume will have noted the regular references to *Record Mirror*, once one of only a few publications providing weekly music news, reviews and interviews. Before my arrival in 1978, it specialised in catering to young consumers and the burgeoning dance scene, or disco. Then punk happened and everything changed forever, including my own life and career. Through *Record Mirror*, I was able to interview many of the artists in this book, from survivors of the old guard to all the new young dudes. More than forty years later, I am proud to still be in touch with many former colleagues, including Mark Manning, aka Zodiac Mindwarp.

During the mid-1980s, Mark went from being a provocative cartoonist to an outrageous parody of a rock god. Having created the weekly strip cartoon for *Record Mirror*, Manning became the art director of *Flexipop!* This is where it all started to go wrong. 'I was sitting in a small room and I kept on seeing these meatheads in groups waltzing in and out of the office, looking as if they were having a much better time than me. I thought, "If these suckers can do it, so can I – it can't be that hard."'

In order to make the transition to Zodiac Mindwarp, Mark had a useful contact in David Balfe, the former songwriter in Teardrop Explodes who went on to start up Food Records. He liked Mark's artwork and. on discovering he had a band, listened to his songs which soon afterwards appeared on an EP, *High Priest of Love*. If the title was typical of the times, so was everything else on Planet Zodiac. The alternative comedian Ade Edmondson was drafted in to direct the first video and Balfe negotiated a huge advance from Phonogram, Food's distributor, when Zodiac Mindwarp and the Love Reaction signed to that label. The cash enabled the band to tour America with Guns N' Roses, who were about to become the biggest heavy rock band in the world, and Alice Cooper, Mark's all-time hero.

Come the next decade, reality set in and the act was dropped. 'In fact, the record company gave us £20,000 to fuck off,' Mark drawled in his flat Bradford accent when we met for a drink in 1991. 'We couldn't really blame them after the amount of money they'd spent on us. We'd have to have sold almost as many records as Michael Jackson, just to break even.' He estimated the amount blown was a whopping £800,000. 'Well it was the 80s, wasn't it?' he wheezed rhetorically, still taken aback by the absurdity of it all. 'Record companies behaved like money grew on trees but it wasn't ours, was it? We never even saw it. It wasn't as if someone gave us a filthy great suitcase full of cash. I suppose it all went on touring and recording, that sort of thing.'

True, part of the money did go on a small cottage in the Cotswolds but even that proved disastrous. 'I bought it at the peak of the property market,' he confessed, 'probably the day before prices dropped. Now I can't sell it – but I'll have to because I owe the tax man a lot.' But it was a good laugh for a while? 'It was like the anti-Christ moving in,' he went on, referring to his decision to leave London for the picture postcard village of Moreton-in-Marsh. 'I immediately got in with the local drunkards and was arrested several times for having fun with squad cars and air pistols, as you do. It was the only bit of excitement amidst the stupefying boredom of country life. I guess I lost control,' he admitted. 'You give somebody from the ghetto a load of money and they do exactly as you'd expect. I created, so then I had to destroy. Not being a careerist, I embarked on a crash course of alcohol abuse.'

The last time I saw Mark was at a *Flexipop!* reunion party in 2015. He'd calmed down a little and looked in good shape for someone who had entered early middle age in a band which made the average Hell's Angel look like a gentleman biker. On seeing former *Record Mirror* editor Alf Martin for the first time in a few decades, he reminded him of the first time they had met, 'I came into the office and saw you editing all the rude bits out of one of my cartoons.'

I guess we were all edited to some degree, not that we would have noticed at the time. Those were heady days, when rock 'n' roll people lived rock 'n' roll lives. Those still young will never see anything like it but I hope you have enjoyed reading about it here. So, to everybody mentioned above, can I just say, thank you for the days and the memories without which there wouldn't be a memoir. I'm happy, hope you're happy too.